STATE, SOCIETY AND ECONOMY IN SAUDI ARABIA

State, Society and Economy in Saudi Arabia

Edited by Tim Niblock

ST. MARTIN'S PRESS NEW YORK

© 1982 Tim Niblock
All rights reserved. For information write:
St. Martin's Press, Inc., 175 Fifth Avenue, New York, N. Y. 10010
Printed in Great Britain
First published in the United States of America in 1981

Library of Congress Cataloging in Publication Data
81-14444

ISBN 0-312-75617-8

CONTENTS

LIST OF TABLES AND FIGURES

Tables

Figures

PREFACE

This book emerged out of a symposium which was held at the Centre for Arab Gulf Studies, University of Exeter, in July 1980. The symposium, entitled 'State, Economy and Power in Saudi Arabia', brought together those working on or interested in Saudi Arabia, whether from a historical, political, social or economic perspective. The selection of articles published here also represents a variety of subject interests and a variety of approaches. The object has not been to provide a comprehensive account of Saudi Arabian politics, society and economics, but rather to make available different insights into particular aspects of these fields. It is hoped that in this way some light can be shed upon the political processes and socio-economic structure of this complex country.

No attempt has been made to render the different contributions mutually consistent; where such contributions lead to incompatible conclusions it has been deemed valuable to retain them — perhaps as an indication of the differing perspectives from which developments within Saudi Arabia can be viewed.

The editor wishes to thank all those who helped to organise the symposium from which this collection of articles sprang, together with the symposium participants whose comments have helped to refine the arguments presented in the articles. Particular thanks should go to the symposium chairman and Director of the Centre for Arab Gulf Studies, Professor M. A. Shaban. Mrs Sheila Westcott typed the manuscript with her customary display of good humour in adversity.

Acknowledgement is due to Croom Helm for permission to reprint the map found on p. 188, and to the American University, Washington, for permission to reprint the maps found on p. 13, p. 14 and p. 216, and the table on pp. 16–17.

Tim Niblock

1 INTRODUCTION

Tim Niblock

Despite widespread recognition of the crucial importance of Saudi Arabia in the world today, comparatively little social scientific research has been conducted on the country. A number of factors account for this neglect: statistical data (outside the purely economic) have often proved difficult if not impossible to obtain, official sensitivity to many of the issues which researchers would care to examine has inhibited research activities, and researchers have encountered little success in penetrating the decision-making apparatus. Research on the political system is inevitably difficult where, as the *Area Handbook for Saudi Arabia* comments, 'little is publicly known about decision-making within the House of Saud', despite this being 'the object of much scrutiny and informed conjecture'.[1] The problems of conducting research on a country which holds so few parallels with other countries (outside the Arab Gulf area) may also have discouraged potential researchers.

Given the state of social scientific research on Saudi Arabia, this book could not — and does not — attempt a comprehensive or exhaustive study of the politics, society and economy of Saudi Arabia. The object, rather, is to provide some insight into these complex fields by means of presenting a selection of articles covering specific (necessarily limited) aspects. The restricted range of aspects covered makes it difficult to draw firm conclusions as to where current developments are leading Saudi Arabia. It remains possible, nevertheless, to delineate some of the critical issues which will determine the country's future prospects.

The origins of the contemporary Saudi state lie in the early eighteenth century. In 1744 a relationship was forged which remains crucial to the nature of the Saudi state. Muhammad ibn Abd al-Wahhab, a religious scholar and preacher calling for a return to the orthodox practices of early Islam, sought and received refuge from the ruler of the tiny Najdi state of Dar'iya, Muhammad ibn Saud. Together they determined to embark on a campaign to spread Muhammad ibn Abd al-Wahhab's message of *tawhid*. The campaign involved an intertwining of the religious with the temporal: the identification of Muhammad ibn Abd al-Wahhab with Muhammad ibn Saud ensured that the latter's

11

temporal authority (which was itself employed to spread the ideas of *tawhid*) expanded in unison with adhesion to *tawhid*. This alliance of the religious and the temporal has been a continuing characteristic of Saudi rule: the *muwahhidun* (followers of the *tawhid* doctrine) have always looked on the House of Saud as their temporal protectors, and the character of Saudi-ruled states has, in turn, been critically affected by the role played within them by *muwahhidun*. The content and nature of Muhammad ibn Abd al-Wahhab's religious teaching is examined in the article by Derek Hopwood which appears in this book (Chapter 2: The Ideological Basis: Ibn Abd al-Wahhab's Muslim Revivalism).

Over the second half of the eighteenth century and during the nineteenth century the territorial extent of the Al Saud's authority depended on the strength of Saudi political leadership, the strength of rival leaderships on the peninsula, and the presence or absence of an externally-backed military force in Arabia. By the time of Muhammad ibn Saud's death in 1765 most of the Najd was under Saudi control, and when Muhammad ibn Abd al-Wahhab died in 1792 that control had been extended south to the Rub al-Khali (Empty Quarter). Al-Hasa was captured in the closing years of the eighteenth century, and shortly thereafter Saudi forces gained their richest prize — control of the holy cities of Mecca (1801) and Medina (1805) and of the greater part of the Hijaz.

The capture of the holy cities, however, provoked a response from the Ottoman government which, in 1814, empowered its Viceroy in Egypt (Muhammad Ali) to free the cities from Saudi control. The campaign in Arabia by Muhammad Ali's son, Tusun, dealt a crushing blow to Saudi power, forcing the Saudis back to the Najdi heartland and, in 1818, even destroying the Saudi capital of Dar'iya. While the House of Saud, under Faisal ibn Turki, was able to rally its fortunes briefly in the mid-nineteenth century, those fortunes were to reach their lowest ebb in the latter part of the nineteenth century. With the Al Saud itself riven by internal conflict, and with the Ottoman government giving support to the rival Al Rashid of Ha'il, the Al Saud were driven from Najd and took up temporary residence in Kuwait.

Two aspects are evident, therefore, in the reconstitution of the Saudi state in the twentieth century. On the one hand, Saudi rule on the Arabian peninsula has a long history; on the other, the reconstitution was initiated from a position of extreme weakness — where the Al Saud had lost even a physical presence in the territories to which they laid claim. Both aspects were to be of significance to the strategy whereby

Figure 1.1: Major Regions of Saudi Arabia

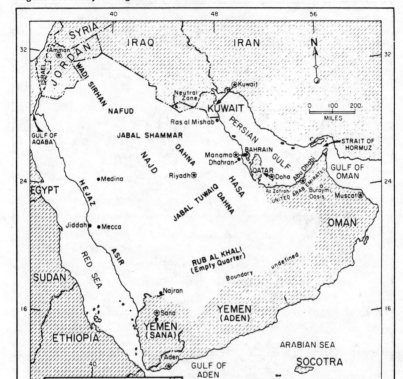

Source: Nyrop *et al.*, *Area Handbook for Saudi Arabia* (American University, Washington, 1977), p. xiv.

the Saudi state was reconstituted: the traditional alliance of the religious and the temporal was retained within this strategy, and the difficulties of regaining control of a territory where opposing forces were strongly entrenched were confronted by developing a new type of military force — the *ikhwan*. The latter, consisting of ex-bedouin settled

Figure 1.2: Saudia Arabia, Transportation, 1975

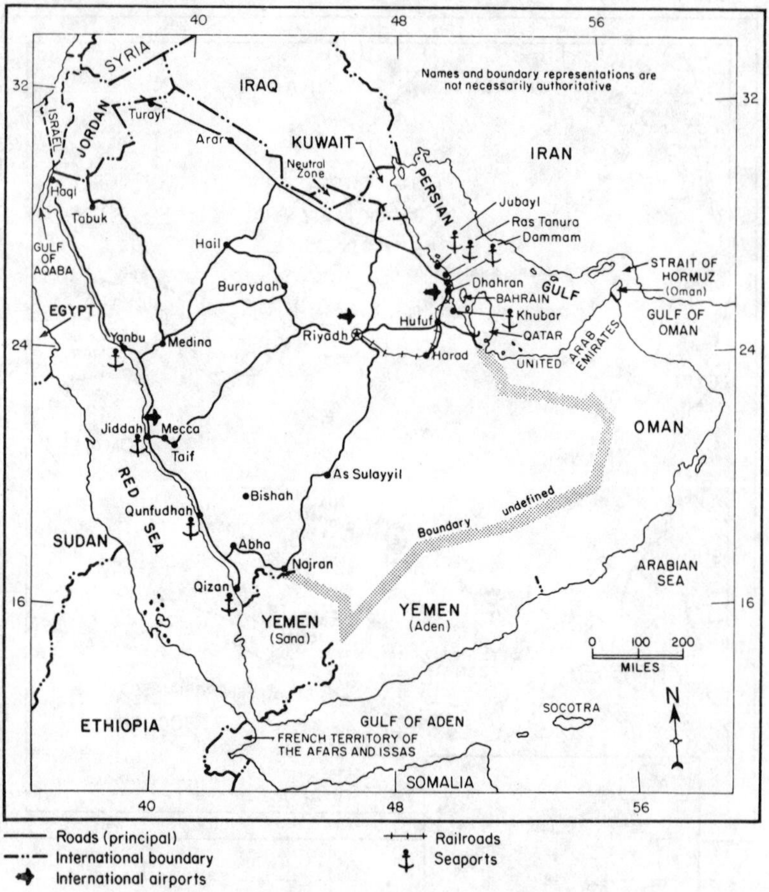

```
───────  Roads (principal)          ┼─┼─┼─┼  Railroads
─·─·─·─  International boundary       ⚓  Seaports
  ◀─┤    International airports
```

Source: Nyrop *et al.*, *Area Handbook for Saudi Arabia*, p. 58.

in agricultural communities and imbued with Wahhabi ideas, reconstituted a force which was 'mobile enough to cross the length and breadth of the peninsula, and sedentary enough to be in a specific locality when they were needed'.[2] The *ikhwan* were not in existence when Abd al-Aziz ibn Abd al-Rahman Al Saud initiated the process of reconstituting the Saudi state — with the capture of al-Riyadh in 1902 — but were created in 1912 when the direct need for such an instrument became apparent.

The territorial extent of the reconstituted Saudi state spread steadily between 1902 and 1926. Between 1902 and 1906 Abd al-Aziz entrenched his control over central Najd; in 1913 al-Hasa came under

Saudi control as a result of the expulsion of the Ottoman garrisons there; in 1919, defeating Sharif Husain of the Hijaz's troops at the battle of Khurma, Abd al-Aziz began to exert pressure on Hijazi territories; in 1920, territory in the vicinity of Kuwait came under Saudi control; in 1921, the independent power of the Al Rashid in northern Arabia was brought to an end and their territory incorporated into the Saudi state; in 1923, Abd al-Aziz secured control of much of Asir, and in 1924 began the campaign which brought to an end the Hashimite presence in the Hijaz. By 1926, therefore, the main part of what is today the Kingdom of Saudi Arabia had been integrated into the Saudi state. The state was known as the Kingdom of Hijaz, Najd and its Dependencies until 1932, when the modern name was adopted.

The analysis of where power and influence lie, and how power has been exercised in the modern Saudi state is the subject of the editor's own contribution to this collection of articles (Chapter 5: Social Structure and the Development of the Saudi Arabian Political System). These issues will, therefore, not be treated in this introduction. All that is necessary here is to give a brief account of the formal structures of power. Power lies in the prerogative of the king, which is bounded only by the injunctions of *shari'a* law. Provided the king upholds the *shari'a* and acts according to its precepts, he is in theory absolute. None of the governmental institutions (which were, in any case, very slow to develop) detract from the royal prerogative.

In 1926, after Abd al-Aziz had secured control of the Hijaz, an Advisory Council (*majlis al-shura*) was established in the latter territory. The Council consisted of the Viceroy (Prince Faisal), his advisers and six notables, and it was empowered to discuss such matters as the Viceroy chose to place before it. The scope of the Council's concern was limited to the Hijaz. No similar institution existed at this time in Najd nor in any other part of the country — although the processes of informal consultation which did take place in Najd were certainly of greater significance than the institutionalised consultation of the Advisory Council (see p. 108 below). The object of establishing the Advisory Council appears to have been to facilitate the integration of the Hijaz into the Saudi kingdom: to convince the population of the newly conquered territory that their Saudi rulers were intent on a co-operative form of government. Once this purpose had been served the Advisory Council seems to have been allowed to wither away. Part of its function, in any case, was taken over by the Council of Deputies which was set up in 1931 (again in the Hijaz, but with responsibilities which could cover other parts of the country) to bring together department

16   *Introduction*

Table 1.1: Formation of Government Ministries, to 1975[a]

Ministry	Established	Significant subdivisions or areas of jurisdiction
Agriculture and Water	1953	Desalinization Irrigation and land reclamation New water sources
Commerce (originally part of the Ministry of Commerce and Industry, established in 1954)	1975	Foreign Capital Investment Commission Director General of Commerce Commercial disputes settlement committees Saudi Arabian Standards Organization[b]
Communications	1953	Deputy Minister for Roads and Ports Saudi Government Railroad Organization[b]
Defense and Aviation (Minister to the king created in 1944)	1953	Military inspection Meteorology Civil Aviation Saudi Arabian Airlines Corporation[b]
Education	1953	
Finance and National Economy (Minister to the king created in 1932)	1954	Director General of Budget Central Statistics Department Institute of Public Administration[b] Public Investment Fund[b] Saudi Arabian Monetary Agency (SAMA)[b] Saudi Credit Bank[b] Agricultural Bank[b]
Foreign Affairs (Minister to the king created in 1931)	1953	Diplomatic missions abroad Western Department Afro-Asian Department Islamic Affairs Department Petroleum Affairs Department Arab Affairs Department
Health	1954	Preventive medicine Curative medicine (hospitals) Director General of Inspection
Higher Education	1975	
Industry and Electricity (originally part of the Ministry of Commerce and Industry, established in 1954)	1975	Director General for Industry Director General for Power Industrial Research and Development Center[b] General Organization for Silos and Flour Mills[b]
Information (originally the General Directorate of Broadcasting, Printing and Publishing)	1963	Director General for Broadcasting Director General for Television Director General for Publications Director General for Press and Public Relations Saudi News Agency

Table 1.1: Formation of Government Ministries, to 1975[a] — *continued*

Ministry	Established	Significant subdivisions or areas of jurisdiction
Interior (Minister to the king created in 1951)	1953	Frontier Force and Coast Guard Passports and nationality Director General for Civil Defense Director General for Investigation Director General for Public Security Internal Security Forces College
Justice	1970	Supreme Judicial Council Sharia court system
Labor and Social Affairs	1961	Deputy Minister for Labor Affairs Deputy Minister for Social Affairs Supreme Committee for Settlement of Labor Disputes Director General for Social Security Director General for Youth Welfare General Social Insurance Organization[b] Saudi Red Crescent Society[b]
Municipal and Rural Affairs	1975	Deputy Minister for Municipalities, Provincial and Town Planning
Petroleum and Mineral Resources	1960	Deputy Minister for Companies and Technical Affairs Deputy Minister for Mineral Resources Comptroller General of Oil Accounts Organization of Petroleum Exporting Countries (OPEC) office Neutral Zone Office General Petroleum and Mineral Organization (Petromin)[b]
Pilgrimage Affairs and Awqaf	1962	Deputy Minister for Pilgrimage Affairs Deputy Minister for Awqaf Supreme Council of Awqaf
Planning (originally the Central Planning Organization)	1975	Economic Experts Office Planning Office Follow-up Office
Posts, Telegraphs, and Telecommunications (originally part of the Ministry of Communications)	1975	Deputy Minister of Communications Director General for Telecommunications Administration Director General for Posts
Public Works and Housing	1975	

Notes:

a. The first formal Council of Ministers was created in 1953.

b. Autonomous agency or public corporation.

Source: Nyrop *et al.*, *Area Handbook for Saudi Arabia*, pp. 179–80.

heads of the skeletal government organisation and advise the king on state policy. The Deputies for Foreign Affairs and Finance seem to have been the main (and sometimes the only) members of this body.

The elaboration of the system of government organisation was brought about by the initiation of oil production. This new sector of the economy made necessary new forms of administration, and the expansion of infrastructure and services which followed from the receipt of oil revenues in turn required a more elaborate administrative system. Details of the establishment of government ministries can be found in Table 1.1. A Council of Ministers was established in October 1953 to co-ordinate the activities of the different ministries and to tender advice to the king. The Council's statutory regulations laid down that 'ministers appointed by the King were to consider the affairs of the Kingdom and recommend decisions to the King, who approved all decisions before they became laws.'[3] New regulations were introduced in 1958 giving the Council a more direct executive power; the overriding royal prerogative, however, remained.

Saudi Arabia's economy is, of course, centred on the production of oil. In 1933 an oil concession was granted, for an initial payment of £30,000, to Standard Oil of California. The company discovered the first commercially exploitable field in 1938 and exported the first oil in 1939. The Second World War inhibited the company from pressing ahead with the expansion of production facilities. It was, therefore, not until the late 1940s that substantial quantities of oil were being exported from Saudi Arabia and substantial revenues were being received. Standard Oil of California had, in the meantime, brought in three other American companies to participate in the extraction of Saudi oil. The resultant consortium was named the Arabian American Oil Company (Aramco). Government revenues followed an astronomical rate of growth as a result of oil production (see Table 1.2).

Despite the influx of oil revenues from the late 1940s extensive development expenditure is a comparatively recent phenomenon. For reasons discussed in the article by J. S. Birks and C. A. Sinclair (Chapter 11: The Domestic Political Economy of Development in Saudi Arabia), the limited sums devoted to development projects in the late 1950s and the 1960s were not of such a nature as to transform the economy. It is only since the oil price rises of 1973—4 brought vastly increased resources into the Saudi treasury that a fundamental transformation of the economy has been attempted. The Second and Third Five-Year Plans (1976—80 and 1980—5 respectively) have laid the framework for this transformation — in the industrial, agricultural and

Table 1.2: Government Revenue in Saudi Arabia between 1944 and 1975

Year	Total government revenue (in million riyals)
1944	c. 80
1948	214.6
1952	756.9
1956	1,610
1962	2,166
1964	2,626
1970	5,966
1972	10,782
1973	13,200
1974	22,810
1975	98,247

Note:

The value of the Saudi riyal has mostly fluctuated around four to the $US — from 1954 to January 1960: 3.75; from January 1960 to December 1971: 4.50; from December 1971 to February 1973: 4.14; for most of the period since March 1973: about 3.55.

Sources: I. al-Awaji, Bureaucracy and Society in Saudi Arabia, unpublished PhD thesis, University of Virginia, 1971, p. 86; and R. F. Nyrop, *Area Handbook for Saudi Arabia* (American University, Washington, DC, 1977), p. 233.

service sectors. The key element in the programme is constituted by the construction of a massive petrochemical industry, based on two 'growth poles': Jubail and Yanbu. H. G. Hambleton's article (Chapter 13: The Saudi Arabian Petrochemical Industry; its Rationale and Effectiveness) assesses the prospects of success in this critical field.

A wide range of different aspects of Saudi Arabian politics, society and economy are covered in this book. These aspects do, however, serve to illustrate a rather more limited set of themes. While the articles in the book progress from the historical through the political and social to the economic, the themes which emerge are not necessarily limited to a single subject-category. Four principal themes emerge.

The first theme is the nature of the Saudi state. How can the dynamics of the state be characterised? What motivates those who determine the broad framework of policy? What forces may bring about a change of political direction? Three articles fall within the purview of this theme, as also does the Appendix. Derek Hopwood (Chapter 2: The Ideological Basis: Ibn Abd al-Wahhab's Muslim

Revivalism) examines the teachings of Muhammad Abd al-Wahhab within the context of other Muslim revivalist movements. Given the central role which Wahhabi thought has played under Saudi rule, placing Muhammad ibn Abd al-Wahhab in comparative context provides a valuable perspective on the Saudi state. Tim Niblock (Chapter 5: Social Structure and the Development of the Saudi Arabian Political System) argues that the most common approach to the analysis of developments in Saudi Arabia, laying emphasis on the interaction of and conflict between the forces of traditionalism and modernism, does not help towards an understanding of the pattern of developments in the country. The forces of modernism and tradition-alism, he contends — far from being in conflict — have often served common purposes and proved mutually supportive. The key to understanding the dynamics which have moved Saudi Arabian politics, rather, is to be found in the interactions between the social structure, the economy and the political process. James Buchan (Chapter 6: Secular and Religious Opposition in Saudi Arabia) looks at the secular opposition to Saudi rule in the 1960s, the religious-based opposition of the Shi'a, and the Muslim fundamentalist opposition of Juhaiman al-Otaibi. He concludes that while the movement among the educated for constitutional reform is today 'listless, fragmented and lacks an ideological framework', religious opposition is so deeply ingrained in the Saudi system as to be to all intents 'structural'. Finally, reference should be made to the Appendix (Opening Remarks to the Symposium on 'State, Economy and Power in Saudi Arabia'), where Abdullah Al Saud emphasises the strength which a conviction of historical legitimacy imparts to Saudi rule.

The second theme is Saudi Arabia's relationship with the international environment (political and economic). An evident paradox arises with regard to Saudi Arabia's international position. It possesses immense economic resources, yet its attempts to convert economic power into international political influence have scarcely been successful. Its closest non-Arab ally (the United States) has provided Israel with the military and economic help that has kept the Israeli state viable; Saudi attempts to influence United States policy in this regard have had scant success. The strength of Saudi Arabia's position economically is stressed by Paul Stevens (Chapter 12: Saudi Arabia's Oil Policy in the 1970s — its Origins, Implementation and Implications). Stevens contends that, despite the widespread belief that OPEC determines the price of oil, oil prices in the mid-1970s were effectively determined by Saudi Arabia. The importance of Saudi Arabia in the world economy, therefore, is not just that she is a major oil-producing country (producing over 13 per cent of world oil output), but that she has at times been able to control the international price of oil. Fred Halliday (Chapter 7: A Curious and Close Liaison: Saudi Arabia's Relations with the United States) locates the key to understanding the paradox outlined above as lying in the vulnerability of the Saudi regime and its need to retain American support. Without sustenance from the United States the regime would fear for its survival; this naturally limits Saudi Arabia's ability to convert its economic power into international political influence. A dependent relationship with an outside power is not a new development for Saudi Arabia, as is evident from the article by Peter Sluglett and Marion Farouk-Sluglett (Chapter 3: The Precarious Monarchy: Britain, Abd al-Aziz ibn Saud and the Establishment of the Kingdom of Hijaz, Najd and its Dependencies, 1925–32). In this earlier period, however, the dependence was based more on financial need.

The third theme is Saudi Arabia's relationship with her Gulf neighbours. The relationship between Saudi Arabia and the smaller Gulf states is bound to have its own particular characteristics — characteristics distinct from Saudi Arabia's relationship with other Arab states. The historical interaction between the states and the peoples of the area, and the discrepancy in size between Saudi Arabia and the other states are two such characteristics. Rosemarie Said Zahlan (Chapter 4: King Abd al-Aziz's Changing Relationship with the Gulf States during the 1930s) shows how Abd al-Aziz came to accept the necessity and desirability of establishing good relations with Kuwait and Bahrain, while failing to do so in the cases of Qatar and the states of the lower Gulf. John Duke Anthony (Chapter 8: Aspects of Saudi Arabia's Relations with other Gulf States) identifies the critical elements determining the nature of relationships among Gulf states as territorial disputes, dynastic competition and the radical–conservative contest. In the light of previous experience he assesses optimistically the prospects for stable relationships to be forged between these states. Finally, Rodney Wilson (Chapter 14: The Evolution of the Saudi Banking System and its Relationship with Bahrain) provides a perspective with some important implications for the development of economic relations between Saudi Arabia and the other Gulf states. His detailed analysis of the development and current structure of the Saudi banking system indicates that (for structural reasons) the latter is uncompetitive when compared with the Bahraini banking sector. A wider point emerges from this: the free movement of goods and capital which currently characterises the main part of Saudi

Arabia's economic relations with its smaller neighbours is liable to lead to severe imbalances, unless the economic (and perhaps related social) structures are brought into greater unison. The character of Saudi Arabia's relationship (economic and political) with its Gulf neighbours will inevitably be a critical element affecting the future prospects of the Arabian peninsula.

The fourth theme is the nature of the economic development currently being pursued, the prospects of its success and the likely effects. The establishment of a successful petrochemical industry in the Gulf area is perhaps a test-case for the prospects of industrialisation in the Third World. If the vast supplies of capital, energy feedstock and raw material are unable to ensure the success of this industry, the prospects of Third World industrialisation as a whole must look bleak. Contrary to some recent assessments, H. G. Hambleton (Chapter 13: The Saudi Arabian Petrochemical Industry: its Rationale and Effectiveness) gives a broadly favourable evaluation of prospects, contending that Saudi Arabian petrochemicals (despite prospective global overproduction) will be able to break into world markets through tying sales to oil entitlements. The cost advantages gained through access to low-priced energy and feedstock supplies will also be of critical importance. As to the social effects of Saudi Arabia's extensive development programmes, J. S. Birks and C. A. Sinclair (Chapter 11: The Domestic Political Economy of Development in Saudi Arabia) examine some of the labour-supply problems which are likely to follow, while Shirley Kay (Chapter 9: Social Change in Modern Saudi Arabia) surveys the general characteristics of the changing society. Ugo Fabietti (Chapter 10: Sedentarisation as a Means of Detribalisation: Some Policies of the Saudi Arabian Government towards the Nomads) looks at the interactions between economic conditions and social policy in the nomadic sector.

Notes

1. R. Nyrop, *Area Handbook for Saudi Arabia* (American University, Washington, DC, 1977), p. 3.
2. J. S. Habib, *Ibn Sa'ud's Warriors of Islam* (Brill, Leiden, 1978), p. 16.
3. I. al-Awaji, 'Bureaucracy and Society in Saudi Arabia', unpublished PhD thesis, University of Virginia, 1971, p. 113.

2 THE IDEOLOGICAL BASIS: IBN ABD AL-WAHHAB'S MUSLIM REVIVALISM[1]

Derek Hopwood

Characteristics of Muslim Revivalism

Islamic history is punctuated with the phenomenon of revival movements. Iran is only the latest of a long line. While some have chosen to use different terms to describe this phenomenon — reform, revolutionary, fundamentalist, resistance or protest movements — 'revival movements' is perhaps the most appropriate, in that they do consistently seek to revive something that has been lost or corrupted. They have occurred at all times and in all places within the Islamic world; they have not always been fringe or heretical movements, and some have been at least as responsible for the maintenance of Islam as have the orthodox *'ulama*.[2]

To understand the nature of Muslim revivalism a number of different aspects of such movements need to be examined:

1. The social, political or economic conditions which form the background and which cause a movement to emerge at a particular time and in a particular place.
2. The prevailing intellectual, cultural and religious climate, and whether there was the expectation of the appearance of a *mahdi*.
3. The character and background of a movement's leader, and the particular path of experience that leads to his 'conversion' or assumption of leadership. We need to assess whether such movements are led by a distinguishable type of man and what factors impel some leaders to proclaim themselves *mahdi*.
4. The processes whereby a movement is started and the mechanics whereby followers are gained, maintained and influenced towards making a radical change in their lives. An understanding of the expectations of the followers is also necessary here.
5. The nature of the message that the leader proclaims.
6. The pattern of development of the movement — whether it leads to the creation of a state, brings about radical change, or peters out.

23

From the study of a number of Islamic movements (and by comparison with other such movements in European and Asian history) it is possible to erect a generally applicable model for the phenomenon – *mutatis mutandis*. Muslims in history have not acted essentially differently from other men; the impulses that have moved them have been the same (the improvement of economic and social conditions, religious salvation), but the ends pursued and their meaning have been expressed in Islamic terms. At times of unrest or decay, whether social, economic or religious, there have been sensitive men of strong personality who have felt their society's problems deeply enough to take upon them-selves the task of giving expression to ideas of reform. After a religious training, often together with a severe emotional crisis, such men can become leaders and articulators, preachers who, with a total conviction and fearless in condemnation, wish to reform society and its members. They preach with threats and promises and pass on their 'fears' to their listeners who may themselves come to share the same convictions. Followers may be gained and their numbers increased by military and other success. The ideology of the movement is *jihad* against an enemy, however defined, and the message is purification of society by a return to the ideals of early Islam, the restoration of what has been lost and the reassertion of the supremacy of the *shari'a*.

The ideology is reinforced by success and those who follow the leader expect of the movement collective salvation and reward in this world and the next. A bond is established between leader and followers which can be strengthened by regular meetings with prayers and preaching, by reassurance, and by the use of specific techniques to reinforce the relationship. The organisation of the movement is important for its success, either as a *sufi tariqa*, a fighting army, or a state – often in alliance with a secular ruler. Such movements become a defence against the outside world and those inside form a new community pledged to each other and to the leader(s). The movement, if strongly established, may outlast the death of the founder.

It is clearly impossible to establish all relevant facts regarding the Wahhabi movement which arose in Arabia in the early eighteenth century and which led to the foundation of the Saudi state. In several respects it resembles other movements but it also has a number of unique features. It was the first of a number of such movements in 'modern' times and carried on the tradition of earlier ones. An interesting comparison is with that of Ibn Tumart in North Africa in the early twelfth century, who returned home after a period of study in the east, burning with the conviction that Islam in his country had been corrupted. By preaching an uncompromising observance of religious obligations and by his learning and piety he found himself the spiritual leader of a movement whose adherents tried to live in accordance with his ideals and who took the name of *al-Muwahhidun* – those who proclaim the unity of God, 'unitarians'. In alliance with a more practical leader, Abd al-Mu'min, a state based on Ibn Tumart's principles was founded which ruled Morocco and Spain. The basis of Ibn Tumart's theology was *tawhid*, a strict adherence to the *shari'a*, and the banning of practices such as the drinking of wine and the playing of musical instruments. The alliance with a strong ruler was a crucial element in the movement's success.

Arabian Background to Wahhabism[3]

Two aspects of the historical background to the Wahhabi movement should be stressed. One is well enough known, but the other has until recently received less attention. The better-known aspect is the low state to which religion had sunk in the Arabian peninsula by the beginning of the eighteenth century. Religious observance was slack and much weight was given to the power of 'holy' trees and the tombs of saints (even the tomb of Muhammad in Medina) and to various other superstitions and talismans. Orthodox Islam regards such practices as *shirk* (polytheism) or *bid'a* (heresy), and it is clear that the precepts of the *shari'a* were in many respects ignored. In Wahhabi parlance the period is condemned as that of *jahiliya* (ignorance), that is a state equivalent to the lack of religion before the preaching of Muhammad.

The other aspect concerns the continuation of the tradition of religious learning in the towns of the peninsula. The political system in Arabia in the eighteenth century was not conducive to a strong religious supervision. A number of petty rulers controlled various towns and their surroundings and there was continuous inter-urban and inter-tribal feuding. The Ottoman writ ran mainly in the Hijaz, in Yemen and on the eastern coast. Central Najd was outside such control. However, in the towns of the peninsula the tradition of religious learning had not been allowed to die despite the political vicissitudes. Medina, Damascus and Cairo were the centres to which scholars travelled from Najd and elsewhere, and where they received at the hands of the *'ulama* the training which they took back and attempted to put into practice in their home towns. Many such scholars became *qadis* to local *amirs* and usually held office at their pleasure. They assured a live tradition of religious learning in central Arabia.

Through this stream of scholars contact was maintained between Najd and the main currents of Islamic learning, usually but not exclusively Hanbali, and Gibb's picture of original Wahhabism as 'a solitary protest in a corrupt world'[4] should now be modified. The *jahiliya* which existed was not among the *'ulama* but among the tribes and the urban populace. *Qadis* of some repute held office in a number of towns in Najd, notably Ushaiqir, 'Uyaina, Dar'iya and al-Riyadh.[5] They were scholars trained in the school of Ibn Qudama (representing the conservative Hanbali tradition in law) and of Ibn Taimiya and Ibn al-Qaiyim who were more radical. One or two in the seventeenth century are known to have been moved to condemn in writing the corruption they witnessed around them. It seems, though, that *qadis* were dependent for their position on the *amir* who was, in turn, subject to political pressures and public opinion and therefore limited in his ability to support the *'ulama* when they expressed dissatisfaction with the moral and religious practices of the people.

This was the tradition from which Muhammad ibn al-Wahhab sprang. His grandfather, Sulaiman, although he himself did not leave Najd, studied under Ahmad b. Muhammad b. Mushrif who had studied in Damascus under a famed Hanbali scholar, Musa al-Hujawi (d. 1560). Sulaiman became an eminent *'alim* and chief *mufti* of Najd and was the author of a number of *fatwas* and commentaries. At the time of his death he was *qadi* in Uyaina where his son, Abd al-Wahhab, who had studied with his father, succeeded him in 1713. Abd al-Wahhab was dismissed by the *amir* in 1727 and moved to Huraimila where he died in 1740. Muhammad ibn Abd al-Wahhab was born in 1703 and in the family tradition studied together with his brother under his father. He was obviously a precocious student of outstandingly rigid views — he quarrelled over his opinions with both his father and brother. He made the *hajj* at the age of twelve and when back in Uyaina he was witness to the corrupt religious practices and tribal feuding of the area, both of which he considered against the true spirit of Islam. He began to condemn such practices in his home town while still in his late teens or early twenties, but to little effect. He was obviously too youthful and unconvincing to make any impression.

The years which followed were the most vital and formative in the career of Ibn Abd al-Wahhab. He left his father in Najd to go to Medina where he established relationships with influential teachers whose teachings helped to strengthen him in his beliefs. After a long period of meditation[6] (and possibly after passing through an emotional crisis), he eventually returned to Najd to preach his message, despite considerable opposition. His most important teacher in Medina was Muhammad Hayat al-Sindi (d. 1751), a Hanafi scholar of *hadith*, whose students came from various different backgrounds and traditions.[7] Most were non-Hanbali and many were *sufis*, mainly Naqshabandi, as was al-Sindi himself. These scholars in Medina had widespread contacts, especially with the eastern Islamic world, and consequently Ibn Abd al-Wahhab was exposed to a number of *sufi* and non-*sufi* influences – among them the current of Islamic revival emanating from India and the Naqshabandi. (Even the ascetic Ibn Taimiya did not oppose *sufism* as such but rather its excesses, and he was initiated into the Qadiri *tariqa*, as was Ibn al-Qaiyim.) Al-Sindi was a traditional teacher of *hadith* in contact with the major movements of his day. The severe spirit of Ibn Taimiya may not have dominated al-Sindi's own thinking but it was certainly part of Ibn Abd al-Wahhab's inspiration as also was a strong conviction of the need for reform which came from the study of *hadith* as presented by al-Sindi.

This, then, was the milieu from which Ibn Abd al-Wahhab emerged as an inspired *iman* or *mujaddid* – the leader and preacher who emerges from time to time in Islamic history determined to revive the observance of religion. Such leaders are often boosted in their self-awareness by prophetic dreams, visions or inner voices. Unfortunately we have no record that Ibn Abd al-Wahhab experienced any of these. It is interesting, though, that one of the *hadiths* which he mentions as being particularly influential on his thinking is prophetic; he seems to have taken it as confirmation of his own role. The *hadith*, found in Ibn Malik, reads: ' "If God desires good for His servant He will use him". They said, "How will He use him?" He said, "He will grant him success in a righteous undertaking before his death".'[8] Later, when persuading Muhammad ibn Saud to join him, he prophesies, with a vision of his own future: 'I bring you good news of glory and power. Whoever holds to and works by the words of *tawhid* will rule through them lands and men.'[9]

Ibn Abd al-Wahhab moved in due course from Medina to Basra where he continued to study and to mix with teachers and students of different *madhabs* and *tariqas*. It is not known how long he spent in Basra, but while there his conviction of the rightness of his ideas must have strengthened for he felt compelled to preach condemnation of current religious practices in Basra. During his studies he had obviously gained sufficient confidence in himself to preach even in the most hostile circumstances. Without support, however, he was doomed and

he was physically ejected from the town.[10] The combination of right
time, place and circumstance necessary for a successful movement was
not present in Basra. The Shi'as and men of trade were clearly
unconvinced by his message and by his call for reform. Such a rebuff
could have dissuaded men less firmly convinced in their call from
continuing to preach. There followed an incident which may have been
of great significance in Ibn Abd al-Wahhab's life. On his way from
Basra to al-Zubair he was walking alone, barefoot, through the desert
and in the midday sun collapsed from heat and thirst. He was,
according to the sources, in his death throes (*mushrif 'ala'l-halak*), when
he was rescued by a passing traveller. Traumatic experiences such as
this seem to have one of two effects on strongly religious personalities.
They are either taken as a warning to desist from further action (and
possibly to retire into a life of meditation) or they serve to strengthen
the individual's conviction (often after a period of retreat) that he is a
man chosen by God. In Ibn Abd al-Wahhab's case, on his recovery he
returned to Najd to spend some months in retirement, largely because
of disagreement with his father, until on the latter's death in 1740 he
began his open campaign which ended only with his own death in
1792.

**Ibn Abd al-Wahhab's Character and Leadership in Comparative
Context**

The most problematical aspect of writing the history of a revival
movement is the attempt to assess the character of the leader. This is a
formidable problem and requires a psychological knowledge of the
processes which lead to conversion and conviction. A number of books
have been written to explain the mental make-up of prominent
Christian personalities (such as St Paul, Luther, Wesley and Christ
Himself) and the picture which emerges may provide some insight into
the psyches of Ibn Abd al-Wahhab and other Islamic *mujaddids*. Such
men become known not so much by signs and miracles as by the inner
logic of their way of life and by their effect on society. They often
have an obsessive temperament which clings tenaciously to ideas once
they have been adopted. This obsessiveness enables them to maintain
their ideas and policies in the face of outright opposition or hostility.
In fact, opposition often makes them cling even more tenaciously to
their convictions. They generally have a hypersensitive conscience and
in some way fear more deeply and consciously what everyone fears in

some form in his inner life. Such men try to master their fears by
reshaping the thoughts of their contemporaries and they live as though
history is making a new beginning with them.

Erikson, the psychologist and historian, has explained how men with
such temperaments have to pass through a mental struggle or an
emotional crisis (or a series of crises) before they emerge as religious
leaders.[11] In some cases this can be little more than an intellectual
struggle with ideas. In others there can be a severe emotional crisis
leading to collapse or illness. Often during this period the future leader
retires from society (for example Muhammad's visits to the mountains)
and it can also be preceded by a period of intense study. What is
happening is that the individual is wrestling with his personality,
passing through an extreme form of the identity crisis which all young
people have to face. This is the period of reassessment when the
influences of tradition fuse with the inner resources to create a new
person. The future leader is seeking a base on which he can stand to
announce his message. He has been seeking that total justification
without which the religious leader has no identity at all. This inner
struggle can be aggravated by external discontent or ideological unrest.

Often part of the identity crisis is concerned with the relationship
with adults, parents or teachers. Ibn Abd-al-Wahhab's relationship with
his father was of crucial importance to the development both of his
character and of his theological views. He quarrelled openly with his
father yet ultimately submitted to his will. The father was of a much
less combative nature than the son and although he condemned
corruption in writing he was not prepared to face public trouble or
opposition caused by himself or his son. (Ibn Abd al-Wahhab's brother
was of a similar character and wrote a tract against his brother's
preaching.) Ibn Abd al-Wahhab respected his father's prohibition —
unwillingly — and, unable to speak out, he left for his period of study
in Medina and Basra. On his return to Huraimila he immediately began
once again, now aged 35, to propagate his views and, according to the
sources, 'there arose between him and his father words (*kalam*)'[12] and
once again he fell silent. To do so when having such a compulsion to
preach shows a rather impressive filial obedience — especially when this
is compared, for example, to the break between Luther and his father.
In this period of silence and presumably meditation, he probably
composed his basic text, *Kitab al-tawhid*. Immediately Abd al-Wahhab
died his son began openly to propagate his *da'wa*.

This attitude of extreme respect and obedience was assimilated into
Ibn Abd al-Wahhab's attitude towards God and into the obedience he

demanded of others towards his message. He tends to sacrifice the idea
of the goodness of God to the idea of omnipotence, and the formulae
he employs define this omnipotence as arbitrary and without restraint.
Obedience to God (*'ibada*) is of the first importance and the believer's
principal duty is to please Him by good works, regular prayer and
performance of religious duties. There must be total service to Him, in
an attitude of love, submission, trust, fear and hope. Perfect love of
God is achieved in the most humble submission to Him. (This doctrine
is, in fact, not far removed from *sufi* teaching.)

Complete submission and obedience implies a rather rigid and
unquestioning attitude towards life. This seems to apply totally to Ibn
Abd al-Wahhab. Once convinced of the rightness of his message, he
demanded total obedience of his followers to it and to him. His *da'wa*
has been seen as rather austere, laying stress on the avoidance of
forbidden things and the restriction of human activities to practices
specifically sanctioned in the Koran. The Wahhabi state pushed to the
extreme the duty to obey; as Ibn Abd al-Wahhab said, 'We teach
complete obedience to the imamate.'[13]

His identity crisis is difficult to assess due to lack of information.
From his early attempt to preach, through his prolonged period of
study, to the proclamation of his *da'wa* at the age of 37, there seems to
have been a steady growth of conviction, not an instant conversion.
From an early age he was not afraid to preach, to suffer persecution
and confront opposition. His problems with his father he transmuted
into obedience to God and it may be that in his periods of silence and
retirement he was coming to terms with his future mission. His closeness
to death in the desert and his period of recovery must have strengthened
his convictions and his urge to preach openly.

A *mujaddid* feels estranged from the compromise patterns into which
his society has settled. He steps aside and isolates himself in order to try
to change society. To fulfil his role he must be able to impart his
message to others who accept him and his call. Without this acceptance
his own personality remains unfulfilled – at least if he has chosen an
active rather than a passive role. Equally the *mujaddid* can have no
identity without a convincing ideology. How does he convince people
of the validity of his ideas and visions, and how does he start a
movement, persuade people to follow him, and maintain his followers'
enthusiasm? Support may be forthcoming when the populace, because
of a common undercurrent of anxiety, feels an intense need for
rejuvenation. It is clear that movements grow up in situations of
uncertainty, dissatisfaction and disturbance – whether economic,

political, social or religious. The *mujaddid* is the man who recognises these floating ideas, focusing and giving expression to society's anxieties. He identifies himself with an image of society as he wants it to be, not as it is. In the Arabia into which Ibn Abd al-Wahhab was born there seems to have been at least an unarticulated feeling of unease with prevailing religious practices.

To gain a response in his community the putative religious leader has to play on the uncertainty of the time and to arouse in his listeners a state of heightened suggestibility, of openness to ideas and exhortations, so that hundreds or thousands of people may fall under his spell. Men become far more open to ideas and less able to respond to them with caution. How do leaders create this heightened suggestibility? Words are the key – the power by which men are swayed. An emotional style of preaching is not, however, necessary. Calm logical preaching, with much repetition, usually presenting men with dire alternatives – conversion or hell – can achieve the desired effect. Such works instil the emotion of fear into men's minds, and words spoken by great preachers have a magical power over their hearers. Ibn Abd al-Wahhab must have had a deep effect on his listeners, with his stress on the necessity of following the *shari'a* and of abandoning the forbidden on pain of dire punishment. He painted vivid pictures of hell and the day of judgement and yet stressed that the sins of the worst sinner could be effaced by good works. A believer's sincerity would be tested on the day of judgement. His message was not dialectical or polemical, his style not emotional, but brief, threatening, to the point and repetitive. It was that of a deeply convinced man. His own certainty must have been transmitted to his hearers. He said of himself: 'I expounded my beliefs to certain idolators, saying "the whole of worship belongs to God alone" whereupon they would all be left amazed and speechless.'[14] Those who knew him reported that he 'aroused great reverence' and that they had 'heard of no-one more tender and less pompous towards those seeking knowledge, questioning him, or in need.'[15]

Once a movement has started, certain techniques can be used to maintain the following and strengthen faith. A bond is established between the leader and his followers which is kept intact by regular meetings and preaching. Religious ritual is observed – the repetition or chanting of the religious formulae and of the name of God, and the rhythmic use of drums to instil religious fervour. When Ibn Abd al-Wahhab had gained followers he stressed the advantages of belonging to the new community and that only those inside would be saved. The first duty of his followers was to wage a *jihad* to make the world of God rule everywhere, and the fight was primarily against unrepentant Muslims. This permanent *jihad* was one method of gaining, keeping and expanding his following. Another was the regular observance of prayer, meeting in *majlis* and the public exposure of backsliders. The adherent was continuously exposed to Ibn Abd al-Wahhab's example and exhortation and to public pressure. As he wrote in his *'aqida*: 'Prayers are true adoration. Fulfil your vows and dread the day of which the evils have been foretold.' It was said of him: 'His tongue rarely abstained from saying *subhanahu*. People waiting for him would hear him coming saying *al-hamdu lillah* and so on'.[16]

Ideology, Message and Organisation

The ideology of Wahhabism and its roots have probably become obvious in the foregoing sections. Most Islamic revival movements have had the same message, although different aspects have been stressed, usually depending on the milieu in which they were preached. Some movements have been more extreme than others, with apocalyptic and messianic elements. Wahhabism was strictly orthodox, Ibn Abd al-Wahhab making no special claims for himself. His message was that Islam had been corrupted and that a return to the pristine conditions of the early days of the Islamic community was necessary. His religious ideas came either directly from Ibn Hanbal, or indirectly from the same source as interpreted by later scholars, especially Ibn Qudama and Ibn Taimiya. For all these men, doctrine was entirely dominated by ethical considerations, by the conviction that the end of all actions is to serve God. Faith is not just a simple body of rites. It is a whole system of moral convictions based on absolute sincerity in the service of God (*'ibada*). Faith includes the feelings on which this service is based, the formulae in which it is expressed and the actions through which it is practised. In his tract, *Al-usul al-thalatha*, which is a kind of official catechism, Ibn Abd al-Wahhab laid out the requirements of the true Muslim. Four things are necessary: a knowledge and understanding of God, the Prophet and faith; action thereon; the profession of faith; patience in affliction in carrying out the faith. The greatest thing that God has commanded is the assertion of His oneness (*tawhid*); the greatest thing He has forbidden is idolatory (*shirk*). The understanding of faith comprises confession and obedience and it has three stages — salvation, belief and finally gratitude. What is striking in Ibn Abd al-Wahhab's message is the insistence on service to God and the close relationship that this implies.

Much has been made of the prohibitions and restrictions of Wahhabism, yet Ibn Abd al-Wahhab insisted that social obligations stem solely from the religious practices which God has explicitly prescribed, and only in the form prescribed (thus outlawing *sufi* and other practices). Nothing can lawfully be forbidden other than practices forbidden by God in the Koran and *sunna.* Everything considered innovative (*bid'a*) was prohibited on this ground, including music, silk, tobacco, wine, and the worship of trees, stones and saints' tombs. Ibn Abd al-Wahhab added nothing to and took nothing away from the teaching of the Prophet, while stressing certain of its aspects – the necessity of obedience to God, of prayer (he quoted with approval the *hadith*: Prayer is the essence of worship), and of a continual *jihad* (of self, tongue and the sword). He emphasised the promise of paradise: 'The elect will see God in paradise as one sees the full moon.'

From Ibn Taimiya he took the notion that religion and state are indissolubly linked. Without the coercive power of the state, religion is in danger, and without the discipline of revealed law, the state becomes a tyrannical organisation. The duty of the state is to bring about the rule of *tawhid* and to prepare for the coming of a society devoted to the service of God. The mission of the *imam* is to build and instil respect for systems of orders and prohibitions which govern the various areas of the life of the community. The *imam* must also bring about and ensure the solidarity of the community in the face of opposition from outside.

This was the basically simple message that Ibn Abd al-Wahhab preached in his attempt to recreate in Arabia a society similar to that of the earliest days of Islam. Those who followed him were promised paradise. Those who did not were threatened with damnation.

There is one final factor to be mentioned regarding the success of Ibn Abd al-Wahhab's *da'wa.* The *mujaddid* is usually a visionary; he is often ill-fitted to the practical tasks of administering a state, organising an army, collecting taxes, and putting the ideas he propagates into practice. Thus, in coming to terms with political reality and political pressures, the religious leader may either develop into a different type of leader or else may enter into alliance with a more secular man to whom practical matters can be entrusted. Ibn Abd al-Wahhab began his preaching in Huraimila without political backing and became so embroiled in factionalism that he was almost murdered by a group of slaves whose conduct he had criticised. He escaped to 'Uyaina where he saw the need to gain the support of a strong ruler.

He first approached the *amir* of 'Uyaina, Uthman b. Mu'ammar, who initially supported the *da'wa* after he had been promised the rulership of 'Najd and its Arabs'. The alliance seemed to work well and Uthman allowed him to preach and to take such practical steps as destroying tombs and holy trees. However, the *amir* later capitulated before protests from another ruler, the chief of the Banu Khalid, and Ibn Abd al-Wahhab had to move on again, this time fortuitously to Dar'iya. The *amir* of Dar'iya, Muhammad b. Sa'ud, proved receptive to him and entered into a pact by which he engaged himself to wage *jihad* on behalf of Abd al-Wahhab's doctrines, to establish the *shari'a* and to enforce the good and forbid the evil. The *mujaddid* had gained the support he needed to be able to preach his message. The Saudis derived legitimacy from Wahhabism as *imams* of the only truly religious community in Islam, while Ibn Abd al-Wahhab needed Saudi political power. The movement which developed from the pact was not simply a religious undertaking aimed at convincing those Muslims in Najd who were dissatisfied with the state of Islam. The Wahhabi message was henceforward linked with the political fortunes of the dynasty which, to promote the *da'wa*, engaged on a campaign of expansion that eventually threatened the power of other rulers in Arabia. Thus the religious message of Wahhabism was perpetuated in a state committed to uphold its principles.

Notes

1. Besides the books and articles mentioned in the other references, the following sources were used in the preparation of this study: M. J. Crawford, 'Wahhabi 'Ulama and the Law 1745–1932 AD', unpublished MPhil thesis, University of Oxford, 1980 (I would like to thank Mr Crawford for his help with sources and his kindness in sharing his ideas with me); Uthman Ibn Bishr, *Majmu'at al-Rasa'il wal-Masa'il Najdiya* (4 vols., Dar al-Manar, Cairo, 1928); H. St J. Philby, *Sa'udi Arabia* (Benn, London, 1955); G. Rentz, 'Muhammad Ibn Abd al-Wahhab (1703/04–1792) and the Beginnings of the Unitarian Empire in Arabia', unpublished PhD thesis, University of California, 1948; G. A. Wallin, *Travels in Arabia (1845 and 1848)* (Cambridge University Press, Cambridge, 1979).

2. The meanings of Arabic words used in this article may be found in the glossary.

3. I shall use this term due to its wide currency, although the movement is more correctly referred to as that of the '*Muwahhidun*'.

4. H. A. R. Gibb, *Modern Trends in Islam* (Octagon, New York, 1975), p. 35.

5. Names of some of these are given in Uthman Ibn Bishr, '*Unwan al-Majd fi Tarikh Najd* (Dar al-Sadir, Beirut, no date); and in Mansur al-Rashud, 'Qudat Najd', *Al-Dara*, vol. 4 (1978–9).

6. There are various stories of his wanderings through Persia and elsewhere

during this period but it is difficult to verify them.

7. See J. Voll, 'Muhammad Hayya al-Sindi and Muhammad Ibn Abd al-Wahhab: an analysis of an intellectual group in 18th century Medina', *Bulletin of the School of Oriental and African Studies*, vol. 38 (1975).

8. Ibn Ghannam, *Rawdat al-Afkar* (Dar al-Manar, Cairo, 1949), vol. 1, p. 32.

9. Ibn Bishr, *'Unwan al-Majd*, p. 22.

10. It is interesting that in the ninth century, Ali b. Muhammad, who was later to lead the Zanj movement, began his preaching in Basra and was likewise quickly ejected. Time and place were not right for him either.

11. E. Erikson, *Young Man Luther* (Faber, London, 1959).

12. Ibn Bishr, *'Unwan al-Majd*, p. 18.

13. H. Laoust, *Essai sur les Doctrines Sociales et Politiques d'Ibn Taimiya* (Institut Français d'Archéologie Orientale, Cairo, 1939), p. 527.

14. Ibn Ghannam, *Rawdat al-Afkar*, vol. 1, p. 33.

15. Ibn Bishr, *'Unwan al-Majd*, p. 83.

16. Ibid., p. 82.

3 THE PRECARIOUS MONARCHY: BRITAIN, ABD AL-AZIZ IBN SAUD AND THE ESTABLISHMENT OF THE KINGDOM OF HIJAZ, NAJD AND ITS DEPENDENCIES, 1925–1932[1]

Peter Sluglett and Marion Farouk-Sluglett

In December 1925, Abd al-Aziz ibn Saud finally captured Jeddah from the forces of King Ali, the son of ex-King Husain of the Hijaz, and brought to an end the struggle between the House of Hashim and the House of Saud which had been pursued intermittently since 1917. St John Philby, who had yet to attach himself more closely to Abd al-Aziz's entourage, believed, in the words of the United States Consul at Aden, that Abd al-Aziz could easily have taken Jeddah whenever he felt like it, but he preferred to wait until that city should fall into his hands 'like an overripe apple'.[2] Sir Gilbert Clayton, who had spent October and early November in the vicinity of Jeddah concluding the Bahra and Hadda agreements with Abd al-Aziz,[3] gave a more convincing rationalisation:

> I think he is holding his hand in order to appreciate more fully the impression which his capture of Mecca (in October–November 1924) has produced on the Moslem world in general, and – as regards Jedda – in fear lest some harm should come to the foreign consuls if he took the place by storm[4]

In this article we shall examine Abd al-Aziz's early attempts to establish himself as effective ruler within his now very considerable domains, and his simultaneous efforts to gain international recognition for himself and his country in the crucial years between 1925 and 1932. As we shall see, many important obstacles had to be surmounted during this short period. The warrior *ikhwan* had to be muzzled; the inhabitants of the Hijaz had to be persuaded or induced to accept the rule of their traditional rivals from Najd; the kingdom had to be kept solvent; and Britain's approbation earned. An analysis of developments in these early years should help towards a deeper understanding of the Saudi state as it emerged.

Since Abd al-Aziz's most crucial diplomatic relations had been, and continued to be, with Great Britain, it is clear that British official perceptions of developments in the Arabian peninsula are of particular importance in providing an insight into the political dynamics of the newly unified state. British official documents must, therefore, form an indispensable basis for the account given here. The main collection is in the Public Record Office in London, but various other documents relating to Sir Gilbert Clayton's missions to Abd al-Aziz have also been preserved in the Sudan Archive at Durham. This article makes use of both of these collections.

It is perhaps worth placing the material presented here within the context of other work undertaken in the same field. Over the last few years, the somewhat gloomy picture of Saudi Arabian historiography presented by Derek Hopwood in 1972[5] has considerably improved, notably with the appearance of three books, by Monroe (1973),[6] Troeller (1976)[7] and Habib (1978).[8] All three add considerably to our knowledge of the early years of the Saudi state before the Second World War. Elizabeth Monroe's *Philby of Arabia* is obviously primarily concerned with its central character, but contains valuable insights regarding the enormous problems facing the young Saudi state. Gary Troeller's *Birth of Sa'udi Arabia* provides a meticulously documented account of the gradual rise of the House of Saud between 1910 and 1926, from Abd al-Aziz's 'first contact with a British official until he conquered the Hijaz from the Hashimites, thus eliminating his chief rivals in Arabia'.[9] It is particularly useful in illuminating the struggles for political influence between the officials of the government of India and the Foreign Office, and the differing perspectives of these two often antagonistic groups. It also shows how Abd al-Aziz was able to direct the energies of those he had recently conquered in Northern Najd to the lure of even brighter prospects in the Hijaz. Finally, John S. Habib's *Ibn Sa'ud's Warriors of Islam: the Ikhwan of Najd and their Role in the Creation of the Sa'udi Kingdom, 1910–1930* shows how Abd al-Aziz set a fanatical force in motion which he was ultimately unable to control, and which might well have destroyed him and his followers but for outside intervention from his British allies.

Although Abd al-Aziz had conquered virtually the whole area which forms the modern state[10] by the beginning of 1926, the more prosaic, and in a certain sense more taxing, task of consolidation still lay in front of him. The transition from a victorious warrior leader, a *ghazi*, perhaps, to the head of a civil government, was fraught with difficulties. In the first place, his closest supporters had to be convinced that such a transition was in any case desirable; secondly, most of the inhabitants of the Hijaz regarded Abd al-Aziz's troops as little more than barbarians, who posed a serious threat both to their normal way of life and to the security of the pilgrimage, their main source of livelihood. Thirdly, his financial situation was (and long remained) extremely precarious, and finally, he desperately needed international recognition, particularly from Britain. Britain's concern with developments in the new state was based primarily on the interests of its Muslim subjects. Incongruous as it must seem now, 'we are', wrote Consul Stonehewer Bird in November 1929, 'the greatest Moslem power in the world, and as such our relations with the ruler of the Holy Places of Islam are bound to be closer and more important than those of other countries.'[11] Needless to say, strategic interests were also involved,[12] but the pilgrimage occupied most of the working hours of three full-time officials in the British Consulate in Jeddah, and its successor the Legation, for five months every year until the end of the 1930s.

The four main problems facing Abd al-Aziz — Najdi—Hijazi relations, the *ikhwan*, the finances of the new state and its international relations — are all interrelated. They will, however, be treated separately, with the main emphasis placed on Anglo-Saudi relations.

Najdi—Hijazi Relations

The most urgent task confronting Abd al-Aziz in 1926 was to effect some *modus vivendi* between his immediate followers and his new subjects in the Hijaz. The two halves of the kingdom were more or less incompatible. The Hijaz, on the one hand, had had many generations' experience of settled, and to some extent orderly, rule under Ottoman suzerainty. It was also extremely cosmopolitan, both in its ethnic composition and in its unique function as host to tens of thousands of pilgrims from the international Muslim community. Najd, on the other hand, had had only the most rudimentary civil government, and was the centre of a puritanical and ascetic Islamic sect whose adherents believed that their own path was uniquely righteous, and that any deviation from it could and should be punished by death. Wahhabism itself, of course, is not so severe, but the troops which Abd al-Aziz had created, the *ikhwan*, were nurtured on a very extreme form of this ideology.

In 1926, then, the *ikhwan* had conquered the Hijaz and driven out the Hashimites. This inevitably posed most critically the question of how the two parts of the kingdom would be related, and made clear one of the fundamental contradictions in the new polity — a contradiction which even the eventual crushing of the 'dissident' *ikhwan* at the end of 1929 did not resolve entirely.[13] The nature of Abd al-Aziz's position within Najd inhibited the role which he could play in the Hijaz. The bond between Abd al-Aziz and his subjects in Najd was both tribal and religious: although he called himself *malik*, king, he was essentially *shaikh al-shuyukh*, as J. J. Malone and others have pointed out.[14] The important distinction is that, in what may be called the traditional and more tribal setting of Najd, allegiance had to be imposed and maintained and, perhaps most significantly, could be lost. Tribes or sections could leave alliances or confederations if they lost faith in or felt dissatisfied with a particular ruler, and in the case of early twentieth-century Najd the position was further complicated by a strong religious element in the political relationship. In the difficult task of consolidating his authority over the Hijaz, therefore, Abd al-Aziz was constricted by the nature of his position in Najd. He spent two years in the Hijaz following the conquest and there is considerable evidence of the Najdi pressures to which he was subject. By December 1928, 'reports that many of the *ikhwan* were deeply dissatisfied with his rule had been current for over a year'.[15]

The Hijaz was, of course, the major potential revenue-producing part of the new kingdom, and it was necessary for Abd al-Aziz to obtain the acquiescence, if not the wholehearted co-operation, of the population of the holy cities and Jeddah in his rule. The task of gaining this acquiescence was facilitated to some extent by popular distaste for the former government of King Husain. The very considerable corruption which had characterised that government had resulted in widespread disillusionment with Hashimite rule. A report from the American Consulate in Aden in November 1923, noted that

> [King Husain] feels himself to be so sure in his position, so far removed from the consequences of public opinion, that no excesses or crimes are too great for him to consider, provided that they are money getters. He lives to rob and the organisation of the Hedjaz kingdom today is a gigantic scheme for the wholesale fleecing of pilgrims.

A year later the same source commented

> the career of Hussein in Hedjaz in Arabia is ended. And he has chiefly himself to blame. His rule was one of oppression, arising from his insatiable avarice . . . He taxed everything he could think of

and held himself accountable to no-one for the disposal of the proceeds . . . Had Hussein's rule been less oppressive, he would have had the unwavering support of all the Arabs of the dominating Sunni sect.[16]

In spite of this, it would have been inconceivable for the Hijazis to have viewed the Najdis, still less the *ikhwan*, as deliverers; both the holy cities had been sacked and then occupied by an earlier Wahhabi invasion between 1805 and 1813. The Hijazis could have had little doubt as to Wahhabi attitudes towards their religious practices, nor as to the determination of Najdi *'ulama* to enforce Wahhabi practices in the Hijaz. As Consul Bullard noted after the capture of Mecca in 1924:

> The account of the alleged agreement between the *'ulama* of Najd and Mecca as to the main articles of faith suggests to what extent Ibn Sa'ud is compelled to countenance the puritannical views of his followers. It is incredible that the *'ulama* of Mecca would ever approve of tenets which are repugnant to most of the pilgrims by whom they live.[17]

This was a reference to Wahhabi hostility to pilgrimages to saints' tombs, intercession and so forth. In the earlier invasion, the Wahhabis had not hesitated to sack the tombs of members of the Prophet's family.

The path which Abd al-Aziz pursued reflected both his appreciation of Hijazi sensitivities and his concern to retain Najdi support. It is significant that although the *ikhwan* took Mecca, they were specifically prohibited from entering Medina or Jeddah when these cities fell to Abd al-Aziz at the end of 1925. Hafiz Wahba, an Egyptian associate of Abd al-Aziz, was made governor of Mecca. Nevertheless, it was not possible for Abd al-Aziz to disregard the feelings and beliefs of his closest supporters, and the Wahhabi *'ulama* of Najd (though not the *ikhwan*) were drafted into the Hijaz administration.[18] An early example of the volatility of this situation and its potential national and international repercussions was afforded in June 1926, when the band accompanying the Egyptian *mahmal*, carrying the *kiswa* or cover for the Ka'ba, was set upon by zealous Wahhabis, to whom the playing of musical instruments was an affront. The Egyptians opened fire in panic, and the incident might have developed even more gravely but for the intervention of Abd al-Aziz's second son, Amir Faisal, who managed to restore order. Diplomatic relations with Egypt were disrupted for ten years following this incident. Coming only a few weeks after the Islamic conference, which in effect gave the seal of respectability to Abd al-Aziz's conquest of the Hijaz, the incident illustrated the difficulty of the King's position as mediator between his own supporters and the international Muslim community.

It is interesting to record that, in the early years of the new state, the newly arrived religious enthusiasts of Najd were only occasionally able to exercise their powers in the Hijaz. On some issues they seem to have been able to exert decisive influence, but not on others. In July 1929, Consul Bond reported that all the non-Hanbali *imams* at the mosque in Mecca had been replaced, by three 'Wahhabis', two of whom were Indian and one Hijazi.[19] A few months later, however, the fourth anniversary of Abd al-Aziz's accession to the throne of Hijaz (which also coincided with the defeat of Faisal al-Dawish) was marked by celebrations which

were organised on an unprecedented scale for Arabia and were obviously intended to impress both foreigners and Arabs alike ... They may be said to mark a definite departure from the rigid precepts which the Akhwan had succeeded temporarily in imposing. Photographs were taken freely: an official photographer had in fact come from Egypt and photographed the Emir (Faisal) on every possible occasion. Smoking was indulged in openly or with only a pretence at concealment.[20]

Three months after the celebrations, the religious disciplinary committees had become active again.

The regulations issued by these committees nineteen months ago had been allowed practically to become a dead letter, and the local citizens, who had been congratulating themselves on the gradual evanescence of these tiresome restrictions were greatly annoyed to find them resuscitated by lictors or special police imported from Najd who carry out their duties with deplorable efficiency ... small boys playing mouth organs have been the first to receive attention. These diminutive miscreants are given a taste of the cane and the offending instruments collected in baskets ...[21]

In May 1930, however, it was reported that 'Jidda remains the home of laxity. The voice of the menaced gramophone is still heard in the land.'[22] As the pendulum swung back and forth, the obvious ambiguities still persisted in December 1930.

A tendency was remarked to increase Nejdi influence in the Hejaz. The use of the Nejdi headdress has now been imposed by Government order upon Hejazi officials. On the other hand, there has been no further attempt of late to impose strict Wahhabi principles. If anything, the tendency to compromise has been a little more in the ascendant. On his return after several months' absence, Sir Andrew Ryan found the gramophone as much a feature of life as before, and choral music, bearing a singular resemblance to Christian hymn tunes, raged relentlessly in the school close to the Legation house apparently in preparation for the celebration of the King's accession day on the 8th January. Mecca also has its school choirs.[23]

Clearly, these reports must be taken with a pinch of salt, but it is interesting to see the same themes reappearing well into the 1930s.[24] The unification of the kingdom was evidently a difficult matter. It may be added that formal administrative unity was only established in 1953, when al-Riyadh was designated the capital; 'Before that date, each of the four traditional areas of al-Hijaz, Najd, al-Hasa and 'Asir were ruled differently as a consequence of their differences in history, environment and contact with outside powers.'[25]

The Ikhwan

As has already been mentioned, the *ikhwan* had played the central role in the military campaign against King Husain. The *ikhwan* had almost killed Abdullah ibn Husain at Turaba in 1919, had stormed Ha'il, and after a few diversionary raids on Iraq, had conquered the main towns of the Hijaz in 1924–5. By the end of the 1920s, however, this powerful fighting vehicle was virtually uncontrollable; the arguments which Abd al-Aziz had used to encourage the *ikhwan* to conquer the Hijaz could now be turned against him with perfect logic; if a *jihad* against the Hijaz was lawful, why not a *jihad* against Iraq? Fortunately for the survival of his kingdom, Britain's interests in this matter coincided with Abd al-Aziz's own.

In their dangerously belligerent mood, the *ikhwan* not only represented a threat to Abd al-Aziz's supremacy in Najd and to the stability of the Hijaz, but also to the careful fence-mending which Abd al-Aziz was undertaking *vis-à-vis* Britain. The details of these negotiations will be dealt with separately, but for the moment it is important to note that from a comparatively early date the *ikhwan* had been raiding Iraq, which was a mandated territory in treaty relations with Britain, and ruled, at least nominally, by Faisal, the son of ex-King Husain, Abd al-Aziz's old enemy from the Hijaz. At the end of 1924 the *ikhwan* launched a particularly savage raid against Iraq, which Glubb has vividly described.[26] In spite of definite prohibitions from Abd al-Aziz, who was well aware of the damage this might do to his relations with Britain, the raids continued into 1925 and 1927. In response, the Iraqi authorities and the RAF proposed the construction of a series of fortifications, at Busa'iya and Sulman, which would be able to provide advance warning of raids and facilitate early punitive action. However, in November 1927, while the Busa'iya fort was actually being constructed, an *ikhwan* raiding party under the notorious Faisal al-Dawish attacked the fort and killed all the building workers on the site as well as the detachment of police who were guarding them. Eventually al-Dawish was pursued into Najdi territory by British aeroplanes.

Even at this stage, well before the *ikhwan* revolt, it was clear that Abd al-Aziz could not control 'his own men'. In seeking to evade the dilemmas which the *ikhwan* raids on Iraq posed for him, Abd al-Aziz took issue with the British over the construction of the forts. He alleged that the forts were a contravention of the terms of Article 3 of the Protocol of 'Uqair, which he had signed in 1922. This stated that no fortifications should be built 'in the vicinity of the frontier', a phrase which, as we shall see, was interpreted in one way in Baghdad and in quite another in al-Riyadh. Abd al-Aziz argued that he could not punish his followers, since they were taking action against military structures that were clearly illegal in the terms of the Protocol. The dangers of a full-scale desert war between the *ikhwan* and the southern Iraq tribes were only too apparent, and the Iraqis, lacking the military organisation and fanatical zeal of the *ikhwan*, were almost certain to be worsted. Clayton, who had negotiated several agreements with Abd al-Aziz, was once more sent to Jeddah by the Foreign and Colonial Offices to try to resolve the dispute.

In the course of the period November 1927–February 1928, nine major *ikhwan* raids took place. As well as causing havoc to the inhabitants of the frontier area, any consolidation of *ikhwan* influence in Southern Iraq would almost certainly pose a severe threat to the Iraq Petroleum Company's scheme for a pipeline and a railway.[27] For his part, Abd al-Aziz alleged that 'the action of the RAF, in invading his territory, has made it impossible for him to inflict on Faisal al-Dawish the punishment he was prepared to mete out when RAF machines flew over and bombed his territory'.[28] However, as the Political Resident in the Persian Gulf shrewdly pointed out, while

> it should not be forgotten by us or by Ibn Saʻud that the origin of [the] trouble was the attack on Busaʻiya — I feel assured that Ibn Saʻud is even more anxious for peace than we are. Unsettled conditions at present contain seeds of danger for him.[29]

In the course of his meetings with Clayton between 8 and 20 May 1928, Abd al-Aziz insisted that the posts should be dismantled, a demand which Clayton was unable to accept. It is interesting that RAF action was singled out again, this time by Clayton, as an important stumbling block:

> if [air action] had been confined to the pursuit of actual raiders across the border, I believe that Ibn Saʻud might have come to an agreement and in any event he would have had a poor case. Continuous raids across the frontier, or forcing back, by means of warning notices and bombs, tribes who had not been concerned in the Busaʻiya raids, have given Ibn Saʻud a useful argument and has hardened the northern tribes in their opposition to the posts.[30]

In the report of his failure to achieve a settlement, sent to the Colonial Office on 10 July 1928, Clayton underlined the dangers of pushing Abd al-Aziz too far.

> it should be borne in mind that the bare rejection of Ibn Saʻud's representations might make it impossible for him to continue to exercise a moderating influence on his tribes. Without accepting his statements at their face value, I feel that, unless he is offered some tangible concession which might enable him to continue his efforts for peace on the border, there is a risk of the situation in Najd getting out of hand.[31]

Conversations were renewed in August 1928, but little further progress was made on the question of the removal or non-removal of the forts.[32] It is clear from the correspondence that Abd al-Aziz was having increasing difficulties with those who might loosely be termed his supporters. He told George Antonius that he had promised the Najdis

that the offending posts would be destroyed, arguing, as before, that
they contravened Article 3 of the Protocol of 'Uqair, which stated that
no fortifications should be built 'in the vicinity of the frontier' (*'ala
atraf al-hudud*). It is difficult to see, in spite of Glubb's sympathetic
explanation[33] how this term could be applied to forts lying 70 miles
within Iraqi territory, but the King was adamant. Antonius reports that
at one point Abd al-Aziz turned to Hafiz Wahba and said 'Would that I
had never mentioned Article Three to them!'[34] Clearly, if he could not
obtain Britain's agreement to the destruction of the posts, he would
run the risk of losing credibility with his subjects.

In the event, of course, neither side was pushed to the brink. By the
winter of 1928—9, Glubb and his colleagues in the RAF had perfected a
technique for obtaining early warnings of raids from Najd, which
enabled aeroplanes to attack an *ikhwan* raid at Jumaima at the edge of
the Neutral Zone on 19 December, and drive them off.

> The defeat of Ibn Ashwan's raid produced a profound effect on the
> Ikhwan exactly at the moment when they were preparing their
> grand offensive against Iraq . . . Had they returned in triumph . . .
> more Nejed tribes would have joined them, and American
> companies might never . . . or not for many years . . . have secured a
> concession to prospect for oil in Arabia.[35]

Furthermore, the British authorities in Iraq had by now come to the
conclusion that it was more important to bolster Abd al-Aziz's
authority than to stand on Iraqi dignity, and that any successful attack
on his position in Najd would bode ill both for Iraq and for Najd's
other neighbours.[36] Eventually Abd al-Aziz managed to inflict a serious
defeat on the rebels at Sibila in March 1929[37] and by the end of
December the combined forces of the King and the RAF had forced
the surrender of Faisal al-Dawish, the most persistent and dangerous of
the rebels.

Finance

From the time of his earliest contacts with Britain, Abd al-Aziz had
always emphasised his need for money. In the course of the First
World War, of course, he had been supplied with a certain amount of
rifles and ammunition, and in fact received a subsidy of approximately
£5,000 per month between 1915 and March 1923. In 1926, when he

had established himself in the Hijaz, his sole sources of income were the Jeddah customs and various taxes taken from pilgrims. Thus the revival of the pilgrimage was vital if the state was to become solvent, and in fact the next few years saw considerable improvements in public security and in transport facilities for pilgrims between Jeddah and Mecca. In spite of this, because of the considerable annual fluctuation in pilgrim numbers, the income of the state was always uncertain: 1927 was a bumper year, but a steady decline set in afterwards, and the world economic depression of the early 1930s made matters even worse (see Table 3.1).

Table 3.1: Number of Pilgrims to the Saudi State, 1927–32[38]

Year	Number of pilgrims
1927	132,000
1928	88,000
1929	82,000
1930	85,000
1931	39,500
1932	29,500

Source: Jeddah report, April 1932: HM Legation, Jeddah, Despatch No. 312 of 29 May 1932.

In fact, through the whole period under review, and until well beyond it, the Saudi state lurched from one financial crisis to another. In 1938, just before the first substantial oil strike was made, one of the leading merchants of Jeddah gave one of the British Legation staff an estimate of the state revenues (see Table 3.2).

Table 3.2: Estimation of the State Revenues in 1938[39]

Source	£ gold
Hijaz customs	600,000
Pilgrims and other revenue	700,000
	1,300,000

Source: Conversation between Muhammad Ali Ridha and Lal Shah, Indian Vice-Consul, Jeddah; Minute of 9 May 1938, FO 905/57.

Later in the same year, 'The police [have been] unpaid for some time and the Saudi Arabian government cannot pay their employees for some months . . . until the arrival of pilgrims for next year's Hajj . . .'[40]

It was the same story throughout the 1930s. In 1930, officials' salaries were substantially in arrears, and the government had borrowed money from most of the commercial companies in Jeddah. Apart from the sheer lack of revenues, the King's personal life-style was necessarily extravagant; one of the fundamental problems of the finances of the kingdom was, according to the Dutch Consul, Van der Meulen, Abd al-Aziz's refusal to allow any separation between the Exchequer and the Privy Purse.[47] Throughout the period there were oblique hints from the Saudi side that Britain might in some way care to come to the aid of the new state.

Early in 1929 Fuad Hamza, the Acting Foreign Minister, intimated that Abd al-Aziz would like to conclude a commercial treaty with Great Britain. It emerged in the course of his conversations with Stonehewer Bird that something rather more positive was desired.

> Fu'ad wished to assure me that no considerations had weighed more with the King than his desire to be loyal to his old-time friendship with Britain. If, however, he were to continue in this course, he would ask for some mark of appreciation from HMG to compensate for the material loss which his policy was causing to the country. I asked Fu'ad what form he considered that this mark of appreciation should take. He replied that the King left this to the generosity of HMG.[42]

The reference here is partly to the cessation of raiding, and partly to Abd al-Aziz's decision to have nothing to do with consignments of Russian goods which were being dumped at Jeddah and greatly undercutting local traders. It emerged a few weeks later from conversations with Hafiz Wahba in Cairo that what was actually wanted was a subsidy.

> It was largely by presents and by lavish hospitality that the tribes could be kept in order. Unfortunately the financial resources of Ibn Sa'ud and his government were meagre, and there was no doubt that he was faced with considerable financial stringency . . .[43]

In fact, no direct subsidies were given, but Abd al-Aziz received arms on very easy terms from the government of India, and paid virtually nothing for the aeroplanes for the Saudi air force (which was started in 1930). There seems to have been some slight fear that the King might turn to 'Bolshevik gold' if his more pressing needs were not satisfied.[44] That unthinkable prospect was averted, but debts did mount up: in

November 1930 the government owed £30,000 to the government of
India, £4,000 to the Eastern Telegraph Company, and £6,000 to the
banking and marine company Gellatly, Hankey,[45] as well as £80,000 to
the King's private banker, Abdullah al-Qusaibi, and £4,000 to the
Governor of Jeddah.[46] In September 1931 the government actually
commandeered the petrol stocks of Gellatly, Hankey, and Philby's firm,
Sharqieh Ltd. Philby was also owed for the wireless stations installed
in the course of the same year.[47] The situation could only have been
alleviated temporarily by the signing of the Standard Oil of California
concessions on 29 May 1933. The latter agreement brought in £50,000
— 'a tidy price for rights the value of which is admitted to be still
entirely problematical'.[48]

As has already been explained, this gloomy state of affairs continued
until the Second World War, and the whole financial structure of the
Saudi state might well have collapsed without the windfall from oil.
Abd al-Aziz's financial difficulties caused some alarm to Britain in the
later 1930s, partly because of fears that the Italians might attempt to
buy him up or bale him out:[49]

> it is clearly to our interest that Sa'udi Arabia should become as
> stable and prosperous as possible. Ibn Sa'ud [is] at present in grave
> financial difficulties and if his financial situation becomes desperate
> he would be the more tempted to . . . accept help from some other
> quarter, e.g. Italy. His lack of resources might well tip the scale in
> turning him against us and the results might be very serious.[50]

This prospect, too, failed to materialise, but it is significant that the
King's financial difficulties remained a major cause of concern both
within the country and to his senior ally throughout the early years of
the new state.

Relations with Britain

Early in November 1925, while negotiating the Bahra and Hadda
agreements with Clayton, Abd al-Aziz intimated that he would like to
regularise his relations with Britain. 'He felt that, as an independent
ruler, dealings between his government and that of Great Britain should
be carried out through the medium of the Foreign Office.'[51] It also
emerged that he wished to renegotiate the treaty of 1915 which still
governed his relations with Britain. Since the war in the Hijaz was still

raging, and Britain had full diplomatic relations with King Ali, it was thought best to delay the matter to a more opportune moment. Although some fairly well-trodden ground may be covered in the process, it is now probably useful to trace the history of Abd al-Aziz's relations with Britain.[52]

In 1913, while acknowledging in a somewhat *sub rosa* and ambiguous fashion that Abd al-Aziz was ruler of Najd, Britain also accepted, as far as her relations with Turkey were concerned, that, since Najd was *de jure* if not *de facto* an Ottoman province, Abd al-Aziz must be considered an Ottoman vassal. Hence Britain declined to conclude a treaty with Abd al-Aziz which would have conferred British protected status upon him, in spite of a clear request from him to do so. The India Office advocated recognition and a treaty, while the Foreign Office felt that its overriding commitments were to Turkey. Rejected by Britain, Abd al-Aziz signed a treaty with Turkey in May 1914,[53] which recognised him as Governor-General and Commander-in-Chief of Najd. Fearing that Abd al-Aziz might actually co-operate militarily with the Turks, presumably against Britain in Mesopotamia, the India Office sent Captain Shakespear to negotiate with him shortly after the outbreak of the First World War. At this stage Abd al-Aziz was occupied in a campaign against his hereditary enemies the Rashids of Ha'il, who were more closely attached to the Turks than he was. Shakespear, as is well known, was killed before a treaty could be negotiated, but by December 1915 'Abd al-Aziz assented to the same status – a veiled British protectorate – as that of the Persian Gulf shaikhdoms nearby'.[54] The general effect of this treaty was to secure Abd al-Aziz's friendship, and to ensure that he did not participate in the war on the Turkish side. In 1917, as a result of a visit by Philby, he was given a subsidy of £5,000 per month and 3,000 rifles, and persuaded to mount an offensive against Ha'il.

At the same time, of course, Britain was subsidising another of Abd al-Aziz's enemies, Sharif Husain of Mecca, in a rather more grandiose design. As Abd al-Aziz grew more powerful in Najd, he began to cast ambitious eyes towards the Hijaz, and gradually extended his authority further and further westwards into what had traditionally been regarded as Hijazi territory. Major clashes occurred in 1918 and 1919 over the settlements of Khurma and Turaba, which both Abd al-Aziz and Husain claimed to lie within their jurisdictions. In May 1919, Husain's son 'Abdullah was ignominiously chased out of Turaba by a force of some 12,000 *ikhwan*, and open warfare was avoided only by Abd al-Aziz's undertaking not to perform the pilgrimage in 1919. In 1920 an armistice was patched up between the two sides, pending British arbitration over the boundary between them.

Between 1920 and 1922 Abd al-Aziz, with the aid of the *ikhwan*, annexed 'Asir, Jauf and Ha'il, and in March 1924, when his subsidy from Britain was terminated and Husain claimed the caliphate, he prepared to attack the Hijaz. In September of that year, the *ikhwan* captured Ta'if, and massacred its inhabitants: Husain called for British support, which was refused, and he was forced to abdicate a month later. In October the *ikhwan* took Mecca without a shot being fired. Throughout the Hijaz war, Britain and the other powers accredited to Husain refused to intervene. Nevertheless, the fact that the Bahra and Hadda agreements were being negotiated before the war had actually finished showed that Britain had little doubt of the eventual outcome.

Abd al-Aziz's first contacts, both with Shakespear and with Sir Percy Cox, who actually signed the treaty of 1915, were officially with the government of India, which had similar relations with other 'independent' Gulf rulers. The treaty was not one between equals; Abd al-Aziz was not to enter

> into any correspondence, agreements or Treaty with any Foreign Nation or Power and further to give immediate notice to the political authorities of the British Government of any attempt on the part of any other powers to interfere with [his] territories.

He also undertook not to interfere in the affairs of Kuwait, Bahrain, Qatar and the Trucial Coast, all of which had similar treaties to his own. The senior British representative in the area was the Resident in the Persian Gulf and Consul-General of Fars, who was responsible to the India Office in his capacity as Resident and to the Foreign Office as Consul-General. When Britain took over mandatory responsibility for Iraq and Transjordan in the early 1920s, the High Commissioner in Baghdad and the Chief British Representative in Amman came under the Colonial Office. As a result of this, the Resident and Consul-General was now instructed to communicate with the Colonial Office on matters, for example, concerning relations between Kuwait and Iraq.

Since the mid-nineteenth century, Britain had maintained a consul at Jeddah for the Hijaz, which was then officially part of the Ottoman Empire. The consul was normally seconded from the government of India, and his duties were mainly concerned with the pilgrimage. In May 1925, S. R. Jordan of the Levant Consular Service took over as British Agent and Consul, now accredited, of course, to King Ali of the

Hijaz, the 'legal successor' of the Ottoman Empire. A few months later, as we have seen, Abd al-Aziz expressed his desire to Clayton to regularise his own position *vis-à-vis* the British government, and to renegotiate the treaty of 1915 on lines which would be more appropriate to his position as a potentially independent ruler. In his despatch to the Colonial Office, Clayton indicated that Abd al-Aziz desired recognition of the independence of Najd, the right to import arms freely into that territory, and a measure of financial assistance: his efforts to prevent his tribesmen raiding into what were now states under British protection had deprived them of a traditional means of subsistence for which they were now demanding compensation.[55]

In the autumn of 1926, therefore, Consul Jordan, now accredited to Abd al-Aziz and the Hijaz—Najd government, was authorised to begin negotiations for the new treaty. In a private letter to Clayton, George Antonius, who was to accompany Jordan, conveyed his misgivings about the mission:

> I do not think that the problem this time is as difficult as at Bahra; and yet I do not anticipate success. Jordan has many qualities and is undoubtedly *persona grata* with Ibn Sa'ud. But the more I see of him, the more convinced I become that he is not the man for the job . . . Shaikh Yusuf Yasin called on me yesterday afternoon and had a chat. He told me that Ibn Sa'ud had been expecting you and wanted to know whether you were coming later to see this thing through.[56]

Antonius's instincts were correct: after three weeks of negotiations near Medina, it was not found possible to conclude a new treaty. There were several points of disagreement, but the real stumbling blocks were the King's unwillingness to make any formal recognition of Britain's special position in Iraq, Transjordan and Palestine,[57] and the question of the boundary between Transjordan and the Hijaz.

On these questions Abd al-Aziz wrote:

> In confirmation of our conversations relating to the recognition of HBM's special position in Iraq, Transjordan and Palestine and the fixation of the frontier between the Hijaz and Transjordan, I desire to assure HMG that I do not intend any harm whatsoever to British interests by not recognising the special position in mandated territory, but that the present circumstances compel me to abstain from intervening in matters with the previous history of which I

have no connection. I believe that by abstaining from entering into this subject I am warding off consequences which would be harmful to our interests and which it is not in the interests of HMG to provoke against us.[58]

By February 1927 the Colonial Office had decided to send Clayton out again. Since he had last met Abd al-Aziz in November 1925 he had attempted, unsuccessfully, to make a treaty between Britain and the Yemen, and had also acted as chief British delegate to a series of meetings in Rome which were designed to settle Italian and British relations in the Red Sea area. Both Britain and Abd al-Aziz believed that the Italians were actively assisting the Imam of Yemen, which would pose a threat to Asir, now under Abd al-Aziz's protection, as well as to the Aden Protectorate. In a meeting in the Foreign Office in London before his departure for the Hijaz, Clayton pointed out that a treaty with Abd al-Aziz would be particularly opportune in view of increased Italian interest in the area; another senior official remarked that if the proposed negotiations failed, Abd al-Aziz might well be tempted to look elsewhere.[59] A letter from Consul Jordan on 23 February confirmed Abd al-Aziz's fears of increasing Italian penetration.[60]

On 4 May 1927 Clayton returned to the Hijaz with Antonius, and the new treaty was signed sixteen days later. An examination of the text shows that Britain had abandoned her insistence on the recognition of her special position in the mandated territories. In the first place, Britain recognised 'the complete and absolute independence of the dominions of His Majesty the King of the Hejaz and of Nejd and its Dependencies'. Other articles concerned the pilgrimage, Abd al-Aziz's undertakings to 'maintain peaceful and friendly relations with the territories of Kuwait and Bahrain, and with the Shaikhs of Qatar and the Oman Coast, who are in special treaty relations with HMG', and the suppression of the slave trade. The former (1915) treaty was allowed to lapse, and the 1927 treaty was to be renewed every seven years.[61]

As far as the other major point of dispute, the Transjordan—Hijaz frontier was concerned, no specific mention was made in the treaty:

At a certain point in the negotiations . . . Ibn Sa'ud informed Sir Gilbert Clayton that he desired to have a personal and private interview alone with him. At this interview Ibn Sa'ud explained his difficulties fully saying quite frankly that he could not sign the protocol (i.e. intimating any agreement over the frontier). He added however that he himself was fully prepared to meet the wishes of HMG and would have done so if the difficulties with which he was beset had not been such as to render it impossible for him to do so. He was prepared to give any secret guarantees which might be considered acceptable provided that he was not asked to put his signature to any public document which could be interpreted by either his friends or his enemies as being a formal and definite renunciation.[62]

Clayton managed to resolve the impasse by suggesting that Abd al-Aziz should simply undertake to maintain the *status quo*, 'to respect the administration of the territories in question by the Transjordan government'. An exchange of letters would be appended to the treaty in which this would be made clear and this solution was adopted. Part of Abd al-Aziz's letter of 21 May reads: 'we desire to express to your excellency our willingness to maintain the *status quo* in the Ma'an-Aqaba district, and we promise not to interfere in its administration until favourable circumstances will permit a final settlement of this question'.[63]

With the conclusion of this treaty, Abd al-Aziz had 'normalised' his relations with Britain. However, the vexed question of channels of communication still persisted: Abd al-Aziz naturally wanted to be approached via the Foreign Office, that is via Jeddah, although when he was in Najd he was actually much nearer to the Resident in the Gulf. There was also the further problem of whether British representatives in Iraq and Transjordan should have the right to communicate directly with him, or whether this had to be done via the Colonial and Foreign Offices.

In 1929, the various inconsistencies inherent in this situation were resolved: Oliphant in the Foreign Office suggested that 'we should take the lead in expressing to the CO and IO the opinion that the time has arrived for converting Jedda into a diplomatic mission and inviting their concurrence'.[64] By October, Bond, then Consul, was appointed Chargé d'Affaires until a more senior official actually took up the appointment. Much to his chagrin, Bond was unable to secure permanent precedence for the British Minister at Jeddah, and was in fact himself pre-empted by his colleague Hakimov, who was elevated to the position of Consul-General and Minister Plenipotentiary for the Soviet Union a few weeks before Bond's own credentials arrived.[65]

Thus when, at the end of April 1930, Abd al-Aziz returned in triumph from his campaign against the rebel *ikhwan* to ride through the arches erected in his honour at the gates of Mecca, he proceeded a few days later to welcome the first British Minister to the Kingdom of Hijaz, Najd and its Dependencies, Sir Andrew Ryan, who arrived at Jeddah on 6 May.[66] In spite of his evident satisfaction in having achieved this objective, the recognition of his status as a fully independent ruler, the change of status seems to have made very little difference to the somewhat haphazard and highly personalised way in which the kingdom's foreign affairs were conducted. Ryan, whose despatches are full of humour, summarised the problem after he had been at his post for a few months:

> Opportunities for discussing really serious questions with the King are reduced to a minimum. When he disappears into the blue, and so far as he is concerned, even Mecca and Ta'if are the blue, we cannot count on any early opportunity of following up the discussions in personal conversations with his Ministers except for an occasional enquiry over the telephone.

Surely, Ryan continued to Fuad Hamza, one of the points of establishing a Legation was to facilitate such contacts?

> Suppose, I said, that King George assumed the sole direction of our foreign affairs: that the Foreign Office were moved to Oxford; that it was considered, in deference to the ancient Christian traditions of that place, to exclude from it Muslims, Brahmins and the disciples of Confucius, and that Hafiz Wahba were confined to London and the suburbs: would the Hejaz Government then think that they were justified in the expense of maintaining a legation in Great Britain?[67]

In spite of the difficulties inherent in the day-to-day conduct of diplomatic affairs, Britain's paramountcy in the Saudi kingdom remained absolute until the arrival of Americans *en masse* during and after the Second World War. The United States granted diplomatic recognition to the new state in 1931, after a three-year campaign conducted by Fuad Hamza, Philby and others.[68] A recent study has shown that, contrary to American suspicions at the time, Britain seems to have been more than ready to let the United States take over as the kingdom's bankers in 1944.[69]

Thus the Second World War marked the watershed, the termination of the special diplomatic relationship between Britain and the Saudi kingdom. In this paper we have tried to show how British co-operation was essential to restrain Abd al-Aziz's recalcitrant followers, and British recognition vital to his international status. For her part, Britain desired peace in Central Arabia, and on the borders of her mandated and treaty territories; only a strong ruler in Hijaz and Najd could provide this. Furthermore, on the west of the peninsula:

> The guiding principle of British policy in the Red Sea is the security of imperial communications with India and the East. For this purpose HMG regard it as a vital imperial interest that no European power should establish itself on the Arabian shore of the Red Sea.[70]

With the co-operation of Abd al-Aziz and at remarkably little cost to herself, Britain succeeded in achieving her objectives in the Arabian peninsula until the passage of time and changing circumstances served to make them redundant.

Notes

1. The research on which this paper is based was made possible by a grant from Durham University Middle East Centre, which is gratefully acknowledged.
2. Vice-Consul Loder Park (Aden) to State Department, No. 109 of 23 December 1925. Reproduced in Ibrahim al-Rashid, *Documents on the History of Saudi Arabia* (Documentary Publications, Carolina, 1976), vol. II, pp. 50–4.
3. In an attempt to define the frontiers between the Hijaz-Najd and Transjordan and Iraq; for details see R. O. Collins (ed.), *An Arabian Diary: Sir Gilbert Falkingham Clayton* (University of California Press, Berkeley, 1969).
4. Clayton to ? (probably Wingate), Bahra Camp, Jeddah, 21 October 1925; Clayton Papers, Sudan Archive, School of Oriental Studies, Durham University (hereafter Clayton Papers), Box 471.
5. Introduction to Derek Hopwood (ed.), *The Arabian Peninsula: Society and Politics* (George Allen and Unwin, London, 1972).
6. E. Monroe, *Philby of Arabia* (Faber, London, 1973).
7. G. Troeller, *The Birth of Sa'udi Arabia* (Cass, London, 1973).
8. J. S. Habib, *Ibn Sa'ud's Warriors of Islam: the Ikhwan of Najd and their Role in the Creation of the Sa'udi Kingdom, 1910–1930* (Brill, Leiden, 1978).
9. Troeller, *The Birth of Sa'udi Arabia*, p. xv.
10. 'Asir was finally absorbed in 1934.
11. Minute by Stonehewer Bird on Great Britain, 6 November 1929, Foreign Office, E 5693/821/93.
12. See the concluding paragraph of this article.
13. See Helen Lackner, *House Built on Sand: a Political Economy of Saudi Arabia* (Ithaca Press, London, 1978), p. 28. Lackner comments that 'there is no account of what happened to the Ikhwan after the end of the rebellion'.
14. J. J. Malone, 'America and the Arabian Peninsula: the First Two Hundred Years', *Middle East Journal*, no. xxx (Winter 1976), pp. 406–24, especially p. 148.
15. J. B. Glubb, *War in the Desert; an RAF Frontier Campaign* (Hodder and Stoughton, London, 1960), p. 196.

16. Consul Davis (Aden) to State Department, Despatch No. 163 of 6 November 1923; Vice-Consul Loder Park (Aden) to State Department, Despatch No. 20 of 7 October 1924. Reproduced in Ibrahim al-Rashid, *Documents on the History of Saudi Arabia*, vol. 1, pp. 138–42, 167–70.

17. Consul Bullard (Jeddah) to S/S Foreign Affairs, Despatch No. 119 of 30 December 1924, Foreign Office, E 354/10/91 (1925).

18. Habib, *Ibn Sa'ud's Warriors of Islam*, pp. 118–20.

19. Consul Bond (Jeddah) to S/S Foreign Affairs, Despatches Nos. 191 of 20 July and 205 of 10 August 1929, Foreign Office, E 3947, E 4208/3947/91.

20. Jeddah report, January 1930; HM Consulate, Jeddah to S/S Foreign Affairs, Despatch No. 42 of 7 February 1930, Foreign Office, E 1014/92/91.

21. Jeddah report, March 1930: HM Consulate, Jeddah, to S/S Foreign Affairs, Despatch No. 82 of 3 April 1930, Foreign Office, E 2280/92/91.

22. Jeddah report, May 1930: HM Legation, Jeddah, to S/S Foreign Affairs, Despatch No. 147 of 21 June 1930, Foreign Office, E 3605/92/91.

23. Jeddah report, December 1930: HM Legation, Jeddah, to S/S Foreign Affairs, Despatch No. 19 of 17 December 1931, Foreign Office, E 528/81/25.

24. For example, in 1936, Indian pilgrims complained to the Indian Vice-Consul at the British Legation that the Saudi government was allowing the playing of musical instruments around the Haram in Mecca. Minute by Khan Bahadur Ihsanullah, 1 May 1936; see FO 905/43.

25. N. A. Saleh, 'The Emergence of Sa'udi Arabian Administrative Areas: a Study in Political Geography', unpublished PhD thesis, University of Durham, 1975, p. 75.

26. Glubb, *War in the Desert*, pp. 123–32.

27. Great Britain, Colonial Office, S/S Colonies to Sir Gilbert Clayton, 59092/28 of 17 April 1928, Clayton Papers, Box 472.

28. Note of 23 March 1928 by Sir Gilbert Clayton (Jeddah), Clayton Papers, Box 472.

29. Resident, Persian Gulf, to S/S Colonies, Telegram 85, of 10 April 1928, Clayton Papers, Box 472.

30. Clayton to Sir Hugh Trenchard, secret and personal, 22 June 1928, Clayton Papers, Box 472.

31. Clayton to S/S Colonies, 10 July 1928, Clayton Papers, Box 472.

32. See Clayton Papers, File 472/8, Box 472.

33. Glubb, *War in the Desert*, pp. 193–4.

34. Note by George Antonius on his meeting with Ibn Sa'ud, 7 August 1928, Clayton Papers, Box 472.

35. Glubb, *War in the Desert*, p. 245.

36. Vice-Consul Brown, to Baghdad, to State Department, Despatch No. 995 of 5 October 1929. Reproduced in Ibrahim al-Rashid, *Documents on the History of Saudi Arabia*, vol. III, pp. 39–41.

37. Habib, *Ibn Sa'ud's Warriors of Islam*, pp. 139–41.

38. Jeddah report, April 1932: HM Legation, Jeddah, Despatch No. 231 of 29 May 1932.

39. Conversation between Muhammad Ali Ridha and Lal Shah, Indian Vice-Consul, Jeddah; Minute of 9 May 1938, FO 905/57.

40. Minute by Lal Shah, 1 September 1938, FO 905/57.

41. D. van der Meulen, *The Wells of Ibn Sa'ud* (John Murray, London, 1957), p. 186.

42. Consul Stonehewer Bird (Jeddah) to S/S Foreign Affairs, Despatch No. 45 of 9 February 1929, Foreign Office, E 1035/381/91.

43. High Commissioner, Cairo, to S/S Foreign Affairs, Despatch No. 243 of 22 March 1929, Foreign Office, E 1668/381/91.

44. Minute by Sir Austen Chamberlain, 29 May 1925 'It seems to me so important to India to do whatever it is possible to prevent the Hijaz becoming a centre of Bolshevik infection that I would at least ask the SS for India whether the Government of India could not make some concession . . .' (this refers to some rifles which the government of India were selling Ibn Saʻud at what appeared an inordinately high price). See Foreign Office E 2631/381/91.

45. Jeddah report, September–November 1930: HM Legation, Jeddah, Despatch No. 368 of 18 December 1930, Foreign Office E 81/81/25.

46. Ibid.

47. Jeddah report, September–October 1931: HM Legation, Jeddah, Despatch No. 465 of 1 December 1931, Foreign Office E 6209/81/25.

48. Jeddah report, May 1933: HM Legation, Jeddah, Despatch No. 169 of 5 June 1933.

49. For example, see FO 905/35 for 1936, and FO 905/50 for 1937.

50. Meeting of Committee of Imperial Defence, 8 November 1937; minute by G. W. Rendel, FO 905/53.

51. Note by Sir Gilbert Clayton, 30 October 1925, Clayton Papers, Box 471.

52. This account is largely based on Troeller, *Birth of Saʻudi Arabia.*

53. See ibid., Appendix II, pp. 248–9.

54. J. C. Hurewitz, *The Middle East and North Africa in World Politics, a Documentary Record*, 2nd rev. edn (Yale University Press, New Haven and London, 1979), vol. II, p. 57.

55. Clayton (Bombay), to L. S. Amery, confidential, of 16 December 1925, Clayton Papers, Box 471.

56. George Antonius (Jeddah) to Clayton, 21 September 1926, Clayton Papers, Box 471.

57. Such as had been made in the (unratified) treaty between King Husain and Britain in 1923; see Hurewitz, *The Middle East and North Africa*, pp. 318–22.

58. Statement by Ibn Saʻud, enclosed in Consul Jordan (Jeddah) to S/S Foreign Affairs, Despatch of 26 January 1927 (E 477/119/91), Clayton Papers, Box 471.

59. See the minutes of a meeting at the Foreign Office on 19 January 1927, Clayton Papers, Box 471.

60. Consul Jordan to S/S Foreign Affairs, 23 February 1927 (E 242/22/91), Clayton Papers, Box 471.

61. For the full text see *Treaty Series* (1927), No. 25, Cmd 2951. The treaty (but not the annexures) is reproduced in Hurewitz, *The Middle East and North Africa*, pp. 383–5.

62. Memo by (?) Sir Gilbert Clayton, April 1927, Clayton Papers, Box 471.

63. See Cmd 2951 (1927).

64. Minute on E 3252/821/91, dated 27 June 1929.

65. Bond to Rendel, personal, of 19 October 1929 (E 5963/821/91).

66. For accounts of his arrival, see Andrew Ryan, *The Last of the Dragomans* (Hutchinson, London, 1951), pp. 256–66, and H. St J. B. Philby, *Arabian Days* (Robert Hale, London, 1948), pp. 274–6.

67. Sir Andrew Ryan (Jeddah) to S/S Foreign Affairs, Despatch No. 184 of 22 July 1930 (E 4309/4309/91).

68. See Foreign Office, Mecca, to State Department, 29 September 1928: Vice-Consul Huston (Aden) to State Department, Despatch No. 40 of 23 October. Reproduced in Ibrahim al-Rashid, *Documents on the History of Saudi Arabia*, vol. II, pp. 219–23, 224–5. See also press release, State Department, 2 May 1931, reproduced in ibid., vol. III, p. 116.

69. B. Rubin, 'Anglo-American Relations in Saʻudi Arabia, 1941–1945', *Journal of Contemporary History*, no. XIV (1979), pp. 253–67.

70. S/S Foreign Affairs to Sir Gilbert Clayton (instructions for his mission to Rome), 28 December 1926 (E 6916/2660/91), Clayton Papers, Box 471.

4 KING ABD AL-AZIZ'S CHANGING RELATIONSHIP WITH THE GULF STATES DURING THE 1930s

Rosemarie Said Zahlan

Introduction

Many of the dominant geopolitical characteristics of the Gulf region today emerged during the formative decade of the 1930s. On the one hand, its three major countries – Iraq, Iran and Saudi Arabia – were in the process of consolidating their respective positions, both internally and externally. On the other, the smaller Gulf states – Kuwait, Bahrain, Qatar and the Trucial States – then, as today, came to be the meeting place for the various competing forces of these three countries, the most dominant being those created by Abd al-Aziz ibn Abd al-Rahman ibn Faisal Al Saud. This paper will attempt to examine how the Saudi relationship with the Gulf states came to dominate all others; it will also describe the changing attitude of Abd al-Aziz to these states during the 1930s.

It was during this period that the geopolitical characteristics of the region as we know them today were being established. The three large countries of the region were in the process of either acquiring independence (as in the case of Iraq), consolidating power (Iran), or in the final stages of establishing a kingdom (Saudi Arabia). It was at this time, moreover, that the central importance of the existence of oil in the entire region was beginning to be recognised. Finally, the decade saw the zenith of British hegemony in the region: the Second World War was to bring on the beginning of the dismemberment of the Empire and with it a gradual decline in Britain's position.

Although Iran, Iraq and Saudi Arabia were undergoing different stages in their political development at this time, they were similar in many basic ways. Their respective economies were beginning to be transformed, and economic changes were accompanied by internal political development. Abd al-Aziz had consolidated his hold over three-quarters of the Arabian peninsula, had disbanded the *ikhwan*, and was proceeding to set up an internal administration in his new kingdom. Iraq had obtained the termination of the mandate, albeit with important limitations regarding the conduct of foreign affairs, and had begun the establishment of a national political administration; it was at this time that Iraq's oil revenues were first used for development projects. Reza Shah had also achieved for Iran full political independence, and had centralised his authority throughout the country.

The international relations of all three countries were beginning to be defined in a modern sense; the governments were coming to identify and consistently pursue certain basic objectives in foreign policy. It must be pointed out here, however, that Britain, the major power of the region, constricted the international dealings of all three countries. Iraq, of course, had the restricting clauses of its 1930 treaty, while both Saudi Arabia and Iran were conscious of the inequality of their respective positions in the face of British strength and opposition.

But while all these changes were transpiring, and while these countries were taking their final shape, the smaller Gulf states by comparison remained comparatively static. All of the latter shared a similar, strangely nebulous, position. They were not colonies or crown colonies; they were not under mandate; they were not protectorates; they existed vaguely within the British Empire 'in special treaty relations with HMG'. In 1928, when the question of establishing protectorates over the Gulf states was raised, the Viceroy of India clearly stated why he thought that such a move was unnecessary. 'Our veiled protectorate over them suffices against European encroachments. So long as we do not alienate Arab opinion by undue Westernisation . . . it suffices also against encroachments by the Wahhabi State. At need it can be more explicitly asserted.'[1]

Bahrain, Qatar and the Trucial States were forbidden to enter into any direct relations with a foreign power other than Britain; and Kuwait was forbidden to receive the agent or representative of any other power except Britain. Their relationship with Britain was plagued by the constant British claims of non-interference in internal affairs while, in fact, a very direct interference could occur in cases involving British interests. An example of the sophistry which could be employed to alter the meaning of non-interference (which was Britain's official and declared policy) is to be found in the words of a Political Resident in 1939 who sought to justify one specific act of interference (in the internal affairs of Dubai). He said emphatically that intervention and non-intervention were abstract principles, and the important thing was to gain British ends with a minimum of interference:

if we could gain our ends by this minimum, there was obviously no point in going beyond it . . . If the minimum of interference did not give us our ends I was always prepared to advocate an amount of interference which *would* achieve our ends.[2]

The rulers, moreover, were subjected to what must have been a bewildering set of admonishments, the definition of which fluctuated almost at random. One of the most central of these was the granting or the loss of 'the good offices of His Majesty's Government', which in the words of an India Office minute, HMG 'have reserved the right to interpret at their discretion'.[3] A good example of the confusing meaning of these 'good offices' occurred after the signing of the 1916 exclusive treaty with Qatar. After much insistence by the ruler, Shaikh Abdallah bin Qasim, an extra article had been added to this treaty to give him further protection. The article (Article XI) stated that: 'They [the British Government] also undertake to grant me good offices, should I or my subjects be assailed by land within the territories of Qatar.'[4] One of the main reasons for the inclusion of this clause was that Abdallah wanted some form of protection from his increasingly powerful neighbour, Saudi Arabia. Although Britain was primarily concerned with the safety of the sea route to India (and in its other exclusive treaties only promised protection against sea attack), it had to include the extra article in order to ensure the introduction of Qatar into the Trucial system — as a means of preventing the tiny peninsula coming under Ottoman control. When, in 1921, Shaikh Abdallah asked the Political Resident to endorse the good offices, he was told they merely signified diplomatic help; to placate him, however, it was recommended that he be given 'a supply of blank ammunition'.[5] That, of course, did not provide the ruler with the security he was convinced he had obtained by dint of the treaty conditions, so once again he approached the British authorities. This time he asked to what extent he would receive British support if, in bringing to heel some of his recalcitrant subjects, the Saudis would rally to help them to attack him. The Political Agent replied to the bewildered Abdallah: '. . . the Government of India do not desire to get mixed up in the internal affairs of Qatar'.[6] In 1928, an India Office memorandum noted that Article XI 'did not . . . in practice impose any very serious liability on His Majesty's Government'.[7]

Although Britain's obligation to provide good offices did not impose any significant liability on HMG, the loss of this facility by a local ruler could be serious. In 1938 the rulers of Abu Dhabi, Ras al-Khaimah and Sharjah lost these good offices; this meant that they and all their people were deprived of travel papers until further notice, that is until the rulers accepted to behave according to the terms laid down by the different British officials.[8]

These examples are merely to illustrate the arbitrary nature of the relationship which the smaller Gulf states had with the only country with which they were allowed to enter into direct communication. At the same time they were being drawn more firmly into the British orbit – particularly during the period under discussion. When Reza Shah's government showed itself reluctant to grant facilities on its southern shores for the important air route to India, it was to the Arab coast that the route was shifted. The deterioration of Anglo-Iranian relations, moreover, brought about the decision in 1936 to move the Residency from Bushire to Bahrain. Finally, of course, the possibility of the existence of petroleum reserves in the Gulf states – particularly after the discovery of oil in Bahrain in 1932 and the 1933 agreement between Saudi Arabia and the Standard Oil Company of California – made it imperative for the remaining concessions to be channelled into British-owned or -controlled companies. The region came under much closer scrutiny. Control of policy was transferred from Delhi to London, first resting with the Colonial Office and later (after 1933) with the India Office. In 1929 the Persian Gulf Sub-Committee of the Committee of Imperial Defence decided that all major decisions on the Gulf should be taken jointly by representatives of the Foreign Office, the Colonial Office, the India Office, the War Office, the Air Ministry and the Admiralty.

But despite the nature of their foreign relationships, the Gulf states were undergoing economic and political change during the 1930s. Three factors will be mentioned here. The most important was the decline of the pearling industry as a result both of the world economic depresssion and of the introduction to the market of the Japanese cultured pearl. Trade began to play a leading role in the economy, particularly in Kuwait, Bahrain and Dubai. A growing merchant class emerged in these places. The trade contacts with open societies and the establishment of schools made the merchants eager to have a say in the political development of their respective shaikhdoms. The culmination of this trend occurred in 1938 when movements calling for reform were established in all three states. Although they were short lived, the reform movements were an important indication of the gradual transformation of their respective societies.[9]

The discovery of oil in Bahrain in 1932 was the beginning of the end of the striking poverty of the region. The subsequent preliminary oil concessions in the other shaikhdoms gave to their rulers annual payments which allowed them to be financially independent of their subjects for the first time. Previously the rulers had had to rely on customs dues and the various pearling taxes for a large fraction of their incomes. This independence marked a departure from the earlier links forged by a ruler with his people: henceforward he would no longer need the co-operation of his subjects to generate his income, although he would still remain dependent on them in order to stay in power. The oil-generated wealth thus began to be an instrument for the consolidation of political power.

Finally, it was during this period that the different radio stations — of Bari, Berlin, Baghdad and London — began to broadcast in Arabic to the Gulf region. The widespread effect of this development cannot be overstated, particularly for a society with a low level of literacy. For the first time, an accessible means was available to convey to Gulf populations national and international viewpoints. This had a definite impact on the changing political scene.

The loosely defined position of the smaller Gulf states was in contrast to the formation of centralised autonomous governments in Iran, Iraq and Saudi Arabia. The latter therefore formulated what I shall refer to as a 'forward policy' towards the former. In 1927, Persia made its formal claim to Bahrain and the following year claimed the islands of the Tunbs and Abu Musa. By the mid-1930s, the influence of Iraq in Kuwait was causing considerable anxiety in British circles, and the shadow of Abd al-Aziz ibn Saud covered most of the Gulf states. Britain, of course, opposed all foreign interests in these states, but in recognising time and again that Saudi Arabia was its natural successor in the Gulf (should Britain ever decide to withdraw), it allowed Abd al-Aziz a certain leeway, which will be discussed in greater detail.

Kuwait and Bahrain

After the conference in Uqayr in 1922, when the Najd—Kuwait boundary was settled — very much to the favour of the former[10] — by Cox, the former British Political Resident in Bushire, the only matter outstanding between Saudi Arabia and Kuwait was the question of trade and customs. Saudi Arabia needed an outlet from Najd to the sea. The feasibility of developing a port within Najdi territory was first examined: Uqayr, Qatif, Jubail and Ras Tanura, in that order, were considered for development. Such a project, particularly when Abd

al-Aziz had little money, was fraught with problems: the physically
difficult conditions of Uqayr and Qatif were one aspect; another was
the fact that Abd al-Aziz would probably have had to pay a subsidy to
any steamship company to convince it to make a regular call there.
Bahrain and Kuwait were the two natural alternatives. With the former,
he reached an arrangement whereby transit goods for Najd were only
subject to 2 per cent customs duties. In the case of Kuwait, however,
which shared a long desert border with Najd, he wished to establish a
Customs House of his own − on the grounds that it would be impossible
to collect customs dues on the desert boundary. The ruler of Kuwait
categorically refused the request, so Abd al-Aziz retaliated by imposing
a trade embargo, thereby bringing about a very serious decline in
Kuwaiti prosperity. Furthermore, Kuwait became subjected to frequent
raids by Saudi tribes, which she was powerless to prevent. Many
attempts were made by the British authorities to end the blockade, but
with no result, and relations between Shaikh Ahmad of Kuwait and Abd
al-Aziz grew steadily more hostile. Shaikh Ahmad was bitter about the
commercial stagnation of Kuwait,[11] and felt responsible for the losses
suffered by Kuwaiti merchants; Abd al-Aziz was disturbed by his
continued dependence on the ruler of Kuwait, and grew to resent this
position with the years.

In 1930 Yusuf Yasin (deputy Foreign Minister) informed British
representatives of the Najdi government's wish to have consular status
for its representatives in both Bahrain and Kuwait. When he was told of
the possibility of this creating a precedent for, say, Iran, he did not
press the point. Abd al-Aziz was not without representatives in these
places, however. In Bahrain the al-Qusaibi family, who acted as his
commercial forwarding agents, were his unofficial representatives, and
the al-Nafisis were his trade agents in Kuwait. The former achieved a
position of what, in 1928, the British officials considered as being an
'objectionable prominence' in Bahrain, it being always understood that
they acted on behalf of Abd al-Aziz. In 1923 they had been expelled
by the Political Resident and only allowed to return on a clear
understanding as to the limitations on their activities.

The bitterness which had developed between Ahmad of Kuwait and
Abd al-Aziz continued to grow. The former felt betrayed by the
British as a result of Cox giving away a large part of Kuwait to Ibn
Saud at Uqayr. Although Ahmad had helped in quelling the rebellion
of the *ikhwan*, moreover, he received no effective aid from the British
in terminating the stifling blockade. When the pearling industry went
into decline in the early 1930s, the Saudi boycott began to assume very

serious proportions. But other developments were taking place which were to change Abd al-Aziz's attitude towards Kuwait and Bahrain: the growing interest of Iraq in Kuwait and of Iran in Bahrain and the Gulf islands; the 1938 reform movements in Kuwait, Bahrain and Dubai; the first discovery of oil (after that in Bahrain in 1932) in Saudi Arabia, Kuwait and Qatar in 1938; and the generally widespread fears that Britain was itself engaged in a forward movement in the Gulf region.

The first Iranian claim to Bahrain during the Pahlavi period was made after the 1927 Treaty of Jeddah (between Britain and Saudi Arabia) was signed, Clause 6 of which stated that Abd al-Aziz undertook 'to maintain friendly and peaceful relations with the territories of Kuwait and Bahrain and with the Shaikhs of Qatar and the Oman Coast who are in special treaty relations with His Britannic Majesty's Government'.[12] The Iranian government emphatically protested against the inclusion of Bahrain in the clause on the grounds that this was an infringement of Persia's territorial integrity.[13] Britain, of course, denied the validity of this assertion, although the Foreign Office and the government of India were unable to agree on a co-ordinated policy towards Iran at this time.[14] The Iranian government persisted in its claims, and in 1930 began to organise the building of a navy with which to strengthen its position in the Gulf waters. Although action on Iranian claims to Bahrain was confined to 'a series of pinprick activities',[15] such as refusing to affix visas for travel to Iran on British passports bearing endorsements for Bahrain or Kuwait, and refusing to recognise Indian postage stamps overprinted 'Bahrain', the effects on Bahrain were destabilising. Arab relations with Iran grew more strained during these years, with little love lost on either side.

By contrast, the relationship between Iraq and Kuwait which began to develop at this time was based on the real ties of Arab nationalism. Iraqi influence on the literate and well-to-do merchant class of Kuwait was particularly strong. It was to Iraq that these merchants sent their children to study, and links between the populations of the two states developed rapidly. An association of Gulf Arabs was formed in Basra in the late 1930s, whose aims were to bring about the unity of Kuwait and Iraq, and to help the other Gulf states in their own political development.[16] Economic interest constituted another strong link, for most of the leading Kuwaiti families owned date gardens there; by the late 1930s some even took up Iraqi citizenship, partly to strengthen their nationalist credentials, and partly to safeguard their property. Moreover, Iraqi newspapers — the only ones to reach Kuwait on a regular basis — and radio broadcasts had a widespread effect. Finally, the strong reaction of the Iraqi government and people to the general strike in Palestine, and the rebellion that occurred there from 1936 to 1939, had a profound impact; the wave of Arab nationalism that swept through Iraq during those three years found echoes in its Gulf neighbour.

The Palestinian issue also acted to polarise the growing opposition to the ruler of Kuwait, who showed great caution in his support for the struggle being waged by the Palestinian Arab population. When the general strike was declared in 1936 the ruler refused a request from Palestinian leaders for financial aid, and forbade any public contributions to the fund. But money was collected and sent to Palestine via a Basra newspaper. A short while later, seven of the leading merchants of Kuwait formed a committee to collect aid for Palestine. The next year, another larger committee of twelve merchants and notables was convened to protest against the publication of the Peel Report which recommended partition; the committee sent telegrams of protest to the League of Nations, the House of Commons and the Colonial Secretary in London. In order to placate public opinion, Shaikh Ahmad appointed Naji al-Suwaydi as his representative at the 1937 Bludan conference.[17] But the opposition was not quelled by such a minor concession, and by early 1938 public demands for reform in Kuwait began to appear in Iraqi newspapers. The Iraqi media continued their campaign, and finally the ruler was obliged to accept the formation of a council to carry out internal reform. The latter council had fourteen members, six of whom had belonged to the earlier committees to aid Palestine. The life of the council was short (six months), but it shook the authority of the ruler of Kuwait in a manner which was very disturbing to Abd al-Aziz's 'stout monarchial spirit. His view was that The People should not be encouraged to acquire political power and the work of governing should be left in the hands of those who were accustomed to rule.'[18] Furthermore, he thought that the 'events in Kuwait had not been in accordance with his conception of institutional procedure in an Arab and a Moslem state'.[19]

Abd al-Aziz's concern with developments in Iraq was, of course, also due to his fears regarding Iraqi influence there. His strong rivalry with the Hashimis gave colour to these fears. Since 1926, when he had driven the Hashimite family out of the Hijaz, his policy had been both to counter Hashimi attempts to gain influence in the peninsula and to contain their designs in the rest of the Arab world. His earlier feelings of hostility towards Shaikh Ahmad gradually began to be replaced by those of sympathy with a fellow ruler; and a fellow ruler who was being plagued by the Hashimis. It must have come as a relief to him when, in July 1939, a Question and Answer in the House of Commons on Britain's commitment to uphold Kuwait's territorial integrity was broadcast on the Arabic service of the BBC.[20] By now, he had started to develop the port of Ras Tanura, but he was not totally convinced of the convenience of its location. He therefore wanted to conclude a trade agreement with Kuwait which would provide favourable terms for Saudi trade and would at the same time strengthen the position of the Kuwaiti ruler. Abd al-Aziz had already started to provide support for Shaikh Ahmad in 1936, when he undertook a visit to Kuwait with a retinue of 700 men, and placed very large orders for goods with Kuwaiti merchants.[21] The trade agreement was concluded in 1942.

Abd al-Aziz also began to show more friendship for the ruler of Bahrain. In 1937 he sent his son Saud to Bahrain on a state visit and in 1939 he went there himself in great splendour.[22] Since Bahrain had also undergone a reform movement in 1938, the King wanted to affirm his support for a fellow ruler. His sympathy for Shaikh Hamad bin Isa also stemmed from the Iranian claims to Bahrain, and from the Shaikh's conflict with Qatar over Zubarah, the outcome of which had been unfavourable to Bahrain.

There were additional reasons for the mellowing of Abd al-Aziz's attitude towards Kuwait and Bahrain. One of these was the apparently widespread belief that Britain was engaged in a 'forward movement' in the Gulf. This belief had been strengthened by the anti-British radio broadcasts of the Bari and Berlin stations, to which Abd al-Aziz carefully listened. The arrangements at his palace in al-Riyadh for receiving news by radio were fairly elaborate. Clerks in the Royal Diwan would write up the broadcasts from the different stations, and every night would prepare a summary for the King. The summary, called *Al-Di'aya*, would then be typed out and issued to the members of the royal family and entourage. When the reform movements in Kuwait, Bahrain and Dubai came to an end in 1938/9, the Axis broadcasts attributed this collapse to a new form of British interference in the internal affairs of the Gulf states. There can be no doubt that Abd al-Aziz was aware of these allegations and of the reports from various Cairo newspapers that Britain was in the process of reformulating its Gulf policy and planning with a view of effecting, amongst other things, the unity of the different shaikhdoms there. His own position in the Gulf therefore had to be reconsidered, particularly since oil had recently been discovered in his country, in Kuwait and in Qatar.

The Trucial States and Qatar

Abd al-Aziz's attitude towards the Trucial States and Qatar was different from that towards Kuwait and Bahrain, for a number of reasons. First, the former large shaikhdoms possessed territories contiguous with his own. Their boundaries with Saudi Arabia were not fixed, as that with Kuwait had been at Uqayr; Abd al-Aziz thus felt there was scope for expansion since the control of the hinterland depended very much on the strength of the individual coastal ruler. Second, he considered the rulers to be of minor importance and not worthy of the new respect he was to show the rulers of Kuwait and Bahrain by the end of the 1930s. Their protection by Britain was a constant irritant to him, but rather than issue a blockade, as in the case of Kuwait, he used more subtle and potent forms of pressure. Although his power in these shaikhdoms was to grow perceptibly during the 1920s and 1930s, there were few incidents that could be pointed to by the anxious British authorities as positive encroachments on their sphere of influence.

During the 1920s, when Abd al-Aziz was in the process of expanding his control over the peninsula, the growing Saudi state constituted a major threat to the stability of the Trucial States, Qatar and Oman. Perhaps the first intimation of Wahhabi influence in these states was recognised in 1921. Abdallah bin Qasim of Qatar appealed to the British Political Resident in that year for help against the growing strength of the *ikhwan* in his shaikhdom. Disaffected members of Shaikh Abdallah's own family had been in constant communication with Abd al-Aziz, who was giving them moral as well as financial help. Their open defiance of the ruler, obviously backed by Wahhabi strength, caused a perpetual state of lawlessness to afflict Qatar. Abd al-Aziz clearly regarded Qatar as part of Saudi Arabia. In 1922 when he was at Uqayr, and about to grant Frank Holmes an oil concession, the maps which Abd al-Aziz used in the negotiations showed the shaikhdom of Qatar as within Saudi territory. Cox sharply rebuked him on this matter, and Abd al-Aziz did not argue the point. Instead he continued to exert pressure on Qatar until Abdallah was finally obliged to enter a secret agreement with the King; in 1930, the ruler of Qatar confessed to the British Political Agent in Bahrain that he had been paying Abd al-Aziz a secret annual subsidy of 100,000 rupees over the years to maintain his own position.[23]

Another direct attempt by Abd al-Aziz to gain some form of control, this time in the Trucial States, occurred in 1925. The turmoil of events and the movements and customs of the tribes involved make it difficult to discern the exact extent of Wahhabi aggression, but there can be little doubt that Abd al-Aziz's forces, particularly those controlled by his cousin Ibn Jaluwi, governor of al-Hasa province, were expanded to an unprecedented level and seriously threatened the internal security of the Trucial Coast, besides providing the motivation for the Imam of Oman to initiate a campaign against the Sultan of Muscat. Abd al-Aziz's methods were subtle and potent: support of one tribe against its traditional enemies, thus isolating the latter; enforcement of the collection of *zakat* on certain tribes to bring them under Wahhabi protection; and muted interference in the internal affairs of the Trucial States.

Throughout his career, Abd al-Aziz displayed a marked ability to recognise an opportunity and use it to his greatest advantage. This was manifested in 1925, when he seized on the weaknesses stemming from tribal conflict in Oman and turned this into a chance to bring pressure to bear on the Trucial Coast and Muscat. He took advantage of the chaos in Abu Dhabi, which had weakened the ruler of Abu Dhabi's hold over the hinterland; of the hostility felt towards the Imam of Oman after the abortive expedition of Isa bin Salih; and of the general weakness of the Sultan of Muscat. By the end of that year, a number of tribes whose allegiance was hitherto given to the ruler of Abu Dhabi, the Sultan of Muscat or the Imam of Oman, were quietly paying *zakat* to him. By thus extending a degree of control over the tribes of Oman, Abd al-Aziz was able to command certain events in the area without making any formal claim to possession and thus incurring British anger.

In 1930, the British Political Resident in the Gulf accurately defined the inadequacy of the British position to protect the Trucial States from Abd al-Aziz by saying, 'We hold the front door to these principalities on the littoral, but we do not hold the back door'.[24] It was through this back door that Abd al-Aziz was able to increase his influence in the Trucial States, for it was in the large inland areas that the extent of jurisdiction of the rulers was determined, and it was there, away from direct British influence, that Wahhabi power was most acutely felt. The enforcement of *zakat*, the technique the Wahhabis used to control the tribes, was later to become important to the issue of formally delimiting Saudi Aradia's boundaries with the Trucial States and Qatar.

Saudi Arabia's granting of an oil concession to the Standard Oil Company of California in 1933 first raised the issue of the definition of

Saudi Arabia's borders with Qatar and the Trucial States. Shortly after the concession was granted, the US government officially enquired of the British government where the eastern frontiers of Saudi Arabia lay. In April 1934 the Foreign Office defined these as being consistent with the Blue Line agreed on under the unratified Anglo-Turkish Conventions of 1913–14. The Saudi government protested, saying that much had changed since 1913, and put forward in 1934 proposals regarding the course of the Saudi frontier with Qatar, the Trucial States, Oman and Aden (the Red Line). The British replied with another proposal the next year (the Green Line), and when this did not meet with Saudi approval, a Foreign Office delegation went to Jeddah to discuss the problem. Little came of the talks, however. This was not surprising, particularly as differences of opinion on this critical question arose even between different departments of the British government: the Foreign Office wanted to retain the goodwill of Abd al-Aziz as a prominent Arab leader on what seemed to be the eve of a major European war; the India Office, by contrast, was against offering any form of compromise to the King. Khawr al-Udayd, which was claimed by the ruler of Abu Dhabi, and Jabal Nakhsh, claimed by Qatar, were central to the controversy at this time.

In 1937 Reader Bullard, the British Minister in Jeddah, suggested that Saudi Arabia be allowed to share in any oil profits which might be obtained from Jabal Nakhsh; and in 1938 the Committee of Imperial Defence suggested that the ruler of Abu Dhabi cede the Khawr al-Udayd to Abd al-Aziz, and that the British Treasury compensate the ruler for the loss by granting him the sum of £25,000.[25] Although nothing came of these suggestions, they provide valuable insight into the attitude of one department of the British government regarding the possibility of reaching a compromise with Abd al-Aziz at the expense of the smaller shaikhdoms in the Gulf.

Abd al-Aziz's own attitude towards the rulers of the smaller shaikhdoms is well reflected in the *mulhaq*[26] (postscript) to a letter which the King wrote to Shaikh Abdallah of Qatar at the time the latter was about to sign a preliminary oil concession with the Anglo-Persian Oil Company (APOC) in 1935. Abd al-Aziz warned the Shaikh not to conclude an agreement until the boundaries between them had been settled. He told Abdallah that, despite the British interference with the Trucial States and Qatar, he did accept the fact that the people of these places were under the formal protection of Britain. He had, he said, already explained to British representatives that the people of these shaikhdoms were his subjects, and that they had been the subjects of his father and grandfather before him, but he deferred to their own wish to be under British protection. There could be no question in his mind, however, of the rulers of these places having claims to anything but the towns; the desert and the allegiance of the tribes roaming that desert had always been under his sovereignty and under those of his ancestors. He made it clear to Abdallah that he had no right to claim an area which he could neither control nor be responsible for, and warned him in no uncertain terms about the consequences of his signing a concession before the formal definition of their mutual boundaries was completed.

Unbeknown to Abd al-Aziz, however, Abdallah had already signed the oil concession two months earlier. The ruler of Qatar had held off his signature until he received formal and explicit assurances of protection from the British government, who were very eager for APOC to obtain the Qatar concession because of the interest in the area by the Standard Oil Company of California. A bargain between the two was struck: the APOC concession was signed and in exchange the British government promised him protection against attacks from outside Qatar, and also formally recognised Abdallah's son Hamad as his heir.[27]

The tone of the above-mentioned *mulhaq* reflected the attitude of a king towards a minor shaikh who needed to be reminded of his tributary status. This attitude was affirmed two years later when the British Minister in Jeddah reported that Abd al-Aziz had no love for any of the rulers of the Trucial States nor Qatar (he claimed that he despised them) and that he liked Abdallah least of all.[28] The other rulers also deferred to Abd al-Aziz, and all secretly corresponded with him despite their treaty restrictions. An enquiry by the Political Agent in Bahrain in 1937 revealed that all the Trucial rulers had agreements with Abd al-Aziz regarding the apprehension and punishment of offenders from Saudi Arabia. Their weak position had precluded their ability to prevent outside raids, so they were compelled to complain to the Saudi authorities; the punishment meted out was invariably satisfactory and much more than what they could themselves have inflicted on the offenders.[29] Since, unlike in the cases of Kuwait and Bahrain, neither Iraq nor Iran had any kind of claim on these shaikhdoms (apart from the islands of the Tunbs and Abu Musa), Saudi influence was not countered by other regional states. Moreover, it is noteworthy that apart from occasional rebukes to Abd al-Aziz, the British authorities did little to stop the growing Saudi influence. There were two reasons for Britain's reticence. First, the realisation of the general decline in Britain's position in the Near East, in line with the degenerating situation in Palestine, and the need, as war threatened Europe, for a powerful Arab ally. Second, the realisation that Abd al-Aziz, and not Iraq nor Iran, was the natural successor to Britain in the Gulf region.

Conclusion

In conclusion, therefore, Abd al-Aziz's attitude towards the Gulf states during the 1930s developed on two levels. For Kuwait and Bahrain, whose rulers he even acknowledged to be distantly related to him, he began to show a new respect. They had both become the recipients of an income from their oil concessions which had liberated them financially. They were becoming increasingly independent of their subjects for the generation of their income, and this placed them in a rank that Abd al-Aziz considered similar to his own. They had, moreover, both been challenged by a group of their subjects, a challenge of which Abd al-Aziz disapproved. Furthermore, their shaikhdoms were being claimed, directly or indirectly, by other Gulf countries, the king of one of which was his everlasting enemy. He had outgrown his former dependence on them and there can be little doubt that they acknowledged his superiority. Neither state had much land he could covet: Kuwait had diminished considerably after Uqayr, and Bahrain was an island in which he had little interest. Both places were fairly densely populated: Kuwait town in the late 1930s had around 60,000 people, and in 1941 Bahrain had a total population of 89,970.[30] The question of the ownership of the Libainat islands, which was in dispute with Bahrain, was not one to warrant undue concern.

The Trucial States and Qatar, by contrast, had rulers whose tribal origins were remote and not of his own noble blood line. They had large territories contiguous with his own, which he could easily have overrun were it not for the British presence. This fact was a constant irritant to him, and became more so once the oil companies wanted to delimit the extent of their concessions. Moreover, even the principal towns of these shaikhdoms were sparsely populated: Doha only had around 12,000 people, Abu Dhabi had 10,000, Dubai had 20,000 and Sharjah only 5,000.

Saudi Arabia's relationship with each of the Gulf states was deeply affected by the British hegemony in the Gulf region. Britain was the only major power with sizeable interests there, and as such, at least until the late 1950s, its position went unchallenged. There were, however, constraints on the role which Britain could play in the Gulf. Maybe most important was its desire to extend the greatest possible influence with the least possible resources. Until the beginning of the Second World War its expenses and commitments were restricted to the presence of one Political Resident, three Political Agents and the six sloops of war which made up the Persian Gulf Division. All decisions on policy were taken with this fact in mind, for there was no wish to extend British expenses in the region.

Another constraint was the divergent positions often taken by the different departments of the government on major policy issues. The Foreign Office and the India Office had fundamentally different factors to consider, and their viewpoints often reflected totally divergent attitudes. This was particularly true with regard to policy towards Iran and Saudi Arabia during the 1930s. There were other, more minor, constraints, though perhaps no less important in their impact. One was the fear that Iran would call the attention of the League of Nations to the position of the Shi'a in Bahrain and thus bring Britain to task over its policy in the islands. Another was the British realisation, particularly towards the latter part of the 1930s, that international conditions required Britain to find a strong Arab ally, that is Abd al-Aziz. This led to Britain's willingness to compromise with Abd al-Aziz in order to ensure his continued friendship.

Despite these constraints, there can be no doubt that Britain provided a stable system of relations within which the forward movements of the three major countries competed for influence in the Gulf states. Britain was directly involved in the actions and reactions arising from the impact of Iraqi, Iranian and Saudi policies in the Gulf states. Britain also had considerable interests in these three countries, not one of which wanted to jeopardise its relationship with Britain for relatively minor gains in the Gulf states. It was thus possible for Britain to placate Iraq, partially appease Iran, and manage Saudi pressures in its sphere of influence not only in the 1930s but well into the 1950s.

The British management of Saudi pressures was undoubtedly less abrupt and explicit than it was towards Iraq and Iran. No doubt the constraint regarding Abd al-Aziz's usefulness as an ally was one reason. Another was the fact that Abd al-Aziz, through his expert knowledge and use of tribal politics, was able to wield greater power than could the governments of the other two countries. The Iranian claim to Bahrain was made through official government channels, and could be contained with relative ease through the same channels. Iraq's chief instrument for intervention in Kuwait was a small group of wealthy merchants whose inability to widen their political base led to the collapse of the reform movement, after which Iraq's forward policy suffered a setback. But Abd al-Aziz's methods were more potent. He knew well the power base of the Gulf states and knew how to manipulate this to his advantage, at the same time remaining within the confines set by British policy. His blockade of Kuwait did not threaten British interests, but did exert effective pressure on the ruler. When the King realised the damaging results of this pressure internally, and externally, he changed course. In Qatar and the Trucial States his powerful tribal position enabled him to extend widespread influence, the payment of *zakat* and the acknowledgement by the coastal rulers of his superiority being two such examples. Once again, there was little cause for official British complaint regarding his methods.

British policy was successful in creating a political order which reflected its interests through the careful balancing of regional forces. The Gulf area was stabilised. The territorial objectives of Iran (in Bahrain and the Gulf islands), Iraq (in Kuwait), and Saudi Arabia (in the Trucial States and Qatar) all failed to achieve success during the 1930s, and none of the conflictual issues was resolved. The tensions became frozen into the political order.

Notes

1. India Office Records: L/P&S/10: P 4535/1928[8]: P 3880/28: Viceroy to Secretary of State, India Office, 23 July 1928 (telegram). Unpublished Crown Copyright material in the India Office Records and Public Record Office transcribed here appears by permission of the Controller of HMSO.
2. R. Said Zahlan, *The Origins of the United Arab Emirates* (Macmillan, London, 1978), pp. 175–6.
3. (IOR) L/P&S/11/178: P 1652/28: Minute on Najd–Kuwait relations, 4 April 1928.
4. C. U. Aitchison, *A Collection of Treaties, Engagements and Sanads Relating to India and Neighbouring Countries* (Government Printing Press, Delhi, 1933), vol. XI, p. 208.
5. R. Said Zahlan, *The Creation of Qatar* (Croom Helm, London, 1979), p. 63.
6. Ibid., p. 64.
7. Ibid., p. 61.
8. The ruler of Sharjah was thus punished for procrastinating over the signing of the political agreement regarding his oil concession; the ruler of Abu Dhabi for general procrastination over the oil concession, although he was told it was because of unsubstantiated reports that the slave trade was being conducted in his shaikhdom; and the ruler of Ras al-Khaimah for discourtesy to the Senior Naval Officer. See R. Said Zahlan, *The Origins of the United Arab Emirates*, chs. 7 and 11.
9. See Muhammed G. al-Rumaihi, 'The 1938 Reform Movements in Kuwait,

Bahrain and Dubai' (in Arabic), *Journal of the Gulf and Arabian Peninsula Studies*, vol. I, no. 4 (October, 1975); and Rosemarie J. Said, 'The 1938 Reform Movement in Dubai', *Al-Abhath* (December, 1970).

10. For Cox's admission that he had given Abd al-Aziz two-thirds of Kuwait's territory, see Gary Troeller, *The Birth of Sa'udi Arabia* (Cass, London, 1976), p. 181.

11. In 1929, the Political Resident remarked that Kuwait's customs revenue, which used to be around 8 lakhs a year, had fallen that year to about 1½ lakhs. (IOR) L/P&S/10/1245: P 447/30: Political Resident to Colonial Office, 15 December 1929.

12. *Treaty Series* (HMSO, London, 1927), No. 25, Cmd 2951.

13. See Husain M. Al-Baharna, *The Legal Status of the Arabian Gulf States* (Manchester University Press, Manchester, 1968), pp. 167–95.

14. R. M. Burrell, 'Britain, Iran and the Persian Gulf: Some aspects of the situation in the 1920s and 1930s' in D. Hopwood (ed.), *The Arabian Peninsula* (George Allen and Unwin, London, 1972).

15. Ibid., p. 184.

16. Ali Humaidan, *Les Princes de l'or Noir* (SEDEIS, Paris, 1968), p. 121. Also see M. Rumaihi, *Bahrain* (Bowker, London, 1978), p. 203 for a mention of the leaflets issued by this Association as having been extant in Bahrain in 1978.

17. For a detailed account of these activities, see R. Said Zahlan, 'The Gulf States and the Palestinian Problem, 1936–48', *Arab Studies Quarterly* (Winter 1981).

18. Charles D. Belgrave, *Personal Column* (Hutchinson, London, 1960), p. 110.

19. (IOR) L/P&S/12/3909: PZ 368/39: Reader Bullard (British Minister, Jeddah) to Foreign Office, 13 December 1938.

20. (IOR) L/P&S/12/4584: PZ 4553/39: Fowle (Political Resident) to Peel (India Office), 8 July 1939. For the parliamentary reference see *Parliamentary Debates*, 5th series, vol. 344, pp. 2155–6;

21. (IOR) L/P&S/12: Coll. 30/29: Report on the trade of Kuwait for the year 1935/6.

22. See Belgrave, *Personal Column*, pp. 108–10, for details of both visits.

23. See R. Said Zahlan, *The Creation of Qatar*, p. 82.

24. (IOR) L/P&S/11/222: P 5027/22: Political Resident to government of India, 18 August 1930.

25. (Public Record Office) CAB23/94: 35(38)10, 27 July 1938.

26. A copy of the *mulhaq* is available at (IOR) L/P&S/12/3848: PZ 6396/35: 6 Jumada I 1354/6 August 1935. Enclosed in Political Resident to India Office, 29 August 1935.

27. R. Said Zahlan, *The Creation of Qatar*, pp. 76–9.

28. (IOR) L/P&S/12/3909: PZ 368/39: Bullard to Foreign Office, 13 December 1938.

29. L/P&S/12/3837: PZ 7019/37. Political Agent Bahrain to Political Resident, 27 August 1937. See also R. Said Zahlan, *The Origins of the United Arab Emirates*, Ch. 8.

30. See Rumaihi, *Bahrain* (Bowker, London, 1978), p. 23.

SOCIAL STRUCTURE AND THE DEVELOPMENT OF THE SAUDI ARABIAN POLITICAL SYSTEM

Tim Niblock

Introduction

Perhaps the most common approach to the analysis of developments in Saudi Arabia is to describe them in terms of a struggle between the forces of traditionalism and those of modernism: the path which events have taken (especially since the discovery of oil) is seen as determined by the interaction of — and ultimately conflict between — these two contradictory tendencies. The most fundamental problem facing the contemporary state, therefore, is described as the likelihood of modern technology (with its associated social attitudes) undermining the traditional foundations of the state. Manfred Wenner, for example, describes Saudi Arabia as a 'patriarchal desert state' and characterises the pursuit of modernisation programmes by the traditional elite as 'the contradiction of Saudi Arabia today'.[1] Robert Crane, similarly, sees the bedouin as providing the 'cultural bedrock of Islamic values' on which the Saudi state is based, and stresses the importance of government programmes which counter the threat that Western technology poses to the traditional foundations of the state.[2] The latter conception echoes one of the themes in the guidelines laid down for the Second Five-Year Plan of Saudi Arabia (1975–80),[3] and is also to be found in the writings of George Lenczowski,[4] Michael Hudson[5] and Stephen Duguid.[6]

This paper will contend that such an approach, laying emphasis on the interaction of and conflict between the forces of traditionalism and modernism, does not constitute a useful means of analysis, and does not help towards an understanding of the pattern of developments in Saudi Arabia (either in terms of explanation, interpretation or prediction). While the approach may have a certain superficial plausibility — in so far as contemporary Saudi Arabia is certainly a mixture of old and new, and the social *mores* advocated by the *'ulama* and imposed by the Committees of Public Morality are frequently at odds with those of the professionally- and technically-trained element in the population — it does not take into account the extent to which the old and the new are interlinked, with both 'forces' serving common purposes. Those parts of the social structure which are usually termed 'traditional' have often played a central role in creating a framework within which 'modern' economic development could proceed; and the modernisation programmes have often constituted a key element in reinforcing the power of the traditional structures of authority. The activities of the *muwahhidun* early in this century in spreading and reinforcing the fundamentalist teachings of Ibn Abd al-Wahhab through the greater part of the Arabian peninsula, far from constituting a simple reversion to the eighteenth or perhaps seventh century, were closely linked to the formation of a political structure which responded to the changing conditions wrought by increased Western economic and political involvement in the area and which was relevant for the protection and expansion of commerce. The large number of highly qualified personnel in the present Saudi Arabian government,[7] while it can be – and usually is – presented as an aspect of modernisation, is also evidence of the capacity and power at the disposal of the traditional structures.

Moreover, the explanation of developments in terms of a contest between traditionalism and modernism is frequently made use of within the context of Saudi Arabian politics to justify and validate courses of action whose principal motivation may lie elsewhere. Attempts to protect and foster 'traditional values' are closely linked with the maintenance of internal security; the emphasis on continuing 'traditional customs' helps to justify resistance to the introduction of political institutions which could broaden the base of political participation and representation; and the slogan of 'modernisation' may be raised by those seeking political and economic changes favourable to their own social grouping.

A more useful approach to understanding developments in Saudi Arabia may be found in delineating the social groupings which have affected the course of events, in tracing how these groupings have been strengthened or given an opportunity to play a role by economic and political developments both within and outside the Arabian peninsula, and in examining the manner in which economic, social and political factors have interacted and shaped the various stages through which Saudi Arabia[8] has passed since the foundation of the third Saudi state in Najd in 1902.[9] This paper will follow such an approach. Utilising secondary material,[10] the interactions between the social structure, the economy and the political process will be examined. The object is to provide a framework within which developments in Saudi Arabia over the past half-century can be explained and understood.

A brief statement of the central themes may help to give coherence to what follows. Despite the prominent military role played by bedouin (and ex-bedouin), the establishment and expansion of the Saudi state was dependent primarily upon the initiative, leadership and support of townsmen. While the needs and objectives which account for the involvement of townsmen were varied, the interests of commerce were a crucial component. The Saudi Arabian state from 1926 (the conquest of the Hijaz) up to 1947 (when oil revenues began significantly to transform the economy), consequently, involved a significant role being given to domestic commercial interests — while the House of Saud, ever mindful of the requirements of security and stability, fostered and maintained a close unison with the *'ulama* and the bedouin tribal leaders. Until 1947, this pattern of political and economic organisation was conducive to a certain equilibrium: although some merchants, together with some of those wielding political power or influence, no doubt grew richer, the country's social structure underwent no radical transformation. Between 1947 and 1958, the substantial influx of oil revenues into a system where authority and influence lay with the elements mentioned above brought about significant changes in the relative prosperity and well-being of different sections of Saudi Arabia's population. The increased level of imports made possible by the revenues, coupled with the failure to devote funds to strengthening the productive base of the economy, affected detrimentally large sectors of the economy — especially agriculture, pastoralism and handicrafts. The declining prosperity (or increasing poverty) of some was in sharp contrast with the substantial profits accumulated by merchants (based on the import trade) and with the spending on luxury consumption by some of those holding, or enjoying access to, political power or influence. By 1958 the trend of developments had created acute problems for the regime, confronting it with growing social discontent — discontent which could find expression in modern forms of political organisation through the involvement of individuals employed in the oil economy or the institutions whose creation had been made necessary by oil production. The period between 1958 and 1962 saw contention within ruling circles as to the most effective means of responding to the situation which had arisen. On the one hand, there were those (associated with Prince Talal b. Abd al-Aziz) who sought to move towards a liberal parliamentary regime, where discontent could be defused by allowing opportunity for its open expression. On the other hand, there were those (associated with the then-Crown Prince, Faisal b. Abd al-Aziz) who sought to

defuse discontent by extensive programmes of industrial and agricultural development accompanied by social welfare programmes –
within a structure which retained, and indeed strengthened, existing
centralised control. The reinstatement of Faisal as Prime Minister in
1962, followed by his proclamation of the Ten-Point Programme,
marked the victory of the latter approach. The political dynamics of the
introduction of development planning in the mid-1960s, and of the
massive programmes of industrial, agricultural and infrastructural
development which followed in the late 1960s and the 1970s, therefore,
are to be found within this context. The economic developments are
themselves now steadily transforming the social structure by expanding
the size and significance of those social groupings on whom the
operation of the economic infrastructure depends. The fundamental
problem posed by the coming stage of Saudi history lies in the nature of
the political role which such groupings will seek, and in how this will
relate to and affect the existing political framework.

Economic and Social Factors in the Establishment and Expansion of the Saudi State, 1902–25

The characterisation of Saudi Arabia as a 'bedouin state', where
authority rests on something akin to tribal leadership, generally stems
from a conception of how the state came to be established – laying
emphasis upon the role of the bedouin in that process. It is of some
importance, therefore, to examine in detail the nature of the social
elements which made it possible for Abd al-Aziz ibn Saud to create a
unified state over the greater part of the Arabian peninsula between
1902 (the capture of al-Riyadh) and 1925 (the expulsion of the
Hashimites from the Hijaz). The contention here is that commercial
interests in the towns played a more crucial role in the creation and
expansion of the Saudi state than did the bedouin. Consequently, even
at the outset a 'modernising element' was both present and prominent:
an element which linked the area to the economy of the industrialised
world and helped to incorporate the Arabian peninsula into the
international economic system. Commercial interests, however, could
only further their objectives through co-operation with other elements
in society.

Some idea should first be given of the nature and significance of
commerce in the peninsula around the time when the Saudi state was
being formed. Of particular relevance is information on trade in Central

and Eastern Arabia, where the Saudi state originated. While the role of trade in the economy of the Hijaz is frequently recognised,[11] that of trade in Najd and al-Hasa is less often acknowledged.

It would be impossible to estimate accurately the amount of trade carried on in Arabia at the turn of the century, but there is sufficient evidence to assert that trade was substantial and growing. The opening of the Suez Canal in 1867, the reinforcement of Turkish power in the Hijaz and the upper Gulf in the late nineteenth century and the continued British presence in the lower Gulf all provided a suitable framework for the entry of increased quantities of European goods into Arabia (part of that general expansion of European commercial involvement in the Middle East characteristic of the late nineteenth century) in exchange for local products.[12] The growth of trade with the outside world, in turn, encouraged intra-peninsular trade. The trade figures for Bahrain between 1894/5 and 1906/7 provide evidence of the significance of Eastern and Central Arabian trade (see Table 5.1), for the

Table 5.1: Figures for Bahrain Trade, 1894/5 to 1906/7

Year	Value (in £000s)
1894/5	387
1895/6	387
1896/7	497
1897/8	503
1898/9	552
1899/1900	642
1900/1	451
1901/2	636
1902/3	888
1903/4	1,027
1904/5	992
1905/6	1,620
1906/7	1,638

Source: B. Busch, *Britain and the Persian Gulf, 1894–1914* (University of California Press, Berkeley, 1967), Appendix F.

bulk of Bahrain's external trade consisted of the re-export trade with Eastern and Central Arabia. Also relevant are figures for the value of pearls exported from the Gulf over this period (see Table 5.2), for although the areas administered by Abd al-Aziz ibn Saud were not themselves involved in the pearl industry or the pearl trade, the rising incomes based on pearl exports in the smaller Gulf shaikhdoms (particularly Bahrain) provided, in turn, a basis for the expansion of commerce throughout Eastern and Central Arabia.

Table 5.2: Statistics of the Value of Pearls Exported Annually from the Principal Emporia of the Persian Gulf between 1893/4 and 1904/5

Year	Trucial Oman (in rupees)	Bahrain (in rupees)	Lingeh (in rupees)	Masqat (in US dollars)	Bushehr (in rupees)	Bandar Abbas (in rupees)	Approx. total annual value (in sterling)
1893/4	5,000,000	3,693,750	4,205,000	50,000	8,440	–	483,767
1894/5	6,000,000	4,658,620	3,903,000	40,000	32,200	–	473,446
1895/6	8,000,000	3,855,000	4,102,000	30,000	–	71,000	458,320
1896/7	10,000,000	5,167,000	3,865,000	30,000	–	–	545,520
1897/8	7,500,000	3,911,000	3,572,000	35,000	–	15,600	481,010
1898/9	5,500,000	4,793,000	3,851,000	40,000	–	20,000	577,523
1899/1900	7,749,990	6,824,430	3,399,900	50,000	52,005	–	689,533
1900/1	4,200,000	3,961,700	2,750,000	55,000	–	–	449,508
1901/2	5,000,000	7,130,100	4,013,500	25,000	–	15,000	741,465
1902/3	8,000,000	8,495,610	7,041,468	52,000	2,025	–	1,307,241
1903/4	9,000,000	10,275,300	4,905,000	22,000	–	–	1,493,975
1904/5	5,000,000	10,488,000	623,800	30,000	1,800	1,000	1,076,973
Totals	132,812,750	122,795,510	112,398,348	1,443,000	276,870	122,600	17,963,310
Averages	4,150,398	3,837,359	3,512,448	45,093	8,652	3,831	561,353

Source: J. G. Lorimer, *Gazetteer of the Persian Gulf, 'Oman and Central Arabia* (Superintendent Government Printing, Calcutta, 1915; republished by Gregg International, Farnborough, 1970), p. 2252.

The elaboration of the picture presented by the sets of statistics (see Tables 5.1 and 5.2) must necessarily depend on such occasional references to Eastern and Central Arabian trade over that period as may be found elsewhere. While the resultant picture is incomplete, some impression of the scale and importance of trade should be conveyed. Lorimer describes the thriving export of dates from Bahrain at the turn of the century as based almost exclusively on dates brought from Eastern Arabia (al-Hasa),[13] and points to Najd as being the only area in the world where the Arabian horse (much in demand for the cavalry regiments of the Indian army) was bred for export in substantial numbers.

> Najd or Central Arabia is the principal horse-breeding country in the Persian Gulf and the only one in the world, except the adjacent Syrian desert, where the genuine Arab is produced on any considerable scale. Horses are most numerous in northern Central Arabia . . . but the export trade depends largely on the more central district of Qasim, where the towns of 'Anaizah and Buraidah are the principal markets. 'Anaizah, supplied principally by the Qahtan, furnishes as a rule animals of higher caste, while at Buraidah, provided chiefly by the Mutair, the number of animals is usually larger.[14]

Commercial activities associated with camels were also significant. First, their breeding for export constituted a fairly widespread economic pursuit, as is attested to by Lorimer.[15] Second, the camel-borne trade crossing the peninsula, from the Gulf ports and Yemen to Syria and back, was of considerable importance to the economy of Central Arabia — most of it being organised by the merchants of Najd and al-Hasa. In the period between Abd al-Aziz ibn Saud's gaining control of the greater part of Najd and the First World War it was tariffs raised on the caravan trade with Syria which provided the main source of funds for the public treasury.[16]

Some evidence of the extent of the commercial networks is to be found in the works of Charles Doughty who, writing of the situation in the late 1870s, estimated that some one-third of the population of al-Qasim province was involved in the caravan trade.[17] This proportion was no doubt higher than would be the case elsewhere in Central Arabia, as the towns of 'Anaizah and Buraidah in al-Qasim constituted the points from which much of the caravan trade between South Arabia and the Levant, as well as between Eastern and Western Arabia, was organised. Nevertheless, commerce did thrive elsewhere. H. St John Philby, writing in the 1920s, described the thriving commercial sector in Shaqra, to the North of al-Riyadh, and referred to the commercial contracts which the Shaqra merchants maintained with their agents in the Gulf ports, Iraq and India.[18] Such commercial networks operated by Central Arabian merchants must indeed have been widespread, for in the early years of the century the town of Zubeir in southern Iraq was inhabited predominantly by Najdi merchants engaged in handling the trade between Central Arabia and the outside world.[19] Trade, moreover, had become a necessity for the settled population of Central Arabia: the wheat crop was insufficient for the needs of the population and thus cereal imports were required (increasingly rice, which was becoming the staple diet of the well-to-do), and the settled population depended almost entirely on overseas sources for clothing.[20]

When the British government complained to Abd al-Aziz during the First World War that the merchants of Central Arabia were keeping the Turkish troops in Medina supplied with provisions (which had been brought to al-Qasim from Kuwait), Abd al-Aziz's contention that these merchants were too strongly entrenched for him to control may have not been wholly unrealistic.[21]

Commerce, then, was of substantial and growing importance in Central Arabia at the time of the creation of the Saudi state. The role which commercial interests played in the creation and expansion of that state is our next concern. The political organisation of the Arabian peninsula was inevitably of great relevance to the conduct of trade: the commercial centres required settled conditions, where communications were free of disputes between local rulers and bedouin tribes, and where the safety and security of the trade routes could be guaranteed.[22] The role played by commercial interests, however, is frequently difficult to separate from that played by other elements of the settled population. The small scale of the societies concerned meant that commercial interests were closely related to other interests: the religious establishment was linked to commerce through family bonds and economic dependence; the town and village leaders often owed their positions to a pre-eminence based on commercial success; such landowning as there was (apart from owner-cultivated land) usually sprang from the acquisition of land by religious leaders, merchants and town or village leaders; and a similar set of local notables would help to mobilise peasant cultivators for a military role when that became necessary.[23] In much of what follows, therefore, it will be appropriate to refer simply to the role of townsmen, rather than seeking always to separate out the specifically commercial element. The importance of commercial interests to the objectives pursued and the activities undertaken by townsmen, however, should not be forgotten.

There can be little doubt that the military power which spread Saudi control over the greater part of the Arabian peninsula was, especially between 1912 and 1926, provided mainly either by bedouin tribes or else by those bedouin who settled in the agricultural settlements (*hujar*) and came to constitute the *ikhwan* movement. A detailed examination of the process whereby the bedouin became involved in the struggle, however, reveals that this movement was largely brought about by and dependent upon the continued support of townsmen. The purpose of the remainder of this section is to place the bedouin military role within the appropriate social setting.

From the capture of al-Riyadh in 1902 by Abd al-Aziz ibn Saud and his forty companions to 1906, the area of Najd controlled by the nascent Saudi state grew steadily.[24] Having strengthened the defences of al-Riyadh, forces loyal to Abd al-Aziz pushed northwards into al-Qasim in 1903, successfully countered the Ottoman intervention on behalf of the Al Rashid of Ha'il in 1904, forced the withdrawal in 1906 of the contingent of Ottoman soldiers (3,000 strong) who had been sent to re-establish Ottoman authority, and, after the defeat of the Al Rashid at Raudat Muhanna in 1906, made it possible for Abd al-Aziz to secure recognition from the Al Rashid of Saudi control of all Najd 'except for Ha'il and its dependencies and the bedouin of the Shammar tribe'.[25]

The nucleus of the military force which accomplished the campaigns just mentioned was composed of townsmen, with bedouin contributing an auxiliary element. At Raudat Muhanna, for example, Abd al-Aziz ibn Saud's forces were composed of 1,000 townsmen and 600 bedouin.[26] Townsmen, moreover, played the central role in the defence of their own towns once they had come under Saudi control, providing the necessary militias and thus eliminating the need for garrisons.[27]

The period between 1906 and 1911 saw only fitful expansion of the area under Saudi control, and the emergence (or re-emergence) of divisive tendencies in the Saudi state.[28] Some of those who had allied themselves with Abd al-Aziz in the conquest of Central Arabia now revolted and pursued their own ambitions. Extensive drought in Najd, with rain in the territories of Shammar, caused some bedouin tribes to transfer their loyalties to the Al Rashid. The Al Muhanna of Buraidah conspired in 1907–8 with other leaders of al-Qasim province and with Faisal al-Dawish, leader of the Mutair tribe, to counter Abd al-Aziz and reassert their own independence of action. The al-Hazzani family sought to regain control of al-Hariq town in 1909 and 1911, and the general dissension was augmented when the rebellious al-Sa'ud ibn Faisal (of the al-Araif — the section of the Al Saud which claimed seniority over Abd al-Aziz's line and which only sporadically accepted the leadership of Abd al-Aziz or his father) attacked some of the areas and tribes loyal to Abd al-Aziz in 1910—11.

The extensive dissension, and the failure to impose convincing authority over the areas conquered, was in part due to the nature of the military force used in the conquest — and to the weakening of that force once the initial conquests were completed. Townsmen generally constituted a dependable element in Abd al-Aziz's informal army, yet the nature of the economic life of the settled population made it difficult for townsmen and villagers to engage in lengthy campaigns outside their own areas. The military force at the disposal of Abd al-Aziz, therefore, became increasingly centred on bedouin contingents. While the characterisation of bedouin fickleness and opportunism may be grossly overdrawn ('Today a sword in the hand of the prince, a dagger in his back tomorrow' — Amin Rihani),[29] it remains true that bedouin contingents were liable to change sides abruptly when the balance of interest shifted. Perhaps the best examples of the latter tendency were at the battle of al-Tarafiya in 1908, where the principal bedouin contingents deserted Abd al-Aziz when he appeared to be losing, only to return when he seemed likely to win; and at the battle of al-Jirab, where some of Abd al-Aziz's bedouin contingents turned on their own allies and plundered them — once it had become clear that the Saudi force would be defeated.[30]

This was the background, then, to the creation of a new military force, whose introduction was required so as to impose a convincing authority on the territories already occupied, as well as to enable a campaign to be launched to dislodge the Ottoman forces from Eastern Arabia (al-Hasa) and to confront the growing activism of the Ottoman-supported Sharif of Mecca. The instrument fashioned for this military role was the *ikhwan.*

As the *ikhwan* constituted the main part — at least the strongest and most disciplined part — of the force which spread Saudi power through al-Hasa, the Hijaz and Jebel Shammar, and cemented Saudi authority in Najd, it is important to consider the significance of the *ikhwan* movement within the social framework. The *ikhwan* are defined by John Habib as 'those bedouin who accepted the fundamentals of Orthodox Islam of the Hanbali school as preached by Abd al-Wahhab

... and who abandoned the nomadic life to live in the *hujar* [singular *hijrah*: agricultural settlement] built for them'.[31] Instruction in the fundamentals of Islam did not by itself qualify an individual to become an *akh*; 'the believer must quit the nomadic life, sell his flocks and migrate to a *hijrah*'.[32] Hafiz Wahbah describes the *ikhwan* as 'those bedouin who abandoned living in tents and became settled in a special place ... and who agree to fight for God and the promotion of his word'.[33]

While the *ikhwan* consisted of settled bedouin, the movement does not constitute the expression of any distinctively bedouin interest or perspective. Rather, the initiation, dynamics and ultimately the decline of the movement must be situated in the military needs of Abd al-Aziz — as outlined above — with much of the inspiration and organisation behind the movement issuing directly from the towns. By creating a force which 'would have loyalties not only to himself but also to an idealism that up to this point apparently played only a secondary role', and which 'would be mobile enough to cross the length and breadth of the peninsula, and sedentary enough to be in a specific locality when he needed them', Abd al-Aziz would be assured of a more stable basis for his military campaigns than had hitherto existed.[34] An ascetic military force was brought into being which 'could be mobilised and demobilised swiftly and which combined the mobility of the bedouin with the political loyalty and reliability of the villager or townsman'.[35]

The objectives of Abd al-Aziz, however, were not sufficient by themselves to create the movement. Rather, the involvement of significant sections of the towns' populations was necessary. The provision of supplies for the agricultural settlements at the outset, together with the skills needed in their initial construction, depended on the support and involvement of commercial and artisan elements in the towns.[36] More important, the process of conversion of the bedouin to the *al-tawhid* doctrines of Abd al-Wahhab, which constituted the impetus behind settlement in these semi-religious, military, agricultural communities, was carried out by *mutawa'in* (missionaries) sent out by the religious leaders in the towns under the overall supervision of the *'ulama* of al-Riyadh. The close connections between the involvement of the religious leaders and the wider objectives of Abd al-Aziz is made clear in the way the bedouin tribes were approached. While the *mutawa'in* were seeking to convert the bedouin, the leaders of the tribe concerned were invited to al-Riyadh as personal guests of Abd al-Aziz.[37] In al-Riyadh, while witnessing the evidence of Abd al-Aziz's growing power (other visiting tribal leaders, foreign representatives holding

discussions, etc.), they would be instructed in the fundamentals of
Islam under the tutelage of *'ulama* adhering to the teachings of Abd
al-Wahhab. Colonel Dickson described the process as follows:

> He would send for the Shaikh and tell him in blunt terms that his
> tribe had no religion and that they were all *'juhl'*. He next ordered
> the Shaikh to attend the local school of *'ulama*, which was attached
> to the great mosque in Riyadh, and there undergo a course of
> instruction in religion. At the same time half a dozen *'ulama*,[38]
> attended by some genuinely fanatical Akhwan, such as Al Duwaish
> the Shaikh of the Mutair were sent off to the tribe itself. These held
> daily classes teaching the people all about Islam in its original
> simplicity . . .
> When the Shaikh of the tribe was supposed to have received
> sufficient religious instruction, he was invited to build a house in
> Riyadh and remain in attendance on the Imam. This again was part
> of the control scheme . . .[39]

The effects of the activities of the *mutawa'in* sent out from the towns
is well described by John Habib:

> Scores of young religious teachers spread out among the bedouin,
> teaching them the word of God and the sayings (*hadith*) of the
> Prophet Muhammad. They painted very vividly the evils of sin, hell
> fire, the wrath of God, punishment, pestilence and other plagues, all
> of which inflamed the imaginations of the bedouin . . . The price of
> [a place in heaven] was only that they adopt the heritage which
> their ancestors lost because of their lack of contact with Islamic
> civilisation. Their nomadic life had weaned them away from their
> heritage and caused them to lapse into 'ignorance' . . . Now all the
> energies of raiding were to be channelled into one rushing course,
> against the infidels; raiding would not be sport alone, but the
> execution of God's will. Instead of trekking across the desert to eke
> out a living husbanding camels, goats and sheep, they would live in
> small agricultural communities where food, if not abundant, was
> adequate. There, the blessings of Islamic learning would be showered
> upon them by the religious teachers who would live in the
> communities to protect them against lapsing once again into
> ignorance.[40]

As will have become apparent from the above quotations, the

common characterisation of the bedouin as constituting the 'repository of Islamic values' or 'cultural bedrock of Islamic values'[41] — following which the religious character of the Saudi state is attributed to the bedouin influence — is, in fact, the reverse of the reality (at any rate with respect to the period when the Saudi state was formed). Abd al-Aziz, in conversation with Colonel Dickson, remarked that before the *ikhwan* movement began 'more than ninety per cent of the bedouin had never heard of religion, their marriages were never solemnised, and circumcision was not practised'.[42] No doubt this subjective assessment was exaggerated, yet the picture is presents of *Islam al 'uruba* — where the legal system was dependent on long-established conventions, practices and customs (*'urf* and *'adat*), and not on the *shari'a* or any other consistently Islamic code of conduct — would appear to be not unrealistic. John Habib quotes a former *akh* as saying that 'the bedouin did not even know the correct posture for prayer, and customary and tribal law were practised alongside with popular medicine and trial by fire and ordeal'.[43] In short, although earlier generations of bedouin had been *muwahhidun* (followers of the *al-tawhid* doctrine), it was in the towns and villages that the ideas of Abd al-Wahhab had lived on.

To state that the *ikhwan* movement developed through the inspiration and organisation of Abd al-Aziz and his townsmen allies is not intended to suggest that the movement did not come to have a momentum of its own. Once the armies of *mutawa'in* organised by Abdalla bin Muhammad bin Abd al-Latif and other *'ulama* had carried their tracts and treatises to the settlements and expounded upon them, there frequently emerged the fanaticism of the newly converted — an enthusiasm which came to despise the more relaxed approach taken by the townsmen, and which ultimately led to the confrontation between sections of the *ikhwan* and Abd al-Aziz between 1928 and 1930.

This, then, was the nature of the movement which constituted the instrument whereby Abd al-Aziz and his allies extended Saudi power into al-Hasa (1913), curtailed Sharif Husain of the Hijaz's ambition to control Khurma (1919), expanded Saudi control of territory in the vicinity of Kuwait (1920), brought to an end Rashidi power in northern Arabia (1921), secured control of much of Asir (1923) and in 1924 launched the offensive which terminated the Hashimite presence in the Hijaz.

The events which led to the decline and eclipse of the *ikhwan* movement revealed once again the nature of the relationship between the movement, on the one side, and Abd al-Aziz and his townsmen allies and supporters, on the other. From providing the crucial military force needed to spread Saudi control through the Arabian peninsula, they became a threat to the security of the state. The urgent quest for international recognition was complicated by the *ikhwan* raids on Kuwait, by *ikhwan* involvement in the *mahmal* incident of 1926,[44] and by some *ikhwan* declaring a *jihad* against Iraq in 1929. Domestic security was endangered by resentment at the civilian massacre which the *ikhwan* forces inflicted on al-Taif after its capture in 1924, by their tendency to discomfit the *Shi'a* inhabitants of al-Hasa in the cause of *al-tawhid*, and by the alienation spreading among the sophisticated urban society of Hijaz due to the excesses of *ikhwan* zeal. The period between 1928 and 1930 saw a deliberate rallying of townspeople — most prominently in the general assemblies convened by Abd al-Aziz in 1928 and 1929 — to counter the independent role which the *ikhwan* (or elements of the *ikhwan*) had assumed. At the battle of Sibila in 1929 a force of townsmen (supported by bedouin contingents which appear to have participated little in the actual fighting)[45] defeated the *ikhwan* and effectively curbed the movement which had run out of the control of its creators. Those parts of the *ikhwan* movement which had remained loyal to Abd al-Aziz, together with most of the agricultural settlements, survived the events of 1928–30; the surviving *ikhwan*, however, no longer had the potential or the opportunity to play an independent role in the state. Under a religious and political supervision which ensured loyalty, they formed the basis of the White Guard (later the National Guard), while the agricultural settlements continued to receive their annual grants of rice financed by the public treasury.

Power and the Social Structure, 1926–47

The examination, in the previous section, of the process whereby the Saudi Arabian state was formed and subsequently expanded is of crucial importance in understanding the political dynamics of the state since 1926. The elements which had helped to unify the greater part of the peninsula continued to play a role in the maintenance of the state. The Al Saud — itself a rapidly growing body[46] which could assert a presence in many different aspects of state life — balanced between, manipulated and allowed state policy to be influenced by the religious leaders, the bedouin tribal leaders and the commercial establishment. The processes whereby influence was exerted, and the effects which this had on the structure and policy of the new state is the concern of this section.

To describe the dynamics of the Saudi Arabian political system between 1926 and 1947 – and, indeed, after this period also – is difficult. The main difficulty springs from the manner in which the most crucial government decisions were taken. Such decision-making was the exclusive prerogative of the King, with the royal *majlis* (the King's audience) and small personalised discussions constituting the channels whereby decisions could be influenced. The informal nature of the channels of influence inhibits any attempt to discover which arguments swayed a particular decision or even who took part in the relevant discussions. Some formal government institutions did exist: in the Hijaz an Advisory Council, whose concern was limited to the affairs of that region, was established in 1926,[47] this was superseded in 1931 by a Council of Deputies, which maintained a spasmodic existence up to 1953.[48] The Council's primary concern was also with the Hijaz, where it was located, but its functions sometimes covered other regions. Neither institution, however, played more than a peripheral role in determining the central aspects of state policy. The only means of gaining some appreciation of the political dynamics of the newly unified state is to bring together such evidence as does exist of the role played by different social elements in particular decisions and to relate this to the kind of policies pursued and the kind of structures created by the state.

The nature of the *majlis* system requires some further explanation before we can usefully examine the means whereby each of the social groupings mentioned earlier exerted influence. The access which citizens had to the King in his daily *majlis* has caused some observers to describe the *majlis* system as a form of democratic representation. This is incorrect, for the ability to express views to the decision-maker is not equivalent to having a share in determining what decisions are made. Abd al-Aziz's attitude towards advice offered to him is neatly summarised in a Koranic text which he frequently quoted to Philby:[49] 'Take counsel among yourselves, and if they agree with you, well and good: but if otherwise, then put your trust in God and do that which you deem best.' Moreover, the principle of free access did not imply giving the mass of citizens an effective channel through which they could affect the whole range of government policy:

There was a clear understanding among the King's subjects that a man did not go to the palace unless he had a particular business with the King, or the visit was a traditional right such as the annual visit of the bedouin. The townspeople of al-Riyadh, for example, never came to the palace unless they had special reason to do so.[50]

The central part of the *majlis* proceedings was the general session, which would last for about 40 minutes and would be attended by some 80–100 people. Although the King would address the gathering on some topic of national concern and answer such questions as might be raised on the subject, most of those present had come either to raise a specific request (which could usually be met by the grant of provisions or funds) or, as bedouin tribesmen who fought for the King, to renew their pledge of loyalty and collect their annual subsidy.[51] Such contact between rulers and ruled no doubt served useful purposes: it did not, however, constitute a channel whereby state policy could be significantly influenced.

Nevertheless, the royal *majlis* did constitute a channel of influence for some. Besides the general sessions there was a small private session in the mornings and a rather larger informal session in the evenings. It was in these two latter sessions that wide-ranging discussion of state policy occurred; participation was restricted to 'prominent individuals in the state — whether owing their prominence to membership in the royal family, to tribal leadership, to position in the religious hierarchy or to commercial success'.[52] Mohamed al-Mana notes that 'the floor was open for anyone who wished to raise a topic for general comment or discussion'.[53] The ability of individuals (or the groupings of which they formed part) to influence successfully a particular policy depended, of course, on a variety of factors: the strength of the King's overall political position, the King's need for support from that particular individual or grouping, the advice tendered by other individuals and groupings and by the King's political committee, etc.[54]

The role of the tribal leaderships in the state structure between 1926 and 1947 is perhaps the most clear: in return for the subsidies provided by the public treasury and the recognition given by Abd al-Aziz to their leadership and administrative authority within their own areas — actions which strengthened the standing of the leaders among their own tribespeople — the tribal leaders secured and maintained tribal (especially bedouin) loyalty to the regime. The assurance of direct and frequent access to the King reinforced the tribal leaderships' involvement with the Al Saud, and the strong loyalties engendered provided a basis for drawing bedouin tribesmen into the White Army (later National Guard). Links were further strengthened by intermarriage between the Al Saud and the tribal leaderships: Abd al-Aziz himself took wives from the leading familes of each of the major tribal groupings.

The strategy of maintaining the loyalty of the bedouin tribal peoples through close co-operation with and support of the tribal leaderships involved an immense system of subsidies, which effectively absorbed a large part of state revenue. Some of these subsidies were paid directly to tribal leaderships for their own use, others were paid to the leaders for distribution within the tribe, and others again were paid directly to the bedouin (although under conditions created by tribal leaders — that is when tribal leaders brought their peoples to attend the royal *majlis*). The main types of subsidy benefiting the bedouin, whether paid directly or through the leaders, were the following:[55]

Al-Sharha — a gift from the King after a visit to the royal *majlis*. In the early 1930s this usually amounted to three gold pounds, a robe and a cloak for each ordinary *bedawi* who participated, and six gold pounds together with better quality robes and cloaks for minor shaikhs within the tribe.[56]
Al-Barwah — a gift of rice, wheat, tea, coffee and sugar from one of the store houses laid aside for this purpose in different parts of the country.
Al-Mu'awanah — funds to meet a particular need for which a special request is made.
Al-Qa'idah — a cash grant to all the *ikhwan* whose names appeared on the King's register as fighters.

The network of subsidies ensured, under the supervision of tribal leaders, continued bedouin loyalty. Confident of this loyalty, the government could then draw the bedouin into a military role (first through the remnants of the *ikhwan*, later through the White Army and finally the National Guard) to strengthen and defend the regime. The co-operative support of the bedouin also enabled the government to pursue policies in nomadic areas aimed at realising national unity — inter-tribal raiding was effectively curtailed (having been formally proscribed in 1925), and in 1925 the government abolished the system whereby tribes were regarded as having rights over particular territory.

The relationship between the King and the religious leaders (those *'ulama* who adhered to Abd al-Wahhab's teachings and among whom the Al al-Shaikh were always prominent) was also one of mutual support and dependence — they helped to shape the nature of the state which emerged and they, in turn, were used by the King in the promotion of his political objectives. The *'ulama* provided the kingdom with something akin to a state philosophy, which played a crucial role in the centralisation of authority. They promoted the expansion of religious education, inculcating a common value system in the rising generation of the new state, and ensured the spread of increasingly uniform legal practices (with the *qadi*, whose adjudication was based on the *shari'a*[57] as interpreted by the Hanbali tradition, taking over the role previously played in the rural areas by the *'arifa*, whose adjudication was based on customary law). The *'ulama*'s involvement in the direct administration of religious education and of the legal system, together with their power to regulate public conduct through the *hay'at al-amr b'il ma'ruf w'al nahi 'an al-munkar* (Committees for Encouraging Virtue and Preventing Vice), placed significant authority in their hands. Yet the philosophy conveyed was one which could be, and was, used to rally political support for Abd al-Aziz.

While the *'ulama* enjoyed ready access to the King's *majlis* they had one further and more effective channel of influence: a regular weekly meeting with the King, held on Thursday afternoons, in which views were exchanged and policy co-ordinated.[58] The *'ulama*'s role in decision-making and in the implementation of policy can perhaps best be appreciated with respect to the management of the *ikhwan* movement. They had initally opposed the inception of the movement, contending that there was no Islamic justification for it.[59] Reassured by Abd al-Aziz as to the leading role which they would play in creating and shaping the movement, however, the *'ulama* actively promoted the project. When the movement began to slip out of Abd al-Aziz's control in 1927–30, they issued *fatwat* (singular *fatwa*: religious pronouncement) intended to strengthen the King's position and they rallied support for the central government in the general assembly convened to discuss the escalating differences with the *ikhwan* in 1928.[60] The importance to Abd al-Aziz of maintaining the support of the *'ulama* is also apparent in his strenuous efforts to persuade them to sanction the introduction of Western mechanical equipment into the country – wireless communications, telegraph and automobiles – and in his willingness to delay the introduction of such machinery until the sanction was given.[61] Furthermore, when the *'ulama* in 1950 objected to the King's plans to celebrate a golden jubilee marking the 50th anniversary (in lunar years) of the capture of al-Riyadh from the Al Rashid, the project was duly abandoned. The *'ulama*'s power to issue *fatwat* on any issue which concerned them was a useful instrument to promote governmental objectives, but so also could that power thwart governmental objectives[62] – hence Abd al-Aziz's need to retain support in that quarter.

The commercial establishment, whose significance within the state was strengthened following the incorporation of the Hijaz with its large commercial sector, enjoyed a similar mutual dependence with the political leadership. The principal sources of funds for the public treasury between 1926 and 1933 (when the first royalties for oil exploration were paid), and continuing as substantial sources of revenue up to 1947, were dues levied on the pilgrim traffic to Mecca and customs dues.[63] Both sources depended upon the continued vitality of the commercial sector to provide the necessary services for pilgrims and to maintain a thriving trade from which duties would be payable. Moreover, merchants were frequently called upon to 'donate' money or provisions for particular purposes — whether to finance a military campaign or to fill the store houses from which grants of provisions were made.[64] Such 'donations' apparently do not figure in the sketchy statistics of government revenue produced at the time.

A further dimension to the importance of the commercial establishment to Abd al-Aziz was the former's close links with local political leaders in the smaller towns and in the villages. The leading families of such towns and villages, from whom the *amir* of the area would be drawn,[65] were often deeply involved in trade and in some cases owed their prominence to commercial success (or else commercial success increased a prominence whose origin lay in the tribal structure of the area). The close intertwining of commercial interest and local political leadership, together with the connections which the latter frequently had with bedouin tribal leaderships, makes it unnecessary to treat local political leaders as a separate category enjoying mutual dependence with the King. They constituted, rather, an element which rendered more crucial to the King the continued support of the commercial establishment and the tribal leaders.

The strength of the commercial establishment is revealed in the developments which ensured whenever Abd al-Aziz sought to take action detrimental to commercial interests (rare though such occasions were). When, following the conquest of the Hijaz, Abd al-Aziz announced that all supplies of tobacco would be confiscated, the leading merchants of Jeddah were quick to impress upon him the economic loss which they would suffer. The scheme was duly abandoned.[66] The same group of merchants, alienated by heavy taxes, had earlier hastened the demise of Sharif Husain of the Hijaz.[67] In 1933, attempting to meet his debts to the Soviet government for the supply of petroleum products, Abd al-Aziz granted a concession to the Soviet Vostgostorg trading company to import freely into Saudi Arabia and undertake its own retailing. The reaction from the local merchant community was strong and immediate; the concession had to be withdrawn.[68] A diplomatic observer noted: 'besides the pilgrimage, the King's most lucrative source of income has been the Jeddah group of merchants, and he cannot remain in power and antagonise them coincidentally for very long'.[69] The steady expansion of commerce between 1926 and 1947[70] reflected the common interest which the merchants and the political leadership had in fostering trade.

The significance of the three above-mentioned elements in the Saudi state between 1926 and 1947 is reflected not only in the policies pursued, but also in the failure to develop certain other policies. As none of the influential social groupings had a specific interest in increasing the state's involvement in economic development, the government structure remained skeletal (only three ministries existed at the end of 1947, and there was no Council of Ministers[71]) and comparatively little attention was given to secular education[72] (which would have been required for a larger bureaucracy). No doubt the failure to engage in a more active development policy was in part attributable to the meagre resources at the King's disposal (see Table 5.3).

Table 5.3: Statistics showing Government Revenue, 1902–47[73]

	Approximate annual government revenue
1902–12	£50,000
1913–25	£100,000
1926–37	£4–5 million
1938–46	£5–6 million
1947–8	£21.5 million

Source: Philby, *Sa'udi Arabia* (Benn, London, 1955), p. 328.

Nevertheless, such funds as were available were not generally devoted to schemes of economic development. They were, rather, channelled into security-related projects (such as the establishment of wireless communications linking the different centres of population to the royal palace in al-Riyadh,[74] subsidies for the bedouin, and maintaining the royal court – an item which involved, among other things, the upkeep of some 250 cars (in 1935) whereby the entire court could accompany the King on his frequent visits to different parts of the country.[75] In short, the main business of government at this stage was 'the preservation of law and order in a divided society', and 'maintaining the *status quo*' rather than pursuing more development-oriented objectives.[76]

The inappropriateness of making a dichotomy between traditionalism and modernism in describing developments in Saudi Arabia is apparent again from the nature of the groupings and tendencies mentioned in this section. While the commercial sector constituted the principal instrument through which Saudi Arabia was increasingly drawn into the economy of the capitalist world and the principal channel through which outside ideas penetrated the country (until the oil sector assumed these roles), the commercial sector was itself dependent on and given encouragement by the 'traditional' framework which surrounded it.

Oil Revenues, Politics and the Changing Social Structure, 1948–58

Authority and influence between 1948 and 1958 remained largely where they had been before 1948. Neither the death of Abd al-Aziz in 1953 and the assumption of power by the less adept Saud, nor the introduction of a Council of Ministers in 1953 (enjoying a purely advisory role until 1958 when it gained some direct executive and legislative powers)[77] substantially altered the political system. Power still rested in the royal prerogative, and the King still needed to take into account the opinions and interests of other members of the royal family, the *'ulama*, the commercial sector and the tribal leaders. The continuing influence of such elements (especially the first two) was evident in the transfer of prime ministerial power – against the wishes of the King – to Prince Faisal in 1958; in the ability of the *'ulama* (apparently in conjunction with commercial interests) to prevent the introduction of a new system of taxation in the late 1950s;[78] and in the King's continuing attempts, through subsidies, to maintain the support of the tribal leaders.[79]

While power continued to be wielded in the same manner as before, the resources at the disposal of those wielding power were vastly greater than before. 1948 was the year in which, oil production now being under way, revenues from oil sales began to transform the revenue at the disposal of the government (see Table 5.4). By 1953 annual revenue had surpassed $100 million and by 1960 it stood at $333.7 million.[81] Not surprisingly, in a structure which was – as explained earlier – not geared to a coherent use of resources for developmental purposes, the vast new resources were not channelled into coherent development. The political processes were neither able

Table 5.4: Pattern of Revenue from Oil Sales Received by the Public
Treasury in 1948

Source of revenue	Revenue in $US	Percentage total revenue
Oil revenue	35,000,000	65.2
Customs	6,250,000	11.1
Other receipts	12,396,750	23.7
Total	53,646,750	100.0

Source: F. Badr, 'Developmental Planning in Saudi Arabia', unpublished PhD
thesis, University of Southern California, 1968, p. 78. [80]

(due to the skeletal government organisation) nor inherently suited
(due to the nature of the groupings wielding influence) to pursue a
consistent development programme. Decisions on disbursement were
taken in a random and uncoordinated fashion, with no clearly
established objectives laid down.[82] Although the country's first
formally organised budget in 1954 did devote some funds to infrastructural development, especially road construction, 35 per cent of
total expenditure went on defence.[83] A large part of the revenue from
oil was spent on luxury projects, such as the two palaces which King
Saud had constructed for himself in al-Riyadh and Jeddah at a cost of
$50 million,[84] and on paying increased subsidies to tribal leaders.[85]

Certain groupings in society — largely those described above as
'influential' — benefited from the influx of funds and their expenditure
in the manner described above, while the economic prospects of others
either remained stagnant or were adversely affected. The effect of oil
revenues on the country's social structure, consequently, was to widen
substantially existing inequalities. The growing wealth of some was, in
fact, directly linked to the deteriorating economic conditions of others.
While the commercial sector benefited greatly from the boom in
consumer demand and from the increased resources available to finance
imports, the rising imports virtually destroyed the handicrafts sector
of the economy and seriously affected the agricultural and pastoral
sectors (by satisfying local demand for the products of these sectors).
Agricultural production appears to have declined in absolute value
during the early 1950s.[86] Those owning land in areas affected by the
boom associated with oil production benefited from the spiralling
prices fetched by such land, while others experienced only the
inflationary effects on the cost of living.

The significance of the growing social stresses following from the
developments just mentioned was increased by the rise of new social

groupings associated with oil production — groupings whose involvement in the process of oil production and whose professional training laid the basis for a consciousness which could be used to channel existing social discontents into new forms of political organisation (as well as to express their own demands for change). There was, first, the Aramco workforce, details of whose changing composition are given in Tables 5.5 and 5.6. The potential for concerted action by the oil

Table 5.5: Nationality of All Aramco Employees in Saudi Arabia, 1952

Nationality	Number	Percentage of total
Saudi Arabs	14,819	61.7
Americans	3,235	13.5
Other Arabs	2,254	9.4
Indians	1,110	4.6
Pakistanis	1,320	5.5
Others	1,268	5.3
Total	24,006	100.0

Source: *Aramco Handbook* (Arabian American Oil Company, Saudi Arabia, 1968), p. 156.

Table 5.6: Nationality of Aramco Senior and Intermediate Staff in Saudi Arabia, 1949—71

Aramco staff	1949	1959	1971
Senior Staff	2,231	2,565	
American	2,201	2,464	935
Saudi Arab	0	44	1,207
Third country	30	57	
Intermediate Staff	364	5,013	
Saudi Arab	80	3,017	4,944
Third country	284	1,986	
Total, all employees	16,909	16,257	10,107

Source: *Aramco Handbook* (Arabian American Oil Company, Netherlands, 1960), p. 211; and Aramco, unpublished paper, 1972.

workers was demonstrated in the 1953 and 1956 strikes.[87] Second, the expansion of government services and administration to cope with the oil economy involved a growing civil service. In addition to the Ministries of Foreign Affairs, Finance and Defence (established in 1930, 1932 and 1944 respectively), a Ministry of the Interior was established in 1951, Ministries of Communications, Education and Agriculture were established in 1953, and Ministries of Commerce and of Health in 1954. A number of governmental agencies were also set up around this time, such as the Department of Labour, and the Directorates General of Petroleum and Mineral Affairs and of Broadcasting, Press and Publications. The ministries were co-ordinated through the Council of Ministers. Some indication of the growing size of the civil service is found in Table 5.7,[88] although the data relate to a rather later period than concerns us here.

Table 5.7: Numbers and Wages of Saudi Workers, 1964

	Number (in thousands)	Average wage (riyals per year)
Industrial		
Petroleum (Aramco)	10	10,700
Other wage earners	8	5,000
Governmental		
Civilian	90	6,500
Military	60	6,500
Non-industrial		
Wage-earners	82	3,500
Self-employed		
Non-agricultural	10	4,000
Agricultural	740	1,000
Total	1,000	

Source: W. Rugh, 'The Emergence of a New Middle Class in Saudi Arabia', *Middle East Journal*, vol. 27, no. 1 (Winter 1973), p. 9.

The deteriorating economic prospects facing some sectors of the population, the growing inequalities and the development of new social groups associated with the initiation of oil production were all crucial to the rise of discontent within the country during the 1950s — a discontent which found expression in the Aramco strikes. The problems facing the government, moreover, were compounded by other issues: the lavish and wasteful scale of expenditure brought on a severe financial crisis in 1957—8; and rising Arab nationalism within the Arab world exerted a powerful attraction on some elements of the Saudi population, especially the 'new social groups' mentioned above. The government's short-term reaction to growing discontent was to suppress the manifestations and the perceived immediate causes of the discontent. The Aramco strikes were terminated by force, conditions for oil workers were improved, and in 1955 Saudis were forbidden to study abroad at any level below that of university.[89] The more fundamental adaptation of the political and economic system to changing conditions, however, was to take place after 1958.

Political Process and Development Strategy, 1958–80

The year 1958 constitutes a critical date in Saudi Arabian political history. The fortunes of the regime perhaps struck their lowest point in that year. On the surface the crisis was caused by the loss of international prestige following the revelation of King Saud's implication in a plot to assassinate Nasser, by the economic mismanagement which had created a heavy governmental debt despite the oil revenues, and by the rising tide of militancy in the surrounding Arab world set in train by the Iraqi Revolution. The response of the Al Saud was to impose upon King Saud, whose increasingly erratic leadership since assuming the crown in 1953 had scarcely helped the regime's reputation, the appointment of Prince Faisal as Prime Minister.[90]

The change in the composition of the government in 1958, however, had a wider significance than as a short-term reaction to passing difficulties. The change constituted the beginning of a concerted effort by leading circles in the regime to confront the situation created by policies pursued between 1947 and 1958 – to defuse the discontent which had been building up. The changing economic and social conditions in the country required government policy to take a fundamentally different direction if the regime was to remain viable. In the period between 1958 and 1962 a struggle emerged within the Al Saud (and among those groupings which enjoyed access to the royal family) as to the kind of adaptation which was required. This struggle was of crucial importance, for its outcome set the pattern for Saudi Arabia's development over the two decades which followed.

One tendency within the Al Saud saw the way forward as lying in political reform and democratisation (accompanied, no doubt, by economic development). The Liberal Princes, of whom Prince Talal bin Abd al-Aziz was the best-known member, talked of a progression towards liberal democracy. If the regime was based on popular support it could, they claimed, be safeguarded.[91] The contrary tendency saw the solution to Saudi Arabia's problems in greater centralised control (both of the economy and of the political system). Discontent would, in this case, be defused solely by a coherent economic and social development programme, catering to the interests of different elements of the population – whether through the provision of employment or through the provision of facilities. Faisal, Prime Minister between March 1958 and mid-1960, was associated with the latter approach. His ability to initiate a coherent programme of economic development at this stage, however, was inhibited by King Saud's earlier profligacy; in the short term, a policy of financial stringency was a necessity.

In June 1960 Prince Talal and the Liberal Princes laid down their programme. They submitted a demand for an elected body with legislative powers, a limited monarchy and a draft constitution.[92] Faisal rejected the demand. It soon became apparent that King Saud was attempting to use the Liberal Princes' initiative as a means to recover some of his authority, and Faisal was forced to resign. Saud immediately formed a new Council 'naming himself Prime Minister and giving the key ministerial posts of finance and national economy to Prince Talal and the new ministry of Petroleum and Mineral Resources to Abdullah ibn Hammud Tariqi, a strong nationalist'.[93] On 25 December 1960, it was announced that the Council of Ministers 'had approved the establishment of a partially-elected national council and an order to draft a constitution'.[94] Three days later, however, this was denied. Evidently Saud, having displaced Faisal, was no more willing to envisage democratisation than was Faisal.

The incident of December 1960 proved crucial to the prospects of the Liberal Princes. Neither King Saud nor the influential groupings within the regime would accept the programme they had proposed. Talal became increasingly critical of the regime, was dismissed from the Council and early in 1962 sought refuge in Cairo. In reaction to King Saud's opportunistic dealings with the Liberal Princes, and to the threat which the Yemeni Revolution of 1962 posed to the Saudi regime, the influential groupings insisted on Faisal's return to power — first as deputy Prime Minister in March 1962 and then, from October 1962, as Prime Minister. Although Saud remained King until November 1964, effective power after October 1962 rested with Faisal.

Faisal's assumption of effective power was marked by the publication of the 'Ten-Point Programme'.[95] Perhaps the most crucial elements in this were those which proclaimed 'the government's solicitude for social matters and education' and pledged a 'sustained endeavour to develop the country's resources and economy, in particular roads, water resources, heavy and light industry, and self-sufficient agriculture'. The ground was laid, therefore, for the massive programmes of infrastructural, industrial and agricultural development which followed in the 1960s and 1970s — as also for the expansion of the government administration required by this scale of economic development.

The contention of this article, therefore, is that the key to understanding the direction of developments in Saudi Arabia — and to explaining the paradox of a traditional regime undertaking a vast programme of economic modernisation — is not to be found in competition between the forces of modernism and traditionalism, but rather in the attempt by leading elements (whether 'traditionalist' or 'modernist') to ensure the continued viability of the regime. The concern of the next stage of Saudi history, therefore, may be as follows: how to ensure the continued viability of the regime in the changing conditions created by the development programmes of the 1960s and 1970s. The demands of social groupings thrown up by the latter programmes may well lead debate back to the issues raised by the Liberal Princes.

Notes

1. M. Wenner. 'Saudi Arabia: Survival of Traditional Elites' in F. Tachau (ed.), *Political Elites and Political Development* (Schenkman, Cambridge, 1975), pp. 166 and 181.
2. R. Crane, *Planning the Future of Saudi Arabia* (Praeger, New York, 1978), pp. 12–13.
3. Central Planning Organisation (Saudi Arabia), *Guidelines for the Second Development Plan, 1975–80*, p. 271.
4. G. Lenczowski, 'Tradition and Reform in Saudi Arabia', *Current History,* vol. 52, no. 306 (February 1967), pp. 98–104; also *Middle East Oil in the Revolutionary Age* (American Enterprise Institute, Washington, 1976).
5. M. Hudson, *Arab Politics* (Yale University Press, New Haven, 1977), see section on Saudi Arabia.
6. S. Duguid, 'A Biographical Approach to the Study of Social Change in the Middle East: Abdullah Tariki as a New Man', *International Journal of Middle East Studies*, vol. 1, pt 3 (1970), pp. 195–220.
7. Of the 64 ministers and deputy-ministers in the Saudi Arabian government at the end of 1979, 19 held PhDs. The proportion of PhD-holders would be even higher if all those with ministerial or deputy-ministerial status — not just those with the formal title of minister or deputy-minister — were included. Information taken from *Saudi Arabia Yearbook 1979/80* (The Research and Publishing House, Beirut, 1980).
8. The name of the contemporary state, 'Kingdom of Saudi Arabia', was not formally adopted until 1932. Between 1902 and 1926 the area under Saudi control was known as the Sultanate of Najd; as a result of the acquisition of new territory in Asir it became the Sultanate of Najd and its Dependencies in 1926. In that same year, with the conquest of the Hijaz, Abd al-Aziz Ibn Saud became King of Hijaz as well as Sultan of Najd and its Dependencies, and in the following year the terms 'Sultan' and 'Sultanate' were dropped in favour of 'King' and 'Kingdom' with respect to Najd and its Dependencies. The dual monarchy was brought to an end in 1932, with the proclamation of the Kingdom of Saudi Arabia. In this paper the term 'Saudi Arabia' will be used loosely to refer to the areas under Saudi control before 1932 as well as after, when the reference is not specifically limited to the pre-1932 period.

9. This concept of Saudi history, involving three Saudi states, is taken from G. Rentz, 'Wahhabism and Saudi Arabia' in D. Hopwood (ed.), *The Arabian Peninsula* (George Allen and Unwin, London, 1972), pp. 54–66. The first Saudi state, established by Muhammad ibn Saud, covered the period 1745–1818, ending in its destruction by the Egyptian forces under Ibrahim Pasha. The second, established by Faisal ibn Turki in 1843 and lasting to 1887, was destroyed by the rising power of the Al Rashid of Ha'il.

10. While specific references will be given as the account proceeds, the works which proved most valuable in constructing the account are as follows. J. Habib, *Ibn Sa'ud's Warriors of Islam* (Brill, Leiden, 1978); L. Goldrup, 'Saudi Arabia, 1902–1932: the development of a Wahhabi society', unpublished PhD thesis, University of California, 1971; D. Edens, 'The Anatomy of the Saudi Revolution', *International Journal of Middle Eastern Studies*, vol. 5 (1974), pp. 50–64; H. Lackner, *House Built on Sand* (Ithaca Press, London, 1978); A. Shamekh, 'Spatial Patterns of Bedouin Settlement in Al-Qasim Region', unpublished PhD thesis, University of Kentucky, 1975; D. A. Wells, *Saudi Arabian Development Strategy* (American Enterprise Institute for Public Policy Research, Washington, DC, 1976); W. Rugh, 'Emergence of a New Middle Class in Saudi Arabia', *Middle East Journal* (Winter 1973); F. Shakir, 'Modernisation of the Developing Nations, the Case of Saudi Arabia', unpublished PhD thesis, Purdue University, 1972; M. Hammad, 'The Educational System and Planning for Manpower Development in Saudi Arabia', unpublished PhD thesis, University of Indiana, 1973; F. Akhdar, 'Multinational Corporations and Developing Countries: A Case Study of the Impact of ARAMCO on the Development of the Saudi Arabian Economy', unpublished PhD thesis, University of California, 1974; I. al-Awaji, 'Bureaucracy and Society in Saudi Arabia', unpublished PhD thesis, University of Virginia, 1971; F. Halliday, *Arabia without Sultans* (Penguin Books, Harmondsworth, 1974).

11. See, for example, R. Baker, *King Husain and the Kingdom of the Hejaz* (Oleander, London, 1979), p. 176.

12. For a detailed treatment of the international factors affecting the Arabian peninsula in the late nineteenth and early twentieth centuries, see B. Busch, *Britain and the Persian Gulf 1894–1914* (University of California Press, Berkeley, 1967).

13. J. G. Lorimer, *Gazetteer of the Persian Gulf, 'Oman and the Central Arabia* (Superintendent Government Printing, Calcutta, 1915; republished by Gregg International, Farnborough, 1970), p. 2297.

14. Ibid., p. 2335. For further information on the breeding of horses in Central Arabia in the later part of the nineteenth century, see W. Tweedie, *The Arabian Horse* (first published 1894; republished by Librarie du Liban, Beirut, undated).

15. *Gazetteer of the Persian Gulf, 'Oman and the Central Arabia*, p. 2335.

16. G. Troeller, *The Birth of Sa'udi Arabia* (Cass, London, 1976), p. 100.

17. C. Doughty, *Travels in Arabia Deserta* (Random House, New York, 1920), p. 312.

18. H. St J. Philby, *Arabia of the Wahhabis* (Constable, London, 1928), p. 106.

19. M. al-Mana, *Arabia Unified* (Hutchinson-Benham, London, 1980), p. 15.

20. For further information on this see H. St John Philby, *Sa'udi Arabia* (Benn, London, 1955), p. 265; H. C. Armstrong, *Lord of Arabia* (Arthur Barker, London, 1934), p. 21; and A. Rihani, *Ibn Saud of Arabia: his People and his Land* (Constable, London, 1928).

21. Troeller, *Birth of Sa'udi Arabia*, p. 103.

22. This should not be taken to imply that the interests of the towns and those of the bedouin were necessarily in conflict. On the contrary, the caravan trade had generally been dependent upon some form of collaboration between the townsmen and the bedouin, and the settled and nomadic elements in the

population of Central Arabia had been mutually-dependent. Nevertheless the roles played by bedouin and by townsmen in the establishment and expansion of the Saudi state can be kept separate. For detailed analyses of the relationship between bedouin, settled populations and state power, see T. Asad, 'The Bedouin as a Military Force: notes on some aspects of power relations between nomads and sedentaries in historical perspective' in C. Nelson (ed.), *The Desert and the Sown: Nomads in the Wider Society* (Institute of International Studies, University of California, Berkeley, 1973), pp. 61–73; T. Asad, 'Ideology, Class and the Origin of the Islamic State', a review of Sulayman Bashir, *Tawazun annaqaid; muhadarat fi-l-jahiliyya wa sadr al-Islam.* I am grateful to Dr Asad for having shown me the text of this review before its publication; and Armstrong, *Lord of Arabia*, p. 105.

23. Doughty, *Travels in Arabia Deserta*, p. 312.

24. For further details of the developments mentioned in this paragraph, see Goldrup, *Saudi Arabia, 1902–1932*, pp. 24–85.

25. Ibid., p. 76.

26. Ibid., p. 73.

27. Habib, *Ibn Sa'ud's Warriors*, p. 15.

28. For further details of the developments mentioned in this paragraph see Goldrup, *Saudi Arabia, 1902–1932*, pp. 86–109.

29. Amin Rihani, *Najd wa Mulhaqatihu* (Najd and its Dependencies), (Dar Al-Rihani Publishing Company, Beirut, 1964), p. 114.

30. Goldrup, *Saudi Arabia, 1902–1932*, p. 95.

31. Habib, *Ibn Sa'ud's Warriors*, pp. 16–17.

32. Ibid., p. 17.

33. Hafiz Wahbah, *Al-Jazirat Al-Arabiyah fi Al-Qarn Al-'Ashrin* (The Arabian Peninsula in the Twentieth Century), (Maktabah Al-Nahdah Al-Masriyah, Cairo, 1961), composite from p. 293 and p. 309.

34. Habib, *Ibn Sa'ud's Warriors*, p. 16.

35. Ibid., p. 6.

36. See Philby, *Sa'udi Arabia*, p. 262; and al-Mana, *Arabia Unified*, p. 80.

37. Al-Mana, *Arabia Unified*, p. 30.

38. The reference should really be to *mutawa'in* (religious teachers or missionaries) rather than to *'ulama* (religious leaders).

39. Quoted in Habib, *Ibn Sa'ud's Warriors*, p. 30. Reference to Dickson, 'Report to the Civil Commissioner', MSS, Foreign Office, vol. 5062.

40. Habib, *Ibn Sa'ud's Warriors*, p. 47.

41. See Crane, *Planning the Future of Saudi Arabia*, p. 12.

42. Quoted in Habib, *Ibn Sa'ud's Warriors*, p. 30.

43. Ibid., p. 30.

44. The *ikhwan* objected to the use of bugles by the contingents of Egyptian soldiers escorting the *mahmal* (the camel-borne frame carrying the elaborately woven covering for the Ka'bah, donated annually by the people of Egypt), because it violated the injunction against musical instruments. They rushed into the Egyptian camp and were fired upon by Egyptian soldiers. The incident created bad relations between Egypt and the new Saudi state, symbolised by the break in diplomatic relations for ten years.

45. Goldrup, *Saudi Arabia, 1902–1932*, p. 425.

46. For further information on this see al-Mana, *Arabia Unified*, p. 242.

47. See al-Awaji, 'Bureaucracy and Society in Saudi Arabia', p. 46.

48. See Shakir, 'Modernisation of the Developing Nations', p. 46.

49. Philby, *Sa'udi Arabia*, p. 292.

50. Al-Mana, *Arabia Unified*, p. 177.

51. Ibid.

52. Ibid. See also pp. 188–9.

53. Ibid.
54. For details of the composition of the political committee, see ibid., p. 191.
55. See T. O. el-Farra, 'The Effects of Detribalising the Bedouins on the Internal Cohesion of an Emerging State: the Case of Saudi Arabia', unpublished PhD thesis, University of Pittsburgh, 1973, pp. 137–9.
56. Al-Mana, *Arabia Unified*, p. 177.
57. The *shari'a*, in turn, is based on four sources: the Koran, *hadith* (the *sunna* traditions based on examples set by the Prophet Mohammad and upon his recorded sayings and actions), *ijma'* (consensus – as decided in the early centuries of Islam by agreement among religious scholars) and *qiyas* (analogy – application of the Koran and *sunna* to new problems for which there is no precedent).
58. Philby, *Sa'udi Arabia*, p. 354.
59. El-Farra, 'The Effects of Detribalising the Bedouins', pp. 127–8.
60. Ibid., pp. 154–5.
61. For a good description of the struggle over the introduction of wireless radio communication see B. D. Arrington, 'An Historical and Descriptive Analysis of the Evolution and Development of Saudi Arabian Television, 1963–1972, unpublished PhD thesis, University of Minnesota, 1972, pp. 47–50.
62. See Philby, *Sa'udi Arabia*, p. 354.
63. See A. Assah, *Miracle of the Desert Kingdom* (Johnson, London, 1969), ch. 2.
64. Al-Mana, *Arabia Unified*, p. 194.
63. Ibid., p. 115.
66. Philby, *Sa'udi Arabia*, p. 304.
67. Baker, *King Husain*, p. 176.
68. See J. J. Malone, 'Involvement and Change: The Coming of the Oil Age to Saudi Arabia' in T. Niblock (ed.), *Social and Economic Development in the Arab Gulf* (Croom Helm, London, 1980), p. 30.
69. I. al-Rashid, *Documents on the History of Saudi Arabia* (Documentary Publications, Salisbury, 1976), vol. 3, p. 172.
70. See Assah, *Miracle of the Desert Kingdom*, ch. 3. Some evidence of the activity of the commercial establishment at this time can also be found in J. R. L. Carter, *Leading Merchant Families of Saudi Arabia* (Scorpion, London, 1979).
71. A listing of the dates of establishment of Saudi ministries is given in R. Nyrop *et al., Area Handbook for Saudi Arabia* (American University, Washington, DC, 1977), pp. 179–80.
72. See M. Hammad, 'The Educational System and Planning for Manpower Development in Saudi Arabia', unpublished PhD thesis, University of Indiana, 1973, pp. 47–81.
73. Philby, *Sa'udi Arabia*, p. 328.
74. See Malone, 'Involvement and Change', p. 38.
75. Al-Mana, *Arabia Unified*, pp. 182–3.
76. This formulation is taken from al-Awaji, 'Bureaucracy and Society in Saudi Arabia', p. 20.
77. See ibid., p. 113.
78. El-Farra, 'The Effects of Detribalising the Bedouins', p. 166.
79. Ibid., p. 172–3.
80. Taken from F. Badr, 'Developmental Planning in Saudi Arabia: A Multidimensional Study', unpublished PhD thesis, University of Southern California, p. 78. Quoted from Kingdom of Saudi Arabia, Ministry of Petroleum and Mineral Resources, *The Impact of Petroleum on the Economy of Saudi Arabia*, (Ministry of Petroleum and Mineral Resources, al-Riyadh, 1963), p. 12.
81. Taken from Saudi Arabian Monetary Fund, *Statistical Summary* (Saudi Arabian Monetary Fund, al-Riyadh, 1978).

82. A good description of the random fashion in which funds were disbursed can be found in Philby, *Sa'udi Arabia*, p. 343.

83. Assah, *Miracle of the Desert Kingdom*, p. 191.

84. Lackner, *House Built on Sand*, p. 59.

85. One of the methods whereby increased funds were channelled towards bedouin tribal leaders is described in el-Farra, 'The Effects of Detribalising the Bedouins', pp. 172–3: 'A given tribe would invite the king and prepare a feast in his honor. The king's advisors estimated the expenses of such a party. Then the expenses would be doubled and handed to the tribe on the spot. The other neighboring tribes did the same and the same was done with them with regard to the expenses. A very limited number of tribal chieftains and tribesmen benefited from such operations simply because only well-to-do persons sponsored those parties and the benefits derived from them were divided among the sponsors, each of whom received an amount of money in proportion to the amount of money he contributed.'

86. Shakir, 'Modernisation of the Developing Nations', p. 129.

87. For detailed information on the origins and conduct of these strikes see ibid., pp. 173–7.

88. Information on the growth of the civil service is found in M. Madi, 'Developmental Administration and the Attitudes of Middle Management in Saudi Arabia', unpublished PhD thesis, University of Southern Illinois, 1975.

89. Shakir, 'Modernisation of the Developing Nations', p. 177.

90. The means by which power was effectively transferred to Faisal is well described in G. De Gaury, *Faisal* (Arthur Barker, London, 1966), pp. 89–93.

91. Shakir, 'Modernisation of the Developing Nations', p. 178.

92. Ibid.

93. Ibid.

94. Ibid.

95. A full account of the Ten-Point Programme is given in ibid., pp. 242–4.

6 SECULAR AND RELIGIOUS OPPOSITION IN SAUDI ARABIA

James Buchan

Introduction

Although the kingdom of Saudi Arabia was founded less than fifty years ago, many believe it to be an anachronism. Formed out of *force main* and religious conviction in a forbidding land, ordered by divine law and a highly developed sense of shame, and governed by hereditary rulers strongly attached to a single of its regions, Saudi Arabia is constantly described as ripe for change.

Yet apart from a prolonged period of political and economic uncertainty in the late 1950s and early 1960s, the people of Saudi Arabia have largely remained united behind the Al Saud inheritors of the founder of the modern kingdom, Abd al-Aziz ibn Abd al-Rahman Al Saud. Where dissent has manifested itself, as in the labour unrest of the 1950s in al-Hasa or in the shattering November 1979 attack on the Grand Mosque in Mecca, it has been isolated from the main body of Saudi opinion.

Whether this will remain the case through the 1980s is quite another matter. At a time of regional and international tension, a host of problems confront the Al Saud. How will the country's rulers control the extravagance and waste that naturally attend high oil-production levels, curb profiteering among their own number, absorb the demands for political expression from a young and increasingly sophisticated population, or soothe anxieties about laxity in social and religious life?

Such questions are not easy to answer — partly because the nature of popular reaction to government policy and to general social and economic conditions is not easy to predict. 'Political stability,' wrote the young Fayez Badr in 1968, 'has been a grim testimony to the fantastic capacity for misery and suffering of the ordinary [Saudi] citizen.'[1] Most observers since the mid-1970s tend to substitute 'the pursuit of wealth' for 'misery and suffering' to arrive at the same comfortable conclusion. To work towards some understanding of the prospects for stability in Saudi Arabia it is necessary to look at the history of opposition to the regime and how the Al Saud have dealt with it. Because of the low level of political expression in Saudi Arabia, the bulk of the written information on the subject is from hostile sources (Nasserite, Zionist or Leftist) and great care must be taken. It is, nevertheless, a contention of this paper that Saudi stability cannot be taken for granted.

Political Framework

Two religious revivals lie at the foundation of the state of Saudi Arabia. The first resulted in the eighteenth-century alliance of Muhammad ibn Saud and the Najdi reformer, Muhammad ibn Abd al-Wahhab; the second occurred in the first three decades of this century and was the springboard for Abd al-Aziz's conquest of what is now Saudi Arabia. To this day, the legitimacy of Saudi rule has been intimately linked with the religious and social message of Wahhabism.

Saudi Arabia is an absolute monarchy, theoretically limited only by the *shari'a* or divine law. The 'fundamental instructions' for the Hijaz of 1926 specifically enthroned the *shari'a* as the supreme sovereign to be obeyed by all, including the King himself. A comprehensive constitutional law (*nizam*) for the whole country was proposed in Article 6 of the Royal Decree creating the Kingdom of Saudi Arabia (September 1932), during the ascendancy of Prince Talal in December 1960, in Faisal's celebrated Ten-Point Programme two years later and, most recently, in an interview given by the Crown Prince Fahd soon after the Mecca incident in 1979. No constitution has yet materialised and there must be some doubt as to whether the Al Saud or the *'ulama* feel the need for a written constitution as far as the rights of the subject and the forms of the administration are concerned. As it is, the *shari'a* is supplemented by a fairly large body of custom (as, for example, that regulating women's behaviour) which has taken on, in many minds, the indivisibility of divine law. The result is that demands for social change take on a political colouring.

Not least because the kingdom was early recognised as a creation of the King's vision, the rule of Abd al-Aziz was a highly personal one. According to all outside accounts, the executive administration of the country was the King's sole responsibility and the revenue of the state was at his personal command — or at least until the 1950s, when the increasing complexity of government and the growing royal family obliged some separation of state and family finance.

There remained a formal limit on the succession to the throne in the institution of *beiah*, the popular oath of allegiance, and as early as the end of 1924, Abd al-Aziz had been responsible for the creation of a consultative council in the more sophisticated political climate of the newly conquered Hijaz. Fuad Hamza, who was later foreign secretary, quoted Abd al-Aziz as telling the Meccans that the council 'of the *'ulama*, the dignitaries and the merchants' would be 'an intermediary between the people and me'.[2] In 1926 this was formalised as a *majlis al-shura*.

While the *majlis al-shura* was essentially a means to reassure the leading figures of the Hijaz of the good intentions of the Al Saud, it did for a while play a role in advising Prince Faisal, the Viceroy of Hijaz. In Najd itself, Philby has left descriptions of the privy council of elders (*majlis al-khas*), yet leaves no doubt that the King's authority, resting as much in his personality as in the throne, was paramount. The same would apply to those formidable figures of the Ibn Jiluwi branch of the family who were local governors of al-Hasa and Ha'il, and enjoyed power of life and death.

In practice, however, the King would consult the leading members of his family (sometimes known to outsiders as the *lajnat al-'ulya* or higher committee), the important tribal figures who had been loyal, the *'ulama* and those merchants on whom he depended for finance. This was partly because the King was always said to respect the Koranic injunction 'Take counsel among yourselves', and partly because these groups had been instrumental in his rise to power and the King still needed their support.

The influence of these various groups has waxed and waned according to the strength of the central authority. In the uncertain years 1958–64, when the family was divided over the fitness of King Saud to rule and over a reform movement headed by Prince Talal, they naturally came to the fore. Fatina Amin Shaker remarks that the *'ulama* and the sixty princes who supported Faisal's assumption of the throne in 1964 'were found to be the major internal groups that had power to support or withhold their support to the King, and thus strengthening the legitimacy of his position or destroying it'.[3] The Al Saud have always been scrupulous about consulting the *'ulama*. Abd al-Aziz saw them every day after the sunset prayer and Khaled receives a delegation of *'ulama* every Monday morning. The effective power of the *'ulama*, especially when central authority was weakened, was reflected in the resurgence under King Saud of the Public Morality Committees (the 'societies for the encouragement of virtue and discouragement of vice') and such Royal Decrees as those that restricted study abroad in 1955 and banned women drivers in 1957. In the period 1977–9, the recrudescence of the committees and the establishment *'ulama* has been much remarked on. Saudi kings (especially Abd al-Aziz and Faisal) have nevertheless on occasions been able to act forcefully against the *'ulama* and the lay zealots (*mutawa'in*), rolling over their opposition to such innovations as public schools for girls in 1960, or television in al-Riyadh in 1965.

In recent years, the influence of the merchants, especially those of al-Hasa and Hijaz, has declined as the royal family has ceased to borrow from them and has begun to compete with them in commerce. Royal businessmen have squeezed the old merchant families out of the most lucrative areas of government contracting. Merchants of Najdi origin, on the other hand, have prospered from the general shift in commercial and political power to al-Riyadh. Although many merchants complain bitterly about the profits made by princes, they recognise that public spending is the sole force within the economy and take great trouble about their relations with the royal family.

An important feature of Al Saud rule, even today, is the responsibility felt towards the tribes. This springs partly from sentiment and partly from the knowledge of the disruptive force of tribal discontent, shown in the revolt of large numbers of disgruntled *ikhwan* in 1928–9. Under Abd al-Aziz, and to some extent still today, the tribal chiefs enjoyed influence in accordance with their role in helping Abd al-Aziz to power. Van der Meulen, in a remarkable passage, nicely establishes the influence of the tribes in the heyday of Abd al-Aziz. The King called a great conclave of *'ulama* and *ikhwan* at the oasis of Marat as he travelled to Jeddah for his trip outside the kingdom. It was December 1944 and he was about to meet Roosevelt and Churchill to oppose the foundation of a Jewish National Home in Palestine. In a lengthy speech, he reminded his listeners of the Koranic antipathy of Jew and Muslim. 'He who recited the words of the Quran was no longer the kind host and King, he was the Arab, the Muslim, the Wahhabi, their Imam and he was preparing to get their assent to the steps *he intended to take*.'[4] In recent years, the relationship with tribal elements has been partially formalised in the National Guard, under the control of Prince Abdullah since 1963. This was originally founded to give employment and cash to Najdi *bedu* but has increasingly developed since the early 1960s as a counterbalance to the regular armed forces. The guard is the royal family's defence of last resort against internal opposition and one must presume that its views are heard on subjects other than subsidies and salaries.

Since the earliest days, the King and members of the royal family have presided over tribal and rural *majalis* (singular *majlis*) to test local feeling and, recently, these have tended to provide the Al Saud with a constituency parallel to, and even occasionally antagonistic to, the bureaucracy. It is often claimed that this highly personal rule has made a formal constitution or system of representation unnecessary. Yet the *majlis* was never intended to work on behalf of the young or women or foreigners or, until very recently, such regional minorities as the Shi'a of al-Hasa, and on various occasions the consultative process has proved surprisingly inflexible.

The Al Saud has always been willing to cede administrative responsibility to men of merchant or other commoner background, especially where their own expertise has been limited. Abd al-Aziz left the administration of royal and state finance, and defence such as it was, to Abdullah Suleiman. In the last year of the old King's life, 1953, a Council of Ministers (*majlis al-wuzara*) was founded. It played an important role in the events of the early 1960s. Yet while technical ministries have been delegated to commoners, portfolios relating to security or enjoying large budgets have remained firmly in Al Saud hands. Those commoners with substantial ministerial budgets have tended to find that they have less than complete control of disbursement. It is simply in the nature of government, nevertheless, that as the bureaucracy has grown, it has become more able to block or disrupt the wishes of individual princes and, in the case of Abdullah Suleiman's successors at the Ministry of Finance, even of the throne itself.

There is no formal political expression in Saudi Arabia, political parties and trades unions are banned and the press receives a subsidy and is liable to closures. According to Helen Lackner, the State Security Law of 1961 prescribes the death penalty or 25 years jail for any person convicted of an aggressive act against the royal family or state. Lapses in ritual and crimes against custom are also subject to severe punishment. If that suggests a climate of repression, the heirs of Abd al-Aziz have also inherited his taste for forgiveness and men like Prince Talal and Yusuf Ahmad Tawil (implicated in the 1969 supposed conspiracy) prosper today as if they had never fallen foul of the regime.

The Al Saud's current conception of the basis of its legitimacy was given expression in an interview which Faisal gave to *Al-Haya'* a few hours after his assumption of the throne in November 1964. He emphasised the integrity of the ruler, prosperity for the ruled and the reciprocity between them as the basis for legitimacy.

The important thing about a regime is not what it is called but how

it acts. There are corrupt (*fasad*) republican regimes and sound
monarchies and vice-versa. The only true criterion of a regime . . . is
the degree of reciprocity between the ruler and the ruled and the
extent to which it symbolizes prosperity, progress and healthy
initiative . . . The quality of a regime should be judged by its deeds
and the integrity of its rulers not by its name.[5]

Secular Opposition, 1953–1979

This article makes a somewhat arbitrary separation between religious
and secular opposition. This is purely for ease of presentation and in
no way suggests the two are mutually exclusive.

The Aramco Strikes

Lackner begins her account of opposition to the throne with a strike
by the old King's drivers in the 1930s.[6] Although the event is attested
by Philby and certainly infuriated the King, it scarcely constituted
political opposition. It is with the year 1953 and the first major strike
by employees of Aramco, the oil company that still produces all but a
fraction of Saudi oil, that the country entered a period of unrest that
reflected the tension in the Arab world between republican rule and
monarchy and the general cold war atmosphere. This was not resolved
until the crushing blow dealt to Nasser's prestige by the Arab–Israeli
War of June 1967.

Yet according to most accounts, including that of the American
oilman Cheney, who was living on the Jebel Dhahran at the time, the
strike that disturbed Abd al-Aziz's last days was not political in
inspiration. According to Cheney, unrest had simmered throughout the
summer of 1953 in Saudi Camp (now demolished), particularly among
those Saudis trained at the company's Long Island language centre, and
was very much focused on the better conditions enjoyed by the
American Aramco employees up on the *jebel*. He claims that it was
only the formation of a Royal Commission by Crown Prince Saud
(acting for his father) and the arrest of the twelve members of the
Strike Committee that changed the complexion of the protest. 'Instead
of a vague discontent,' Cheney wrote, 'Saudi labor now had a specific
cause and a ready-made set of martyrs.' Again, 'the strike was now
directed against the Government.'[7] The protest fizzled out at paytime
in the third week and the Royal Commission stepped in to provide
improvements in the pay and conditions of the Saudi employees.

Certain conclusions can be drawn from these events. First, Prince Saud refused to countenance the settling of the dispute through negotiation between employer and strikers. With the governor Saud ibn Jiluwi, in Cheney's rueful words, 'fortunately out of the country', the Royal Commission was a natural extension of the Al Saud's role as resort of all grievance. At the same time, the government showed it would not tolerate any form of disturbance by despatching some 5,000 troops and tribal levies. In recent strikes by foreign labour, Prince Naif, the Interior Minister, has tended to leave the matter in the hands of the companies and governments concerned. For example, the Korean government was made responsible for handling the extraordinary explosion of violence among Hyundai's workers at Jubail in March 1977. But the bias against any form of organised labour appears to be as strong as ever.

Second, the collapse of the strike heralded a period of repression. In April 1955, the Mecca newspapers published a Royal Decree restricting study abroad. Meanwhile in al-Hasa, according to Cheney:

> Local officials took to disappearing suddenly. An increasing suspicion of foreigners became very evident and particularly of our bedevilled Palestinian employees. A hundred of these refugees were bagged in a midnight round-up by local cops and deported, without trial of course, as being members of a Pan-Arab political movement known as the PPS which was unpopular with national governments. Another batch was expelled on the grounds they were communists.[8]

At the same time, Saud began organising the rump of the *ikhwan* into an internal security force of a more effective nature than mere tribal levies. 'They looked better organized – and I hoped better disciplined – than the original *ikhwan*, but their spiritual kinship was plain though they went under the name of *mujahiddin*.'[9] It was also plain that the King put 'more trust in his corps of rural irregulars than he did in the vaunted new national army', the *nizam* forces which British and American advisers had been training since the late 1940s. Ultimately, the *mujahiddin* were absorbed into the National Guard.

Third, Cheney points to the growing influence in the kingdom of movements active elsewhere in the Arab and Muslim worlds. Nationalist fervour similar to that which had led to 'the dismal fate of the Anglo-Iranian oil company' was rising.[10] It is significant, therefore, that the second major Aramco strike, which occurred during Saud's visit to al-Hasa in June 1956, apparently had no major economic demands, but 'rather displayed nationalist and anti-imperialist slogans'. The strike, Cheney writes, was swiftly broken by Saud ibn Jiluwi 'with some of the leaders reportedly beaten to death in the process', while a Royal Decree of 11 June outlawed participation in a stoppage on pain of imprisonment.

Increasingly, such issues as the US lease of the Dhahran air base and Saud's acceptance of the Eisenhower Doctrine were to help make a gulf between the monarchy and 'progressive' Arab thought. Arab nationalist and anti-Western feelings became a feature of demonstrations in al-Hasa from the Suez crisis and Nasser's visit to Dammam that autumn to the 1967 war. According to Lackner, the Strike Committee members who became communists were the nucleus of the National Reform Front in 1956, the National Liberation Front in 1958, and finally the Saudi Arabian Communist Party in 1975.[11] It appears they have no power base in the kingdom today.

Aramco itself could never be described as a nest of political opposition to the throne, although both Nasser Said, the founder of the Nasserist Union of Peoples of the Arabian Peninsula (UPAP) and Abd al-Aziz al-Muammar, who spent much of the 1960s in gaol, began their careers at the company. The company has pursued a careful and generous labour policy (which has been, incidentally, highly beneficial to the Shi'a of al-Hasa).

The Liberal Princes and the 1960s

The years 1955–7 saw growing chaos in the financial administration of the country. The progressive devaluation of the Saudi riyal and King Saud's implication in a bribery scandal over the Egyptian–Syrian union the next year caused the royal family to invite Faisal to take over day-to-day management of the country as premier.

It was during this first period of Faisal's stewardship that the first major 'legitimate' demand for constitutional reform was made. The demand was presented in June 1960 by a group of princes and educated commoners. Under the influence of Arab nationalism, they proposed 'a draft constitution and called for a more limited monarchy and a partially elected Parliament', according to the *Area Handbook*.[12] Somewhat opportunistically, Saud allied himself with this group, of whom his half-brother Talal was the chief, and Faisal felt himself obliged to withdraw from the scene. In the new Council of Ministers, Talal took over the Ministry of Finance and Abdullah Tariqi, a forceful technician and one of the founders of OPEC, became Saudi Arabia's first Minister of Petroleum and Mineral Resources.

Yet, the 'Liberal Princes', as they became known, soon fell foul of the remainder of the Council and the King, and the announcement on Mecca Radio on Christmas Day, 1960 that the Council 'had approved a partially-elected national council and an order to draft a constitution' was denied three days later. Talal became increasingly frustrated, took to advertising the country's disunity abroad and was ejected from the Council of Ministers. In the autumn of 1962, Talal and his brothers Badr, Fawwaz, Nawwaf and Abd al-Mohsen and his cousin Saad ibn Fahd left for Cairo where they started broadcasting on behalf of a national liberation front.

By that time, however, a *coup d'état* had been staged against the new *imam* in Yemen, Muhammad Al-Badr, and four Saudi air crews defected to Egypt. By mid-October, Faisal was in a position to demand a *carte blanche* in forming an emergency Cabinet. Khaled, Fahd and Sultan were important members while Adbullah's support of the new order was consolidated the next year when he was made commander of the National Guard. Between 1962 and 1964, the civil war in Yemen between royalists and republican forces, backed up by Egyptian troops and the strident attacks from Cairo radio, created a climate too hostile for the impetuous Saud to be tolerated. On the request of sixty princes and after a ruling by the *'ulama*, he was obliged to abdicate in March 1964.

There can be no doubt that the failure of the reform movement exposed the regime to criticism from 'progressive' sources both within and outside the country. What is not so easy to identify is the extent to which internal opposition was organised. Various writers have detailed a bewildering variety of opposition groups which professed to flourish in the Saudi Arabia of the mid-1960s. Apart from Nasser Said's UPAP and Talal's front, which collapsed in 1964, we hear of a branch of the Baath Party and even, according to Sana'a radio station, a group called the Popular Front for the Liberation of the Arabian Peninsula. There must, however, be real doubt whether many of the organisations had any presence 'on the ground' at all.

Early in 1966, nineteen 'communists' were jailed and another thirty-four given royal pardons. Later that year, there were reports of bombings in al-Riyadh and Dammam. These were ascribed at the time to infiltrators from Yemen and, indeed, in March 1967, seventeen Yemenis were executed for planting bombs at government installations and royal palaces — including that of Prince Fahd, the Interior Minister. Nasser Said proclaimed the innocence of the Yemenis on the grounds that the UPAP was responsible; however, he also claimed responsibility for the attack on the Grand Mosque 12 years later for which there is not a shred of evidence. There can be little doubt that, as Richard Johns has it, the authorities were well aware that 'there was considerable clandestine activity in the Hijaz and, more particularly, in Hasa'.[13]

Yet the crushing blow to Nasser's prestige constituted by the Egyptian defeat in the June 1967 war with Israel, and the ignominious withdrawal of Egyptian forces from Yemen clearly undermined Arab nationalist opposition. Those in favour of a shift towards Nasserist government saw the ground disappear from beneath their feet. It is an irony that the regime was not to hit out strongly at dissidents until 1969, when Faisal's own authority was mounting rapidly, Nasser was approaching death, and the Arab nationalist threat had greatly diminished. 'The underground political opposition,' Richard Johns has written, 'though disquieting, appeared to be too fragmented and embryonic in such a far-flung country to mount a coup, unless it received the fullest backing of the armed forces.'[14]

By the summer of 1969, Arab armies had added insurrections in Libya and Sudan to their string of coups in Egypt, Syria and Iraq. The Saudi regime was certainly anxious about revolutionary instincts in the army and the Royal Saudi Air Force. Its worst fears seemed to have been confirmed in June 1969 when both the Central Intelligence Agency and the Saudi intelligence service, headed by Kemal Adham, received information about a conspiracy of officers and civilians.

The authorities acted with despatch. In a single night, some 150 men were arrested. The RSAF was temporarily grounded and its officers purged. A sweep was made through the Shi'a villages and a number of intellectuals, including Saleh Amba, the head of the Dhahran Petroleum College (whose brothers-in-law had been implicated in a 1967 bombing), were gaoled. It seems that at least one officer died in gaol, while the final group of those arrested did not see the light of day until King Khaled announced an amnesty soon after his accession in 1975. It is probable that the armed forces have never regained the position of trust they hitherto enjoyed.

Yet former officers of the CIA now feel that the agency overrated the threat while Prince Naif, who was Prince Fahd's deputy at the Interior Ministry and is now the minister, has said that 'the majority just professed to be misled'.[15] What conspiracy there was appears to have revolved around a Jeddah merchant called Yusuf Tawil, who was found in possession of explosives, and a group of RSAF officers who had been indiscreet in their Nasserist or quasi-Nasserist sympathies. It seems more than likely that the General Directorate of Intelligence did

not scruple to arrest men on mere suspicion — even if only of professing
Nasserist sympathies during the period of Talal's ascendancy. Both
Tawil and Hashim S. Hashim, who was RSAF commander but in no
way implicated, are now rich businessmen and enjoy royal patronage.

On the whole, then, the authorities found little to justify the round-
up, the men's families were looked after and they themselves were
released in a series of amnesties over the next six years. While the
clamp-down may have contributed to the general collapse of
'progressive' opposition, it should be remembered that after the death
of Nasser in 1970 and, most notably after the 1973 oil embargo, Faisal
emerged as an Arab national leader *par excellence*. Lackner remarks,
rather superfluously, that the absence of loyalties to class, rather than
to tribe or region, precluded the possibility of Marxist revolution and
that the revolutionary potential of the armed forces was well balanced
by the conservatism of the National Guard.[16]

If there is a lesson to be drawn from the unrest of the 1960s, the
Saudi royal family has learned it. The disfavour of radical regimes in the
Middle East can be perilous for the internal stability of the kingdom and
the Al Saud's policies on the Palestine Question, its rather *sub rosa*
relationship with the US and its response to the Iranian Revolution
have shown how well it recognises this. Such a realisation has been
evident in Prince Fahd's refusal to provide public support either for US
use of Omani bases or for Washington's quarrel with Iran. Only in the
crucial area of oil policy has the Al Saud pursued actions that seem
more in the interests of consumers than its radical brethren in OPEC.

Recent Secular Trends

Common sense would suggest that the legitimacy of the Al Saud rests
as much on traditional control and rising standards of living as on the
broad consensus of *'ulama*, tribal leaders and *tujar* behind their rulers.
The vastly increased national wealth since the quadrupling of oil prices
in 1973—4 and a haphazard but reasonably effective spreading of this
wealth should have increased the government's popularity and the
people's pride in their rulers. In fact, a depressing international
situation, rapid change in the physical fabric of the country and a
certain confusion of values have combined to trouble large numbers of
Saudis.

A recent characteristic of the Saudi political scene has been the talk
of Saudi, as opposed to Arab, nationalists in the government and the Al
Saud. These are apparently opposed to squandering a wasting asset on a
world that is slow to conserve, generally hostile in its attitudes and

listless over Palestine. They are said to regard oil in terms of national patrimony and strategic use, not as the engine of the world's economy. The most extreme advise caution over the US attitude; clearly, the Soviet Union does have a long-term interest in Saudi oil but it is the United States and Europe that need it *now* and may therefore pose the current threat. These opinions are expressed quite openly among educated Saudis. Their effect on Saudi oil-production levels has so far been extremely limited, although the regime does pay lip service to the notion of Saudi oil as a national patrimony. Even over the long-term question of production in the late 1980s and 1990s, the sharply reduced targets are the result of parsimony and technical problems, not concerted bureaucratic or family opposition.

There is, in truth, considerable grumbling about profiteering by princes and senior commoners and about the conduct of the royal family in such matters as the extra-judicial killing of Princess Mishaal bint Fahd in the summer of 1977. Discussion of these issues came out in the open in the winter of 1979, when Juhaiman al-Otaibi's strident condemnation of royal corruption, the feeble handling of the Mecca siege and the royal family's failure to provide a coherent account of events upset a great many Saudis.

Clearly, the question of corruption and royal behaviour will grow in importance as the family itself proliferates, while the failure in consultation appears more glaring as the standard of political awareness rises. The Saudi leaders seem to recognise that these problems require some more exact constitutional definition of the royal family's position and of the law. Prince Fahd, the Crown Prince, promised both *nizam* and *majlis al-shura* soon after the end of the siege. It is too early to say whether the promise alone is considered adequate. There is certainly no organised movement to press for constitutional change, and to find an ideological framework and organisation which can translate grumbles into active opposition we must look among the Shi'a and the religious zealots.

Religious Opposition

Problem of the Shi'a

Despite the impression of a monolith given by Saudi Wahhabism, there are many local differences in religious observance in Saudi Arabia. The Wahhabism of Asir would scarcely pass muster in Najd, while there are pockets of schism among, for example, the Bani Yam of the Wadi Najran. Yet there is no minority to compare with the Shi'a of al-Hasa, either in size or activity. Numbering as many as 400,000 souls in its own villages of Qatif, Safwa and Seihat and in the main al-Hasa oasis itself, the Shi'a constitutes a very significant minority in the Eastern Province and a substantial proportion of Aramco's Saudi employees. Alienated as it is from the religion and custom of Najd, the Shi'a of al-Hasa look for guidance to the great Shi'a shrines of Kerbela and Najaf in southern Iraq and to the *mujtahids* (exemplars) of Iran.

As early as May 1913 the Shi'a, then under the control of a somewhat isolated Turkish garrison in Hofuf, had been fearful that the expansion of Abd al-Aziz's power and, more particularly, the wayward *ikhwan*, posed a threat to their safety. The Sheikh of Seihat wrote to the British Political Agent in Bahrain asking for the protection of the British government.[17] It was not, of course, forthcoming and Hofuf fell to the Saudis the next year.

There can be no doubt that the immense and awesome authority of the Ibn Jiluwi governor and the King's peace helped to prevent real mischief among the Shi'a. None the less, the suspicion and distaste felt by the Najdi *'ulama* and the more zealous *ikhwan* for the Shi'a was advertised on several occasions. The *'ulama*'s and *ikhwan*'s attitude found expression in the *fatwa* of the February 1927 congress, convened by Abd al-Aziz to patch up his differences with the dominant elements of the Utaibah, Mutair and Ajman.

> As to the Shi'a, we have told the Imam that our ruling is that they must be asked to surrender to true Moslems and should not be allowed to perform their misguided religious rites in public. We ask that the Imam should order his Viceroy in Hasa — ibn Jiluwi — to summon the Shi'a to Sheikh ibn Bishr, before whom they should undertake to follow the religion of God and his Prophet, to cease all prayer to the saintly members of the Prophet's house . . .
>
> Any places specially erected for the practice of their rites must be destroyed and these practices forbidden in mosques or anywhere else . . .
>
> With regard to the Shi'a of Qatif . . . we have advised the Imam to send missionaries and teachers to certain districts and villages which have now come under the rule of the true Moslems . . .[18]

In the years that followed, Shi'as were excluded from advancement in the armed forces and civil service. It is only recently that they have begun to take part in the service and contracting boom that has accompanied Aramco's oil operations since the early 1950s.

It was almost certainly for the Shi'a's own good that successive Ibn Jiluwi governors of Hasa refused the community permission to stage the most self-conscious of their ceremonies in public. The experience of Bahrain would have shown them that the mourning procession on Muharram 10 for the Imam Hussein, always an emblem of the Shi'a's sense of historical oppression, often unleashes sectarian violence. As in Bahrain, too, the martyrdoms of history carry more meaning than actual present suffering. If the Shi'a have done comparatively badly in recruitment to government organisations, playing only a tiny role in the civil service and armed forces, and have only lately profited from the retail and contracting boom, this has been partially offset by the jobs Shi'a men have taken in the oil company. The company was, in the words of a former chairman, 'colour blind': it did not specifically favour the employment of Shi'a, but was simply resorting to the only convenient source of domestic labour.

In the course of the 1970s, a shift in Saudi government attitudes could be detected. If the Shi'a suffered in the wave of arrests in 1969–70, this was primarily because of a sort of institutional nostalgia at the Interior Ministry and the General Directorate of Intelligence. By 1976, a Shi'a from the Island of Tarut, off Qatif, had been appointed to head the Jubail Industrial Project – designed to become al-Hasa's second largest employer by the middle of the 1980s. It is widely expected that a substantial number of Shi'a will be employed on the project – indeed, many of the junior employees currently at the site are Shi'a. In the royal family, Prince Sattam, the deputy governor of al-Riyadh, and Prince Ahmad, deputy Interior Minister, have both spoken up for the grievances of the Shi'a before foreign listeners.

Even without the strident calls from Tehran radio, it was inevitable that the Iranian Revolution would produce a new consciousness among the Saudi Shi'as. The first notice came in the summer of 1979 when the *mujtahids* of Qatif announced they would stage the Ashura ceremony which the Ibn Jiluwi had always banned. The demand came at a time when the General Directorate of Intelligence, now headed by Prince Turki al-Faisal, was acutely concerned at possible subversion by Iranian pilgrims both in the *haramein* (Mecca and Medina) and in the villages. As it turned out, the pilgrimage passed relatively quietly; the Ashura on 28 November, coinciding as it did with the attack on the Grand Mosque in Mecca, did not. An attempt to hold a procession in Seihat found the security forces extremely jittery and in 24 hours of rioting there and in Qatif, seventeen Shi'a lost their lives. Prince Ahmad, the deputy Interior Minister, made an attempt to mediate; promises and arrests were made; on 1 February, the anniversary of Imam Khomeini's triumphant return to Iran, violence broke out in Qatif once again and four demonstrators lost their lives.

The government in al-Riyadh now recognises that the al-Hasa Shi'a are a potentially restive element in the oil-producing province and Saudi newspapers regularly carry notices of new public works for Qatif and the villages. Yet active Shi'a discontent will probably depend more on the Saudi government's relations with Iran and, to a lesser extent, on the internal politics of Iraq where a Shi'a majority is ruled by a predominantly Sunni leadership. Events in Bahrain may also be influential.

At the time of writing, the Saudi leaders were providing support for the Iraqi regime in its war with Iran — presumably on the grounds that the Iranian revolutionaries pose an unacceptable threat to the stability of the Gulf and al-Hasa. Yet should the Iraqi venture backfire, and there is no evidence that the rank-and-file Shi'a in the Iraqi army are fighting with any energy, there could be repercussions in southern Iraq which would surely spread to al-Hasa.

Revolt of Juhaiman

The November 1979 siege of the Grand Mosque in Mecca, carried out under the leadership of Juhaiman al-Otaibi, can only be properly understood within a historical context. Accounts of Abd al-Aziz ibn Saud's unification of the peninsula this century differ in the weight they accord the forces of religious reform. Nevertheless, it is quite clear that both the *'ulama* and the zealots of the towns and *ikhwan* settlements (*hujar*, singular *hijra*) played an important role in the revival of Saudi power and could expect their influence to persist in the kingdom. Much of the recent history of the kingdom is a tale of conflict between religious zeal and the Al Saud's notions of political expediency and social progress.

The conflict stretches back to Abd al-Wahhab himself, but for our purposes the conquest of the Hijaz in 1925 provides a convenient starting point. Abd al-Aziz, who recognised that he needed the good opinion of the Hijaz merchants and the Muslim powers, installed a relatively tolerant administration; the *ikhwan* turned their *jihad* north and east, where they rapidly came into conflict with the forces of Abd al-Aziz's British allies. Hafez Wahba, one of the King's advisers, reported that the leaders of rebel *ikhwan* proclaimed through the *hijras* that they, and they alone, were the defenders of the true faith and the supporters of the Law which Abd al-Aziz was seeking to destroy. Abd al-Aziz wanted power and conquest, they alleged; he was a friend of infidels and a party to all their activities.[19]

Military force was used to bring these *ikhwan* to heel, although the fires of the revolt continued to smoulder into the 1930s. The defeat of the *ikhwan* allowed Abd al-Aziz to introduce such innovations as wireless, telegraphy and motor cars, which the *'ulama* and *ikhwan* rebels considered heretical but Abd al-Aziz saw as crucial for the administration of the Court and the growing realm. It also made possible the grant of an oil concession to a non-Muslim company in 1933 – although, typically, the first notice related to this in *Umm Al Qura*, the Mecca newspaper, called for Muslim applicants to come forward. At times, the conflict between religious zeal and political expediency led to violence, as at the opening of a girls' public school in 1960 or at the al-Riyadh television station five years later. None the less, as royal authority increased so did the monarch's skill in treating with the *'ulama*; Faisal expressed his displeasure in no uncertain terms when the blind theologian, Shaikh Abd al-Aziz ibn Baz, published an article with a pre-Copernican account of the universe. Later in the 1960s the creation of such institutions as the Ministry of Justice helped to identify the *'ulama* more closely with the administration.

In recent years, the pendulum has seemed to swing back the other way in such sensitive areas as the role and conduct of women and the presence of large numbers of foreigners. This is no doubt because the Al Saud have responded to the revivalist atmosphere throughout the Muslim world and because, in the confusion of ideals caused by rapid social and economic change, the Wahhabite tradition has strong sentimental and national attraction.

Juhaiman ibn Seif al-Otaibi, the leader of the revolt in Mecca, belongs firmly within this tradition. His followers were termed *ikhwan* and though this is a common enough designation in the language of Islamic reform, Juhaiman was himself born in the *ikhwan hijra* of Sajir in Qasim and his men emulated the outward show of their original zeal with long beards and cut-off robes.

Juhaiman's preaching, concerning the legitimacy of the Al Saud and the appearance of the *mahdi*, can be found in four pamphlets, signed by him. While these still await the study of a competent Islamic scholar – and were almost certainly designed as texts for exegesis rather than as manifestos — a brief summary of the pamphlet numbered 'one', and probably published early in 1978, gives the flavour of his thought.

There are two classes of ruler, one who follows the Koran and the *sunna*, and the other who forces the people to do his will. The people are not obliged to obey the second class of ruler even if they rule in the name of Islam.

All Muslim rulers must be from the Quraish. Present Muslim rulers are co-operating with infidels and those who deny God.

The present trouble began when the people accepted Abd al-Aziz, who hated the *jihad* against the Turks and betrayed King Hussein (of the Hijaz).

The royal family is corrupt. It worships money and spends it on palaces not mosques. If you accept what they say, they will make you rich; otherwise they will persecute and even torture you.

The *'ulama* have warned the royal family about its corruption but Abd al-Aziz ibn Baz is in the family's pay and has endorsed their actions.[20]

While the theory of government is classical, the reference to *jihad* evokes the first *ikhwan*. As for Ibn Baz, he and other religious figures are castigated throughout the pamphlets as creatures of a corrupt regime. Juhaiman and nearly 100 of his band were arrested in al-Riyadh in June 1978 and questioned by the *'ulama*, including Ibn Baz, who found them harmless and had them released after six weeks.

If the pamphlets, numbered one to four, represent a chronological sequence — only number three is dated '1399' (1979) — it is only in the later pamphlets that the notion of a *mahdi* comes to the fore. The concept of a 'rightly guided' redeemer for the Muslim world is alien to Wahhabism, having its origins in Christian and Persian tradition. One explanation for the change is provided at the beginning of the third pamphlet, where Juhaiman describes the various reforming groups he had encountered and how he had exposed their weaknesses. These ranged from the *jamiat al-tabligh*, originally from the Indian subcontinent, the *jamiat al-Islah*, a group active in Kuwait, the *Ansar* of Sudan, and so on.

The band of 200 or so men, women and children who took over the mosque on the first day of the Islamic year 1400 included large numbers of foreigners, from Egyptians and Kuwaitis to an American Black

Muslim and a Guyanese. It was subsequently revealed that many of these had been students at the Islamic University of Medina, founded under the influence of Muslim Brothers who had fled Nasser's Egypt, and headed since the late 1960s by Ibn Baz as rector. Medina's role in the pilgrimage and the government's aid for students of religion and the law has a natural attraction for foreign students and for their extreme opinions; they make up over three-quarters of the student body in Medina. According to Hamud ibn Saleh al-Uqail, the *imam* of a royal mosque in al-Riyadh

> An atmosphere favourable to heresy existed because of the presence of large numbers of foreign students. A group appeared calling for a rejection of 'interpretation' in favour of a return to the basic Koran and *sunna*. The authorities expelled the foreigners and rehabilitated the Saudis but after the death of King Faisal, the heresies started again.[21]

It is difficult to give a coherent account of Juhaiman's career because of the wildly conflicting reports on this subject which are current. One account, for example, describes Juhaiman as attending Medina University where, after a period of close association with Ibn Baz, he broke with his master in 1974 and led ten followers off to Qasim. Another account tells that while serving with the National Guard in Qasim, he assumed the head of a band of students expelled from the university. The pamphlets themselves say that the band came together in Qasim. The government has been keen to portray Juhaiman as illiterate and wholly unqualified to interpret the law, and to play down the anti-Saud teaching in favour of the more universal doctrine of the *mahdi*.

Whatever actually occurred, the *ikhwan* who took part in the attack ranged from such deracinated bedouin with sentimental links to the original *ikhwan* as Juhaiman to the more sophisticated heirs of generations of Islamic extremism in Egypt. As Prince Naif, the Interior Minister, has constantly repeated, 'their numbers were extremely limited'; but in a country where religious opposition to the throne is deeply ingrained and whose borders are, by necessity of pilgrimage, open to extremism from abroad, the threat has not disappeared.

Conclusion

This article concludes with five points drawn from the preceding account. First, the collapse of secular opposition at the end of the 1960s was brought about both by the round-up of 1969–70 and by Faisal's subjugation of Nasser. Even today, the Al Saud remain extremely nervous of triggering Arab or Islamic nationalist disfavour. Second, the movement among the educated for constitutional reform is listless, fragmented and lacks an ideological framework. Third, the Al Saud, while encouraging social and economic development, have proved unwilling to cede a significant measure of political reform. Fourth, religious opposition and the problem of the Shi'a are so deeply ingrained in the Saudi system as to be to all intents 'structural'. Fifth, Saudi Arabia's role in the pilgrimage and its tendency to *da'wa* make it vulnerable to religious extremism from non-Saudi sources.

Notes

1. F. Badr, 'Developmental Planning in Saudi Arabia', unpublished PhD thesis, University of South California, 1968.
2. F. Hamzah, *Al-Bilad al-Arabiyah al-Saudiyah* (Mecca, AH1355/AD1937), pp. 90–1, quoted in G. Rentz, 'The Saudi Monarchy' in W. Beling, *King Faisal and the Modernisation of Saudi Arabia* (Croom Helm, London, 1980), p. 28.
3. F. A. Shakir, 'Modernisation of the Developing Nations: the Case of Saudi Arabia', unpublished PhD thesis, Purdue University, 1972.
4. D. Van Der Meulen, *The Wells of Ibn Saud* (John Murray, London, 1957), p. 158.
5. G. de Gaury, *Faisal, King of Saudi Arabia* (Prentice-Hall, New Jersey, 1967), p. 138.
6. H. Lackner, *A House Built on Sand* (Ithaca Press, London, 1978), p. 90.
7. M. S. Cheney, *Big Oilman from Arabia* (Heinemann, London, 1958), pp. 264–6.
8. Cheney, *Big Oilman from Arabia*, p. 284.
9. Cheney, *Big Oilman from Arabia*, pp. 284–5.
10. Cheney, *Big Oilman from Arabia*, p. 319.
11. Lackner, *A House Built on Sand*, pp. 103–4.
12. N. C. Walpole *et al.*, *Area Handbook for Saudi Arabia* (The American University, Washington, DC, 1971), p. 154.
13. R. Johns *et al.*, *The House of Saud* (Sidgwick and Jackson, London, to be published 1981).
14. Johns, *The House of Saud*.
15. Johns, *The House of Saud*.
16. Lackner, *A House Built on Sand*, pp. 106–7.
17. M. Field, *Financial Times Survey of Saudi Arabia* (28 April 1980), p. xxii.
18. H. Wahba, *Arabian Days* (Arthur Barker, London, 1964).
19. Wahba, *Arabian Days*.
20. Juhaiman ibn Seif al-Otaibi, *Rules of Allegiance and Obedience* (Misconduct of Rulers).
21. *Al Riyadh* (4 December 1979).

7 A CURIOUS AND CLOSE LIAISON: SAUDI ARABIA'S RELATIONS WITH THE UNITED STATES

Fred Halliday

Introduction: The Necessity of the Alliance

The relationship between Saudi Arabia and the USA is, by conventional standards, amongst the most important linking any Third World country to an industrialised nation. Whilst the foreign policy of most countries is a compound of different factors — strategic, military, political, economic — that of Washington towards Saudi Arabia is more overtly and massively founded on economic interest than in almost any other comparable case. The US concern with Cuba, affected as it may have been by sugar, cannot be reduced to that substance. America's intervention in Vietnam was determined by factors far weightier than control of rubber plantations. Even its concern with Iran was, in the context of the whole post-war period, determined less by concern over oil than by the strategic position which Iran occupied. All these junior allies could, with reluctance, be abandoned. In the case of Saudi Arabia, however, oil provides an urgent reason for its indispensability.

Despite the enormous increase in the levels of co-operation between the two countries over the past decade, this central component of the US–Saudi relationship was unambiguously established as early as 1943. Long before there was any hint of a serious energy shortage, Washington, under pressure from the American companies, decided to establish a direct link to the Saudi state and Roosevelt declared that the defence of Saudi Arabia was a US national interest. In the ensuing decades, this attachment has served three functions. First, even in the years when Saudi oil exports went exclusively to Europe and Japan, it was American firms that were able to reap the profits from this energy source whilst the flow of oil to other industrial economies fuelled the post-war boom. Second, once the USA became a net oil importer, it had comparatively secure access to Saudi crude which made up 8 per cent of US consumption by 1980. But the bond always had a third function, that of *exclusion*: not the current concern to keep the Russians out, but the more long-standing one of preventing the British and French from enjoying direct access to this source of raw materials.[1]

While rivalry with the Europeans constituted an important factor shaping US policy in the 1940s, anxiety about the US position being eroded by disloyal allies in Europe is one that has still a certain role to play in US calculations of its policy towards Saudi Arabia.

On the Saudi side, support from Washington has continued to play a central part in the preservation of the royal family's rule. Yet here there is an important discontinuity. In the 1930s and 1940s, the Saudis needed financial support – from the American oil companies and from the US Lend–Lease funds – to stabilise their budget. There was no great sense of the Al Saud being threatened from the outside, and thus no need for major assistance in defending the security of the kingdom. The deteriorating state of the Saudi economy during the depression led to the US oil companies gaining an entrée in 1933, but it was Saudi economic needs during the Second World War which brought in the US state. While the British had been accommodating allies in the 1920s and 1930s, they were overcommitted in the war period itself and were unable to provide sufficient funds. The ideological conservatism of the Saudi family precluded it from establishing permanent ties with the country that was the first to recognise the new kingdom (in 1926) and to offer economic assistance, namely the USSR. It was these considerations that led it to establish links with the USA, thereby enabling the Americans to make the first breach (outside the Far East and Liberia, in the system of colonial dominance that the Europeans had constructed in Asia and Africa.

Whilst the early period of the relationship was defined by the internal economic weakness of the Saudi kingdom, the later period, which began in the 1960s, was marked by the enormous financial strength of Saudi Arabia. The new economic power, however, did not emancipate Saudi policy from the USA since it came together with two counter-vailing factors which more than offset the security benefits from the new oil revenues accruing to al-Riyadh. The first was the rise of Arab nationalism, which posed an apparent threat to the Saudi royal family. Despite Saudi criticism of some US actions, the Iranian Revolution has had a similar effect of emphasising the need for the alliance. The second factor was the change in the world oil market. This made the Gulf in general, and Saudi reserves in particular, of far greater importance to the industrialised world than they had been before. The resultant vulnerability of the Saudi state in this new international political and economic context has made it more reliant than ever on sustenance from the USA. This is a form of support which, with the increased oil import needs of the USA, Washington has been eager to provide. The kingdom's new wealth, therefore, has created a situation in which this originally independent, if poor, dynastic regime has had to find an external patron to protect it in its new wealthy condition.

Yet if this relationship is so vital to both sides, it is also an anomalous and a persistently troubled one. In one sense, the US link to al-Riyadh fits easily into the established patterns of relations with influential Third World countries, whether that of the Nixon Doctrine, enunciated in July 1969, that of the Trilateral Commission, which became dominant with the advent of the Carter Administration to power in January 1977, or that of the need to build an anti-communist 'strategic consensus', which was the guiding concern of the Reagan Administration in 1981. Whilst the first stressed the delegation of regional power to strong junior allies, the second laid greatest emphasis on the need to build up a three-way partnership (USA, Europe–Japan and 'regional influentials', that is strong Third World states) in order to handle economic as well as strategic issues and to break the constrictions of the bipolar US–USSR conflict. The third sought to rally conservative powers agianst social upheaval in the region. But Saudi Arabia is singularly ill-fitted to work within these frameworks: although its financial power and religious character give it definite forms of influence in the Arab world and beyond, Saudi Arabia is in certain essential aspects an extremely weak country, far more so than the other countries that have been incorporated within the Nixon Doctrine. In population terms in the mid-1970s it was relatively insignificant − 5 million, compared to Iran's 36 million, Egypt's 40 million, Brazil's 120 million, or Indonesia's 137 million. The small size of the population, moreover, is not compensated by qualitative factors: a quarter of the population remains nomadic, literacy is perhaps 30 per cent, modern skills are rather scarce, and life expectancy is still only about 40 years. Economically, Saudi Arabia has little except its oil, nor, despite much polite coverage in the world's financial press, is either Saudi agriculture or industry likely to reach the standards of productivity or levels of output of even a modest developing country over the next generation. Militarily the kingdom is powerless, incapable of mounting any but the most symbolic operations outside its own frontiers, and reliant on a mass of foreign technicians to sustain its purchased equipment. It was easily humiliated by the well-organised and tenacious seizure of its holiest religious site in 1979. Poorer countries like Jordan, Morocco or Pakistan are in military terms far more credible candidates for Nixon Doctrine adoption or regional influence than is Saudi Arabia.

This anomaly of financial strength and productive and military debility affects the Saudi place within US foreign policy. It also goes quite a way towards explaining what might appear to be the surprisingly discordant nature of Saudi—US relations. Two countries that need each other so much, and which share a common anti-communist perspective, should, at first sight, be able to handle their relations more calmly than has been the case. In the 1950s there was a prolonged period of disagreement over the lease on the Dhahran base and over King Saud's association with Nasser. After the 1962 Yemeni Revolution the Americans recognised the Yemen Arab Republic, whereas the Saudis refused to do so. After the 1967 Arab—Israeli War, and following accusations of US involvement in the Israeli attacks upon Egypt, the Saudis switched their arms purchases for a time to France. In 1973 the Saudis joined in the Arab states' oil embargo on the USA and forbad Aramco to sell oil to its American associates.[2] Although the embargo was lifted before any of the original conditions were met (not an inch of Palestinian land had been released by Israel), it did provoke tension in US—Saudi relations. In the mid-1970s successive US attempts to produce a full Saudi—Iranian defence pact and to resolve the suspicions between the two countries foundered on the rock of Arab, including Saudi, resistance. In 1978 and 1979 new disagreements came into the open, with the Saudis criticising the Americans for their supposedly weak-kneed response to the gains in Soviet policy, for their failure to save the Shah, and for the attempt to make Saudi Arabia participate in the Camp David process.[3] Nor did events in Iran, and a common US—Saudi hostility to the new revolutionary regime, lead to a co-ordinated stand on matters relating to Iran: the Saudis openly criticised the US attempt to release the hostages in April 1980, calling it 'an affront to the sovereignty of the countries of the area, which jeopardized the area's security and stability'. Moreover, in June 1980, two new issues emerged which led to renewed controversy in the USA: first, the Saudi government requested new equipment to arm its F-15 fighters, and secondly, the Saudis indicated that they would reduce supplies of oil to the USA if this was being used merely to build up the US strategic petroleum reserve.[4] At the same time there was increasing dissatisfaction within Saudi Arabia, including among some members of the royal family, about the failure of the USA either to do more on Palestine or to exert leadership in the Gulf, and the Saudi authorities were irritated by official US briefings which indicated that the regime in Saudi Arabia might soon be crumbling. With the advent of the Reagan Administration to office in January 1981, US—Saudi relations appeared to be heading for considerable tension. The new Administration did agree to sell some of the new F-15 equipment but withheld bomb-racks, and seemed too optimistic about Saudi willingness to join a new alliance with Egypt and Israel. As on earlier occasions over the previous decades, the Saudis were therefore beginning to cast around for other allies and for ways of distancing themselves from Washington's policies. Whether such dissidence would meet with indulgence in the USA, given the new 'imperial' mood in fashion there, remained to be seen.

These conflicts spring from the anomaly of Saudi strength/weakness in at least two ways. First, despite their enormous financial wealth, the Saudis have not yet been able seriously to influence US policy on Israel. Given the long-run US interest in Saudi oil and the, at least temporary, damage that the Saudis could inflict upon the US financial system by withdrawing their reserves or abandoning use of the dollar for oil payments, the degree of change in US policy has been remarkably slight. The US has certainly done nothing to prevent the increasing intransigence of the Israelis, let alone reverse their territorial advance. This failure is largely due to Washington's knowledge of the extent to which the Saudis are reliant on US support for their very survival – a support which results from the Saudi royal family choosing to continue to rule in the peculiar and vulnerable manner which it has so far favoured. Secondly, the very political vulnerability of the Saudis to Arab nationalism prevents them from making the kinds of strategic accommodations that the USA would like: the Saudis feel they cannot support the Camp David process, and they cannot give the US overt and adequate military bases, because both would provoke further difficulties for them and broadcast their client status rather too loudly. Even in a case like the North Yemen crisis of February 1979 the Saudis were unable to find an appropriate means of mobilising US support; the US decision to send $380 million worth of emergency aid to Sana'a, and a token flight of jets to Saudi Arabia, was again too public for Saudi ease. Whereas US disputes with some other allies reflect the strength and the room for independent manoeuvre of these countries (France, Turkey and Argentina, to name but three), Saudi disagreement with Washington is rather a reflection of the weakness of that country. Indeed, the limited influence which Saudi Arabia exerts on the USA can be illustrated by contrasting it with that of another US ally in the region, namely Israel. The former is rich in oil and finance, the latter is dependent for its day-to-day survival upon US military and financial support. Yet it is the superficially weaker state, Israel, which has been able to condition US policy in the 1970s, whilst the Saudis have produced little net change of direction in Washington. Part of the explanation certainly lies in the workings of US internal politics, but the weaknesses of the Saudi regime itself are also a major factor.

Saudi exposure is evident in another respect, namely the intermittent indication that the USA is prepared to seize the eastern Saudi oil fields by force. Initially voiced in the mid-1970s, in response to the 1973–4 oil embargo, the idea of a US invasion was revived in 1979–80 after the riots in the eastern province of Saudi Arabia and the seizure of the Mecca mosque. Many qualifications have been made about this project – that it is only floated by extremist elements in the USA, that enormous logistical problems would arise, that the oil fields would be sabotaged before the US troops got there. No doubt any US administration would prefer not to have to resort to such a course of action. But in the last resort there can be no doubt that, if access to Saudi oil was seriously threatened for any period of time and by whatever political circumstances, the USA would send forces to seize the wells; nothing inside Saudi Arabia, nor in US politics would prevent this, and both the military supply problems and the engineering challenge of restarting oil production could be overcome. At that point the present constraints upon US action in the Middle East, namely the response in the Arab world and the survival of the Saudi ruling family, would become irrelevant since the sanction of Arab displeasure would no longer have any force. US intervention would, of course, be made more likely by a political convulsion involving the Saudi ruling family's fall from power. The alarm felt in US and European circles about a 'Saudi Qaddafi' indicates that these circles are none too optimistic about the family's future. Were a major threat to emerge in this context the oil wells would be seized. If this is of little comfort to the Saudi ruling family, it does underline once again the vital importance of Saudi oil to US economic policy.[5]

Non-Military Collaboration: Oil, Trade, Diplomacy

The relationship between the Saudi government and Aramco has been one of sustained success on both sides: in generating income for the Saudis (from $1.2 billion in 1970 to perhaps $80 billion in 1980), in generating profits for the American companies in the consortium (Exxon, Texaco, Mobil and Socal), and in preventing other European or Japanese competitors from gaining significant access to supplies of Saudi crude. It took from 1972 to 1980 for Saudi Arabia to nationalise

Aramco, and the understanding, even now that full nationalisation has come, is that the Aramco companies will retain a preferential position in the Saudi market, as servicing agents and as purchasers of Saudi crude. A 1976 agreement on this could be revoked by the Saudis, but unless major new conflicts arise it will form the basis of a continued and close partnership.

The US oil industry has tried to prevent the Saudis from gaining independent access to consumers. In the early 1950s the companies successfully prevented the Saudis from using Onassis's ships to transport their crude.[6] They were not indifferent to the attempts by Abdullah Tariqi, the first Saudi oil minister and one of the inspirers of OPEC, to assert greater producer control. Although control at the point of production is no longer as ominous or as important as it was judged to be in the 1950s, and producer interest in downstream activities has declined, serious conflicts could emerge in the future if Petromin, the Saudi oil company, was able and willing to make a serious effort to establish its own network of distribution within the industrialised countries.

One effect of the Aramco–Saudi relationship – from the 1940s onwards – has been to bring the US government into the picture. The relationship between US companies and the Washington bureaucracy is not always without friction, but the Aramco–US government partnership is one of the most striking, given the image of free enterprise and autonomy which both sides like to cultivate. It was the Socal president, Harry Collier, accompanied by Texaco chairman, Star Rogers, who visited the US Interior Secretary in February 1943 to persuade Roosevelt to grant the Saudis Lend–Lease aid, and thereby cemented the state-to-state relations.[7] In the 1950s US tax laws were organised so that the royalties paid to the Saudi government by Aramco were deductible from the companies' taxes payable in the USA. A substantial company–Washington clash emerged in 1973 when the US companies obeyed the Saudi embargo order, but even this had its benefits for the companies, enabling them to boost prices and cut out independent firms, and there is considerable doubt as to how effective the embargo on the US ever was. Since 1973 Saudi oil policy and the activities of Aramco have been a source of concern to the US government which, given the shortfall in US domestic output, has now come to take a major role in determining oil policy. In the complex interactions of Arab–Israeli diplomacy, Saudi output decisions and US domestic politics, the lines of communication between Washington and the oil companies have been extremely busy.

The US government has also come to play a major role in promoting other economic links between the two countries. Between 1947 and 1980 Saudi Arabia bought $56 billion-worth of US goods, $34 billion of which was for military items. The Joint United States–Saudi Committee for Economic Co-operation set up in 1976 is overseeing contracts worth over $650 million,[8] and in 1978 Saudi Arabia imported nearly $4.4 billion-worth of US goods, making it the seventh largest US export market. According to some reports, up to 50,000 Saudis are now studying in the USA. Most important of all is the Saudi willingness to support the dollar: they use it in most of their foreign transactions and bank the majority of their reserves in the USA. Precise figures on Saudi foreign investment are not available, but one estimate in 1979 was that $35 billion were held in American government securities, and another $24 billion in other US investments.[9] In all of these diverse activities, the US government has sought to use the disposition of reserves in such a way as to co-ordinate economic support for the Saudi government and to encourage Saudi support for the US economy.

Active diplomatic collaboration between the USA and Saudi Arabia goes back to the mid-1960s when the two countries faced a common enemy in Nasser's Egypt. Although there was an initial divergence over recognition of the Yemen Arab Republic (YAR), with Washington establishing relations with Sana'a, there was no long-term difference on this issue. From early 1963 the US policy shifted to one of quietly supporting the Saudis in their arming of the royalist tribes in North Yemen. Later, in 1965, with the assistance and collaboration of a number of other pro-American states, King Faisal launched his Islamic Pact. It was in the aftermath of the 1967 war, however, that the greatest success of Saudi diplomacy began – the weaning of Egypt away from the Soviet Union. Whilst the main cause of the Egyptian move lay in the internal processes of Egyptian society itself, the Saudi financial and diplomatic offensive certainly played an important part, beginning in the time of Nasser and bearing fruit under Sadat. Saudi 'riyal diplomacy', as the Americans sometimes call it, has had other notable successes, where it has found local situations that are independently ripe for such approaches: in Sudan, Somalia, Syria and Jibuti. Saudi finance has helped the Afghan rebels, the Islamic forces in Bangladesh and the more conservative forces within the PLO. It has sustained tribal and right-wing elements in North Yemen, and contributed to the survival of the Moroccan monarchy. Saudi money financed the despatch of Moroccan troops to Zaire in 1978. Until its war with Iran, Iraq has not needed Saudi finance, but political and security co-operation between the two has helped to inflect Baghdad's policies to the right especially in the wake of the Iranian Revolution[10] and once the war began the Saudis were willing to extend substantial credits to the Iraqi government.

Problems of Strategic Co-ordination

Within this wide-ranging alliance, a number of substantial problems have come to the fore. First, despite its large productive capacity, Saudi Arabia has not been able to exert the domination over OPEC which the USA would have expected. Saudi Arabia did help to keep down the price of oil in the 1974—7 period and was doing so again in 1980, but the Saudis find themselves unable to prevent the overall rise in oil revenues that has been the objective of US government policies. Conversely, the Saudis find their willingness to sustain a high rate of output — 10.4 million barrels a day in early 1981 — unmatched by what they consider to be helpful US moves even on oil: the USA has still not launched a serious oil conservation programme, and congressional pressure to build up the strategic reserve is explicitly aimed at making the USA less dependent on OPEC, and specifically Arab, pressures.

Second, the major diplomatic concern of both the Americans and the Saudis remains the Arab—Israeli question. This is not just for reasons specific to each side (US strategic perception, Arab solidarity) but also because both sides realise that the continued failure to resolve the Arab—Israeli dispute is the greatest single cause of political instability in the Middle East. No amount of oil pacts or theatrical demonstrations of US willingness to 'confront' the Soviet Union can make up for the impasse on this matter and for the Saudi refusal to endorse US policy. Despite the closeness of their alliance, both sides misjudged the other over Camp David: the Saudis expected that their new influence would move the Americans more that it did, and the Americans imagined that Saudi reliance on the USA would produce greater responsiveness in al-Riyadh.

Third, Saudi 'Nixon Doctrine' activities in Egypt and elsewhere have certainly been successful, but they have not been as successful as the scale of Saudi aid might initially have indicated. The saga of Saudi relations with Egypt is indicative of one way in which this can go wrong, with Washington 'kidnapping' Sadat after the Saudis had financed and promoted the break with Moscow. North Yemen is

another case in point: for, despite the dependence of the YAR government apparatus on Saudi financing, and the challenge from the People's
Democratic Republic of Yemen (PDRY), the authorities there decided
in 1979 to switch back to Soviet military equipment. Whilst one reason
for this may have been the technical fact that the officers and technicians
were more used to Soviet equipment, Yemeni hostility to the way in
which the Saudis handled the deal whereby they had formerly financed
arms purchases from the US must also have played a part. The Saudi
record in South Yemen is even more debatable: having tried, from 1969
to 1973, to challenge the PDRY government by encouraging subversion
along the border, Saudi Arabia switched to a 'riyal diplomacy' policy
in 1976, offering the South Yemenis financial inducements to turn
away from Moscow. But, precisely because the internal conditions
present in other countries were not present in Aden, this policy failed.
Indeed, the attempt to win President Salem Robea Ali, with offers of
financial aid, only precipitated a crisis in which he was deposed and
killed in June 1978.

Fourth, in certain situations Saudi intervention has, if anything,
provoked *greater* problems from the US point of view. A clear case in
point is Somalia, an interesting subsection of the US–Saudi relationship.
As early as 1974 the Saudis offered financial aid to the Somali government on condition that they expelled the Russian military personnel in
their country. This project was supported by the then US Ambassador
to Saudi Arabia, James Akins, but vetoed by Kissinger, on the grounds
that the Soviet presence in Somalia was a convenient legitimation for
the build-up of US facilities on the island of Diego Garcia.[11] When
Carter came into office, the situation changed and the Saudis went
ahead with their plan to win over Somalia. Carter voiced his hope that
Somalia would change over and break with the Soviet Union. In the
event the Somalis saw what they thought was their long-awaited chance
– not just to win Saudi aid, but, what for them was more important,
to attack Ethiopia and re-occupy their lost lands in Ogaden. The result
was that a low-level Soviet presence, in the rather small country of
Somalia, was replaced by a much larger Soviet and Cuban presence in
the strategically more important and ten times more populous country
of Ethiopia. The Saudis had created a new problem many times larger
than the one they had originally proposed to remove. Similar risks can
be detected in Saudi initiatives elsewhere: the Soviet intervention in
Afghanistan was not, as Moscow claims, the result of 'direct' foreign
activity against the Kabul government. But it was the result of a tribal
uprising that would not have reached the scale it did had it not been for

the support the rebels received from a Saudi-supported Pakistan and from Arab funders in Saudi Arabia and Kuwait. Again, an apparently offensive Saudi move, clothed in suitable evocations of Islamic solidarity, produced a response that rather qualified initial Saudi hopes of success. In the Gulf itself it may well be that similar if less spectacular reversals will occur: the Saudis seem to have been rather pleased with the manner in which political pressure upon Kuwait and Bahrain forced those two countries to close down their national assemblies in 1975 and 1976 respectively. Yet resentment at Saudi interference in those situations has sustained opposition movements whose activities show no signs of abating.

Fifth, the Saudi–US relationship has caused difficulties within the US governmental apparatus itself. One problem is the nature of the Saudi political system which cannot, even in the most euphemistic of terms, be held to approximate to the ideals of the Founding Fathers. At the time of the 1943 link-up, Roosevelt's special adviser, Harry Hopkins, was heard wondering 'how we can call that outfit a democracy',[12] and in the 1950s US officials became adept at drawing a veil over the continued presence of slavery in the Saudi kingdom.[13] At that time the US representative at the UN Economic and Social Council blocked new anti-slavery regulations in order to facilitate the post-Suez reconciliation of al-Riyadh and Washington. This problem has, however, never reached the scale it has done in the case of some other US allies, such as Iran or Chile. One reason is that those countries had to allow greater journalistic and academic observation than Saudi Arabia ever did. But part of the explanation must also lie in the comparatively lower level of *direct* political repression (that is imprisonment, political trials, executions), combined with the relatively less viable nature of the oppression to which the inhabitants of the Wahhabi domain have been subjected. There are not, it seems, thousands of political prisoners in Saudi jails, while the fate of women or of illiterate migrant workers, and the elimination of dissident army and air-force officers, has only rarely been broadcast to the world. The problem of how to justify support for a patently undemocratic government has, however, remained a recurrent one, and came rather comically to light in the dialogue between Kissinger and a pro-Israeli Congressman during the 1978 hearings on the F-15 jet fighters.

Mr Rosenthal Could you tell us a little bit about what kind of government Saudi Arabia has?

Mr Kissinger Well, I don't quite know how to answer that

question. Saudi Arabia is governed by the royal family. In my
experience their policy has been one of friendship for the United
States and moderation.

Mr Rosenthal That is not my question, Mr Secretary. My question
is if you were teaching a high school civics class, how would you
describe the government?

Mr Kissinger Well, I would describe the government as one in
which the country is run by a royal family. It was originally, before
the discovery of oil, a society based on beduin tribes, which is now
in the process of modernization. And I think that they are going
through a very complicated process.

Mr Rosenthal When did they last have an election?

Mr Kissinger They have not practised elections in recent
centuries.[14]

A number of US government agencies have, on occasion, questioned
specific features of Saudi policy, such as the almost complete ban on
the recruitment of Jews and women to work in Saudi Arabia, and the
operation of the boycott against Israel. Another matter of dispute has
been the code of conduct in commercial dealings and, in particular, the
commissions paid to middlemen in commercial transactions between
the USA and Saudi Arabia. Since both Saudis and Americans have been
willing partners in this practice the question of apportioning moral
blame, on which so much energy has been expended, is not so relevant.
But as an irritant in US–Saudi relations, especially after the Senate
Hearings of 1975 on Multinational Corporations, this has been a
significant and by no means closed issue.[15]

Military Linkage

Military links between the two countries began in July 1943 when a
US mission arrived to assess Saudi military requirements.[16] The first
US military training mission was established in April 1944 and by 1946
the USA had constructed Dhahran airfield, the largest US airfield
between Germany and Korea and a major link in its world-wide
transport network in the cold war period. During the 1950s the
Americans provided military aid in return for continued use of the
Dhahran base: the first tanks were purchased in August 1956, and in
1957 an air-force training programme using F-86 jets was launched.[17]
At this stage, however, the scale of US–Saudi military collaboration

was limited, and it was the Yemeni Revolution that really set the programme in motion. Although the USAF had departed from Dhahran in 1962, jets returned in a demonstration of US support in 1963 (Operation Hard Surface) following Egyptian raids across the border with Yemen, and in 1965 what was to be a massive commitment was entered into with the US Army Corps of Engineers for the construction of military facilities. Although the Saudis at this time bought British Lightning jets in preference to US ones, this choice was partly at the suggestion of the Americans who saw the sale of British material to Saudi Arabia as a way of compensating for Britain's decision to purchase US jets.[18] Moreover, whilst the Saudis bought jets from Britain, they none the less went to the US firm Raytheon for their Hawk Air Defence System. In 1966 the Saudis signed another long-term arrangement: initially known as the Saudi Arabian Mobility Programme, it has since been renamed the Saudi Ordnance Corps Programme and involved the provision of over 9,000 tactical and general-purpose vehicles to the Saudi army, and the training of some 4,200 Saudis by 1977.[19] In 1971 the Saudis began negotiations for a new range of jets, the American F-5s, and in 1972 they signed a ten-year naval expansion programme, designed to add 25 new ships to the 4-ship Saudi navy then in existence. In 1973 they contracted for a major National Guard modernisation programme. In 1976 the US Corps of Engineers set up a special Middle East Division, moved its headquarters outside the USA from Germany to Saudi Arabia, and became involved in a massive new military construction programme, at the centre of which lay three new 'Military Cities'; at al-Batin, near the Iraqi border, Khamis Mishayt, near the North Yemeni border, and Tabuq, near the Jordanian and Israeli borders. By 1980 the Corps was overseeing work totalling between $22 and $25 billion, although much of it was contracted to European or Middle Eastern firms. (See Table 7.1 for details of projects under way in 1976.)

The scale of this US involvement is enormous and its effects are as yet incalculable. It reflects both the anxieties of the Saudi regime, and the regime's increased purchasing power; Saudi military purchases from the US totalled over $34 billion in the 1971–80 period (see Table 7.2). It also reflects the strictly commercial desire of US arms manufacturers to sell as many weapons as they can to the Saudis, as they did to the Iranians; not just to boost their sales as such, but also to lower the unit costs on items being manufactured for the US and other markets. The military programmes have led to a massive influx of US personnel into Saudi Arabia: of the 30,000 or so Americans estimated to be in the

Table 7.1: US Corps of Engineers Activities in Saudi Arabia

	Estimated cost (in $ million)
Projects under planning and/or design (as of October 1976)[a]	
King Khaled Military Cantonment (Al Batin)	3,378
Saudi Naval Expansion Programme (SNEP) Jeddah, Jubail	1,200
MODA Medical Centre, Al-Kharj	3,500
MODA medical air evacuation network	100
MODA medical materials depot system	1,500
Taif General Hospital (expanded)	1,900
Phase II medical support facilities — Tabuk, Khamis, and Jeddah	30
Airborne and physical training school, Tabuk	169
Cantonment additions, Tabuk	113
Family housing, Khamis Mushayt	150
Infantry centre, Khamis Mushayt	213
Artillery centre, Khamis Mushayt	211
Cantonment additions, Khamis Mushayt	300
Military museum and library, al-Riyadh	6
MODA headquarters building rehabilitation, al-Riyadh	35
RSAF headquarters building, al-Riyadh	121
King Abd al-Aziz Military Academy (expanded)	2,000
Combined operations centre, al-Riyadh	12
SANG vehicle management programme (VMP)	357
SANG modernisation programme	893
SANG headquarters complex	156
MODA military sea ports	300
RSAF Academy (site not selected)	25[b]
Peace Hawk phase V (estimated)	300
Total	16,944
Status of projects	
Completed	572.2
Currently under construction	1,723.4
Requests for proposals	79.3
Under design	9,508.9
In planning stage	5,907.0
Proposed but not yet approved	2,036.0
Total	19,827.1[c]

Notes:
a. Projects expecetd to be completed within the next ten years.
b. Could actually reach $1 billion to $2 billion.
c. Totals differ because costs are estimated and subject to significant revision, as e.g. Royal Saudi Air Force Academy listed above.
MODA — (Saudi) Ministry of Defence and Aviation.
SANG — Saudi Arabian National Guard.
RSAF — Royal Saudi Air Force.
Source: House of Representatives Committee on International Relations, *United States Arms Policies in the Persian Gulf and Red Sea Areas: Past, Present and Future* (Washington, 1977), p. 28.

Table 7.2: US Arms Sales to Saudi Arabia[a]

Type of arms sale	1971	1972	1973	1974	1975	1976
Foreign military sales agreement	15.245	305.426	1,152.03	2,048.234	5,775.999	7,742.087
Commercial sales	20.799	3.649	5.65	18.031	20.151	92.670

	1977	1978	1979	1980	1971–80
Foreign military sales agreements	1,888.115	4,121.519	6,468.701	4,536.777	34,054.179
Commercial sales	44.050	166.278	34.631	28.985	273.944

Note: a. The dates referred to are fiscal years, and the figures are in millions of dollars.
Source: *US Security Interests in the Persian Gulf*, Report of a Staff Study Mission to the Persian Gulf, Middle East, and Horn of Africa, to the Committee on Foreign Affairs, US House of Representatives, 16 March 1981.

country in 1980, many were on military programmes. Yet the majority are not direct employees of the US defence apparatus, but ex-military personnel contracted by civilian firms. The National Guard Modernisation Programme is subcontracted to the Vinnell Corporation, General Electric and Cadillac-Gage.[20] Vinnell, which handles infantry training, is widely held to be a CIA front company.[21] Lockheed handles maintenance on the C-130 transport planes supplied to the Saudis. The Ordnance Programme has been run by the Bendix Field Engineering Corporation, and Raytheon have maintained the Hawk Air Defence System. The CIA also maintains liaison teams with various units of the General Information Department (*al-Mokhabarat al-'Ama*), the Saudi intelligence network.

Perhaps the most controversial of all the components of the US military sales programme has been the F-15 sales decision; in 1978 the US Congress authorised the sale of 60 of these jet fighters to Saudi Arabia in conjunction with the sale of other jets to Egypt and Israel.[22] As early as 1974 the Saudis had begun asking for a replacement for their F-5s and Lightnings, but the decision to ask for F-15s provoked a major conflict in the US Congress, which the Arab side finally won. The delivery of the planes was to begin in 1981, and would involve the provision of US technicians into the early 1990s, at least. Yet the F-15 decision was won at considerable cost, with the US imposing restrictions upon the Saudis. Most serious was the US requirement that the planes were not to be equipped with major offensive capabilities. The Saudis were supplied only with interceptor variety planes, with a limited range: whilst the normal 'ferry range' of an F-15 is 2,800, those supplied to al-Riyadh could fly only about one thousand miles. Since the Saudis were prohibited from stationing them at Tabuq, the airfield nearest Israel, the planes could not in theory reach that country.[23] It is these limitations which the Saudis tried to remedy in June 1980 with a request for bomb-racks, for an advanced air-to-air missile, the AIM-9L, and for airborne warning and control craft that could direct the fighters once they were in a combat situation. Subsequent Saudi requests for new fuel tanks and for KC-135 tankers that could refuel the planes in mid-air also indicated a desire to break away from the congressional limitations.

The F-15 issue highlighted what has been an underlying feature of the Saudi military procurement policy, namely the predominance of politics over military concerns. The Saudis made it clear at the time, as they did over the subsequent June 1980 request, that they would take the US response as indicative of Washington's overall attitude to the kingdom. They know as well as anyone that these planes cannot adequately assure the security of Saudi Arabia. The Israelis knew this too and therefore accepted Reagan's decision to meet part of the Saudi request. Of the 60 F-15s only 45 are actually combat planes, the rest being trainers;[24] as with the earlier jets, these fighters are virtually blind on their own, relying on ground support systems which are manned by foreign personnel. While the large figures of US arms sold are apparently comparable to those for US arms sales to Iran or Egypt, the programmes concerned are rather different in effect. The level of technical skill available in Saudi Arabia is far lower than in the other cases; thus the absorptive capacity for new weapons systems is more limited. A high percentage of the total level of US military provision is not for straight arms sales at all, but for military-related construction and infrastructure expenditure, such as the three military cities. One estimate for the mid-1970s reckoned that 50 per cent of Saudi military purchases were for construction, 28 per cent for training and only 22 per cent for arms themselves.[25]

Problems of the Military Alliance

First, the most immediate problem of the US arms sales programme is that of manpower. Neither in absolute numbers nor in technical proficiency is the Saudi population able to absorb the large supplies of equipment which the USA is eager to supply. Reports on US training programmes, although phrased in muted tones, underscore problems of unfinished training schemes, widespread absence-without-leave rates, schedule runovers and the like.[26] No figures are available to indicate how much of the Saudi air force could really be put into the air at any one time. It has proved unexpectedly difficult to implement the F-5 programme, and there are strong reasons for doubting the feasibility of the more demanding F-15 programme, once it gets under way. In 1977 it was calculated that if Saudi Arabia were to receive no more military equipment it would take six years for existing personnel to be able to use equipment already bought;[27] yet no such moratorium was imposed, and the likelihood is of continued foreign, and specifically US, military activity in Saudi Arabia for many years to come.

Second, the Saudis can calculate that this is not a situation they necessarily want to avoid: US personnel lessen the likelihood of a coup and act as some guarantee that the Israelis will not attack. (Although this is not an absolute guarantee, as the crew of the USS *Liberty* found out in June 1967.) The presence of several thousand military-related US personnel, however, is certainly also an embarrassment, as can be seen from the government's reluctance to allow the US formal base facilities. The US military presence has been somewhat more prominent than al-Riyadh allows: it was not just a symbolic flight of F-15s that was arranged during the 1979 North Yemen crisis, but also the stationing of US aerial intelligence planes. Similarly, there have been repeated reports of squadrons of US fighters, manned by over a thousand men, being positioned in Saudi Arabia and four AWACS reconnaissance planes were supplied when the Iraq–Iran War began in September 1980.[28] Yet none of this amounts to the kind of recognised base facilities that the USA has been requesting and which it seems to have acquired in Oman.

Third, the weakness of the Saudi armed forces – totalling around 60,000 in 1979[29] – is reflected not only in the country's inability to conduct military policies abroad and its reliance either on financed surrogates (North Yemeni tribesmen) or on other regional powers (the Shah's Iran going into Oman). It also necessitates the importing into Saudi Arabia of military personnel from other Third World countries, and in particular from Jordan and Pakistan. The latter is probably the largest reserve of skilled and combat-experienced troops in the Muslim world, outside Egypt, and has for some time played a growing role in providing technical service to the Saudi armed forces. But in the aftermath of the Mecca incident a more wide-ranging agreement between the two countries has been worked out, under which the Pakistanis would provide several thousand troops in return for increased Saudi military aid. Events on Pakistan's north-western frontier have naturally increased the attractiveness of such a link to both countries, yet the presence of increasing numbers of foreign forces, in addition to those from the USA involved on specific projects, may generate political problems inside Saudi society.

A Tentative Balance-sheet

Leaving aside the absolute Saudi need for oil revenues, which it could presumably satisfy from other sources, and at much lower levels of output, al-Riyadh would appear to request four things from the USA:

1. supplies of arms and personnel to protect the Saudi state;
2. assistance in its economic development programmes;

3. progress on the Arab-Israeli question;
4. an active anti-communist role in the Middle East.

The second of these has presented relatively little difficulty. The first
is somewhat restricted by internal US pressures, but is more crucially
limited by Saudi absorptive capacities. The third and the fourth are
areas of considerable Saudi disappointment. Perhaps the announcement
of the Carter Doctrine, the despatch of new US forces to Diego Garcia,
the base agreements with Oman and Kenya and the new militancy of
the Reagan Administration will go some way to allaying Saudi fears;
but since these actions have themselves in part contributed to the
revolutionary climate in the region, and since Saudi apprehensions are
in the first instance a product of the country's internal political
weaknesses, there is little that the USA can do to satisfy them in the
longer run. The US failure to make substantive progress on the Arab–
Israeli question reflects the pressures within US domestic politics and
Israeli intransigence, and there is no great likelihood of these factors
diminishing in importance in the next months or even years.

For its part, the USA can be said to have seven major requirements
of Saudi Arabia:

1. continued and guaranteed supplies of oil at levels determined not by
   Saudi income needs, but by Western levels of demand;
2. near-monopoly supply rights for US oil companies, even after
   nationalisation;
3. continued support for the dollar;
4. exertion of a moderating role in OPEC;
5. purchases of US exports, particularly in the military field;
6. an active and supportive regional role;
7. permission to station US forces.

Of these, three are relatively straightforward and seem, at the present
time, to involve no great difficulties: the preservation of a preferential
position for US companies (especially the Aramco consortium), the
support for the dollar and the purchase of US exports. On the other
hand, one US objective, namely the ability to station forces in Saudi
Arabia, seems unlikely to be satisfied. Hopes of Saudi Arabia being
able to play a moderating role inside OPEC have not been entirely
dashed, but Saudi control over that organisation has been less than the
USA in particular, or the West in general, might have hoped. The level
of oil output has remained high for some time, but there are increasing

demands from within Saudi Arabia for a lower level of output.[30] As for Saudi Arabia's regional role, it has been a mixture of success and failure from a US perspective: successful in encouraging the rightward drift of a number of countries, rather counterproductive in the cases of Somalia and North Yemen, and uncooperative in the case of the Arab–Israeli dispute. Both countries would seem to need each other, yet the closeness of their collaboration has not prevented these substantive areas of disagreement from persisting.

Do the two countries have any other options? The Americans have never relied on the Saudis to play a military role in the region: that was the function of the Shah, and US military attention is now focused upon Egypt. The only real alternative for oil supplies in the next decade or two is Mexico, but, even assuming its supplies are capable of rising to meet US requirements, there are major political problems involved. The Mexicans, who had the first social revolution in this century and successfully nationalised their oil in 1938, are jealous of their independent control of oil and not willing to produce at the rate dictated by the industrialised importers. The Saudis, on the other hand, do have other options: they could greatly reduce their oil output, to a level sufficient to meet their own development needs, and they could turn to other countries, such as France, Germany, Britain and Japan, for their arms and economic development assistance. In early 1981, for example, the Saudi authorities seemed to be warning that such a reorientation was in the offing: faced with an apparently strong supporter of Israel in the person of Ronald Reagan, and with Iraq preoccupied by its war with Iran, the Saudis used the occasion of the Islamic summit in January 1981 to present themselves as leaders of a new Third World bloc more independent of the USA. They also signalled dissatisfaction with Washington by opening talks with West Germany on the sale of Leopard II tanks to the Saudi army. If the Western Europeans are not acceptable, the Saudis could even turn for many of their requirements and for that peace of strategic mind which they so lack, to their first friend, the Soviet Union. But the price of breaking the bond with Washington that has been nurtured for nearly four decades would appear to be too high a one for the House of Saud to pay. The convenience of the relationship, for both al-Riyadh and Washington, remains.[31]

Behind the diverse requirements of the US relationship with the Saudi ruling family, there lurks the ultimate inequality of power between the two countries which could, in the midst of a political crisis, be demonstrated in the most obvious way, namely by a US invasion. If this prospect was merely an extremist rumour in the mid-1970s, it has become somewhat more realistic in the light of the political tensions which arose within Saudi Arabia in the late 1970s and of a more overt US preparation for such an action. Were this to occur it would not only jeopardise the forty-year liaison between Washington and the House of Saud, but it might also hasten the break-up of that heterogeneous country which the Saudi conquerors created in the 1920s. This ultimate assertion of US power would ensure the energy supplies of the industrialised West, but at the possible price of bringing about the disintegration of Saudi Arabia itself.

Notes

1. A detailed study of this period is given in Barry Rubin, *The Great Powers in the Middle East 1941–1947* (Frank Cass, London, 1980), pp. 34–72. Rubin shows that, whilst the British had no objection to the US playing a larger role, US oil-company officials urged an active exclusion policy upon the US government. Other accounts can be found in Joe Stork, *Middle East Oil and the Energy Crisis* (Monthly Review Press, New York, 1975), pp. 30–4; Anthony Sampson, *The Seven Sisters* (Hodder and Stoughton, London, 1975), ch. 5; Gabriel Kolko, *The Politics of War* (Weidenfeld and Nicolson, London, 1969), pp. 294–313.

2. Stork, in *Middle East Oil*, pp. 222f, shows how in practice the embargo amounted to far less than was publicly claimed on both sides.

3. Abdul Kasim Mansur, 'The American Threat to Saudi Arabia', *Armed Forces Journal International* (September 1980); Anon, 'A Gulf of Anxiety', *Newsweek* (8 January 1979).

4. *International Herald Tribune* (18 June 1980). During the closing stages of the 1980 presidential campaign, President Carter indicated that he would refuse the Saudi request for additional F-15 equipment. This appeared to be a means of trying to increase his following amongst Jewish voters, and did not bind the subsequently elected Reagan Administration.

5. Abdul Kasim Mansur, 'American Threat to Saudi Arabia'; Michael Klare, 'Is Exxon Worth Dying For?' *The Progressive* (July 1980).

6. Robert Engler, *The Politics of Oil* (Aldine, Chicago, 1961), p. 180.

7. Kolko, *Politics of War*, pp. 295–6; Rubin, *Great Powers in the Middle East*, p. 39.

8. Adeed Dawisha, *Saudi Arabia's Search for Security* (International Institute for Strategic Studies, London, 1979), p. 28.

9. Dawisha, *Saudi Arabia's Search for Security; International Herald Tribune*, Saudi Arabia Supplement, February 1980. Critical overviews of Saudi–US relations are contained in Abdul Kasim Mansur, 'American Threat to Saudi Arabia' and Joe Stork, 'Saudi Oil and the US', MERIP Report, no. 91 (October 1980).

10. Dawisha, in *Saudi Arabia's Search for Security*, gives a detailed account of Saudi foreign policy implementation in this area.

11. US Senate Subcommittee on Multinational Corporations, *Multinational Corporations and US Foreign Policy* (Washington, 1976), pt 14, pp. 430–4.

12. O'Connor, *World Crisis in Oil* (Allen and Unwin, London, 1962), p. 327. A potential source of difficulty in this regard arose when, under the Carter Administration, the US State Department began issuing its annual reports on

human rights. But these reports tended to rely on the reports sent to Washington by the US Embassies in the countries concerned, and the analysis of Saudi Arabia was of an appropriately indulgent kind. The 1981 report, for example, repeated conventional claims about the virtues of the *majlis* system of consultation, and about the absence of pre-publication censorship in the country. (*Country Reports on Human Rights Practices*, Report to the Committee on Foreign Relations US Senate, and Committee on Foreign Affairs US House of Representatives by the Department of State, 2 February 1981, pp. 1083–9.) It did, however, report on the absence of political parties and the ban on trades unions.

13. Engler, *The Politics of Oil*, p. 254.

14. US House of Representatives Committee on International Relations, *Proposed Aircraft Sales to Israel, Egypt and Saudi Arabia* (Washington, 1978), p. 157.

15. For discussion of US–Saudi controversy on this score, and the involvement of members of the royal family in contentious business dealings, see *International Herald Tribune* (24 April 1980), and Stork, 'Saudi Oil and the US'.

16. US House of Representatives Subcommittee on the Near East and South Asia, *New Perspectives on the Persian Gulf* (Washington, 1973), p. 16; and House of Representatives Committee on International Relations, *United States Arms Policies in the Persian Gulf and Red Sea Areas: Past, Present, and Future* (Washington, 1977), pp. 17–49. Abdul Kasim Mansur, 'American Threat to Saudi Arabia' also surveys US–Saudi military relations.

17. House of Representatives, *New Perspectives*, p. 16.

18. Anthony Sampson, *The Arms Bazaar* (Hodder and Stoughton, London, 1977), pp. 160–2.

19. House of Representatives, *United States Arms Policies*, p. 35.

20. Ibid., p. 31.

21. *Washington Post* (17 September 1975).

22. For background documentation on the F-15 sale see note 14 above. The F-15 sale agreement was hailed in the Middle East and by the Arab–American lobby as 'an Arab victory'. This was, however, a specious claim. First, it merely strengthened the hand of *some* Arabs, namely those in al-Riyadh, against that of *others*, such as those in Aden, who disagreed with Saudi policies and who were forced to take new measures to protect themselves against this new threat. Secondly, it was not a sign of a substantive change in US policy on the Palestine issue, so much as a sop to Arab opinion. It produced the impression of a shift, whilst none had in fact taken place. Since the same congressional hearings authorised new sales to Israel the sale of F-15s to Saudi Arabia did not alter the military balance between the two sides.

23. J. Taylor (ed.), *Jane's All the World's Fighting Aircraft 1979–1980* (Macdonald, London, 1980), pp. 383–4, gives the 'ferry range', i.e. the distance it can fly *in toto*, as 2,878 miles. But the F-15s supplied to Saudi Arabia had a substantially lower range and could only reach targets around 450 miles away before returning to base; i.e. their 'ferry range' must have been in the region of 1,000 miles (*International Herald Tribune*, 18 June 1980). Hence the Saudi request for new fuel facilities in 1980 was designed merely to give their planes the conventional flying capacity.

24. Ibid., pp. 383–4.

25. House of Representatives, *United States Arms Policies*, p. 27.

26. Ibid., p. 22.

27. Ibid., p. 39.

28. *International Herald Tribune* (13 October 1980), for 1979 and 1980 AWACS missions.

29. International Institute for Strategic Studies, *The Military Balance 1979–1980*, (IISS, London, 1980), p. 44. This figure includes 20,000 National Guards,

amongst whom absence-without-leave rates of up to 50 per cent or more are believed to obtain.

30. For a forceful statement of the 'low-production' case see Hayyan Ibn Bayyan, 'Open Letter to Saudi Arabia', *The Nation* (New York) (4 April 1981). He suggests a reduction of Saudi output to 4 million barrels a day, over five years.

31. The consequences of the Iranian Revolution for US–Saudi relations are too recent to be fully discernible at the time of writing. Whilst the US raid in April 1980 to rescue the hostages was, as noted, condemned by Saudi Arabia, the Saudis showed little sympathy for the Iranian regime and took advantage of the Iranian challenge to permit an increase in the US military presence inside Saudi Arabia (*The Economist*, 13 October 1979). In the Iran–Iraq War that began in September 1980 they supported Iraq, providing it with substantial loans, but also insisted that the US despatch aerial reconnaissance planes immediately when hostilities broke out (*International Herald Tribune*, 13 October 1980). The Saudis must, however, have been alarmed at the eventual outcome of the US–Iranian dispute over Iranian assets frozen in the USA which demonstrated how successful the US banks and government could be in a combined attempt to defeat a Third World country's political challenge by seizing its assets. The possibility of seriously using Saudi financial power against the West in a future dispute about Palestine would therefore appear to have receded.

8 ASPECTS OF SAUDI ARABIA'S RELATIONS WITH OTHER GULF STATES[1]

John Duke Anthony

Introduction

Public commentary in the past decade over expanding Great Power interest and involvement in the Gulf has often laid greater emphasis on Iran's role in this region than on those of Saudi Arabia and the other littoral states. One of the most far-reaching consequences of the October 1973 war, however, has been a fundamental shift in the focus away from Iran and toward the Arab actors in the region. A principal reason for the change was the Arab oil embargo, together with the associated production cutbacks and the subsequent steep rise in petroleum prices. Owing to these factors, plus the concomitant rapid accumulation of monetary wealth by Saudi Arabia and several other countries, greater attention has been paid to the Arab states in the Gulf.

There should be little surprise at the increasing attention given to the Arab states of the Gulf: seven of the eight littoral states are Arab (counting the seven members of the United Arab Emirates as a single state). Moreover, throughout this period it has been primarily Saudi Arabia and its immediate neighbours, not Iran, who have produced and exported most of the area's oil, have possessed the overwhelming majority of its petroleum reserves, have controlled the bulk of its impressive financial holdings, have played the most important roles within OPEC on matters pertaining to the price of oil, and have exercised a determining influence inside OAPEC on questions pertaining to industrialisation and regional economic co-operation.

An analysis of Saudi Arabia's relations with other Gulf states requires a clear understanding of the regional dynamics of the area. This is essential to any assessment of Saudi Arabia's future role in Gulf and international politics. Such an understanding, moreover, is crucial not only to assessing the kinds of contributions which Saudi Arabia and its neighbours might make towards the goal of regional security. Equally, it is essential to an appreciation of the context in which both foreign and local interests in the area can be pursued.

This paper examines three questions bearing on the local and regional aims and concerns of Saudi Arabia and the other Gulf states

148

and the way that these questions shape relations both amongst the kingdom and its neighbours, on the one hand, and between them and outside powers, on the other. The first concerns the nature of political interaction (at the governmental level) among these states. The second focuses on the continuing contest between conservative and radical forces in the area. The third examines the ongoing connection between these states and the Arab—Israeli conflict.

General Political Interaction among Gulf State Governments

In general, political interaction between and among the kingdom and its neighbours has been and remains a complex mixture of historical, economic and political competition and co-operation — a pattern which has been critically affected by dynastic, national and territorial issues, as also on occasion by ethnic, sectarian and tribal sentiments. With the arrival of a succession of foreign powers in the Gulf, the conflict side of the interaction subsided but did not disappear. Indeed, even during and after the long period of British domination in territories adjacent to Saudi Arabia, elements of conflict based on the above-mentioned factors continued to affect the political processes of the area.

In contrast to the relative lack of constraints operating on Iran and Iraq during the early and middle years of this century, any practical significant role for the kingdom of Saudi Arabia in the Gulf region, beyond the extension of monetary and other forms of support to counter radical trends in the area, was effectively foreclosed until the 1970s. The reason for this state of affairs stemmed less from the absence or presence of the requisite Saudi diplomatic, administrative or military capabilities for such a role than from constitutional and structural considerations. In short, the long-standing special treaty relationships between Great Britain and most of the smaller Gulf states constituted an imposing limitation. In practice, this meant that the defence and foreign affairs responsibilities for ten of the states lying along the eastern Saudi Arabian periphery from Bahrain to Muscat were, for the most part, conceptualised and administered by London instead of the ten states themselves, or, for that matter, by al-Riyadh, Baghdad, Kuwait or Tehran.

In the east Arabian reaches of the Gulf, only in Abu Dhabi, and to a lesser extent in Oman, did the Saudis extend themselves externally to a significant degree before the 1970s. Even then, however, the kingdom was not engaged in promoting its interests in the areas situated along the shores of the maritime Gulf. Rather, its concern lay in pressing claims to territories situated along caravan routes that led to certain oasis regions which, at the time, were thought to contain promising petroleum deposits. Problems arose from the fact that the areas in question lay deep within territories also claimed by Abu Dhabi and Oman. As is well known, the kingdom's endeavours to expand its eastern frontiers were largely unsuccessful. A far-reaching consequence of the episode itself, however, was the setback it dealt Saudi Arabia's interest in forging good relations with its neighbours. In the case in question, the result was to make it much more difficult for the kingdom to build up a relationship of trust and confidence with two other Gulf states which, in time, would themselves become important actors in Gulf affairs.

The strained feelings that accompanied the mutual feelings of suspicion and distrust engendered by these and other disagreements between Saudi Arabia and a number of its eastern neighbours were to last far longer than might have been anticipated. Indeed, from the time of the forced eviction in 1955 by British troops of a Saudi police detachment from Abu Dhabi's eastern province (from where the detachment had also encroached on the writ of the Omani Sultan in nearby territories), it was to take a full sixteen years before events would permit the normalisation of relations between the kingdom and the Sultanate of Oman. This proved true despite the fact that during six of these years (1965–71) a guerrilla war was being waged in Oman that sought to overthrow not only the regime in Muscat but, eventually, others in the region as well. And it was to take nearly twenty years before the border dispute with fellow OPEC and OAPEC member Abu Dhabi was resolved. Only then did it become possible to establish diplomatic relations and a more institutionalised means of pursuing the range of regional interests shared between the kingdom and the seven-member United Arab Emirates.

The source of much of the interaction between Saudi Arabia and its neighbours in the Gulf, to be sure, has been a quest for control of the region's limited economic resources. Prior to the discovery of petroleum, various groups within the area struggled with one another incessantly over such survival-related issues as control of maritime and overland trade, offshore fishing and pearling rights, access to grazing lands for their flocks and control over strategic water holes. In conjunction with these encounters, and continuing up to the present day, there have been other kinds of contests, such as those which have often occurred within and among the ruling elites of these states over questions of territory, commercial pre-eminence, military prowess and dynastic leadership.

The discovery of oil, and the subsequent realisation that millions (nowadays often billions) of dollars were at stake, added a new and vastly different dimension to these cleavages. While not completely superseding the traditional forms of competition, the disputes now have an increased significance both within the Gulf itself and in the eyes of the outside world. This significance — which brings in its wake the meddling of every foreign interest group conceivable — is likely to remain valid as long as the issues contested remain unsettled.

A major component of the dynamics of the relationships between Saudi Arabia and the other Gulf states, then, has long derived from their competing claims to disputed territory. The most important among such disputes that remain — most of which have involved outside powers in support of one or more of the parties to the conflict — are the following.

(i) Saudi Arabia and Kuwait over their maritime boundary;

(ii) Saudi Arabia and Southern Yemen over the lengthy, undemarcated boundary between them and specifically in the al-Wadi'a area where armed clashes (and the capture and subsequent exchange of prisoners by both sides) have occurred;

(iii) Saudi Arabia and Oman over the waterhole of Umm Zamul and surrounding territory in the undemarcated border area covering the northernmost reaches of the Rub'al-Khali desert;

(iv) Saudi Arabia and Egypt over the ultimate disposition of the island of Sanafir in the Straits of Tiran which, previously under Egyptian suzerainty, fell to Israeli control in the June 1967 war but is supposed to revert to Egyptian control under the Camp David Accords of 1979, although sovereignty over Sanafir has long been claimed by the kingdom;

(v) Iraq and Iran over the exact location in the Shatt al-Arab of their common maritime frontier, a dispute which the world was informed had been 'settled' when the late Shah was still in power by the terms of the March 1975 Algiers Accord, the provisions of which were declared null and void by Iraqi President Saddam Husayn in September 1980;

(vi) Iraq and Syria over control and use of the Euphrates river;

(vii) Iraq and Kuwait over their common frontier and the question of control over Warbah and Bubiyan, two strategic islands lying in their offshore waters;

(viii) Bahrain and Qatar over the Hawar Islands group, located in the
Bay of Salwa, and over the village of Zubarah on the west coast
of the Qatar peninsula;
 (ix) the United Arab Emirates (on behalf of Ras al-Khaimah and
Sharjah) and Iran over the Greater and Lesser Tunbs islands and
the island of Abu Musa;
  (x) Sharjah, Ajman, Umm al-Qawain and Iran over offshore waters in
which petroleum was discovered in 1972, near Abu Musa Island;
 (xi) Sharjah and Fujairah over their respective land boundaries, a
dispute which re-erupted in June 1972 and resulted in the death
of some two dozen Sharjan and Fujairan tribesmen and, as the
1980s began, still necessitated the intermediating presence of a
United Arab Emirates Defence Force battalion;
(xii) Dubai and Sharjah over territory being considered for commercial
development along the border between them;
(xiii) Ras al-Khaimah and Sharjah over a valley area situated in
disputed territory between them which is believed to contain
potentially lucrative deposits of phosphate;
(xiv) Ras al-Khaimah and Oman over their respective land and offshore
boundaries on the Musandam peninsula.

In addition, there are other territorial disputes that are less well known
but, like those cited above, have the potential to re-erupt and alter the
future regional balance of power.

Territorial disputes, formerly centred on issues of land and water
usage in and between states with sizeable bedouin populations, are
nowadays more frequently centred on questions of sovereignty over
strategic island and border areas. The pattern of petroleum discoveries
and Western legalistic notions pertaining to concessions and national
boundaries have been the principal factors in this shift in focus. In
areas adjacent to the eastern reaches of Saudi Arabia, Great Britain in
the 1950s attempted to resolve such boundary disputes as were then
preventing the granting of oil concessions and drilling operations in the
seven states which were long known as the Trucial States but which
now comprise the United Arab Emirates (UAE). British officials
proposed final resolutions for some two dozen of the nearly three
dozen cases pressing at the time, most of which were accepted by the
parties involved. To this day, however, a dozen or more conflicting
claims to land boundaries in the UAE, in addition to disputed claims to
half a dozen offshore boundaries among these states plus the other
Arab Gulf states, and, as noted, between some of them and Iran, remain
outstanding.

On the other hand, it is important to note that substantial progress has been achieved in the past decade in close to a dozen offshore disputes, most of which were resolved in conformity with the principle of the median line. Some of the settled disputes, as for example in establishing the maritime boundaries and the sharing of offshore oil revenues between Saudi Arabia and Bahrain and between Abu Dhabi and Qatar, were resolved with a minimum of difficulty.

By contrast, the question of sovereignty over Abu Musa island, which involves a number of similar legal issues, has not been so easily managed. In the early 1980s that dispute, the handling of which contributed directly to the assassination of the Ruler of Sharjah in 1972, was no nearer to *de jure* resolution than in the late 1960s, when Britain and other countries were engaged in a concentrated effort to effect its resolution. But in that case, unlike most of the other disputes, there have been the additionally complicating factors of religious differences (that is Sunni v. Shi'a) and competing nationalisms (for example Iraq plus Ras al-Khaimah and Sharjah *cum* UAE, *inter alios* v. Iran). Rendering the dispute still more intractible in terms of regional security concerns is the geopolitical significance which many have attributed to both Abu Musa and the Tunbs islands and a putative strategic role accruing to whoever controls these islands. This is due to the islands being located near the route which oil tankers and most other maritime traffic uses *en route* to and from the Straits of Hormuz at the head of the Gulf.

Dynastic Competition

A second category of political interaction concerning Saudi Arabia and the other conservative Gulf states centres on dynastic rivalries. These rivalries occur both within and among the area's twelve ruling families. Popularity contests and the non-violent jostling for position within a given dynastic pecking order (such as those with which much of the Western media is preoccupied) are not the object of our concern here. Indeed, such competition – most of which is natural given the size (for example 7,000 members in Saudi Arabia) of some of the dynasties and by all accounts is conducted almost altogether along peaceful lines – has its positive as well as negative features. In any case, in no instance to date has the phenomenon been a matter of concern comparable in terms of the magnitude or gravity of its impact on regional and domestic political dynamics as the kinds of manoeuvres that have actually resulted in the forceful displacement of one Arabian ruler by another. Such displacements can have far-reaching implications for relations among Arab Gulf states.

The most recent intradynastic challenge occurring in a state immediately adjacent to Saudi Arabia took place in Qatar in January 1972, when the emirate's then Deputy Ruler and Heir Apparent, Shaikh Khalifa bin Hamad Al Thani, ousted his cousin, Shaikh Ahmad bin Ali, and seized the rulership for himself. In this instance, Saudi relations with Qatar, which had been exceptionally close under Shaikh Ahmad, managed to remain unimpaired. This was not the case, however, with Qatar–Dubai relations. Indeed, the previously strong ties between these two states – due in large measure to Shaikh Ahmad's marriage to the daughter of the ruler of Dubai and a host of interlocking relationships which followed as a consequence – underwent a prolonged period of estrangement. This estrangement was to last in some manner until the death of the former Qatari head of state in 1979 in Dubai, where he had been granted asylum following his ousting from Qatar.

Other such events can be recounted. In July 1970, for example, Sultan Qabus, thirteenth member of the Al Bu Said dynasty to serve as ruler of Oman, came to power following a palace coup in which he replaced his father, Sultan Said bin Taymur (ruled 1932–70). In Abu Dhabi in 1966, Shaikh Zayid bin Sultan of the Al Nahyan overthrew his ruling brother, Shaikh Shakhbut (ruled 1928–66). In the case of Oman, Saudi Arabia decided not to embrace the new ruler, Sultan Qabus, immediately upon his accession to power even though he was desirous of Saudi recognition. The reason for this was the kingdom's long-standing support for a different, ostensibly more religiously-oriented, group of Omanis who had opposed the former Sultan. The political asylum which Saudi Arabia had extended to the opposition grouping, combined with traditional Arabian peninsula notions of civility (in this case to the asylees) served to forestall for a year and a half any Saudi move towards establishing closer relations with the new Sultan. After relations were established, however, Saudi aid to the insurgency-ridden Sultanate began to flow. A comparable resolution was not forthcoming, however, in the aftermath of the 1966 change in the rulership of Abu Dhabi. There, the new ruler, Shaikh Zayid, like his Omani counterpart four years later, was also anxious for the Saudi blessing. In contrast to Sultan Qabus, however, Zayid was not so eager for recognition by al-Riyadh as to yield on certain matters in dispute between Abu Dhabi and Saudi Arabia, and nearly a decade passed before the issues in contention between these two states were reconciled.

While the dispute between Saudi Arabia and Abu Dhabi was primarily over territory, it was also the outgrowth of a clash between the strong personalities of two men: Shaikh Zayid and King Faisal. For Zayid, the heart of the contested area had always been a very special oasis. It had long been the centre of the emirate's eastern province where, at the village of al-'Ayn, he spent most of his formative years prior to becoming ruler. Until well into the 1970s, it had also remained a major source of much of the capital's water supply, even though it was 90 miles away. For Faisal, equally, the dispute over the area was of special significance. To him it was an issue of pride and honour, a reminder of past Wahhabi glories, and, during his own lifetime, of a humiliating defeat inflicted by Zayid and the British when the Trucial Oman Scouts drove Saudi forces from the area in 1955.

By the mid-1970s, neither Saudi Arabia nor Abu Dhabi was any longer considering a possible confrontation over the areas in dispute. Both states increasingly shared an overriding interest in the perpetuation of traditional rule in the area and in the establishment of a UAE capable of defending itself against external threats. Accordingly, in a move widely interpreted as a sincere effort to end the conflict, high officials from both states agreed on 29 July 1974 to a formula whereby the issues in dispute between them were resolved peacefully.

According to the agreed formula, the two states acknowledged in principle that Abu Dhabi sovereignty would be recognised over six of the villages in the so-called 'Buraimi Oasis' region previously claimed by Saudi Arabia; that the territory which includes the rich Zararah (Shaybah) oil field previously in dispute would be divided between them, and that Saudi Arabia would obtain an outlet to the Gulf through Abu Dhabi in the Khawr al-'Udayd area.[2] The ratification of the accord, as noted earlier, paved the way for the establishment of diplomatic relations between these two states and facilitated what had hitherto been a rather unorthodox means of co-ordination of joint policies towards such questions as oil and regional security. In addition, the ending of the dispute removed the last barrier delaying completion of construction on the road network linking Abu Dhabi and the other UAE states to the northern end of the Gulf.

In Saudi Arabia, the replacement of one ruler by another in March 1975, when King Faisal was assassinated, was of a different nature than the cases mentioned above, and as such had little significance for relations with other Gulf states. In this case the assassin, although a member of the ruling Al Saud household, is acknowledged by both the Saudis themselves and outside observers to have acted alone, with the overriding goal in this instance being the assassin's intent to settle a personal grievance against the King. By all accounts, the succession to the rulership of the incumbent King Khalid (the late King's younger brother and since 1965 his Heir Apparent) took place without incident and in strict accordance with a procedure agreed to a decade earlier by the dynasty and its key allies within the kingdom's elite structure.

Throughout much of the 1970s, intra-dynastic competition among leading ruling family personalities figured predominantly in the political dynamics of Saudi Arabia, Kuwait, Qatar, and most of the seven UAE states. In the first three states, the selection of Heir Apparent — Fahd Al Saud in Saudi Arabia, Saad Al Sabah in Kuwait and Hamad Al Thani in Qatar — was determined in 1975, 1977 and 1978 respectively. As the 1980s began, however, most of the outsiders and many insiders viewed such matters in the case of Oman and the UAE with much less certainty.

Intra-regional dynastic tensions have expressed themselves on occasion as well, the issue in dispute often being irredentist in nature. An example of this was the tense relationship between Saudi Arabia and Iraq when the former country's King Abd al-Aziz and the latter's King Abdallah were alive. Such tensions have involved competition between individual rulers for power and prestige in the area. Differences on policy issues, giving expression to a quest for regional pre-eminence — however muted and good-natured the competition may be on the surface — have occurred frequently between Saudi Arabia and Kuwait. Kuwait has pursued a foreign policy quite different from Saudi Arabia's on various matters of regional importance. To cite but four cases in point: the question of maintaining diplomatic relations with the Soviet Union, the pricing and production of OPEC oil, the lending of various kinds of support to the government of the People's Democratic Republic of Yemen (PDRY), and the relative freedom of expression within Kuwait permitted to such militantly radical groups as the leftist-oriented Arab Nationalist Movement.

Inter-dynastic competition was much less evident in the early 1980s than during the mid to late 1970s when, fostered by the infrastructural boom in Saudi Arabia and a number of other Gulf states, the pheno-menon was at its zenith. Dynastics came to seek their own aggrandise-ment in the infrastructural development of their states. Variants of this dimension of regional political dynamics were instrumental in Bahrain,

Qatar and the United Arab Emirates achieving independence separately in 1971 — much to the chagrin of Saudi Arabia and Kuwait which had laboured long and hard to promote a nine-state federation, instead of the seven-state UAE which did emerge. To some extent the same dynamics have continued to influence the degree to which these and other Gulf states have been able to co-operate with one another in such matters of mutual concern as regional security and economic integration. Saudi Arabia appears increasingly to be opting out of dynastic competition in infrastructural development. As but one indication of its growing willingness to co-operate in these areas, the Saudi government, in the spring of 1980, cancelled its plans to build an aluminium smelter in order not to compete with the already existing smelters in Bahrain and Dubai. In this context, the kingdom, as a principal regional power, has been confronted with no easy task in its efforts to forge a coherent and cohesive set of policies towards its neighbours, not only in pursuit of its own national interests but in the context of regional concerns as well.

The competition between Abu Dhabi and Dubai, at war with one another as recently as 1948, is historically rooted in the fact that the ruling family of the latter seceded from Abu Dhabi in the early nineteenth century and settled in Dubai. The heads of these two states, Shaikh Zayid of Abu Dhabi and Shaikh Rashid of Dubai, compete with each other for influence in the UAE, in which they hold the posts of President and Vice-President/Prime Minister, respectively. The competition between neighbouring Qatar and Bahrain, which lies behind the failure to demarcate the borders between the two countries, is founded on the still outstanding claim of the ruling family of Bahrain to sovereignty over portions of Qatar, territory it once controlled, and, more recently, in their different attitudes towards regional political integration in the Gulf. The heads of many of the smaller emirates have had and continue to have similar, though less dramatic, disagreements among themselves and with Iran and Oman.

Saudi Arabia, being ruled by a family that traces its own roots back at least 500 years, if not longer, is on familiar ground when it encounters the genealogical dimension of status and prestige among its neighbours. Saudi policy in the Gulf area, therefore, in seeking to ensure regional stability and create co-operative relations among the Gulf states, has had to take account of such factors as ancestral lineage as an additional aspect of inter-Gulf state relations. The ruling families of Sharjah, Ras al-Khaimah and Bahrain, for example, have been accused of putting on airs, as it were, in considering themselves of more noble pedigree than some of their neighbours. In the case of Bahrain, the aristocratic self-perception of certain members of its ruling family (the Al Khalifa) contributed to the island state's reluctance, and ultimately its refusal, to enter into an equal political relationship with the neighbouring dynasty (the Al Thani) of Qatar during the negotiations between 1968 and 1971 for a nine-state federation in the Gulf. The continuing legacy of this facet of the historical relationship between Bahrain and Qatar diminishes the likelihood of their combining to form the kind of political union that Saudi Arabia and Kuwait, only a decade ago, worked so diligently to achieve. Ras al-Khaimah's relationship with other Gulf states has also been subject to influences stemming from genealogy. Shaikh Saqr of Ras al-Khaimah has long bridled at having to occupy a subordinate niche to the rulers of Abu Dhabi and Dubai in the government of the UAE. Despite being the beneficiary of substantial amounts of Saudi economic assistance, he has been unable to turn this favoured position into advantage for his emirate inside the UAE.

The foregoing examples of the manner in which Saudi Arabia and a number of its neighbours relate to one another illuminate the uneasy equilibrium which persists between different forces in the area. These forces, whether in the form of conflicting territorial claims or inter- and intra-dynastic competition, testify to the uniqueness of the kingdom and its neighbours in terms of international relations, and lie at the root of how these states relate to one another politically. At the same time, these forces do not exist in isolation. Rather, their manifestation usually occurs alongside other phenomena, including those associated with the ongoing contest between revolutionary and traditional forces in the region.

The Radical–Conservative Contest

Whether the vantage point has been al-Riyadh, Baghdad, Muscat or one of the emirates of eastern Arabia, a major dimension of the competition between radical and conservative forces in the area has been the asymmetry of the contest – until the Iranian Revolution. For example, until 1979 only one state, Iraq, could be classified as 'radical' in terms of its political values and orientation toward the rest. The other Arab Gulf states were 'conservative' or 'moderate' states. To this day these polities are ruled by dynasts whose foreign policies and official attitudes have by and large been quite friendly not only to Western countries, but to the evolutionary forces of political and socio-economic change operating in the Gulf, the Middle East and elsewhere. With Saudi Arabia at the forefront, the internal political and legal systems of the Gulf's conservative Arab states continue to leave little room for manoeuvre to the as-yet small minority of the citizenry and non-national residents who harbour radical or revolutionary sentiments. To be sure, the revolution in Iran and the seizure of the Grand Mosque in Mecca by religious fanatics in 1979 has served to heighten the anxieties of all the Gulf regimes. In the aftermath of these and other events, the rulers have gone to some length to indicate their determination to anticipate and accommodate as many legitimate demands for change and/or conservation as possible. Their goal is to provide a means of preventing extremist groups from gaining − or, where this has already occurred, from retaining − a foothold of any significance in the area.

Among the Gulf's Arab actors, one of the most important points to underscore is the striking numerical imbalance in the ratio of radical to conservative states. Indeed, this fact has long been such an obvious constant in the interplay of regional forces that it is often discounted by outsiders, especially among many strategists and economists who view the area in impersonal terms. Yet in practice its implications pose a formidable array of obstacles to the area's actual and would-be dissidents. Iraq's geographic and ideological isolation are but two factors which place constraints on its capacity − not to mention its interest or willingness − to foment internal unrest in the other Arab states of the Gulf. Another is the fact that of the 'overseas Iraqis' − individuals whose numbers in these states are tinier than miniscule − few have demonstrated an interest or inclination to become involved in an effort to topple the area's traditional regimes.

Saudi Arabia, Kuwait and Iran all have, of course, lengthy borders with Iraq. This, however, has not enhanced significantly Iraq's opportunities to foment internal dissidence in these states or even to contribute substantially to forces seeking to foster instability in those countries' border regions. On the contrary, throughout most of the 1970s, Iraqi subversive activities were largely offset by Iran's capacity − as, for example, through the assistance it lent the autonomy-minded Kurds in the northern part of the country − for creating a wide range of problems for the Iraqi government. Of no small concern to the Iraqi government following the overthrow of the Shah of Iran in 1979 was the powerful attraction of Ayatollah Rouhollah Khomeini and other Iranian revolutionary leaders to the politically disgruntled Shi'a Muslims in Iraq.

In the case of Saudi Arabia, although Iraq shares an extensive boundary with that country, territorial ambitions *vis-à-vis* the kingdom have not played a major role in the Baghdad regime's calculations of how best to enhance the pursuit of Iraqi interests in the region. Furthermore, any putative Iraqi desires to subvert the Saudi regime would be constrained, at least in part, by the Baathist government's limited capacity to instigate or influence political, social or economic disequilibrium inside the kingdom. The real deterrent to this capacity has not been Iraq's limited abilities to foment disequilibrium in Saudi Arabia so much as it has been the capacity of the Saudi government, to date, to meet the demands of its domestic constituency.

To be sure, in common with most of the rest of the world, elements of domestic dissatisfaction in Saudi Arabia, as in neighbouring traditional states, do exist. In terms of composition, they cut across the social and political spectra and include portions of the newly educated, the military, the tribes, regional ('nationalist') groups such as the Front for the Liberation of the Hijaz and various members of the ruling House of Saud. Even so, and notwithstanding the November 1979 seizure of the Grand Mosque in Mecca by rightist radicals, all of these groups have been relatively small in numbers and poorly organised. More importantly, they have been heavily outweighed by a combination of conservative and moderate reformist forces which, on balance, favour a policy of working for such changes as are necessary from within the existing political, social and economic structure.

In the case of Kuwait, the situation is substantially different. Indeed, Kuwait's capacity to deter a putatively expansionist Iraq rests not so much on religious or military factors — it is doubtful, for example, whether Kuwait's armed forces by themselves could successfully resist an Iraqi invasion — as on considerations of a political and diplomatic nature. To wit: not a single Arab dynasty, and least of all the House of Saud, would be expected to support or condone any hypothetical or actual Iraqi attempt to violate Kuwaiti territory. The record on this to date has been clear — Iraq has stood completely alone in its attempts to occupy Kuwaiti border outposts and in its demands for control over the Kuwaiti islands of Warbah and Bubiyan, in exchange for recognition of Kuwait's sovereignty.

Of related significance during the 1970s was the fact that Kuwait received both official and private assurances of support from Saudi Arabia and other nearby Arab states. An even greater deterrent was the support it received from monarchical Iran, the one country which, up until the last year or so of the Shah's rule, had the means, the will and the tacit approval of all the other Gulf states to do whatever necessary to contain Iraqi expansionism. As a further deterrent, the mutual defence clause of the 1961 Britain–Kuwait Treaty, invoked when Iraq attempted to seize control of Kuwait in 1961, remained intact.

Iraq, in short, despite its perceived role as a bastion of anti-monarchical sentiment and revolutionary socialism in the area, has all along been far more isolated, both militarily and politically, than many foreign analysts and policy makers, especially Americans, have been prone to acknowledge. Compounding Iraq's isolation has been the fact that, from the beginning, the radical secularist ideology espoused by the Baathist leadership in Baghdad has been rejected *in toto* by all the other Gulf states, Arab as well as Iranian.

In addition to the external limitation discussed above, any would-be activist role for the Baghdad regime in an effort to spread its brand of Baathist radicalism to Saudi Arabia and the other Gulf states remains inhibited, at least in part, by the distraction of Iraq's ongoing ideological cleavage with the rival Baathist Party in Syria. On more than one occasion various manifestations of this dispute have had repercussions in the other Arab Gulf states, causing substantial embarrassment to Iraq. For example, in October 1977 UAE Minister of State for Foreign Affairs Sayf Ghobash – widely recognised as one of the brightest and most talented government officials in the area – was accidentally assassinated at Abu Dhabi International Airport. At the time of the incident, Ghobash was seeing off Syrian Foreign Minister Abd al-Halim Khaddam who, according to the gunman, was the intended victim. Under interrogation, the latter admitted to having acted upon orders from Baghdad.

Until Camp David, then, and more specifically prior to 'Camp Baghdad' in 1979, Iraq's role was severely circumscribed owing to reasons of geography, politics, ideology and demography. In practice, the regime's policies were far more cautious and conservative than many observers of developments in the Gulf were aware. During the period in which the Shah of Iran was still in power and it was by no means certain that Egypt would galvanise Arab reaction by signing a separate peace treaty with Israel, Iraq's role was a relatively modest one. In general, Iraq was limited to occupying its traditional position as a cultural pole for many Arab students from the area who enrolled in its universities; to holding the sites of several religious shrines venerated by the area's Shi'a Muslims; to giving support (often together with Iran) inside OPEC for higher oil prices; to pursuing its commercial ties, mainly with Kuwait and Bahrain; and to the training and other forms of support it had extended over the years to radical groups operating in the Gulf. Following the March 1975 agreement – the 'Algiers Accord' – between Iraq and Iran, the latter facet of Iraqi influence ceased to be operative. Opportunities for Iraq to encourage subversion in the area thereafter continued to exist, to be sure, but the country's revolutionary potential was none the less no longer a volatile issue (to the extent that it ever was) with which either the rulers or the key administrative elites in Saudi Arabia, Kuwait, Oman and the nine emirates were preoccupied. On the contrary, as the 1980s began, most of the leaders of the latter states drew solace from the close monitoring of former Iraqi-sponsored radicals by their armed forces, intelligence and internal security personnel and the nearly region-wide view that even had Camp David and the fall of the Shah not transpired, there appeared to be little prospect of a revolutionary challenge emanating from Iraq in the then foreseeable future.

There was, moreover, evidence that Iraq had been redefining its relationships with all the Arab Gulf states for quite some time. Some, no doubt, remained suspicious of the Iraqi government's ultimate intentions towards Saudi Arabia and the other Gulf states, but many of these sceptics conceded that the redefinition had at least had a salutary effect on the cause of enhancing the prospects for increased co-operation between Iraq and other Gulf states on regional matters pertaining to security. In this regard, the Baghdad regime's attitudes and policies had moved closer to those of Saudi Arabia than most analysts would have imagined or predicted possible half a decade earlier.

Officials of the still highly secular and socialist-oriented regime held to the view that Iraq had moved inside the so-called 'arc of crisis'. In so doing, the regime renounced, in effect, its previous role (as perceived both in the region and in a substantial segment of the Western, especially American, foreign policy establishments) as one of the 'encirclers'. The importance of the shift was not lost on Saudi Arabia and its other Gulf neighbours. In short, there was a genuine and welcomed tendency towards pragmatism and away from radicalism in Iraq's dealings, not only with the Gulf dynasties but also, further afield, with a number of Western countries as well. At the regional level, the strategic and political significance of these developments was twofold. In the first instance, Iraq joined with Saudi Arabia and most of the other Gulf states in opposition to the Camp David accords. Secondly, the Baghdad regime emerged as the centre-piece of a nearly region-wide consensus regarding the dangers attendant on any growth in the rivalry of the superpowers in the Gulf. These two factors combined to lessen the likelihood in the immediate future that Iraq would place any great emphasis on the further spread of radicalism in the region and, concomitantly, to enhance the prospects for greater regional security co-operation among the Gulf states themselves.

What needs to be added now is an account of the interests that the kingdom and its neighbours have in common which, despite differences, tend to promote their collaboration. First, among the dynasties there are at least five categories of shared concerns which transcend their aforementioned differences and competition for influence in the area. Briefly, these encompass their interests in: the perpetuation of their respective monarchical regimes; the prevention of radical groups and movements from gaining footholds and momentum in the area; the continuation of an uninterrupted flow of the Gulf's oil resources to markets outside the region; securing the highest value possible in exchange for their oil, whether this is measured in economic or political terms, or both, and whether the means be through the pricing mechanism or production limitations; and finally, keeping the Gulf free from superpower rivalry. Throughout the 1970s, Saudi Arabia and the other eleven Arab dynasties in the area shared these five interests not only amongst themselves but also with Iran.

Moreover, despite the ideological antithesis between the ruling household of Saudi Arabia and its fellow dynasts in the Gulf, on the one hand, and Iraq as the sole socialist-oriented regime, on the other, some common interests do exist here also. The interests of conservative and radical forces tend to coalesce on the issues of keeping superpower rivalry out of the Gulf and on pursuing ways to increase or protect the value of their oil incomes. Moreover, especially since Camp David and in a continuing fashion since the Iranian Revolution, two particular interests – the preservation and enhancement of Arabism and orthodox Islam – have helped the governments of Saudi Arabia, Iraq and their neighbours to surmount their ideological differences. In this context, Saudi Arabia, Iraq and the other Arab Gulf regimes stand in unison against Iran whenever the policies or practices of Tehran are perceived as detrimental to Arab interests. This kind of solidarity, notwithstanding the 'radical versus conservative' contest between Iraq and the dynastic Arab states of recent years, has occurred in reaction to Iran's claims to sovereignty over Bahrain prior to 1970; to events in 1971 when Tehran pressured the ruler of Sharjah to sign an agreement permitting Iranian occupation of Abu Musa island and then directed Iranian naval forces to seize the Greater and Lesser Tunbs islands from

Ras al-Khaimah; in a more generalised fashion, to the close relationship, much of it clandestine, which Iran maintained with Israel up to the time of the overthrow of the Shah in 1979; and in response to Iranian leader Ayatollah Rouhollah Khomeini's subsequent attempts to export revolution to these states.

Regarding the religious factor, theological considerations are once more serving as a unifying force within and among the officialdom of these states. This factor, however, also creates greater unity among those who oppose the region's incumbent regimes. It is none the less important to stress that differing versions of Islam are adhered to by the government of Iran and its counterparts among the Arab states of the Gulf, that is all of the latter are officially orthodox Sunni and thus at doctrinal odds with Iran, the citadel of heterodox (Shi'a) Islam. Both factors, the national-ethnic as well as the religious, tend to forge even greater solidarity among Saudi Arabia and the other Gulf states with respect to the Palestine problem.

Linkage between the Arab–Israeli Conflict and the Gulf

The linkage between the Arab Gulf states and the Fertile Crescent (confrontation) states most directly involved in the Arab–Israeli dispute continues to occur within several different contexts. One of these has been in the realm of specific events that occasionally take place in one of the areas – for example the sabotage inside Syria or Lebanon of an oil installation involved in the trans-shipment or refining of oil from Saudi Arabia or Iraq, or, more recently, the embargo by Iran of oil sales to Israel – that have had a direct impact on developments in the other area. A second context has been that of the bilateral relationships between Gulf states and confrontation states. Examples have been the relations between Egypt, Jordan, Syria and Lebanon, on the one hand, and Saudi Arabia, on the other, and, until 1979, between both Jordan and Iran, and Israel and Iran. A third context has been the extent to which the mineral and monetary might of Saudi Arabia and the other Arab oil-producing states in the Gulf has been perceived, and in certain instances used, as a political and economic arm of the Arab–Israeli conflict.

The linkage between the confrontation states and the Gulf in the context of specific events pre-dates the 1973 war. Saudi Arabia and the other Arab states of the Gulf both prior and subsequent to that event have repeatedly exerted pressures aimed at regaining the Arab lands seized by Israel in the June 1967 war. They have supported UN resolutions 242 and 338, which call for Israeli withdrawal from territories occupied during the conflict (in exchange for recognition of Israel's right to exist), and, in addition, they have insisted on Israeli evacuation of the old quarter of Jerusalem. Without exception, all of them have also demanded recognition of the legitimate rights – among them the right to exercise the principle of self-determination – of the Palestine people.

Since the Khartoum conference of Arab heads of state in September 1967, called to assess the lessons learned from the June war, Saudi Arabia and Kuwait, in particular, have disbursed generous sums to the 'front line' (bordering on Israel) states of Egypt, Jordan, Syria and, to a lesser extent, Lebanon. Their payments to the first three countries enabled them to pay for much of the damage inflicted by Israeli forces in the course of the war. They have also funnelled millions of dollars yearly to the Palestinian guerrillas, and have contributed heavily to the funding and staffing of the 30,000-man Arab peace-keeping force in Lebanon.

During the 1973 war, Saudi Arabia and other key Gulf states adopted their most effective position to date on the Arab–Israeli conflict when they imposed the oil embargo and production cutbacks against countries supporting Israel. They regarded American security assistance to Israel during the war as tantamount to direct US intervention. From 10 October (four days after the hostilities began) until the final cease-fire on 25 October, the US Air Force made over 550 flights to Israel, bringing arms and supplies. Especially provocative, in the Saudi view, was the White House request to Congress for $2.2 billion in emergency aid to the Jewish state while the fighting was still going on. King Faisal took this as a personal betrayal by President Nixon. His response came on 18 October, when Saudi Arabia joined Libya, Iraq, Kuwait and other states in agreeing to curtail its oil production. Two days later the Saudi government proclaimed, as several of its neighbours had already done, an immediate and total embargo of oil to the United States. This action deprived the United States of nearly 650,000 barrels per day of Saudi crude, the largest single component of America's Arab oil imports.

Saudi Arabia and its neighbours have been able to sway attitudes toward Israel – in the United Nations, in African and Asian capitals, and increasingly within the European Economic Community – only in part through the implicit threat of another embargo in the event of a resumption of hostilities between Israel and one or more of its neighbours. Additional leverage in these matters has been exercised through their influential positions with respect to oil prices and production levels and through the generous use of their impressive financial resources. Following the example first of Kuwait, then of Libya and Saudi Arabia, Iraq and such other Gulf states as Abu Dhabi and Qatar have for several years been in the front ranks of those Arab oil producers who have used their wealth to counter Israeli diplomatic influence in Africa.[3] They have invested heavily in economic ventures in African and Asian countries, viewed not only as states with substantial numbers of kindred Muslims, but also with governments that, in general, have been sympathetic to their position regarding Palestine.

Since the 1975 Sinai accords — and especially since the Camp David agreements — there has been a large measure of unity between the Arab Gulf states and other Arab states with regard to policy on the Arab–Israeli dispute. The inability of diplomacy during the 1973–80 period to deal effectively with the Palestinian problem, which lies at the heart of the Arab–Israeli conflict, has been and remains especially troublesome for all these states. More than any other problem, this lies at the root of the ongoing uncertainty among Saudi and other Gulf state leaders as to the future of their relationship with the West. The continuation of this relationship itself could prejudice their security. Long perceiving the dynastic Gulf states' policies *vis-à-vis* the Arab–Israeli conflict as overly moderate, some among the more militant elements within the Palestinian diaspora have advocated sabotage of the Arab Gulf states' oil facilities to demonstrate this disenchantment. Others have argued in favour of undermining these regimes and their sources of wealth as a means of indirectly striking at Western powers — particularly the US — which are supporting Israel.

One of the most vexing sources of concern in this context has, of course, been Egypt. Since Egyptian President Sadat's surprise visit to Jerusalem in November 1977 a radical change has occurred in the relationship between most of the Gulf states and Egypt. Cairo's conclusion of a separate peace treaty with Israel — along lines far short of being comprehensive as far as the future of either the Palestinians or the status of Jerusalem is concerned — contributed directly to the distance which Saudi Arabia and other Gulf states placed between themselves and Egypt following the Camp David accords.

In short, one of the consequences of the Egyptian–Israeli treaty was the termination of what, until then, had been a growing linkage between the Gulf states and Egypt at the strategic and military levels. Jordan, like Egypt, has long had both economic and related political interests in the area. Indeed, Jordan has been particularly active in contributing to the maintenance of the existing governmental systems in the Gulf — a contribution that has not gone unnoticed or unrewarded by Saudi Arabia. As the 1980s began, Jordanian army officers and police and intelligence personnel on secondment and private contract, for example, continued to hold key positions in the defence and internal security forces of Bahrain, Qatar and the United Arab Emirates. These Jordanians were generally acknowledged by the conservative Arab regimes as among the most respected and trusted of the various expatriate groups working in the area. In return for the Hashimite kingdom's multifaceted role in enhancing the security and development of the emirates, Jordan received important political, diplomatic and financial support from these states in inter-Arab councils.

Linking the Arab states of the Gulf to the confrontation states in the Arab—Israeli conflict even more directly for a lengthy period were the extensive Iranian—Israeli ties. These two countries had long enjoyed a close political relationship and had collaborated to a significant degree in military and economic matters as well. After the June 1967 war, for example, military equipment bearing Soviet markings found in the Kurdish areas of Iraq bordering Iran was discovered to have been provided to the Kurds not by the USSR but by Iran *via* the Sinai peninsula, where Israel had recovered considerable amounts of abandoned Soviet-made weaponry in June 1967. The relationship between Iran and Israel in petroleum grew to be especially close during the 1970s and, for that reason, it came as all the more heavy a blow to Israel when its oil supply from this quarter was terminated in early 1979. Following the Sinai II Agreement of September 1975, the importance of Iranian oil to Israel had increased dramatically until, at one point, Iran accounted for nearly 90 per cent of Tel Aviv's oil imports.

Lastly, it remains clear that the countries directly involved in the Arab—Israeli conflict will continue to consider the oil of the Gulf states, and that of Saudi Arabia in particular, as an important political and economic arm of the dispute. This sentiment persists despite growing Arab financial and economic interests in the West which could be jeopardised if another oil embargo were imposed. The linkage between the Palestine problem and the Gulf states, moreover, nowadays extends beyond the Middle East to the basis and kinds of relations these states seek with the US, Europe and Japan, the most important customers for their oil. Indeed, Saudi Arabia and other Gulf oil producers have repeatedly indicated that their willingness to raise or, in some cases, even to maintain existing levels of oil production to help the consuming countries solve their energy problems cannot be taken for granted. For reasons relating to their own national security interests, they have stressed that such co-operation in the future may be made contingent upon the willingness of these countries to use the various means at their disposal to bring about a restoration of legitimate Muslim rights as pertains to the sacred Islamic shrines in Jerusalem; the cessation of Israel's policy of colonising the occupied territories of the West Bank, the Golan Heights, and the Gaza Strip; an end to the intervention of Israel in the affairs of Lebanon; and, more generally, a just and lasting settlement of the problems of the Palestinian people.

Concluding Perspective

As the foregoing attests, much change has occurred in the past decade in that area which, while including Saudi Arabia as a principal power in the region, actually encompasses a much larger sphere extending from 'republican and revolutionary' Iraq and Iran to the eleven dynasties of eastern Arabia. Coups have occurred; revenues among the oil-producing states of the area have more than quintupled; the transition from the strong, highly personalised rule of the late King Faisal to the *de facto* duumverate of King Khalid and Heir Apparent Fahd in Saudi Arabia, and conversely, from the weak, almost totally nominal reign of the late Shaikh Sabah to the more dynamic rule of former Heir Apparent Shaikh Jabr in Kuwait, took place without mishap. Further, a decade-old insurgency in Oman was brought to an end as, likewise, was the Kurdish rebellion, a conflict of even longer duration, in Iraq. Most momentous of all, the dynasty in Iran, the one country in the area throughout this period with a military apparatus, population base and socio-economic infrastructure both larger and more developed than Saudi Arabia and most of the other Gulf states combined, was toppled.

Even so, amidst these changes — in the case of Iran and oil, changes that were truly epochal and revolutionary in scope — there have been and remain important themes of continuity. Iraq retained the secular and socialist orientation of its government and economy but, of greater importance and for the reasons delineated earlier, brought its foreign policies into greater harmony with those of the other Arab Gulf states, especially Saudi Arabia. In the dynastic states of Arabia, although these

have been portrayed incessantly for the past half-decade by Western
and especially American analysts as ruled by inherently unstable
regimes, coups did not occur (and of greater significance, notwithstanding the seizure of the Grand Mosque in November 1979, none
were attempted). Compared to the more advanced societies of the
industrialised and allegedly far more developed and progressive West,
these polities evidenced less theft, less divorce, fewer rapes and other
crimes of violence to persons or property; less unemployment; fewer
political demonstrations, and fewer related societal problems as those
manifested through apathy and alienation born — as in most of the rest
of the world including Western Europe, Japan and the United States —
in a milieu perceived by many to be one of limited educational,
economic and social opportunities.

The institutions relating rulers to ruled throughout the region were,
of course, constantly being challenged. But, for the most part, fewer
than expected were found to be seriously wanting. Western and other
biases against the forms of rule in the area under examination notwithstanding, a close look at the substance of political, social and economic
life within these states revealed what, as the 1980s began, was accepted
almost as a truism: that most of them were in one way or another
insecure, in common with the lot of most other developing countries.
In as many other ways, however, they were revealed to be as resilient
and responsive as most other developing countries — if not more so —
to the societal strains of countries caught up in the throes of change
along a broad front. To be sure, such emotionally charged issues as
moral probity, economic inequality and popular participation in the
political process constituted the substance of much discussion and
debate within these societies as they entered the 1980s. There appeared,
moreover, to be regionwide agreement that rapid modernisation was
not only psychologically stressful but, as the seizure of the Grand
Mosque dramatically demonstrated, that some were less able to cope
with the associated strains than others. However, a consensus appeared
to hold, however begrudgingly in some instances, that the great
majority of the region's regimes were probably as accessible, accommodating and accountable (if, again, not more so) to the overall
concerns, needs and interests of their citizenry as most other governments. With respect to the latter, this included not only those of the
much more austere and authoritarian 'revolutionary free officers' or
'Islamic republic' models, but also, for that matter, many of those more
frequently associated with Western-style 'democracies'.

Political interrelationships between and among Saudi Arabia and its dynastic counterparts elsewhere in the Gulf, on the one hand, and between these states, both individually and collectively, and Iraq and Iran, on the other, have thus often been exceptionally complicated, as this essay has sought to demonstrate. A comprehensive understanding of the impact of what has and has not taken place in the region continues to elude the grasp of most outside observers. As valid as this statement has been and remains for the state of knowledge about intra-Gulf relations, it is becoming increasingly applicable with respect to the changing relationships between these states (again both singly and jointly) and more distant powers. Once more, the most portentous transformations have occurred in the post-1973 period. Perhaps nowhere has such a range of events affecting the role of the Middle East in regional and world affairs occurred as in the area encompassed by Saudi Arabia and the other Gulf states examined herein.

Notes

1. An earlier, substantially different, version of this paper was submitted to the US Congress Joint Economic Committee, for internal use by its members and staff.

2. The word 'obtain' is an accurate description of the Saudi view of what transpired; 'permitted' would be a more correct rendition of Abu Dhabi's sentiments as to what was agreed. There is, of course, a considerable definitional difference between the concepts that lie behind these words, especially as pertains to the vexsome notion of sovereignty.

3. Black African recipients of Israeli aid have included Ethiopia, Nigeria, Kenya, Uganda, Chad and the Ivory Coast. Most African states severed diplomatic relations with Israel in the aftermath of the October 1973 war. Since then, in international and regional organisations, they have consistently backed Arab-sponsored resolutions condemning Israel. These include the UN's 1973 'Zionism is a form of racism' resolution and its recognition in 1974 of the PLO. In more recent years, Saudi Arabia and other Arab oil-producing states have underwritten the Arab Bank for Economic Development in Africa as a means of further consolidating their influence in the sub-Saharan region.

9 SOCIAL CHANGE IN MODERN SAUDI ARABIA

Shirley Kay

Introduction

'Then came the wealth and the power, thanks be to God', an Arab
merchant remarked to me, commenting on the experiences of the
1970s. He might equally well have said: and then came the wealth and
the problems, for as fast as a sudden massive influx of wealth solves one
set of problems, it creates another. The latter are the more worrying to
deal with in that they are new, often unforeseen, sometimes almost
without precedent and therefore cannot be solved by example. A tidal
wave of prosperity swept Saudi Arabia in the 1970s. I spent three of
those years in Jeddah and it is on that experience that this article is
based. The object is to provide an overall perspective of the differing
aspects of social change occurring in modern Saudi Arabia.

The life of virtually the whole nation has been upheaved by sudden
wealth. It is relevant, however, to take a glimpse at the realities of the
old existence, to banish romanticised notions of the 'good old days'.[1]
For most of the population life was simply a struggle to survive:
drought meant starvation, infant mortality was high, sickness could
easily and arbitrarily spell death, an injury or toothache brought
unrelieved pain (of all the hardships experienced by one of the early
travellers in the desert, the pressing need to pull out his own tooth to
relieve pain was the one which most impressed me, for it was the one
most easy to comprehend). Once when I reproved a British-educated
Jeddah merchant for allowing his old coral-built family house to fall
into disrepair, he rounded on me: 'If you had lived there with no
running water, no drains, no air conditioning, you would want to
forget all about it too.' Jeddah in September is anyway a nightmare of
heat and humidity; without the modern comforts which he mentioned
it was a fight against sickness and boils, lethargy and frayed nerves, the
inability even to hold a pen or a sewing needle so damp was the hand.

Nevertheless, the impact of wealth and the foreign experiences
which have come with it have been particularly abrupt and difficult to
digest. Statistics from Saudi Arabia are often elusive and misleading.[2]
I shall quote few of them, but those for the income from oil are
particularly striking and worth remarking: in round figures Saudi Arabia

171

received about $1.5 million from oil in 1940, $334 million in 1960, $1,214 million in 1970, and about $80,000 million in 1980.[3] Twenty years ago, under King Saud, the kingdom reached near bankruptcy. Only six years ago, from 1974 onwards, did massive wealth begin to percolate through all strata of society. In the wake of wealth came foreigners. Saudi Arabia had, of course, always known the annual influx of pious Muslims coming for the pilgrimage, but non-Muslims had been little seen, outside perhaps of Jeddah. At the turn of the century a handful of seasoned explorers had criss-crossed the peninsula; by the beginning of the Second World War Philby commented that some eight European women had visited al-Riyadh; in 1951, when he visited Tayma (which is now on the main western road into the interior of Saudi Arabia) he could name the five Westerners who had been there before him.[4] Today there are estimated to be 1.5 to 2 million foreigners working in Saudi Arabia — Asians, Europeans, Americans, as well as Muslim Arabs and Pakistanis — and they have fanned out into the most remote and isolated districts.[5] The example of their relatively comfortable lifestyle, even in the loneliest desert (air conditioning, transport, medical attention, film shows at night) is only one of the many factors which are draining the indigenous population from the desert and country districts and drawing them irresistibly to the cities.

The major cities, particularly, exert a magnetic attraction. Jeddah, al-Riyadh and the Dammam–Dahran–Al Khobar complex have seen a real population explosion. Jeddah, for example, has increased from a population of 60,000 20 years ago to an estimated 1 million today.[6] The pattern of tight family life is breaking up in face of this extreme mobility: the men move to the cities first, the young people being the most ready to go. Wives and children may stay in the village or tent, coping with the fields or animals, to follow later perhaps. The old people are often left alone in their original environment; if they are fortunate one of their children will stay on with them, but for how long?

The Pastoral Setting

The bedouin, who are now thought to number only a little over half a million, have been opting fast for settled life.[7] The first step is often semi-settlement. All around the fringes of the desert one sees villages of huts built of large tins or new breeze-block houses, with a black tent pitched beside each. The options are thus kept open — if settlement fails they can go back to the desert; meanwhile they may practise semi-nomadism. A Japanese anthropologist, Motoko Katakura, was able to study in depth a settlement of this kind in the Wadi Fatima between Jeddah and Mecca.[8] She found that education was much sought after and over 70 per cent of children were in primary school. It had been an important factor in leading many of the families to settle; another factor leading to settlement had been that many of the families had not been very successful as nomads anyway.

Although such a village would seem to be a natural first stage in moving to the city, in fact many bedouin make the change in one leap, going straight into a shack on the outskirts of Jeddah or al-Riyadh. There fellow tribesmen will help find them a home and a job, or they will take to taxi- or truck-driving which seem to be preferred occupations because of the independence and mobility which they offer. In the Eastern Province settlement has often been through employment by Aramco and so is rather different.

Young bedouin have proved remarkably adaptable and there are many whose ambition has taken them to the top in a surprising variety of fields. I have met men who spent their early years in a tent and who today are civil servants, army officers, a jet pilot, a deputy minister; one young woman, whose grandparents were still in the desert, was a successful broadcaster, in Arabic and English.

Even those who have stayed in the desert, and are therefore presumably the more conservative, have adopted new ways which have greatly changed their way of life. Most important of these is motor transport. A combination of subsidies, gifts and loans have made ready cash available to such an extent that virtually every family now has a pick-up truck and many camps own a large truck for transporting animals, and a water tanker. When I first started to explore the deserts in early 1975 it was still easy to follow the tracks and find one's way about. By the time I left in late 1977 tracks fanned out like a spider's web in every direction, leading as often as not only to an abandoned camp site, and the only way to find one's way through them was with a compass. This was what the desert dwellers themselves were also starting to do.

Trucks give the bedouin a new independence and security. They can move flocks rapidly from one place to another to find the grazing. They can stay at some distance from a water source, carting the water by truck. This, along with other factors, is causing severe over-grazing in places and may, in turn, force more bedouin to settle.[9] Their tents, too, are becoming more and more cluttered with belongings, such as sewing machines, cold boxes, tin trunks and binoculars, which make semi-nomadism at any rate appear more attractive. Empty oil drums serve to store water, primus stoves heat it, tinned foods (especially sardines, tomato paste, tuna and milk powder) add flavour and sustenance to the diet. An abandoned camp site is no longer marked solely by the ring of blackened stones of the hearth; you will find it by the litter of punctured tyres, oil drums and rusty tins.

The power of the tribes has clearly diminished. The National Guard aims to integrate the tribesmen into a corporate body and break down age-old rivalries.[10] It is difficult to say to what extent the tribes today could represent a threat: the siege at the Grand Mosque in Mecca in November 1979 showed that such an attack could still be tribally-based and that the tribes are quite well armed. It was led and largely manned by members of the Otaiba tribe, a numerous tribe whose rangelands extends from Najd to the western region. Juhaiman al-Otaibi, leader of the revolt, was from a settled family of this tribe.

To people in the cities, however, the bedouin have all but faded into oblivion. 'But there are no bedouin left', I was frequently told when I asked about them. Their existence, once so threatening to the sedentary population, seems now so distant (in time rather than in space) that it is difficult to visualise among the paraphernalia of late twentieth-century city life with its tower blocks and traffic jams. It could, it seems, more easily belong to the fantasy world of video films, with which the city population is far more familiar.

The Urban Setting

The changes in desert life are completely insignificant in comparison to the changes which have ravaged the small, quiet walled towns of 40 years ago. In those days the pace was gentle, as befitted life led in great heat, and the quietness of the desert pervaded the town where even a football was muffled in the sand of the alleyways; above all everyone knew each other (the men, that is, at any rate). That peaceful existence is shattered today: Saudi towns are among the noisiest I have experienced, with every driver keeping his hand on the horn, every taxi driver treating his passengers to a continuous stream of pop music, and pedestrians often dominating the background din with their own transistors held close to the ear. Houses which, 30 years ago, looked out onto sand and passing gazelle, are now practically in the town centre; houses which were out in the desert when I arrived in Jeddah in 1975 are now in the inner suburbs.

Throughout this period roads were being laid, asphalted, dug up to allow for drains, or water pipes or cables, re-asphalted, dug up again, etc.,[11] creating a hectic environment in which it was very straining to live. The well-to-do merchant families moved further and further out from the city centres. The great old family houses, which had sheltered the extended family under one roof, had usually been abandoned in the course of the past 20 or 30 years, when the old patriarch died. It was he who had held the family together and insisted that sons and grandsons ate at his table and slept under (or in summer, on) his roof. Nuclear-family villas proliferated and with them loneliness for the women and children.

Life in the old houses in the 1940s and early 1950s was described by Marianne Ali Reza who was the first Western wife to live in a Saudi household.[12] The women and children of the family lived upstairs, the men had their offices and reception rooms below. In the old Banaja house in Jeddah a wooden bridge across a corner of the courtyard enabled the women to pass from one wing of the house to another without showing themselves. When Marianne and her companies wanted to visit the garden it took considerable organisation to remove all the men working there, and ensure that none should be allowed to enter. Yet the women and children were never lonely and the women went out of their way to support each other in misfortune. They had known no other life and did not fret for a freedom they did not know existed. Since they neither read nor saw films, their horizons were closely limited.

The introduction of modern comforts has led to more and more luxurious villas (luxury bathrooms are especially popular in a land where water itself is a luxury); class divisions and social snobbery are becoming more apparent as wealth is shown in possessions. Comfortable living is subsidised: when the cost of electricity was lowered the demand for air conditioners rose, causing problems for the electricity suppliers, but bringing relief to even relatively humble homes; desalinated water (produced at an estimated cost of around $2 per gallon) is distributed free, but when the distribution network breaks down one must purchase water at rather more than the local cost of petrol.

The merchant families have acquired the taste for comfort and luxury and spend an increasing part of the year travelling abroad, primarily in London. One wealthy merchant remarked that he went abroad every weekend (in his own plane, of course), because he felt the lack of any cultural activities at home. I asked why he did not spend some time and effort trying to introduce theatre, cinema or concerts to Saudi Arabia but his immediate reply was that the people were not ready for it. Abroad the educated rich can enjoy the things they miss at home but which might disturb their strongly Islamic society, while their wives enjoy a degree of freedom from veiling, segregation and boredom which makes them loath to return before the first days of school term.

Despite the fact that these families have moved out of their old family homes they continue to work as a family unit. Business is almost always kept within the family, the children being taught a variety of skills and languages which will forge a useful business team. Most families also donate a member to government service, ensuring that he does not suffer too greatly from the financial point of view through a discreet participation in the family business activities. The old business principles prevail: trust brothers and cousins before outsiders, and trust outsiders whom you know rather than newcomers. The old manners prevail too: Saudis are inherently polite, they cling to an introductory conversation on generalities to establish rapport, and the token of hospitality is the offer of a cup of green coffee.

Some of the merchant families who had scattered to their own villas are now trying to regroup in family compounds, where each has his own house but within the same outer wall. 'A united family is a strong family', one merchant remarked, explaining why he was offering plots of his extremely valuable building land to his brothers and cousins at a fraction of market price. The family compound seems to have much to offer: while individual families can retain their own privacy, the women will not be lonely during the daytime, and the children will grow up together and become friendly with the cousins among whom they will, in all probability, find their future spouses.

Children are greatly cosseted in Saudi families and the toddlers are petted and carried about by everyone. Their upbringing is the subject of considerable concern and Saudi families have maintained a strong control over their offspring which makes teenage violence and delinquency unknown. In the past, when modern education was not available in Saudi Arabia, wealthy families sent their sons, and sometimes their daughters, abroad to school. Victoria College in Egypt has produced an influential group of graduates, both businessmen and government officials (now in their 30s and 40s),[13] who are as close knit as by any British old school tie. But today those very men are sending their own sons to Saudi schools, to have them grow up 100 per cent Saudi before sending them to the United States to university and business school. During school holidays, however, even the young children of merchant and professional families are sent off to summer school in England, and later Switzerland, to acquire a fluent command of languages.

Young graduates returning from university abroad often find it hard to adapt to the enveloping family atmosphere and strong paternal and religious discipline. This is especially true for the women who return to a life very different from anything they have known abroad (there was, in fact, an announcement in 1980 that Saudi girls would no longer be allowed to go abroad to study, following the showing of the *Death of a Princess* film).

The Role of Women

It is difficult to write on so emotive a subject as the life of women in Saudi Arabia and, as a woman, I cannot pretend not to be *parti pris*. However, social change in Islam affects the women first and foremost, and Saudi Arabia is no exception. Until 20 years ago life for the women was largely as described by Marianne Ali Reza, circumscribed and led almost entirely within the home. A few girls of wealthy families were sent abroad to school and university and it is these women, now in their 30s and early 40s, who take the lead in the field of education for women and in the struggle to acquire some emancipation.

The first schools for girls were opened in 1957 (Dar al Hanan and the small Nassif school in Jeddah). State schools came soon after and the story is well known of King Faisal's need to call in troops to ensure the opening of the girls' school in Buraida in 1960. Today there are girls' primary schools throughout the country and secondary schools in the towns. About half as many girls as boys attend school, some 300,000 girls in primary schools and 100,000 in secondary schools.[14] There are several women's teacher training colleges and strictly segregated women's sections at most of the major universities. Education for girls is rapidly increasing in popularity: at least one of its advantages is that of improving a girl's marriage prospects. The widespread tendency for Saudi boys to acquire a foreign wife during their studies abroad had become a source of considerable concern. In the mid-1970s regulations forbidding their bringing foreign wives back into Saudi Arabia were enforced and it became very difficult, though not impossible for the well-connected, to circumvent these. At the same time the need to educate Saudi girls was stressed and the number of university places for them was greatly increased.

Literacy does not give them, however, a free run of world literature. Girls' education is carefully controlled; it is the responsibility of the religious, not the education authorities, under the Directorate-General of Girls' Schools, founded in 1960, and girls spend more time on religious studies at school than do the boys. In the universities girls have restricted use of library facilities (either books are brought out for them from the boys' library or they have a smaller library of their own); at home, by and large, they will find very few books on the family shelves, for censorship in Saudi Arabia is strict.[15] Nevertheless, their education, at whatever level it is terminated, does open their eyes to other possibilities than a life led within their own walls. They are eager and diligent students and now tend to outshine their brothers in examinations. They are also determined; many women students continue to study despite the birth of their babies.

The problems can start when they finish university — which may have prepared them for a life they cannot lead. The employment possibilities are severely limited. Girls are now encouraged by the government to work in girls' schools and colleges (as teachers or, more popular, as administrators) and in women's hospitals as doctors or nurses. They are not allowed to work in any place where they will meet men. In practice, before I left Saudi Arabia at the end of 1977, a number of girls were working in offices and the number seemed to be increasing each year. There were, however, periodic purges and these seem to have become more thorough after 1978. Moreover, many families are against their girls working outside the home. Since women are not allowed to drive, transport is a major problem unless they can afford a car and chauffeur, which is becoming more expensive and is now strictly a luxury for the rich. It is estimated that something like 1–2 per cent of Saudi women have jobs;[16] the desirability of employing Saudi women rather than foreigners, however, has several times been aired in public, and was returned to in the outlines of the new plan, if only suitable work could be found . . .[17]

Meanwhile most Saudi women stay at home, trying to enjoy a life which offers more interest than that of their mothers did, but which cannot satisfy their new awareness. They marry rather later, perhaps about 18 rather than at 13 as in past generations.[18] They may immediately then have to cope with their own household, instead of moving in with mother-in-law, and this can mean housework for the first time for the better-off. Until 1963 reasonably wealthy families had slaves (who were more members of the household than slaves were in the West). Afterwards these slaves stayed on as servants, or else

Yemeni, Sudanese or Ethiopian servants were hired. But with the sudden rise in wealth servants became not only a very expensive luxury but also nearly unobtainable, in part due to the numbers employed by foreign companies. A neighbour of mine was saved from scrubbing her own floors for the first time in her life by a young black woman whom she had brought up as a slave girl, who volunteered to come and help her until she could find someone permanently.

For the wealthy woman, however, the days are long and the quickest way to get through them is to sleep. Many sleep till lunch-time; Rosemarie Buschow recorded that in the palace where she lived the princesses slept until 5.00 p.m.[19] The telephone is a new and much appreciated blessing. Families keep in touch with lengthy daily telephone chats from one continent to another, engaged couples who have barely been allowed to meet can get to know each other quite well by phone, women can spend their afternoons chatting to their women friends whom they have no means of visiting, the really bored can dial at random for the thrill of a chat with a stranger.[20] Television and more especially video films have added a new dimension to life within the home. Many women spend six hours or more a day watching video; the films available often give them a thirst for, but a distorted view of, romantic life in the West.

Mixed social life has been accepted in the past decade by many educated families and is certainly on the increase. Such couples are especially cautious about going to dinner parties with other Saudis whom they do not know, for if one man brings his wife then he must be sure that the others will do the same. They prefer to mix only with their own family and circle of close friends, thus avoiding embarrassing encounters. These beginnings of social life can give a little hope to women who are divorced, or who for some reason failed to get married at the accepted time. I was twice asked if I could not arrange suitable meetings, as though by accident, at my dinner parties; the women concerned would, of course, have been escorted by a brother or close relative.

At such functions the women will invariably be dressed in the height of fashion, in exquisite dresses bought in Paris or London. Young Saudi women are often extremely beautiful and they have a highly developed fashion sense. It is a far cry from the days described by Marianne Ali Reza when bolts of cloth were brought home from the *suq* and made up into dresses for all the women in the household; the four wives of Finance Minister, Abdullah Suleiman, she remarked, invariably wore dresses in the same material. Today it is rare for a leading Saudi to have more than one wife, and inconceivable that if he did they should be dressed alike. Outside the house Saudi women invariably still wear the black '*abaya* in Saudi Arabia (though many dispense with it abroad). They cover their hair, either with the '*abaya* or with a head scarf, but increasingly they are not veiling their faces. It seems often to be a family decision to abandon the veil: 'the women of my family stopped veiling about five years ago', one young women remarked to me. In the Jeddah *suq* one evening I counted that about half the women were not veiled, though the sample would be weighted by the many Egyptian and Palestinian women there, and by the fact that women in the *suq* might well be from the more liberated families. The sight of a woman's face has become more acceptable in recent years, with the insistence in 1975 on passport photographs for women (brought about by the fact that women were previously travelling on any passport available, and importing foreign maids on their own passports).

Traditionalism and Modernism

The relaxation of traditional customs does not imply that the social restrictions of Wahhabi Islam are being swept aside in a wave of modernisation. Foreigners often gain the impression that modernisation in Saudi Arabia is a case of 'one step forward, two steps back', but middle-aged Saudis assert that the change in their own lifetime has been enormous. The authorities appear anxious, however, to maintain prohibitions until such time as the forbidden activity is so widely accepted that permitting it will cause no stir. I was on several occasions shown the site of a future cinema or theatre, although no such entertainments are at present permitted. As David Holden wrote, 'King Faisal adopted the classic position of the conservative and led his people backwards into the future.'[21]

A flexible attitude has thus developed towards widespread breaches of religious regulations, which to foreigners appear as hypocrisy but to Saudis seem simply to be a practical way of avoiding social conflict. While I was there contraception was prohibited, but every brand of pill was openly available and on display in the chemists. Alcohol was prohibited, yet was widely available for those who could afford it (prices for whisky rising to around $100 a bottle); although any bottle brought in through the airport was ceremoniously emptied down the drain, large quantities were brought in through the ports and a telephone call, 'The chickens have arrived, how many do you want?' would alert those on the net. It also came in overland by truck and a crisis developed in the market when trucks were searched one winter for arms. Deviations from accepted behaviour were charitably accepted so long as they did not engender public fuss or scandal, or lead others astray. One often had the feeling that those who fell foul of the authorities were punished rather for setting a bad example, that discretion was all that was really demanded.

This cautious approach to change comes as much from the Western-educated sector of the population as from the religious authorities themselves.[22] Young men with American doctorates may hope eventually to introduce some of the advantages of Western life, but they have been shocked too by much that they have seen in the West. They are appalled by the violence and crime which they consider to be the result of our 'soft' attitude to punishment. They cannot accept full freedom and equality for women and hence the agonised debate over just how much work women may be permitted to undertake. They have no desire to shake the strong, authoritative, social structure of family and religion. Hence the tendency to go abroad more and more to enjoy the comforts and pleasures of the West, alternating with the more austere life, but reassuring security of the strongly moral society at home. It is noteworthy that few Saudis fail to return home in the end.

That the morals are different from ours can lead foreigners to accuse them of hypocrisy or immorality. A state handling billions of dollars with growing sophistication must, we feel, be corrupt if it does not run on our lines. Yet traditional values have come through into the modern state in Saudi Arabia: a man's first loyalty is to his family, then his tribe, then his country. Nepotism is a virtue and it would shame a man to refuse to help or give a job to a close relative. Bribery is a widely accepted way of obtaining contracts and spreading wealth; it does not cause the same moral agonising that it does in the West. 'One good turn deserves another' could well be a Saudi adage.

Punishment is often tied more to retribution, restitution, or the need for public example than it is to moral guilt. The payment of blood money can free a murderer (or a driver involved in a fatal road accident) from further punishment, irrespective of his responsibility. The latter may also be differently assessed from the way it is in the West: a fire engine came out of a side road one day, hit a lorry, ricocheted off and killed some pedestrians on the pavement. The lorry driver was held part-responsible; had he not been there at the time, the pedestrians would not have died. A passenger in a taxi is held part-responsible for the driver's accident, since it was he who had chosen the road which led to trouble.

There have been some widely publicised cases in recent years of foreigners sentenced (though rarely subjected) to caning for alcohol offences. Most of Jeddah society serves alcohol at their parties, but discreetly in their own homes. Those sentenced to punishment have usually called attention to themselves (as in the case of the British party in Jeddah in 1979 at which two expatriates died) or have been selling liquor. It is the public nature of the offence which calls for a public example to be made. As a *Sunday Times* article (18 June 1978) so aptly put it: 'You have to be bloody stupid or bloody-minded to get caught.'

A case of punishment which has caused an even greater international stir was the execution in 1977 of Princess Mishaal for adultery. As in any society, adultery is not unknown in Saudi Arabia (though it is not common for women there). In this case, however, the Princess through being caught at the airport had made public her attempted escape with her lover. Her family decided that an example must be made. The punishment was controversial: the King refused to order a public execution but the Princess's grandfather, Prince Muhammad (the King's older brother), had the authority to carry out the execution by his own command and without recourse to legal processes. As a result the execution was carried out on a Saturday, and not on a Friday, the official time.[23] Many Hijazis were shocked by this action, which they regarded as a return to tribal ways.

Hence foreigners who go to live in Saudi Arabia must tread warily and do well to keep a low profile. Their presence is increasingly resented as their numbers increase and their influence is feared. Asians, who are less assertive and seek little recreation beyond their work, are more readily accepted — but are often despised. Westerners, whose way of life is more distinctive, and to many more desirable also, can be more disruptive. The relative freedom of Western women is seen as a bad example for Saudi youth and a source of discontent among Saudi women, but if Western men are employed 'on bachelor status' the problems with alcohol can easily increase. Saudi employers hover in their choice as to which is the lesser of the two evils, but are driven to opt for one or other by their need for technology and competent management. The pace of rapid development, once embarked on, cannot readily be checked. How to carry it through without sacrificing the essential values of their own society is seen as one of their major problems by those who rule Saudi Arabia.

Notes

1. See for instance C. Raswan, *The Black Tents of Arabia* (Hutchinson, London, 1935) for a description of drought; C. Doughty, *Travels in Arabia Deserta* (Duckworth, London, 1888) for a description of privation; Jaussen and Savignac, *Coutumes des Fuqara* (Belfond, Paris, 1914) for illnesses and the bedouin's attempted remedies; A. Musil, *The Manners and Customs of the Rwala Bedouins* (American Geographical Society, New York, 1928) for diseases, injuries and attempted cures; H. Muhsam, 'Fertility and Reproduction of the Bedouin', *Population Studies*, vol. IV, no. 4 (1951) for infant and maternal mortality.

2. The size of the population is, for example, a subject for debate. See Ministry of Finance and National Economy, Central Department of Statistics, *Population Census, 1974* (Dammam, 1977); J. S. Birks and C. A. Sinclair, *Arab Manpower; the Crisis of Development* (Croom Helm, London, 1980) for well-informed discussion of census figures; P. Iseman, 'The Arabian Ethos', *Harpers* (February 1978).

3. E. Monroe, *Philby of Arabia* (Cass, London, 1973), p. 24, for early incomes; D. E. Wells, *Saudi Arabian Revenues and Expenditures* (American Enterprise Institute, Washington, DC, 1974); J. P. Cleron, *Saudi Arabia 2000* (Croom Helm, London, 1978); SAMA estimate for 1980, quoted in the *Financial Times* Saudi Arabia Survey (28 April 1980).

4. See H. St John Philby, *Sheba's Daughters* (Constable, London, 1939), p. 4; and H. St John Philby, *The Land of Midian* (Ernest Benn, London, 1957), p. 76.

5. Yemenis are the largest component of the foreign workforce. Their numbers have been quoted at between 0.5 and 2 million (the latter figure by President Hamdi, in *The Middle East*, August 1977). The *Financial Times* Saudi Arabia Survey (28 April 1980) gives 250,000 Pakistanis, 80,000 Phillipinos, 80,000 South Koreans, 25,000 British, 35,000 Americans, 200,000 Lebanese, and 80,000 Palestinians. This survey also reports that the foreign component of the workforce is to be reduced to 1.7 million. See also Birks and Sinclair, *Arab Manpower*; and H. Lackner, *A House Built on Sand* (Ithaca Press, London, 1978).

6. The *Population Census, 1974* gave the following estimates for the major cities: al-Riyadh 666,840, Jeddah 561,104, Mecca 366,801, Tayif 204,857, Medina 198,186, Dammam 127,844. In 1980 Jeddah town-planners estimated the population of the city at 1 million (*Financial Times*, 28 April 1980). Al-Riyadh has grown at least as fast and the urban complex of the Eastern Province has also witnessed very rapid development.

7. Central Planning Organisation, Kingdom of Saudi Arabia, *Second Development Plan 1395–1400 AH*, (al-Riyadh, 1975) gives an estimate of 635,000 bedouin in 1975. Sample surveys have shown an estimated outmigration from the desert of 2 per cent per annum – see H. Lackner, *A House Built on Sand*. Also personal communication.

8. M. Katakura, *Bedouin Village* (University of Tokyo Press, Tokyo, 1977).

9. See Central Planning Organisation, *Second Development Plan* (1975); UNESCO, *Nomadic Populations in Selected Countries in the Middle East and Related Issues of Sedentarisation and Settlement* (UNESCO, Beirut, 1970); S. Kay, *The Bedouin* (Crane, New York, 1978); and *Financial Times* (28 April 1980) for the situation in Asir.

10. Numbers for the National Guard are somewhat below those of the regular army. *The Encyclopaedia Britannica* in 1974 estimated the number at 35,000 for the regular army and 30,000 for the National Guard. J. Bedore, in 'Greatness Thrust Upon Them', *Middle East International*, no. 79 (January 1978), quoted 80,000 for the combined forces. The *Financial Times* (28 April 1980), gave 44,500 for regular forces and 26,500 for paramilitary forces (largely National

Guard). See also D. P. Cole, 'The Enmeshment of Nomads in Saudi Arabian Society' in C. Nelson (ed.), *The Desert and the Sown* (Institute of International Studies, Berkeley, 1973).

11. See for instance *SAMA Annual Report 1979*, which lists sewage projects for Mecca, Medina, Jeddah, al-Riyadh, Dammam and al-Khobar as completed at a cost of SR 3.5 billion; expansion of utilities (water supply and storm water drainage) in al-Riyadh at a cost of SR 721 million, in Jeddah and Mecca at a cost of SR 332 million. See also development plans for individual towns, and *Arab News* supplements on Jeddah (23 January 1977) and on al-Riyadh (29 March 1977).

12. Marianne Ali Reza, *At the Drop of a Veil* (Houghton-Mifflin, Boston, 1971).

13. Linda Blandford, *Oil Sheikhs* (W. H. Allen, London, 1976) gives an example of this (p. 87).

14. In 1960 113,176 boys and 5,224 girls were at school; by 1970 the numbers had risen to 385,841 boys and 126,230 girls. *SAMA Annual Report 1979* gives the following figures for 1977–8:

	Males	Females
Primary	474,639	278,569
Post-primary	193,003	93,927
Higher	32,429	9,155
Technical	4,967	–

University students, both male and female, increased by 30 per cent from 1976–7 to 1977–8; of women university students 84 per cent are at Jeddah or al-Riyadh universities. In the same period the numbers of women students at teacher training colleges (*kuliyat*) rose by 66 per cent; seven new colleges were opened.

15. For instance, an *Arab News* report on women's education (9 September 1976), stated: 'The provision of books that would meet the needs of Saudi Arabia's young girls has also been a major factor of interest. It has been necessary to carefully screen books produced in sisterly Arab–Islamic countries to assure that the texts are of the required quality, and special texts have been commissioned to meet Saudi Arabia's needs.'

16. The *Guidelines for the Second Development Plan, 1975–1980* (Central Planning Organisation, Kingdom of Saudi Arabia, 1975) gave an estimated 1 per cent in 1970, expecting this to rise to 3.5 per cent in 1975; the *International Herald Tribune* (30 May 1975), quoted 1.5 per cent for 1975; Lackner, *A House Built on Sand*, gives an estimate of 1.5 per cent for the mid-1970s; and Birks and Sinclair, *Arab Manpower* in 1980 quote the figure as 2.7 per cent.

17. Director of Main Labour Bureau in Western Province, Sayed Ahmad Yahya, quoted in *Saudi Economic Survey* (2 April 1975): 'it is better from the economic point of view, therefore, that consideration should be taken to exploit their [the women's] portion of the labour force through ideal methods, in accordance with the traditions, customs and labour laws, instead of resorting to recruitment from abroad'. Shaikh Hisham Nazer, Minister of Finance, is on record as saying that by the end of the third plan 40,000 women graduates would be available and that their right to work, provided it did not mean mixing with men, had been accepted by the *'ulama* (*Financial Times*, 28 April 1980).

18. E. Rutter, *The Holy Cities of Arabia* (Putnam, London, 1928), p. 386, states 13 or 14 years; M. Katakura, *Bedouin Village*, p. 86, gives 'about 14' for recently settled bedouin; D. P. Cole, *Nomads of the Nomads* (Aldine, Chicago, 1975), p. 73, gives 'about 18' for the Al Murrah; women of Hijazi merchant

families told the writer that the geneallly accepted marriage age for their girls was now 18 or 19.

19. R. Buschow, *The Prince and I* (Futura, London, 1979).

20. S. Kay and M. Basil, *Saudi Arabia Past and Present* (Namara Publications, London, 1979), p. 51; Iseman, 'The Arabian Ethos', p. 43.

21. D. Holden, *Farewell to Arabia* (Walker, New York, 1966).

22. For example, some 17,000 Saudi students are at present studying in the USA on Saudi government fellowships; 5,000 of those are taking higher degrees.

23. For an account of life in the princess's family and of this event see R. Buschow, *The Prince and I*.

10 SEDENTARISATION AS A MEANS OF DETRIBALISATION: SOME POLICIES OF THE SAUDI ARABIAN GOVERNMENT TOWARDS THE NOMADS

Ugo Fabietti

Introduction

Some recent studies of nomadic pastoral communities have emphasised the significance of the social and political environments within which these communities exist: the fact that these communities are by now more or less stably included inside centralised political structures.[1] Placing the nomadic pastoral communities within larger economic and political systems, today equivalent to the structures of nation states, is a phenomenon that cannot be analysed in formal terms. The phenomenon, known as encapsulation,[2] is not just the simple super-imposition of larger economic and political structures on the 'more limited' structures that are characteristic of the nomadic pastoral communities. On the contrary, encapsulation causes changes and new social dynamics within the encapsulated communities, acting in particular on the mechanisms which assure their reproduction and social cohesion. The case of the nomadic communities in Saudi Arabia is typical.

In this article I propose to examine some of the policies carried out by the Saudi Arabian governments towards the nomadic pastoral population, to indicate the nature of these policies, and finally to illustrate their effects on the reproduction and social cohesion of the communities in question. With this aim in mind I will concentrate on the programmes for the sedentarisation of the bedouin because, even if these do not cover the whole range of methods adopted by the Saudi Arabian government in their detribalisation policy, they certainly form the most important part of this policy. I will try to demonstrate, in the following order:

1. that sedentarisation as such is a phenomenon closely linked to the productive instability and deficiency of pastoral nomadism in this region;
2. that by promoting intervention policies, both at present and in the

past, the Saudi Arabian government has always exploited the
productive instability and deficiency to serve its detribalisation
policy;
3. that state intervention aiming to make the nomads settle has been
   more successful when it has managed to alter the traditional system
   of access to resources.

Sedentarisation, in the Middle East, is a phenomenon linked
structurally to the nature of pastoral nomadism. The pastoral nomadism
of the bedouin in the Arabian peninsula can be considered as a multi-
resource system, according to Salzman's well-known definition of this
type of appropriation of natural resources.[3] Pastoral nomadism, then,
is not a productive system that can alone supply the necessary resources
for the survival of the groups that practise it. The productive deficiency
of pastoral nomadism in this area is due both to the unstable ecological
conditions and to the vulnerability of the animals which are bred to
diseases. As a result the nomadic groups have always tended to
integrate their pastoral activities, which have always been the basis of
their subsistence, with other types of productive activity. Among these,
an important role was played in the past by cattle stealing from other
groups – which enabled the nomads to re-establish an endangered
productive equilibrium.[4] Another important source of subsistence in
the past was offered by merchant caravans and pilgrimages, usually by
providing the caravans with escorts or by controlling tribal territories
which could only be crossed after reaching an agreement with the
groups that professed to own them. The control of small oases could
also be a source of income, but only in cases where these were not in
the areas of influence of centralised political organisations, for example,
those characteristic of pre-Islamic Arabia.
   The multi-resource character of the nomadic communities' productive system, then, is the effect of adaptation to the productive
discontinuity of pastoral nomadism. This adaptation played, and still
plays, a role of vital importance in the social history of the Arabian
peninsula. It has contributed to the inclusion of the nomadic groups in
a close network of relationships with the sedentary populations who,
however, have very often managed to impose their own political and
military hegemony.[5] Due to the nature of pastoral nomadism the
relationship between the nomads and the sedentary populations has not
been one of simple opposition; pastoral nomadism has been responsible
for a continual flow of men and goods between the desert and the areas
of permanent settlements. In the past the roles of the nomad and

Figure 10.1: Approximate Location of Major Tribal Grazing *Diras*

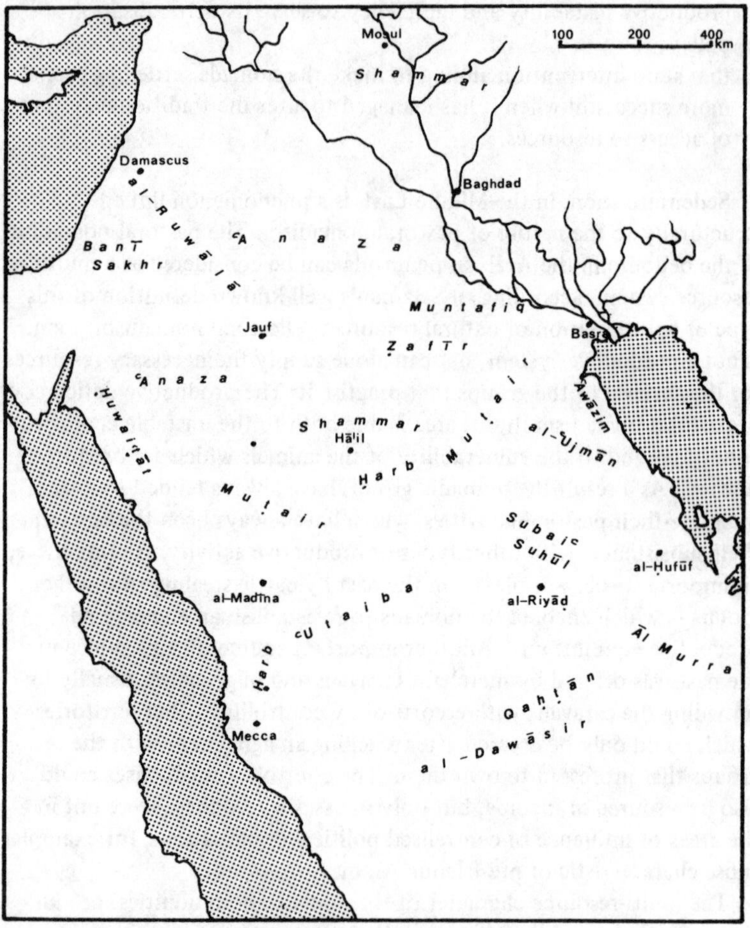

Source: C. Moss Helms, *The Cohesion of Saudi Arabia* (Croom Helm, London, 1981), p. 50.

sedentary have been easily interchangeable since, instead of being the expression of the existence of two types of communities with markedly different economic, social and ideological characteristics, they have reflected a situation of productive instability. This can be seen clearly in the case of tribes whose population is one part nomadic and one part sedentary (for the most part farmers). The population of the Shammar tribe in the centre and north of Arabia, for example, can be divided into the purely nomadic, who live in the Nafud desert, and the sedentary, living in villages near the town of Ha'il. The tribe's separation into nomadic and sedentary elements does not correspond to social groups formed on such ideological bases as lineage or fraction (*fakhd*), but it is rather a distinction based on a division of labour stemming from 'fluid' productive conditions. These productive conditions, in turn, stem from unstable ecological factors, such that some groups in the past were forced to change the fundamental part of their production from pastoral activity to agriculture, and others *vice versa*. There has been a constant interchange between the desert and the village, and we can therefore say that the type of sedentarisation which has occurred is structurally connected to the ecology of pastoral nomadism. Abandonment of the nomadic way of life can be the consequence of a significant fall in productivity, but it can also signify the opposite, that is that benefiting from higher than average productive margins, the group in question chooses to settle in one place in order to be able to undertake other productive activities and thus protect itself from the instability of pastoral production. In both cases sedentarisation appears to be a phenomenon linked to the productive discontinuity of pastoral nomadism.

The relationship between sedentarisation and the characteristics of pastoral nomadism is worth emphasising in order to show how, in a situation of non-encapsulation, sedentarisation may occur spontaneously. This type of sedentarisation contrasts with that favoured by the Saudi Arabian state for its detribalisation objectives. The latter type will here be referred to as 'guided' sedentarisation.

The tribal identity of pastoral nomads in the Arabian peninsula is the ideological correlate of a social form of exploitation of the natural resources — involving community rights of access to the resources of a particular area (*dira*) over which one group asserts its control at the expense of others. The tribal identity of a group, therefore, reflects the level of political and ideological integration which serves to exploit the resources. Detribalisation policy, directed towards strengthening the centralised state, has necessarily affected all the bases of nomadic life — juridical, ideological and economic. In this respect, sedentarisation in an encapsulated community has significantly different aspects than sedentarisation in a non-encapsulated community. Whereas in the latter case the process of sedentarisation has little effect on the social structure of the community, 'guided' sedentarisation does affect the social structure — especially with regard to social differentiation. The introduction of an external factor, that is the intervention of a centralised state, alters the nature of the available resources and the modes of access to them, thereby creating the possibility of wider inequalities.

Early Sedentarisation Policy

The first attempt at 'guided' sedentarisation of the bedouin occurred in the early years of the Saudi Arabian state. It was linked to the development of the *ikhwan* movement and to the beginnings of Saudi Arabian expansionist policy in the peninsula. Through the creation of a series of agricultural villages (*hujar*), with a population made up from various different tribes, Abd al-Aziz, the founder of modern Arabia, aimed at creating a military force that possessed both the qualities that are typical of sedentary groups (easily controllable, immediate mobilisation) and the characteristics of the bedouin groups (mobility, aggressiveness).[6] This was made possible by freeing these groups from the necessities imposed on them by pastoral production. The *hujar*, in fact, were never self-sufficient from a productive point of view, but survival was assured their populations by government assistance,[7] and by the benefits deriving from raids carried out against enemy groups and from the spoils of war. In the period following the elimination of the *ikhwan* as a military and religious movement, the *hujar* underwent a rapid process of decline and depopulation. The bedouin who had settled in the villages in response to the appeals made by Abd al-Aziz and the religious hierarchy went back to the nomadic way of life or moved into the cities looking for jobs in the National Guard. The detribalisation process linked to sedentarisation and the fusion of elements of heterogeneous origin was thus frozen. In this phase of the history of the Saudi Arabian state, then, the attempt to weaken tribal solidarity was pursued by means of substituting widely dissimilar activities for the productive base on which this tribal solidarity was founded. The state intervened, manipulating the aggressive characteristics of the bedouin and channelling them into a holy war (*jihad*). Tribal solidarity was not altered by affecting the mechanisms which sustain it — that is the modes of access to the resources. In this kind of situation the process of detribalisation is limited to the extent that the groups concerned are able to return to traditional pastoral activities. The sedentarisation of the *ikhwan* worked as a decisive factor in the process of amalgamation of the groups (and therefore in the detribalisation process) up to the moment when the inhabitants of the *hujar* were able to do without the activities linked with pastoral nomadism. It is only when the state can alter the mechanisms that control access to resources that there can be a real process of detribalisation.

The second experiment in guided sedentarisation was the policy of big agricultural projects launched at the end of the 1950s. This policy was made possible by the increasing availability of financial resources which permitted the introduction of new agricultural technology. In this case, sedentarisation was intended to give the nomadic shepherds access to new resources made available by the state and to transform the productive bases of the bedouin communities in the areas concerned. The projects (Wadi Sirhan, Harad and Jabrin) were launched after a period of drought during which the nomads suffered a fall in productivity. The Wadi Sirhan project (1958) was launched after a very long period of drought in the area had deprived several nomadic groups (above all the Shararat) of the greater part of their livestock. The sedentarisation of the bedouin in Wadi Sirhan was intended to transform the foundations of their subsistence through substituting agriculture for their pastoral activities. The project failed due to a series of planning errors, the worst of which were the insufficient technical preparation given to the bedouin and the low degree of their involvement during the project's preparatory phase. When the ecological conditions of the region returned to normal, making pastoral activities possible once again, the majority of the bedouin went back to a nomadic existence, while the remainder moved to urban centres, looking for employment in the army or National Guard — exactly as the bedouin settled in *hujar* had done at the end of the *ikhwan* movement. The bedouin's return to the nomadic way of life, and therefore the failure of the project, was blamed on their low disposition to a sedentary way of life.[8] We have seen, however, that pastoral nomadism has certain productive characteristics which make integration with other activities necessary and that bedouin will choose sedentarisation when facing either a deficit or a surplus in pastoral production. Rejecting 'psychological' explanations for the failure of the project, therefore, we must assert that bedouin are not *a priori* refractory to a sedentary way of life, but rather that they have an attitude towards it inspired by very practical criteria: they adopt this way of life every time, failing other possible alternatives, it seems to be worthwhile.

Neither at Wadi Sirhan nor in any of the other projects covered here was the state's intervention capable of altering the mechanisms of tribal solidarity. As with the *hujar* the authorities aimed at a substitution of the productive system and not an alteration of the modes of access to the resources upon which tribal solidarity is based. One paradox arises with relation to these projects. Each one was highly homogeneous — composed, not necessarily of the same tribe, but at least of tribal groups traditionally present in the area.[9] No doubt the project organisers hoped that this would facilitate the transition to sedentarised life, but, in fact, the characteristic accounts for the ease with which many nomads returned to pastoral activity after the project had failed. During the whole period in which the bedouin remained sedentary, they never in fact abandoned animal husbandry. Only two years after the beginning of the Wadi Sirhan project, when its failure was already on the cards, some groups were already returning to a nomadic way of life.

Sedentarisation Policy Based on Altering Access to Resources

In contrast to the two experiments mentioned above, we will now show how state intervention, aiming to settle the nomads, achieved greater success in detribalisation when it managed to alter the traditional system of access to the resources. This concerns the policy of distributing land to the bedouin, under the 1968 law, which has been carried out by the government during the last decade — an intervention in the nomadic sector which is of a qualitatively different kind compared to previous state activity. Unlike the former cases, the present policy involves an intervention which could be defined as *juridical*, capable of causing profound changes in the mechanisms of integration of the tribal units. The 1968 law on the distribution of land is not the first intervention of a juridical character made by the state in the nomadic sector. In fact, it is part of a longer-established programme for the progressive dispossession of tribal space, carried out by the state at the expense of bedouin groups. In 1925 the exclusive rights of the tribes in their own *diras* were virtually abolished. In this way anyone who wanted to was given the possibility of utilising resources (pasture and water) in tribal territories. While it is difficult to trace the precise effects of the 1925 law, it seems probable that the law did not, in itself, cause an immediate alteration in the models of nomadic life and the use of the natural resources. Trespassing in other tribes' territories was, moreover, a habitual practice even before this law, and the utilisation of the resources of different tribal territories had been possible under precise inter-tribal agreements (without which conflicts might arise).[10]

The 1925 law did, however, have some significant effects in the longer term — in conjunction with the greater freedom of movement which motorised transport brought to the bedouin. The introduction of motor vehicles has caused a real change in the relationship between the bedouin and pastoral space. It has simplified the means of supplying water to the camps and animals, and finally led to more frequent contact between the nomads and the population of the urban and agricultural centres. Given these factors, only now may the law abolishing the exclusive rights of utilisation of the *dira* be able to produce its most significant results. It is quite common today to meet isolated families or whole fractions of tribes several hundreds of kilometres away from their traditional pastoral territories. This fact certainly also reflects the diminished interest which the tribal units have in conserving their exclusive rights on the use of resources in their own territory. The development of new sources of income (work in the public sector, the army, the National Guard, commerce, etc.), the marketing of small-size animals raised on cultivated fodder, and state assistance are factors which today play a decisive role in the life of the bedouin, whose subsistence is less tied than it once was to the exploitation of natural resources. The natural resources are no longer subject to the type of management and defence that was characteristic of the period when the bedouin were more dependent on a pastoral economy based on big seasonal migrations. In 1965 a Saudi Arabian expert had already noted how the relaxation of tribal control on the *dira* risked creating ecological degradation in certain regions[11] — that is the lack of a centre of management of the resources was likely to cause damaging effects on pastoral productivity. Today the areas in Saudi Arabia suffering from this degradation process are numerous, but the shift from breeding dromedaries to breeding sheep (on cultivated fodder) has at least rendered the modification of the ecological equilibria of minor importance.

The aim of the 1925 law, then, was to promote access to the resources in a manner which contrasted with the system of traditional rights of utilisation of the *dira*. Besides affecting the bedouin's migration patterns the law was intended to undermine the tribes' political independence. It replaced the practice of agreements and alliances between the tribes, upon which the tribes depended in order to be able to exploit the resources of another *dira*, with an all-embracing code. In this way the state asserted its right to intervene in a field which until then had been the domain of tribal politics. Thus the tribes lost one of their principal functions, that of protection and management of the communities' interests as regards access to the resources. Today this process of weakening the tribes' functions has been reinforced by the law of 1968 on the distribution of land.

In order to describe the effects of the 1968 law on the tribal cohesion of the groups that benefited from the allotment of land, the writer will rely on his own research experience in the Ha'il region.[12] As regards the nomads, the law is most relevant to those areas where the presence of very deep water-bearing strata of ancient formation allows for a type of agriculture to be developed using irrigation. The al-Khotta region, an administrative subdivision of the province of Ha'il, enters into this category. The water-bearing stratum situated in the subsoil of this plain on the southern edge of the Great Nafud was formed as a result of a multi-millennial process of infiltration and collection of rainwater. Since 1970, the year in which a settlement was established there, the government has distributed several hundred parcels of land (100 dunum each – about 23 acres). The Bank of Agriculture made the necessary loans, half of them without security, to cover the initial costs of developing agricultural production, that is enclosure, well-drilling, and the purchase of water pumps and seeds.

In theory, all the citizens of the kingdom can apply to the competent authorities for a piece of land in a region like al-Khotta; in reality, land distribution is based on criteria of tribal membership. Al-Khotta is in the ancient *dira* of the Shammar tribe and all the bedouin who have benefited from the 1968 law belong to the Abde fraction, one of the big *fakhds* which make up the tribe. Some subgroups of the Sinjara *fakhd*, benefiting from the law, have obtained land in the area to the south of al-Khotta. Within the Abde fraction distribution seems to depend on such factors as the closeness of parentage to the local *amir* dealing with the land distribution, and possession of influential friends inside the Ha'il emirate or al-Riyadh's ministries. Naturally distribution on this basis cuts off many families, belonging to the same *fakhd* as the assignees, from access to the land.

The pattern of distribution can have significant effects on tribal solidarity. On the one hand, distribution takes place according to a traditional system – and this tends to strengthen group solidarity and tribal sentiments. But, on the other, some families are cut off from access to the resources, which is likely to create considerable social differentiation. The disaggregating effects of the policy of land distribution do not appear immediately and in fact only emerge as a result of a different kind of land appropriation, which will now be described.

It is quite common on the al-Khotta plain to find bedouin who, due to the low profitability of certain crops or to the possibility of obtaining other larger sources of income elsewhere, have alienated the land that was allocated them. The 1968 law, in fact, established that the land becomes the property of the assignee three years after he begins to cultivate it (right of *usus* and *abusus*). This is an application of the Islamic principle of vivification. Once the land has been allotted, it can be sold under this condition. Usually, in the al-Khotta settlement, the land is bought by rich businessmen from Ha'il or by farmers who want to enlarge the area of land they already possess. The land is then cultivated using salaried farm labourers – recruited through special employment bureaux in the Saudi Arabian embassies in foreign countries (Egypt and Pakistan in particular). The new owners do not necessarily belong to the tribal fractions that originally took possession of the land nor to other *fakhds* of the Shammar tribe. It is, therefore, only at the level of the first appropriation that the criterion of tribal membership is respected. When the land is alienated this criterion is no longer the decisive factor for obtaining access to the agricultural resources. The right to private property substitutes the traditional collective right of access to the land. In fact, the 1968 law makes possible the emergence of a market for land in a society where once there were only collective rights as regards the exploitation of the resources.

This is the first important effect produced by the 1968 law on the system of community rights which are the pillars of tribal cohesion and solidarity. The most significant aspect of the law, therefore, is not the distribution of land as such, neither is it that the availability of land favours the sedentarisation of the nomads or gives them the possibility of exploiting different resources than those deriving from pastoral activities. These are all factors that do not alter *per se* the social dynamics of the bedouin communities, whose productive system is a multi-resource system. Unlike the Saudi Arabian state's previous sedentarisation policies, that carried out through the distribution of land is not based either on the fusion of elements coming from different tribal units, nor on the substitution of the productive base of the nomadic communities, but rather on the effects of the individual appropriation of the resources inside tribal territory.

The bedouin families which first received land in the al-Khotta plain started to cultivate it, first, in order to develop a type of animal husbandry that lessened the risks of traditional pastoral production, and secondly, to exploit the possibility that fodder production gave them of increasing the breeding of small animals. The latter activity, given the growing demand of the home market, is reasonably profitable. Very often the cultivation of fodder, generally alfalfa (*bersim*), has brought in the same level of income as sheep rearing. Surplus fodder is sold on the market at Ha'il to those bedouin who, even though they are unable to cultivate their own fodder, have undertaken the breeding of sheep and goats as a consequence of the almost total monetarisation of the pastoral economy. The breeding of small animals is a kind of husbandry which has provoked a growing impoverishment of the natural pastures, making the purchase of supplementary fodder a necessity. The fodder market owes its highly profitable character to the fact that there are sheep breeders, in fact the majority of them, who have been denied access to the land.

The distribution of land, therefore, has introduced an element of disturbance to the bedouin communities' typical tribal cohesion and solidarity. It has laid the foundations for the individual appropriation of resources which previously were managed along community lines, and this has, in turn, led to the development of a market in land resources. In this way the conditions have been created for a rapid process of differentiation within the bedouin communities, based on wealth.

Talal Asad, in an article written in 1979,[13] has queried whether the social systems of the pastoral nomadic populations are indeed egalitarian. He has noted how their inclusion in a larger national setting, that is their encapsulation, can lead to a division of labour involving real class differences. The bedouin of the Arabian peninsula, it is true, have never constituted a separate society. Today, nevertheless, when the presence of the state can be felt in all sectors of the pastoral nomadic communities' existence, from the economico-political to the ideological-religious, their social system is increasingly influenced by the wider setting. The action taken in the last few years by the Saudi Arabian state at a juridical level has altered the social dynamics of the bedouin communities – through private ownership of the land, individual management of resources which originally were collective, and the exclusion of one part of the population from certain privileges linked to the development of a market. Encapsulated nomadic communities tend to witness the growth of differences of status which favour the tribal leaders who are in a better position to exploit the relations with the state[14] and therefore to acquire privileges regarding access to the new resources made available by the government. Sometimes the bedouin communities react to this situation with passive resistance. The failure of the Harad project, for example, was partly due to bedouin reluctance to take part in enterprises in which individuals belonging to powerful fractions were given the possibility of obtaining greater benefits than the others.[15]

The encapsulation of the nomadic communities, therefore, often leads to the groups' losing control of their means of production. Probably the social dynamics which characterise these groups today will mark the beginning of a new kind of social differentiation based on a new social division of labour.

Notes

1. See, for example, R. Fazel, 'The Encapsulation of Nomadic Societies in Iran' in C. Nelson (ed.), *The Desert and the Sown* (Institute of International Studies, Berkeley, 1973); and T. Asad, 'Equality in Nomadic Social Systems? Notes towards the Dissolution of an Anthropological Category', in Équipe Écologie et Anthropologie des Sociétés Pastorales, *Pastoral Production and Society* (Cambridge University Press, Cambridge, 1979).

2. See F. G. Bailey, *Stratagems and Spoils* (Blackwell, Oxford, 1970).

3. P. C. Salzman, 'Multi-Resource Nomadism in Iranian Baluchistan' in W. Irons and N. Dyson-Hudson (eds.), *Perspectives on Nomadism* (Brill, Leiden, 1972).

4. See L. Sweet, 'Camel Raiding of North Arabian Bedouins: A Mechanism of Ecological Adaptation', *American Anthropologist*, vol. 67 (1965).

5. T. Asad, 'The Bedouin as a Military Force: Notes on Some Aspects of Power Relations between Nomads and Sedentaries in Historical Perspective' in Nelson (ed.), *The Desert and the Sown*.

6. J. S. Habib, *The Ikhwan Movement of Najd: its Rise, Development and Decline* (Brill, Leiden, 1978), p. 25.

7. T. O. el Farra, 'The Effects of Detribalizing the Bedouins on the Internal Cohesion of an Emerging State: the Kingdom of Saudi Arabia', unpublished PhD thesis, University of Pittsburg, 1973, p. 136.

8. Economic Intelligence Unit, 'The Nomadic Community – a Policy Framework', unpublished working paper, al-Riyadh, no date.

9. See ibid.

10. A. Musil, *The Manners and Customs of the Rwala Bedouins* (American Geographical Society, New York, 1928), p. 533.

11. K. M. Al-Gosaibi, *The Programme for Bedouins* (Central Planning Organisation, al-Riyadh, 1965), p. 6.

12. The fieldwork was carried out as part of a study of the pastoral nomadic communities organised by the Société d'Études pour le Développement Économique et Social with the collaboration of the Saudi Arabian government's Ministry of Social Affairs (July 1978–March 1980).

13. T. Asad, 'Equality in Nomadic Social Systems?'

14. D. Cole, 'The Enmeshment of Nomads in Sa'udi Arabian Society: the Case of Al Murrah' in Nelson (ed.), *The Desert and the Sown*, p. 121.

15. D. Cole, *Nomads of the Nomads* (Aldine, Chicago, 1975), p. 157.

11 THE DOMESTIC POLITICAL ECONOMY OF DEVELOPMENT IN SAUDI ARABIA

J. S. Birks and C. A. Sinclair

Introduction

This article will attempt to make a broad assessment of the direction of economic development in Saudi Arabia, and highlight some areas of growing political and social stress.[1] Prior to 1970, development was financially and geographically limited, the result of Saudi Arabia's limited oil revenues and the physical size of the country. Extensive economic development is recent in origin and has been effected at a rapid pace. Partly as a result of which rapidity of development, it has been primarily the urban populations which have participated in and experienced the effects of it. About half the national population has been bypassed by it, remaining, for a range of social and economic reasons, locked into the rural economy. Productivity in this sector is low, but cash incomes, derived from a miscellany of sources, are comparatively high — high enough to persuade rural Saudis that their self-ordered existence on farms is preferable to the trauma of urban life.

Managing development is becoming increasingly a question of trading off one pressure group against another. The non-participation of a large proportion of Saudi Arabian nationals, the burgeoning ranks of foreigners (both Muslim and non-Muslim), and the restrictions imposed by the branch of Islam followed in Saudi Arabia, all combine to create discord and unease. Events have progressed to the point where now no alternative is stress-free: every alternative carries social, economic or political risks. An abandonment of development in Saudi Arabia would have more serious consequences for the outside world than did the collapse of Iran. While there is no sense in which this article predicts a collapse of development, it does enumerate some potential contributory factors to that result.

Growth of the Modern Economy

Most contemporary comment on and analysis of Saudi Arabia focuses on the economic and political power and influence of the kingdom.[2] Whilst this is a valid perspective for many purposes, here analysis stems from a different viewpoint; it is important to realise how tiny the Saudi Arabian economy was until the early 1970s and how quickly it has grown since then. This is not simply an academic observation (although as a case study in development Saudi Arabia is fascinating to the economist), but one of immense practical significance. Because of the rapidity of growth, many Saudi Arabians have been left behind, stranded in the traditional sector. Moreover, religious leaders and traditionalists have had very little time to come to terms with 'modern development'. Their reaction to it is pitched correspondingly.

Prior to 1970, Saudi Arabian oil revenues, although large by Middle Eastern standards of that time, were only a fraction of their post-1970 dimensions: revenues rose from $1,150 million in 1970 to $29 billion in 1975, and are estimated to have reached $60 billion in 1980. Indeed, at the end of the 1960s, so little had the focus of the Saudi Arabian economy moved towards oil that the annual pilgrimage to Mecca (*hajj*) remained a significant source of government income and employment for the national population.[3] The high prestige of employment based on the *hajj* and the periodic nature of this work remain an influence on the employment patterns of Saudi Arabian nationals even today, as will be shown. So limited were oil revenues at the end of the 1960s and in the early 1970s that their impact in this large kingdom within the modern sector was accounted for virtually completely by the small urban surrounds of Jeddah, al-Riyadh, Damman and Dhahran. In character, this limited modern sector consisted of a modest – though growing – government bureaucracy, a general proliferation of small-scale construction activity and innumerable trading concerns, some small, some large.

It was only with the accession of Faisal to the throne in 1964 that modern development really began. The enormous size of the country, together with the relatively modest oil income prior to 1970, however, made rapid development impossible. Communications, infrastructure and social services absorbed much of all government expenditure. Other constraints – such as the lack of manpower (quantitatively and qualitatively) together with inadequate roads and ports – also slowed down the pace of development. Moreover the natural conservatism of Saudi Arabia's leaders meant that modern development proceeded cautiously: there was protracted debate about the impact of modernity upon moral values. The extent to which the large majority of the Saudi Arabian population was unaffected by modern sector

development even in 1970 can be illustrated by the large proportion
then still working in the (rather ill-defined) sector 'agriculture and
nomadism': in 1970, as in 1966, virtually one-half of the Saudi Arabian
economically active labour force was in this sector.[4]

In 1970, the 'agriculture and nomadism' sector was essentially
traditional in nature. Its organisation was little changed, and its
technology largely that of subsistence hill farming, with a much smaller
proportion of the population engaged in semi-nomadic and, to a lesser
extent, nomadic herding. Numbers of the 'bedouin' (nomads) in Saudi
Arabia are almost always overstated in assessments of the Saudi Arabian
population. Even United Nations' estimates have slipped into the trap
of exaggeration, reporting in 1967 that 'there were some 3,000,000 of
the nomadic population who had escaped enumeration in the 1962/63
census'. In fact, the majority of the rural population are settled farmers,
and have been so for some decades; farmers in the wadis and hills
outnumber the semi-nomadic goat herders of the mountains and better
watered plains areas. Only a relatively small proportion of the rural
population was truly nomadic even in the 1960s, and this group has
been declining in numbers as they have settled. In settling, though, the
erstwhile bedouin have not become modern-sector farmers − rather
they have exchanged one form of subsistence income for another.

It was the sheer size of the kingdom and the virtually complete lack
of infrastructure which militated against any major change in the rural
way of life in Saudi Arabia until 1970. Apart from other factors, the
general lack of water set strict physical limits on what could be
achieved without massive infrastructural investment. Where modern-
sector agricultural projects were instigated, their impact was only local
and not really expanding. Thus, in 1970, the 440,000 economically
active Saudi Arabians living in rural areas mostly enjoyed only low
incomes, and lived a largely traditional life.

In sharp contrast to this was, of course, the nature of the oil
industry, in 1970 almost exclusively represented in Saudi Arabia by
Aramco. Although growing paramount as an earner of government
income, the oil industry only employed small numbers, many of whom
were non-nationals in 1970. The low levels of educational attainment
and limited modern-sector employment experience of Saudi nationals
meant that there were few opportunities for the latter to work in the
oil sector. The various arms of government and public administration
represented the principal alternative to farming for most Saudi Arabians
− thus, in 1970, their employment options were much the same as they
had been for the past century. Indeed, so limited was development

expenditure that there was not even much expansion in these traditional non-farming opportunities. Terms of service and conditions in
the police, army and civil service did, however, improve significantly.
Many Saudi Arabians of urban background continued to follow private
trading pursuits.

Overall, though, most of the population in Saudi Arabia in 1970
had experienced relatively little change since the receipt of oil revenues,
either in transformed incomes or way of life. The pace of growth that
was to characterise the 1970s had not begun. Ironically, the concern
at the time, despite the limited impact of modernity, was that change
was proceeding too rapidly. The lobby for more and faster economic
growth had not yet gained real voice. In 1970, despite the receipt of 31
years of oil revenues, only some 480,000 workers in Saudi Arabia were
employed in modern-sector activities. Even more surprisingly, many of
these, even outside the oil sector, were expatriates.

Nascent Modern Sector of the Early 1970s

Despite its small scale in 1970, the Saudi Arabian modern sector had
begun to emerge in the 1950s. Its features were similar to the nascent
modern sectors in neighbouring Kuwait, Bahrain, Qatar and Abu Dhabi.
Construction of new roads, government buildings, new dwellings, urban
infrastructure and social amenities such as schools, hospitals and clinics
composed the main focus of development expenditure. Urban areas
enjoyed the majority of investment expenditure in Saudi Arabia, as
they did in the neighbouring countries. In Kuwait, Bahrain and Qatar
modern development had an almost immediate impact upon the total
population. The mass of the populations in these neighbouring states
was able to participate because of the small size of the states —
effectively city states. In Saudi Arabia, though, the size of the country
and the difficulties of communication, meant that the impact of
development was confined to urban areas where only a small proportion
of the population lived. The bulk of the Saudi Arabian population
neither saw the changed urban skyline, nor felt an appreciable change
to their way of life; indeed, it would have been surprising, in view of
the widely dispersed nature and the paucity of spending in rural areas,
if the rural population had felt the effects of modern development.

Beginnings of Dualism

This isolation of the rural population from the modern sector was
thought, in an illogical way, to stem from a sound policy pursued by
the ruling family who, whilst desiring modernity, felt that too great an

involvement of nationals, particularly those from more traditional environments, would be harmful to the kingdom.

There was another set of reasons, though, accounting for the small number of Saudi nationals in the modern sector. The typical rural Saudi Arabian found it difficult to enter the modern sector, even had the knowledge of it and the desire to enter it been present. The modern-sector development required a workforce with skills and also, importantly, with aspirations that Saudi Arabians did not possess in the 1950s through to the 1970s. Few nationals had professional qualifications, and only a small proportion had received secondary or even primary education. Primary education was not widely available in rural areas of the kingdom as late as 1970. Even in 1974, the educational attainment of Saudi Arabian nationals was such that 70 per cent of those aged ten years or more were illiterate. Some 13 per cent of this age-group were classified in the census as 'educated'. Nationals were therefore excluded from all but the most unskilled of modern-sector occupations. It was these jobs which, if any, Saudi Arabians were least likely to desire to fill.

Migrants and the Modern Sector

In the 1950s, troubles in Oman, essentially surrounding the collapse of the Imamate, resulted in the movement of Omani refugees and exiles into Saudi Arabia, where they were welcomed. Many of those displaced from Omani villages went to Saudi Arabian towns, where they participated in modern-sector development. At about the same time Yemenis, mostly from North Yemen, began to enter Saudi Arabia. This movement of Yemenis into Saudi Arabia in the 1950s continued through the 1960s. It was part of a wider dispersion during which Yemenis travelled and settled as far afield as Detroit (USA), Sunderland (UK), and in the Philippines and Indonesia. Out-migration was increased by the intense disruption of North Yemen during the 1960s. These Yemenis, like the Omanis, moved to the towns and worked either as builders or traders.

Another group significant in seizing with alacrity modern-sector opportunities for the unskilled in Saudi Arabia was the pilgrims. Each year throughout the 1950s, some 200,000 pilgrims converged upon the Hijaz. Many arrived as paupers, but had modern-sector work experience and sought job opportunities to pay for their journeys home. Some pilgrims found work at higher occupational levels, but most worked as unskilled labour in the gently expanding urban modern sector of the 1950s, 1960s and early 1970s.[5]

These groups together virtually excluded the Saudi Arabian nationals from the modern sector. In any case, the low motivation of Saudis, who did not desire manual work, limited their participation to military and quasi-military employment and government administration.

Economic factors — the ready availability of a non-national labour force in the urban areas — had combined with a general and rather ill-defined political desire in the palaces to exclude the mass of Saudi Arabians from 'immoral' modern-sector development and to isolate the rural Saudi population from the transformation of their towns. This almost exclusive reliance of the modern sector upon immigrant workers has continued into the 1970s. Accurate data on the number of migrant workers in the kingdom are scarce. The overall picture, however, is one of slow but steady growth of migrant workers through to 1975, after which their numbers have grown almost exponentially.

Table 11.1: Employment of Migrants in Saudi Arabia, 1962/3 to 1985

Year	Migrant employment
1962/3	60,000
1966/7	240,400
1975	723,400
1980	1,023,600
1985 estimate	1,314,400

Sources: J. S. Birks and C. A. Sinclair, *The Kingdom of Saudi Arabia and the Libyan Arab Jamahiriya: The Key Countries of Employment* (World Employment Programme Research Working Paper, ILO, Geneva, May 1979); Ibid., *Arab Manpower: The Crisis of Development* (Croom Helm, London, 1980), ch. 5, Tables 20.3 and 20.4 and authors' estimates.

One important point emerges from all the data on employment: the number of migrant workers reflects closely the expansion of the modern sector. Throughout this period, migrant workers absorbed a high proportion of modern-sector jobs. Meanwhile, Saudi Arabian nationals retained a very constant distribution of employment between economic sectors — even in 1974, 52 per cent were recorded in the census as farmers. Of course, the number employed in government rose, though surprisingly slowly. Outside public service, however, penetration of the modern sector by Saudi Arabians was minimal. Thus, contrary to popular opinion, in 1975 Saudi Arabia still had a relatively small modern sector. Even more surprisingly, the mass of the population took little part in this small modern economy, which was staffed almost exclusively by immigrants.

Accentuated Dualism in the Economy

The sudden spurt of growth in the economy which occurred with the implementation of the 1976–80 Development Plan, and the corresponding increase in the importation of migrant workers, served to reinforce the dualistic pattern of development. Even during the Second Plan, Saudi Arabians tended to remain on the farms.

Urban labour markets developed which required labour of all levels and types prepared to accept poor working conditions. Saudi Arabians were neither qualified to participate in these labour markets, because of their continued lack of modern-sector experience, nor willing to endure long working hours. They were, moreover, unable to pay the high rents necessary to secure housing in the urban areas. Much, then, deterred their leaving rural areas for the towns. At the same time, access to housing grants, agricultural loans and other cash benefits available as largess in rural areas served as a very strong economic incentive to farmers to retain their rural life-style. Curiously, the government's recent attempts to transform farming in Saudi Arabia (other than by instigating large-scale projects) by giving loans and grants to smallholders with the aim of promoting their modernisation are crucial in the preservation of a subsistence-based traditional rural sector. Loans and grants are accepted by farmers, but often are spent on consumption. If invested, then the capital so provided remains under-utilised, either because of mismanagement or for want of sufficient labour inputs. Thus gifts and loans to farmers, directed towards investment in small-scale agriculture, are taken as income by the farmers. This income does not require intensive labour inputs and so is highly prized. Indeed, as income in cash, it alleviates partly the need to derive income from the farms themselves, which are allowed to stagnate or decline further. Thus, moneys directed towards modernisation of small-scale farming may have the contrary impact to that which is intended: they withdraw labour inputs from the land, but ensure that the population remains rurally orientated. As a result, the agricultural sector is preserved in its relatively unproductive form.

Unearned income in these rural populations, then, is surprisingly high. This often removes the incentive to gain regular formal employment. One source of 'unearned income' has already been mentioned – the loans and gifts from banks and other development institutions. This is only one form of several such non-wage-related incomes that are received by those in this sector. Social security payments are now common; payments of compensation for drought and other hardships from government agencies also contribute to rural incomes. Less formalised, though perhaps yet more substantial, incomes unrelated to wage earning include payments resulting from clientage, traditional obligations and loyalties, and rents from family properties and land. For instance, rent from a single dwelling owned in one of the major cities comprises substantial income to a family dwelling in a village in rural Saudi Arabia. Such families, owning property in urban areas but choosing to remain in rural parts, are not uncommon; although having property in the cities, they are little tempted to move there. These families are reluctant to forgo the income from their property – which they would lose if they moved into it – and wish to avoid the high costs of living in towns. Therefore, despite being landlords of property in towns, they are not potential rural–urban migrants; their urban connections serve to reinforce and facilitate further their desire to live in rural areas.

None of this mattered when the prevailing official opinion in Saudi Arabia was that nationals were not required to contribute to modern-sector development. However, with the spirit of economic development which has accompanied the effecting of the 1976–80 plan, and the adopting of a far less cautious attitude towards economic development, the government has taken a different attitude towards the participation of nationals in economic development. Strenuous efforts are being made to encourage Saudi Arabians to work in the modern sector. Changing government policy in this sphere stems not only from an ideological change towards a more 'progressive' philosophy, but also from awareness of the extent of reliance upon non-nationals in the modern sector, and the dependence that this implies.

Market forces, however, have continued to work strongly against full participation of nationals in the modern sector. As long as development is executed by private bodies, and as long as these employers are concerned to maximise profit, then development in the kingdom will always be executed using the most cost-effective labour available. While alternative supplies of Egyptian, Jordanian, Syrian, Pakistani, Indian or South-East Asian labour remain easily available, Saudi Arabians will not be employed widely in the private modern sector.

Political Economy of Future Development

Planners in Saudi Arabia respond to social as well as economic pressure. The economic motive behind Saudi Arabian development at its rapid post-1975 pace is essentially that the sooner the economy is diversified away from its narrow oil base, the more economically independent (especially from the industrialised Western nations) and therefore the stronger economically will the kingdom become. Moreover, Saudi Arabia is under considerable international pressure (as a major exporter of oil) to recycle oil revenues; domestic industrial development is one way of achieving this. It is also a way of investing oil revenues such that considerable control is maintained over assets. An oil state which has invested financial assets in banks or real estate outside the country does not have the same degree of control as it does over domestic assets. The freezing of Iranian assets in the USA has shown the truth of this. Furthermore, the more vigorously Western economists predict world recession, the greater the incentive for Saudi Arabia to keep investing in domestic industry.

There are also considerable domestic pressures within Saudi Arabia that wish domestic economic growth to continue, even to accelerate. These 'pro-growth protagonists' not only include the more bizarre empire builders of Saudi Arabia who feature in the Western press, but also the more humble entrepreneurs with small industries and businesses in Saudi Arabia. It is significant that most members of the royal family fall firmly within the pro-growth class; their economic interests throughout the kingdom have become formidable, and will be furthered by more economic progress. Indeed, economic strength and political power within the royal family have become increasingly closely interlinked, a modern counterpart to the political strength and tribal allegiances of the past, with princes wielding influence by manipulation of their economic interests in the form of financial capital and employment, rather than by control over numbers of fighting men.

A second grouping in Saudi Arabian society which has also sampled modernity is rather more equivocal about continued economic growth. This comprises those Saudi Arabians who have been through higher education abroad. These new technocrats and academics, generally thought of as being in favour of economic expansion, do include some who question the nature and direction of Saudi Arabian change. One thing is clear, though; few of these highly educated individuals have much to gain from any reversion to the traditional order. Their doubts stem more from a questioning of the present structure of growth, rather than from doubts that modernity, in some form, should be accepted by Saudi Arabian economy and society. The group is most easily characterised by the PhD graduate from California. He is widely perceived as owing nothing personally to the establishment; his attitudes are feared as being atheistic and anti-establishment.

In many respects, the technocrats and academics occupy a position intermediate between, on the one hand, the entrepreneurs and, on the other, the religious fundamentalists and reactionaries. Many of the latter question whether economic growth should continue at all. The ideas of religious fundamentalism are strong among large portions of the uneducated rural population who have, over the past two decades, developed a disdainful attitude towards modern-sector change — partly a rationalisation of their *de facto* exclusion from it. Such ideas are also influential among the more educated *mutawa'* (religious teacher) class, and have become entrenched within substantial portions of the Shi'a minority. Ironically, in Saudi Arabia the Shi'a are concentrated in the eastern region around Qatif and al-Hasa. This is a sensitive area both politically and economically, since Dammam, Dhahran and Ras Tanura are in the vicinity. Many Shi'a are employed by Aramco, and work on oil installations. Despite the fundamentalism — and the vociferousness — found in this quarter, however, the Shi'a do not hold that much sway in the kingdom, though they do comprise a substantial wedge of the most conservative opinion, albeit with differing perspectives from the Wahhabis.

In bowing to pressures for further change, the government has to deal carefully with religious leaders and opinion. It is by an unholy alliance between the ultra-conservative religious group and the overseas-educated intellectuals that radical change is most possible and most feared, particularly since this might be comparable to the Iranian recipe for change. So far, the pro-growth lobby has been more success-ful in placating this conservative group than the Shah ever was in managing the religious reactionaries of Iran. For example, in the spread of television, great care was taken to ensure that the Wahhabis and their close cohorts in society were always consulted. The power of television to carry and reinforce Islam within the kingdom has been acknowledged and used from the start.

Other examples of official sensitivity to conservative religious opinion include the progressively harsher restrictions on the employ-ment, freedom of movement and educational opportunity of women, as also the strict adherence to laws concerning alcohol. Of great significance are the close tribal and family links of the Saudi royal family with widely dispersed tribal groups in Saudi Arabia. These contrast markedly with the ethnic and racial isolationism of the Peacock Throne; it is these tribal, blood and political relationships, reinforced by selective largess and sinecure employment, by which the Saudi royal family feels the pulse of and controls Saudi Arabian society. Probably such factors are effective in maintaining the loyalty of most nationals, and the system would act as a sensitive warning mechanism of any significant dissent, although they apparently did not do so prior to the take-over of the Grand Mosque. Perhaps one of the most imminent threats to stability in Saudi Arabia comes from within the royal family itself. The very size of the family — numbering some 2,000 princes — which gives it strength in monitoring and manipulating Saudi society at large also engenders disagreements and marks fundamental differences based on traditional alliances.

It is significant that the surprising and alarming attack on the Grand Mosque was accomplished with a substantial number of non-nationals. Of this diverse group of people — with widely differing perspectives and interests in their host country — the ruling family's cognisance is limited. Moreover, the family's ability to manipulate migrants by means other than the law, deportation and, implicitly, force is severely limited. Ostensibly exposed to deportation and economic downturn, the non-national community is generally thought of as being economically progressive, secular and pragmatic. This denies the heritage of Saudi Arabia's history within Islam. Many of the migrant workers were economically motivated migrants only in a secondary sense, and arrived primarily as pilgrims. Saudi Arabia's international influence through Islam, therefore, could prove a double-edged sword.

Typically immigrants are looked down upon by Saudi Arabian nationals who generally mistrust and suspect other Arabs, are contemptuous of Asians, and regard Far Easterners as 'infidels'. This attitude of superiority, based upon the Saudis' view of themselves as Islam's chosen people, makes the Saudi national insensitive to the tide of feeling amongst non-nationals, about whom the myth continues that 'our kingdom can be rid of them whenever we choose'. Yet the Saudis do feel threatened by the non-nationals. Already groups of Koreans, Philippinos, Indonesians and other South-East Asians are present in the peninsula in such large numbers that fears of their representing 'a potentially hostile army' are often voiced amongst Saudi Arabians of influence and weight. Indeed, this concern reached the point in the late 1970s where it became of major influence, nominally, on the Third Five-Year Plan (1980–5). During 1980 special measures to limit migrants' family size and to prohibit wives of certain groups joining husbands in Saudi Arabia were announced.

Migrants are in reality indispensable to the economy of the kingdom. This point can be clearly seen by looking at the Third Five-Year Plan outline. Total expenditure, including defence and aid, will total

$363,000 million at constant (1980) prices. Total spending in the Second Plan was $133,000 million. The emphasis in the Third Plan will be more on expanding production, and relatively less on infrastructural projects. Human resources development and rural areas emerge as two areas planners see as of key importance. Industrialisation will continue at Yanbu and Jubail, the large petrochemical projects will proceed, and several of the large projects such as King Khaled Military City, al-Riyadh University and the Causeway to Bahrain will be effected. Most of these projects have their origins in the Second Plan.

Employment grew annually at 4.8 per cent under the Second Plan (Table 11.2). Some sectors grew more quickly than others, notably transport and communications (15 per cent), construction (10 per cent) and manufacturing (10 per cent). By interpreting the stated objectives of the Third Plan, from a knowledge of the projects presently ongoing and from the trends of employment from 1975 to 1980, we have constructed a pattern of growth, shown in Table 11.2. The construction sector is assumed not to grow any larger in employment terms, although manufacturing employment grows more quickly: this reflects the objective of moving investment away from infrastructure and towards production. The agricultural sector, which was declining previously, begins to grow in employment terms as large sums are invested in rural infrastructure and in agriculture. Services, notably government, continue at the comparatively high rate of employment growth of 6 per cent, reflecting the continuing growth of government administration, health and education provision, as well as defence and national security. The growth of utilities will moderate slightly, but remains quite high. Overall, employment would then grow at 4 per cent per annum under the Third Five-Year Plan.

Essentially, the growth of employment envisaged here is consistent with announced Plan expenditures, erring possibly on the conservative side. The construction projects envisaged in the Third Plan may require an even larger workforce than 385,000 persons; productivity on construction sites may be lower than we anticipate. The administration of this ever more complex and diverse country may require yet more staff; the expansion of schools and hospitals may proceed still more quickly. However, it is estimated here that total employment will grow from 2.2 million in 1980 to 2.7 million in 1985, an increase of some 500,000 persons.

Table 11.3 shows the growth of the national workforce from 1.0 million persons in 1975 to 1.4 million in 1985, an annual rate of increase of some 3 per cent. Deducing the expatriate element in the

Table 11.2: Saudi Arabia: Employment in 1975 and Estimated Employment Growth to 1980 and 1985

Economic sector	All employment in 1975	Annual employment growth rate, 1975–80 (percentage)	All employment in 1980	Estimated annual employment growth in Third Plan, 1980–5 (percentage)	All employment in 1985
Agriculture and fishing	585,550	−2	529,300	+2	584,380
Mining and quarrying	27,000	+5	34,460	+5	43,980
Manufacturing	65,900	+6	88,190	+11	148,600
Utilities	20,350	+10	32,770	+7	45,960
Construction	239,300	+10	385,390	0	385,390
Trade and finance	204,200	+5	260,620	+4	317,080
Transport and communications	103,800	+15	208,780	+5	266,460
Services	503,700	+6	674,060	+6	902,050
Total	1,749,800	+4.8	2,213,570	+4.0	2,693,900

Source: Data for 1975: based on J. S. Birks and C. A. Sinclair, *Arab Manpower* (Croom Helm, London, 1980), ch. 5, Table 5.13, p. 108; data for 1980 and 1985: authors' estimates.

Table 11.3: Saudi Arabia: Employment by Nationality in 1975, 1980 and 1985

	1975	1980	Annual rate of increase	1985	Annual rate of increase
All employment	1,749,800	2,213,570	4.8	2,693,900	4.0
Nationals' employment	1,026,400[a]	1,189,990	3.0	1,379,530	3.0
Expatriate employment	723,400	1,023,580	7.2	1,314,370	5.1

Note: a. There is some uncertainty about this figure and over the national population for 1975. It might be rather higher than the present figure suggests. However, adjusting the national workforce would not affect the figure for the non-national workforce.

Sources: Data for 1975: national total based on J. S. Birks and C. A. Sinclair, *Arab Manpower* (Croom Helm, London, 1980), ch. 5; expatriate total based on ibid., *International Migration and Development in the Arab Region* (ILO, Geneva, 1980), Table 10, p. 134; data for 1980 and 1985: authors' estimates.

workforce is not simply an arithmetical task, for reasons outlined earlier in this paper. There are some spheres where nationals are unwilling to work, others where they are unqualified to work and still others where only nationals are entitled to work. However, in a broadly based assessment such as this one, we make the assumption that we can deduce expatriate employment by subtracting the supply of national labour from the total labour requirement. Thus while expatriate labour increased from 1975 to 1980 at an annual rate of 7 per cent and by some 300,000 persons, it is projected here as increasing annually at the reduced rate of 5 per cent, and by some 291,000 persons from 1980 to 1985.

An Expatriate Manpower Growth Constraint of 1 Per Cent Per Annum?[6]

The stated Third Plan expenditures are both well within the country's fiscal capacity and conservative in that the government is likely to be tempted to spend more rather than less. Projects may prove to be more costly, but also both internal and international pressures will be exerted on the Saudi Arabian government to maintain high levels of development expenditure. Local merchants and the national populace benefit from government expenditure, and the Third Plan aims to distribute wealth more evenly. Saudi Arabia is a major supplier of oil to OECD countries; a regular energy supply is essential for their economic growth. Within OPEC, Saudi Arabia extends her influence often by raising oil production. The demise of Iran as a major oil producer and the disruption of Iraqi production following the war with Iran will have a growing impact on the oil market. Iran and Iraq have been major oil producers. In 1978 their combined production was 8 million barrels a day, equivalent to Saudi Arabian production. For as long as the war continues their combined production may fall to 1 million barrels a day. The net effect of this will be to encourage Saudi Arabia to increase oil exports. The high price of oil will ensure enormous revenues and, even at presently envisaged levels of development expenditure, Saudi Arabia will accrue large surpluses. To diminish the task of recycling these surpluses, she will be under pressure from the international community to maintain high levels of domestic expenditure.

The expatriate manpower requirement to 1985, as envisaged in this article, is some 291,000 persons, an annual increase of 5 per cent. To reduce this to 1 per cent implies one of two things: either a spectacular increase in productivity or a greatly reduced level of domestic expenditure. Constraining expatriate manpower growth to 1 per cent per annum would be equivalent to virtually halting development, a situation certainly not envisaged in the Third Plan.

Conclusion

In many ways the kingdom has come to terms with the simultaneous experience of wealth and dependence. The last thirty-five years have seen almost uninterrupted stability of government and domestic harmony; the last ten years have seen the economy transformed. However, the strain on Saudi Arabian society and economy of enormous oil wealth and rapid economic growth have recently become more obvious. The present domestic consensus of opinion that development is acceptable and appropriate to the kingdom depends on the alliance between the religious establishment and the ruling family: religious and political authority are in unison. The unrelenting inflow of migrant workers and their families weakens this alliance. Managing the migrant community is therefore a very important, if not the primary, task of government.

Notes

1. Views expressed in this paper do not necessarily represent those of any organisation or agency with which the authors have been, or are, associated. The authors alone are responsible for views and opinions expressed.

2. P. Hobday, *Saudi Arabia Today: An Introduction to the Richest Oil Power* (Macmillan, London, 1978); F. Al Farsy, *Saudi Arabia: A Case Study in Development* (Stacey International, London, 1978); see also Y. A. Sayigh, *The Economies of the Arab World* (Croom Helm, London, 1978), ch. 4.

3. This point is shown by S. H. Hitti and G. T. Abed, *The Economy and Finances of Saudi Arabia* (IMF Staff Papers, Washington, vol. XXI, 1973), Table 16, p. 282.

4. Further discussion of employment data is given in: J. S. Birks and C. A. Sinclair, *Arab Manpower: The Crisis of Development* (Croom Helm, London, 1980).

5. Further detail on migration in the region is given in J. S. Birks and C. A. Sinclair, *International Migration and Development in the Arab Region* (ILO, Geneva, 1980).

6. This limit on manpower growth was outlined in the Third National Development Plan. See 'Saudi Arabia's Third National Development Plan 1980–5', *MEED* (7 November 1980), pp. 7–12.

12 SAUDI ARABIA'S OIL POLICY IN THE 1970s — ITS ORIGINS, IMPLEMENTATION AND IMPLICATIONS

Paul Stevens

Introduction

There are numerous aspects to Saudi Arabia's oil policy, some of which are complementary and some of which are contradictory. The difficulty lies in identifying the strands of policy and then deciding the relative importance of each strand in terms of the varied objectives which oil policy is intended to achieve. The initial problem is therefore one of identification and this can be very complex.

There are three sources which can assist in the identification of policy strands. The first source is a clear source of evidence derived from ministerial policy statements given in press releases, conferences, etc. The difficulty with using this source is concerned with the degree of Machiavellian interpretation to be put on the statements. Does the statement mean what it apparently says or does it mean something else? Freud once remarked that sometimes a cigar is just a cigar. The same is true of ministerial statements, but the problem is deciding when the cigar is merely a cigar and when it carries more exotic overtones.

The second source of identifying policy is what might be termed circumstantial evidence. In this situation an action to implement policy can be indicative of what the policy is intended to be. The problem here is that the action may be open to many interpretations and may be intended to achieve more than one aim. For example, in May 1980 Saudi Arabia increased the price of the marker crude by $2. Was this because of a desire for higher prices, to restore the price-differential structure, to offset the high profits of the Aramco partners or to punish the US for showing *The Death of a Princess* the previous Monday, or some combination?

The final source of identifying oil policy is what might be termed mere hypothesis. Here one takes other objectives of policy which seem apparent, for example with respect to domestic economic development, and then from this imagine what oil policies would logically follow given the position of oil with respect to these other spheres. The problem, of course, with this approach is that it assumes that the

214

author and the oil minister have read the same textbooks on economic
development.

The reason for mentioning these three sources from which the
researcher can divine policy is that policy-making for oil in Saudi Arabia
(as in all the other OPEC countries) is a matter of the highest secrecy
and results in a complex set of policy objectives. Therefore, in order to
decide what the oil policy actually is, it is essential to make use of all
three sources in an effort to find a policy orientation which satisfies
all three as evidential sources. This article, therefore, is not based
entirely on hard evidence to which the author can refer the reader to
check. Rather, as will become apparent, it is based on a mixture of bits
and pieces — many of which it is impossible to reference.

Finally, two points of definition. The focus of this article is on the
international aspects of Saudi Arabian oil policy, although as will
emerge the domestic ramifications play a significant role in determining
this international policy. Secondly, primary attention will be given to
the period from mid-1973 to mid-1978, for reasons that will become
apparent, but reference will be made to the periods before and after
this in order to provide supporting evidence.

The article begins by examining what role Saudi Arabia's oil policy
plays in the international scene. Then the policy-making mechanism is
outlined, followed by the policy tools available to the Saudis and the
constraints on the use of those tools in achieving policy objectives.
Having set the context of the discussion, the paper then suggests what
the objectives of oil policy have been and how the policy tools have
been used to attain the objectives.

Importance of Saudi Arabia's Oil Policy

At one level the importance of Saudi Arabia's oil policy needs little
elaboration or explanation. In 1978 Saudi Arabia accounted for over
13 per cent of world oil production and about 40 per cent of Middle
East oil production,[1] and Saudi Arabia's reserves of oil account for
some 17.5 per cent of the world's oil reserves.[2] Finally the financial
reserves which are recycled or held by the Saudis are simply enormous.
At the end of 1978 Saudi Arabia's foreign assets were $60 billion
compared to $28 billion for Kuwait, $9.3 billion for the UAE, and $8.6
billion for Iraq.[3] All this is well known and frequently stated; the
implications are obvious in a world where, rightly or wrongly, the big
issue of the 1970s and 1980s is energy and more specifically oil.[4]

Figure 12.1: Oil Fields and Facilities, 1975

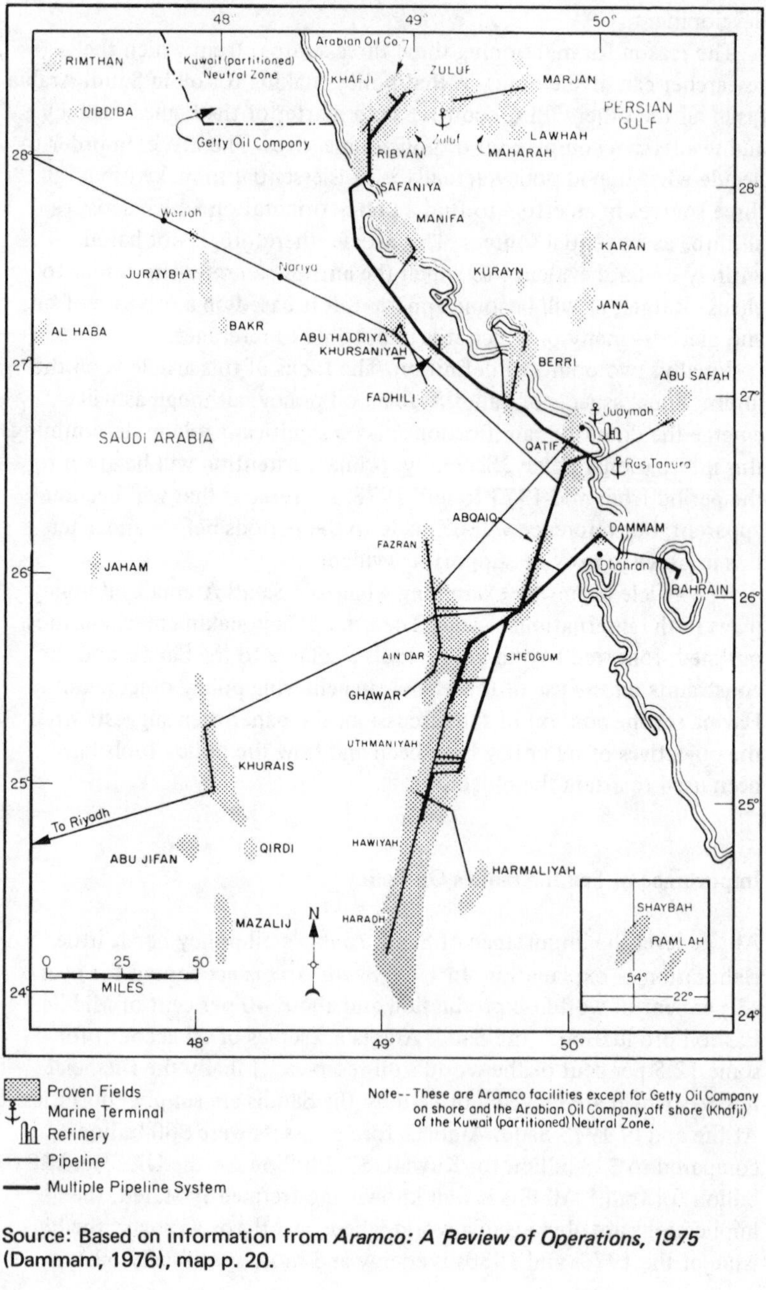

Proven Fields
Marine Terminal
Refinery
Pipeline
Multiple Pipeline System

Note-- These are Aramco facilities except for Getty Oil Company
on shore and the Arabian Oil Company.off shore (Khafji)
of the Kuwait (partitioned) Neutral Zone.

Source: Based on information from *Aramco: A Review of Operations, 1975*
(Dammam, 1976), map p. 20.

However, there is another side to Saudi Arabian policy which is little known and is not well understood. This other side has been of crucial importance since mid-1973. The heart of the matter can be stated quite simply. Since mid-1973 and up to the third quarter of 1978 (with one exception to be described shortly), OPEC has had little or nothing to do with crude pricing. Rather, Saudi Arabia has set the price of the marker crude according to its own lights, and the market place (albeit imperfect and manipulated by companies or others) has done the rest with the marker crude as the starting point. Order has been kept in the market place (or prices manipulated, depending on your preferences) by the companies in conjunction with the threat of Saudi Arabia's spare capacity. This departure from the conventional wisdom needs further elaboration.

The marker crude (Arabian Light 34° API) is the standard crude from which other crudes are then priced according to a notional OPEC formula based on the differences in the quality of the crudes with respect to gravity, sulphur content, freight advantage and other quality factors. Before each OPEC 'price-setting' meeting, Saudi Arabia has decided on the level at which this crude should be set. What determines the basis of this decision on the price is the central concern of this article. Certainly the companies are very closely consulted, since they are the only organisations which have a relatively clear idea of the current state of supply and demand and what the market will bear. Thus the Saudis enter the OPEC meeting with the marker price fixed. This needs a qualification, for often they enter the meeting not with one price but with a price band ranging from low to high. The meeting then takes place but is merely so much talk since Saudi Arabia will not go above the upper limit. On one occasion they did, in the Tehran meeting held in December 1973, when Shaikh Yamani allowed himself to be pushed above the upper limit;[5] he duly had his knuckles rapped.[6]

The price of the marker is then set and duly announced to the world as an OPEC price decision. What then of the other crudes? As mentioned earlier, there is a notional OPEC formula which determines the differential prices. This formula is cumbersome, complex and virtually ignored.[7] The other OPEC members charge whatever they can get for their respective crudes, as determined by what the market will bear. This, in turn, is determined by whether the companies, who are the ultimate disposers of the crude by virtue of their downstream facilities, will lift the crude or not. What happens if a country sets prices too high? The company is buying in one of several circumstances. If it is buying on the spot market, and the price is too high, it simply refuses to buy the tanker load or whatever at the asking price. If it is buying on a short-term contract it grits its teeth for a short while and refuses to renew the contract at the higher price. If it is buying on a longer-term contract in some form of buy-back arrangement, then it accepts the right of the country to increase the price mid-contract — since there is a clause in the agreement allowing the country to do just that. However, it then invokes the clause a few paragraphs down which allows it (over a relatively short period) to reduce its lifting. In many of the contracts the company can, over a six-month period, reduce liftings by as much as 50 per cent.[8]

The latter course, naturally, would mean that the company is going without oil, but the company can then appeal to Saudi Arabia for crude from its excess capacity and — usually — obtain it. If too many companies appeal to this excess capacity then it would mean that the country was (or the countries were) in fact pricing right in the first place and the companies were trying to be too clever or too greedy, or both. In this system the country must price in such a way that the crude slate into the refinery which is blended from different crudes is priced in line with blends from alternative crudes. This is set by the market and the chemistry of the blend. If the countries get together in subgroups to set prices in an effort to break out of this system, then they end up with spare capacity and the mini-cartel goes the way of all mini-cartels. Libya, Algeria and Nigeria have been playing this roundabout for some time.

The outcome of this system has been that the market has remained relatively stable, with Saudi Arabia calling the tune and the companies 'grassing' on any country which got out of step. Attempts to break out of the system, such as occurred after the price split in 1976, came to nothing. The beauty of the system was that Saudi Arabia did not need to actually supply disgruntled companies. The mere threat was sufficient to keep differential prices in line, albeit at times a slightly ragged line.[9]

In 1978, however, two factors broke the system. First, Iran's production was lowered and in order to offset the shortage, Saudi Arabia had to produce to the limit. This left Saudi Arabia with little or no capacity to retaliate if the other countries pushed up the price of crude — which, of course, is precisely what they did.[10] Second, considerable doubts began to be cast on the technical ability of Saudi Arabia to produce at very high levels over a long period of time (of which more will be discussed later). The system broke down and prices rose sharply. Since then the market has been in a chaotic situation.

Prices now are determined solely by supply and demand, although the producers have been controlling the supply curve on an individual basis. Predictions are rife that prices will fall in the face of a supply surplus,[11] but this need not happen if countries voluntarily cut back production. They may, in fact, choose to cut back production in the face of a lower domestic need for revenue, arising both from accepting a slower pace of development, so as to avoid religious-based unrest and from a realisation that investing surplus revenues abroad looks less and less attractive.[12]

The last few months have seen reports in the various trade magazines that Saudi Arabia is in the process of expanding its capacity. If this is the case then it may well be that the Saudis will be able to regain control of the oil market; it is not necessary for them actually to produce 12 million barrels per day, merely the threat is enough.

If the above is accepted as an approximation to reality (and it is a controversial interpretation) then the importance of Saudi Arabia's oil policy can not be overstated. That policy has, in effect, determined the world cost of energy, the rate at which substitutes will be developed, and the general stability of the world economy. Even if the above version is rejected then the reader can still accept the importance of Saudi Arabia's oil policy since the levels of production and reserves alone gives the policy a crucial place in the world energy scene.

Formulation of Oil Policy in Saudi Arabia[13]

Theoretically all decisions in Saudi Arabia are the prerogative of the King. In order to cope with this, however, there is an infrastructure of advisers, information sources and consultation. At the top of this 'back-up triangle' is the Higher Committee,[14] which consists of princes of the royal blood and in effect acts as the liaison between the royal family and the King. The terms of reference of this Committee are limitless. Under King Faisal it tended to concentrate on internal affairs, but since the accession of King Khaled it has concerned itself increasingly with foreign affairs. There is no regular schedule for meetings, but the committee is convened by command of the King. In practice the recommendations of the Higher Committee are binding on the King.

The next step below is the Council of Ministers – the cabinet of government ministers which can make recommendations to the King. Oil policy, however, seems largely to be kept outside the concerns of the Council of Ministers. With the Saudi government's take-over of control of oil matters in the early 1970s at a *de jure* level, and given the general importance of oil in the affairs of the kingdom and the enormous ~~enormous~~ complexities of the oil industry, it was felt that oil should be dealt with in a more specific and specialised way. As a result in April 1973 the Higher Petroleum Council (HPC) was formed, to concern itself with broad issues of policy. It meets on a regular monthly basis and has a sufficiently wide membership to allow examination of all the policy implications which follow from a particular oil-policy orientation. These bodies, then, are concerned with setting the broad lines of policy and deciding how this policy may be executed. Below this level is the Ministry of Petroleum, which provides information to the Higher Petroleum Committee and then translates the decisions of that body into specific action which is then monitored by the HPC.

Petromin as a national oil company began with a very wide brief of action, which was, in effect, to be the spearhead of the country's industrialisation. Since it succeeded admirably in that role it consequently became involved in a great many varied activities and as a result became extremely unwieldy. In December 1975 the responsibility for petroleum, gas and mineral projects was transferred to the Ministry of Industry and Electricity, leaving Petromin free to concentrate on marketing, refining and distribution. Petromin retained only three of the related companies (ARGAS, the Arabian Drilling Company, and Marinco).[15]

Two other executive institutions are worthy of note. In January 1976 a Gas Council was set up to supervise the kingdom's gas affairs, initially for three years, and in August 1976 the Saudi Basic Industries Corporation (SABIC) was set up to supervise precisely what its title implies — which in the oil context covers petrochemicals.[16] The relative significance of all these parts of the policy-making machinery is very difficult to assess. There is a great deal of overlapping in the membership of the various institutions and clearly policy will be a compromise between the variety of views held. One point worth emphasising is that the system is rather clumsy and is incapable of taking rapid decisions of a basic policy nature. Saudi oil policy is the result of long, slow and careful deliberation, as befits a traditional monarchy. I will not spend much time on the policy-making machinery for two reasons. The operations of the top end are highly secret and as a result are the subject of rumour and speculation, with very little by way of hard fact to guide a researcher. Secondly, the bottom end of the structure is still in the process of changing and will change again presumably when the take-over of Aramco is actually implemented. Dr Abd al-Hadi Taher of Petromin indicated in January of this year, for example, that the birth of a Saudi National Oil Company was 'imminent'.[17]

Policy Tools and Constraints

Before examining the actual objectives of Saudi Arabia's oil policy, it would be helpful to discuss in general terms what tools are available to implement policy, since this will influence what policy options are feasible and what the constraints are upon the operation of these tools. Three policy tools can be identified — production levels, prices and forms of availability. While each will be discussed separately, the three are clearly interlinked.

Production as a policy tool arises from the ability of the Saudis to set the production levels either in minimum or maximum terms. Since Saudi production is such a large part of the OPEC output this gives the Saudis the ability to determine the general availability of OPEC crude supplies. There are, however, specific technical constraints on this ability. Any maximum level has to be set in the light of existing production capacity. This includes not only the rate of flow from fields but also such factors as the loading capacities at the ports and the ability of the Saudis to make use of the associated gas. If the gas-processing capacity is not available then the gas must be flared. It was noticeable that when Saudi Arabia increased its allowable production level to 9.5 million from 8.5 million (a maximum which had been set in March 1974),[18] the extra crude had a premium charged — allegedly because the associated gas from the extra million would have to be flared. Further technical factors may also mean that a productive capacity on paper may not be technically feasible without incurring well damage: the slower the recovery rate, the more oil is eventually extracted.

There is considerable discussion at the moment about what the technical upper limit to Saudi oil production is.[19] The current allowable ceiling is 9.5 million barrels per day. During 1979 it was assumed that the potential technical maximum was between 10 and 10.5 million. Recent reports,[20] however, suggest that this could be increased to 11 million barrels soon and could reach 12 million by the end of 1981 as a consequence of large-scale investment in 1979. It is worth noting that under a plan drawn up in 1978, a capacity of 12 million was not due to be reached until 1983. The speeding up of the capacity expansion (assuming it is real) could be explained in terms of the Saudis' desire to maintain (now regain) control of the oil market.

Considerable doubt has been cast upon the ability of Saudi Arabia to increase this maximum and indeed even upon the ability to attain the supposed maximum (this was a key factor in loosening Saudi control of the oil market). The doubt began to be expressed in the mid-1970s as a result of hearings from the various US Senate Committees, the most recent being that of the Church committee in 1979 which threw serious doubts on Saudi Arabia's ability to maintain higher production levels.[21] At various other points in time the issue has been raised. For example, rumours of technical problems were printed in the *New York Times* in late 1977, prompting the Chairman of Aramco to write a letter in January 1978 denying any such problems.

These rumours were fuelled by two other facts. First, the apparent failure of Saudi Arabia in the first quarter of 1977 to increase output to the 11.8 million barrels which Aramco had then said was possible, which would have been the only way to force the OPEC 'hawks' back into the fold after the Doha split in December 1976. This was supposed to be the result of a combination of field problems and bad weather at Ras Tanura hampering loading, although Prince Fahd subsequently stated[24] that Saudi Arabia had no intention of solving the pricing split by means of increased production. The second factor was the announcement in 1978 that liftings of Arabian light were to be limited to 65 per cent of liftings (which resurrected the rumour of problems in the Ghawar field). These rumours of technical difficulties were strongly denied by the Saudis in so far as they related to anything unusual outside of the normal course of a field getting older.[23]

There are also technical/economic factors which limit the use of production levels as a policy tool. Apart from revenues (which will be discussed under pricing) the main constraint arises from gas. At present Saudi Arabia is in the process of developing a gas-gathering system[24] which will cost at the last estimate $16 billion. That estimate was in late 1976; it will be considerably higher on completion. At the same time gas processing for export is being developed in a big way and contracts signed for delivery. Less oil production means less gas production which, in turn, means large numbers of unhappy customers and a horrendous amount of idle equipment. A decision to reduce oil production, therefore, cannot be taken lightly.

The effects of the production tool are also uncertain for two reasons.

The first is the problem of time lag. Turning the tap on increases oil output, but it can be a considerable time before this increased output begins to emerge on to the market, and the precise time is a function of a great number of variables such as tanker availability, storage facilities, etc. Because of the uncertainty over time it is quite conceivable that use of production levels to regulate price, for example, could actually aggravate fluctuations.[25] The second reason for uncertainty over the effect of production policies is that Saudi Arabia is in the classic situation of oligopolistic uncertainty. Thus, an increase in production could be met by a reduction by other OPEC producers (or an increase), which means that the effect of a change in Saudi production levels on the whole energy equation is uncertain.

The pricing tool is the result of Saudi Arabia's right to set the price of the marker at whatever level it sees fit; the impact of this on the oil scene in general has already been outlined. We must now examine the factors which determine the level of prices set by Saudi Arabia prior to the OPEC meetings, and the degree of flexibility which exists on pricing. Specifics revolve around the question of what the market will bear. This depends primarily on the general oil supply and demand equation, which is why the oil companies are consulted. Such consultation is necessary because the oil companies are the only organisations with anything approaching the total picture. I would not like to give the impression of a highly formalised meeting, but merely of unofficial contacts. The pricing decision here, of course, cannot be divorced from decisions on production levels. The Saudis are faced with supply and demand curves. The main difference from the other producers is that they are in a position to significantly shift the global supply curve. This means they are far from constrained by what the oil companies tell them. If the market will not take a price increase because of over-supply, the Saudis can still increase the price provided they lower production. A second influence on the pricing decision is the price of substitute energy forms. There are two possible views. Given Saudi Arabia's reserves and productive capacity, the country has the longest life of any oil producer and correspondingly great world influence. The rapid development of substitutes would undermine that position and so, in one view, it is in the interests of Saudi Arabia to keep the price at such a level as to slow down the rate of substitution. The other view is that oil is too precious to burn and should be used as a chemical input, in which case a price should be set to speed up the development of alternatives. Officially the Saudis follow the latter view of the world, but their enthusiasm for a future in which the Saudi voice, lacking the influence wielded by an energy supplier, would be reduced to a whisper could well be questioned.

Other factors influencing price levels include the impact of inflation, exchange rates, the general health of the industrial countries and many others. The effectiveness of the pricing tool as a policy instrument is very much a function of the oligopolistic uncertainty mentioned with respect to production. The main point being that Saudi Arabia can influence the others by virtue of its role as price leader with excess capacity. Without excess capacity the position of Saudi Arabia in terms of its ability to control prices is very uncertain. This can be clearly seen from the two recent price increases by Saudi Arabia, each of $2. Both intended to restore order to price differentials and both had unforeseen consequences, that is the other OPEC members simply increased their prices, which annoyed the Saudis considerably.[26]

The final policy tool is a variant of production levels and concerns the form in which the crude is made available. As Shaikh Yamani succinctly pointed out at the end of 1979, 'the problem . . . is definitely not the price of oil so much as its availability'.[27] 'Availability' in this context concerns the method by which the crude is exported. For most of the 1970s Aramco produced and disposed either through its own integrated channels or via arm's-length deals with other companies. More recently the Saudis have been showing a greater interest in the disposal mechanism. In October 1979, for example, the Saudis warned Aramco that despite the shortages of that period, the less developed countries must get their contracted supplies come what may.[28] Moreover, Petromin has been becoming increasingly involved in direct sales of crude and in 1979 these reached some 1.4 million barrels a day. This gives the country an enormous leverage in foreign policy, since it can now directly determine who gets what, and if a customer in some way embarrasses the Saudi government, as happened over the Petromin—ENI oil agreement, then the perpetrators are liable to face oil shortages. However, direct marketing could well tie the hands of the Saudis with respect to production policy. There has been much discussion of the possibility of oil entitlements linked to money spent on industrial projects by foreign companies in Saudi Arabia. Figures have ranged from 1,000 barrels a day per million dollars equity to 200 barrels a day per million for refineries. Given the size of the planned projects this ties up a substantial amount of oil.

Apart from the constraints which are specific to the policy tools of production, price and forms of availability, there are other constraints which apply in more general terms. These can be divided into international political factors and economic factors.

At an international level there are the problems of sanctity of contract. This can limit action not only on production levels but also on prices charged. Although contracts are usually short term, from one to three years (or shorter), they do inject considerable inflexibility into policy-making in a rapidly changing scene. Aside from mere legal considerations, there is also the desire to be seen as a good international citizen who wishes to promote peace and stability, and as Prince Fahd has remarked 'World economic stability is the most important pillar of world peace.'[29] A good citizen is one who does not rock the boat too often. Finally there is the brutal reality that the West is too dependent on Saudi Arabia to allow too drastic a revision of oil policy. The industrial West quite simply could not take a Saudi production level of 4 million barrels overnight without total collapse. Faced with economic and political collapse or the removal of a government, it is not hard to imagine the response of the West — despite the consequences.

The economic constraints provide an array of limitations on policy formulation. Domestic revenue needs influence both the minimum level of oil production desirable and the maximum.[30] The minimum constraint is set by the need for expenditure. At present the Third Five-Year Plan is emerging and there are reports that this will involve expenditures totalling 783 billion riyals with an extra 50 billion for inflation, compared to 623 billion in the Second Five-Year Plan.[31] In addition arms expenditures are rising rapidly, from $570 million (constant 1973 $) in 1970 to $3,653 million (constant 1973 $) in 1978.[32] Clearly such activities place a limit below which revenues cannot fall. In terms of revenue maximum, this follows from a fear that excessive revenue will either lead to domestic unrest (that is resulting from over-rapid development based on the expenditure of this revenue), or else (if the revenue is invested abroad) that inflation and a weakening dollar will diminish the value of resultant assets. The former concern is prominent following the demise of the Shah. At the same time the fact that so large a proportion of Saudi foreign assets are in dollars means that any action which could damage the dollar would also damage the Saudis' own interests. Of course, the trade-off might be worth it, but none the less it is a trade-off which must be taken into the calculations.

A more recent constraint is the level of profits achieved by the Aramco partners as a result of the Saudis' present policy of under-pricing Saudi crude relative to other crudes. In the fourth quarter of 1979 Exxon's earnings were up 60 per cent, Mobil's 72 per cent,

Texaco's 62 per cent and Socal's 66 per cent.[33] This has proved a source of both annoyance and embarrassment to the Saudis whose largess was intended, according to official statements, to help the consumer.

We have described the importance of Saudi oil policy, who makes it, how it can be implemented and the constraints on this implementation. The next step is to begin to attempt to identify what the objectives have actually been, how the tools have been used to achieve those objectives and whether or not they have been successful.

Objectives of Saudi Arabia's Oil Policy

The problems in identifying policy arise from the fact that 'objectives' is plural rather than singular. In other words, overall policy is a mixture of different objectives which together form 'the' oil policy. The relative emphasis of these different strands is both uncertain and in a constant state of flux as both personnel and circumstances change. In attempting to identify the various policy objectives this analysis will make use of all three sources outlined in the introduction, but the qualifications with respect to the reliability of these sources must be emphasised.

While this article has been emphasising the international aspect of oil policy, in reality it is impossible to distinguish between international and domestic objectives since they are merely different sides of the same coin. In the same way oil policy also has to be considered in the light of other facets of government policy.

Saudi oil policy has two overriding objectives. The first is the maintenance and strengthening of the security and stability of Saudi Arabia. Whether this objective arises from a sense of altruism with respect to the people or from a desire to secure the position of the House of Saud makes little difference to the outcome of the analysis. The second objective is to increase the voice of Saudi Arabia in world affairs in general and the Arab world in particular. To achieve these two objectives (which would also apply to other fields of Saudi Arabian policy such as foreign policy and economic policy), oil policy carries a set of sub-objectives more specific to oil. While the degree of emphasis of these sub-objectives varies, they must ultimately assist in the achievement of the two main objectives.

The first main objective, that is security and stability, can be expressed as the need to safeguard the long-term economic health of the country. This implies two sub-objectives for oil policy — pursuit of the country's long-term interests as an oil producer and the carrying out of economic diversification. Aspects of the long-term oil-producing interests have already been mentioned and imply a continuation of the crucial role for oil in world trade, with Saudi Arabia acting as the key supplier. This means pricing in such a way that, while substitutes for oil as energy develop, they do not appear on the scene too quickly. Attaining the objective is also dependent on the general economic health of the customers, which means in effect the industrialised West. If Saudi oil policy changed in such a drastic manner as to present a real threat to the economic basis of Western society it is just not realistic to expect the Western countries to accept this, despite the consequences. At the same time a slow change in policy direction which led to a gradual reduction of supplies or excessive cost would inflict damage on the Western economies, and this, in turn, would affect the markets for Saudi crude (or products). A better example of a symbiotic relationship is difficult to find.

A policy objective which emerges from the above analysis is the provision of sufficient crude at prices which can realistically be paid. What is realistic is, of course, a matter for discussion. Much has been made of this aspect of the 'reasonableness' of Saudi Arabian oil policy. The Saudi government has been accused of being a puppet of the USA, and there have been reports of secret agreements between the USA and Saudi Arabia concerning the favourable placing of funds in return for maintaining price rises.[34] As an aside on the existence of such agreements, it is worth questioning why Saudi Aarbia would want to tie its policy options up in the most rigid manner imaginable until 1984 in return for a few extra percentage points of interest. Price moderation and expanded production by Saudi Arabia have been dictated by self-interest. (There are some who would argue that the pricing policy has not been moderate when the difference between cost and price is considered. However, this attitude tends to ignore replacement cost and the cost of substitutes.)

The long-term health of the economy also depends on the ability of the country to diversify away from dependence on crude-oil exports. This has created two sub-objectives. The first has been for the Saudi government to gain control over the oil industry within Saudi Arabia. This was achieved at a *de jure* level in the first half of the 1970s by gaining an equity majority in Aramco, although to obtain *de facto* control will take considerably longer.[35] The reason for gaining control is — at least in theory — to direct the oil sector towards the role of a leading development sector with all that implies, in particular maximising linkages.[36] The decision of where to locate processing plants, for example, is the prerogative of the disposer of the crude — hence the recent expansion of refinery plans in Saudi Arabia.[37] The second objective is to integrate oil more fully into the economy, which implies gaining access to technology and expertise. This can be done via the inducement of oil availability and/or by spending revenues.

The objective of increasing the importance of Saudi Arabia in the world carries with it several sub-objectives. The first is to appear as a responsible and considerate member of the international community whose voice will be listened to and whose opinion will be sought. While this appears a rather unlikely objective in a world of Realpolitik, it is a theme which constantly reappears in policy statements. Indeed one can make out a good case for maintaining that Saudi policy overpricing, availability and especially recycling has precisely been responsible and considerate. The ulterior motives are obvious and are linked to the previous discussion of the need for a stable situation in the industrial West. This objective is reinforced by the Saudis' deep hatred of Communism and their fear that instability in the world arising from Saudi 'unreasonableness' will promote Communism. This obsessive dislike of Communism arises mainly from religious considerations, but if one wanted to be more cynical one could also point to the position of the House of Saud and its future in terms of the Marxian dialectic.

A second sub-objective concerns the settlement of the Arab—Israeli conflict. This objective is motivated by a variety of factors, some of which are deep-rooted 'national' and religious factors. When King Faisal expressed the desire to pray in Jerusalem before he died, it was genuinely meant. There are two other less 'moral' reasons for desiring a settlement. First, the Palestinians play a very powerful role in the Arabian peninsular by virtue of their provision of skilled manpower and they can act as a source of considerable influence and pressure. Secondly, failure to solve the problem has, among other things, generated instability which has tended to promote 'left-wing' movements in the Arab world. The latter are, as already stated, anathema to the Saudis.

A third sub-objective is to promote and encourage Islam throughout the world. Two motives for this can be suggested. The first is a sense of missionary zeal to encourage and protect Islam where it has come under pressure — the oil agreements with, and financial aid to, the Philippines are a case in point. The second motive is more obscure and concerns the sources of legitimacy on which the House of Saud can call to justify its position. During the formation of the kingdom under Abd al-Aziz ibn Saud, the source of legitimacy was force. After taking control of the holy places in the Hijaz, however, a new source of legitimacy emerged by virtue of the House of Saud becoming protector of the holy places. The greater the importance of Islam the more significant are the holy places, and correspondingly their protectors.

These, then, are among the more important objectives towards which Saudi Arabian oil policy is working, in conjunction, of course, with foreign policy, etc. Many of the sub-objectives are complementary, although there is also some degree of conflict between the objectives. There are, for example, clear problems in implementing a diversified development programme based on oil processing and at the same time maintaining a relatively high production level as a 'reasonable citizen' – which reduces the country's life as an oil producer and therefore processor. To build oil refineries for when the oil runs out smacks of black humour rather than development policy.

Use of the Tools to Achieve the Policy Objectives

To achieve the objectives enumerated above it is necessary to direct the policy tools mentioned earlier towards those stated goals. Before the summer of 1973 policy options were relatively limited because the government rejected the use of oil as a political weapon, which effectively meant that the potential weapons of price and production were determined solely by technical considerations. Before the participation agreement, moreover, while Saudi Arabia could in broad terms influence the actions of Aramco, subject to an upper limit, Aramco determined offtake levels.

The summer of 1973 saw a major shift. In April 1973 Shaikh Yamani warned the US that Saudi Arabia would not increase production[38] unless the US changed its policy with respect to the Arab–Israeli issue.[39] In July King Faisal repeated the warning.[40] This culminated in the imposition of the Arab oil embargo in October 1973. Three factors caused this switch. First, intense pressures for a new approach to the problem were being exerted by the other Arab countries and the Palestinians. Second, there was within the Saudi government increasing frustration with the insensitivity of the US government. Finally, the embargo plan which had been carefully worked out over some time was a very subtle and clever piece of political manoeuvring.[41]

The use of the oil embargo created a precedent which meant that oil could be used again as a political weapon. In practice it was not directly used, but the threat was periodically unsheathed and waved. In 1974, for example, Shaikh Yamani indicated that while Israel remained intransigent 'offtake levels must remain victims of political constraints'.[42] The possibility of using oil as a weapon was not confined to leverage in the Arab–Israeli dispute. In 1975, for example, Shaikh Yamani threatened to abandon Saudi Arabia's 'moderating role' in OPEC if the developed world provoked a confrontation, following the failure of the early North–South talks in Paris.[43] How far this policy tool was actually operated in a political context is uncertain. While Shaikh Yamani argued recently that 'oil is a political weapon . . . In fact we have never stopped using this weapon',[44] to translate this into specific instances is very difficult due to the problem of ascribing motives to specific actions. It may be suggested, therefore, that while oil has been used as a political lever, threats to use oil in this manner have never been implemented in any grand fashion after October 1973.

The use of pricing as a policy tool has gone through various stages. Up to October 1973 the decision to increase price was simply to take advantage of a combination of circumstances which allowed the price of oil to rise to a level which the Saudis regarded as fair and reasonable. Thus the increase in price was a reaction rather than a specific policy tool, that is it was an end objective in itself. The change came in December 1973 when Shaikh Yamani was faced with the option of going along with the majority of OPEC or causing a split. He chose the former, which led to a price increase. The members of the HPC appear to have been unhappy over this because they felt it too high in the context of Western stability. After the December 1973 price increase, the Saudi position became for a time somewhat ambivalent. On the one hand, they wished to reduce the price, while, on the other hand, they saw that there was an opportunity to extract concessions from the West (and the USA in particular) in return for a reduction in price. The carrot of a reduced price was offered. In the summer of 1974, for example, Shaikh Yamani indicated that Saudi Arabia would auction 1.5–2 million barrels a day at whatever prices the market would take. This was tantamount to offering a reduction in price. It was subsequently rumoured that Shaikh Yamani was reprimanded by the HPC for making this offer.[45] This seems highly improbable since it is unlikely that Shaikh Yamani would make such an offer on a mere whim. A more likely explanation is that the carrot of reduced prices was offered but no *quid pro quo* was forthcoming. It was later suggested that the auction was dropped in return for an agreement with

Algeria to freeze prices.[46] Whatever the truth of these rumours, it seems fairly clear that there was general unease over an oil price which was believed to be too high.

In March 1975, with the death of King Faisal, there was a subtle but significant change of policy – whereby the present level of prices was declared reasonable. Indeed, in May 1975 Prince Fahd specified that the government would now seek to maintain the real value of the oil price. In the climate of inflation and currency changes this implied a nominal higher price.[47] The basic change was that the policy 'carrot' was no longer a reduction in price, but rather a reduction in the size of price increases. In September 1975 the Saudis pushed the marker price up by 10 per cent. From then on Saudi pricing policy, at least publicly, was claimed to depend on the behaviour of the West with respect to a variety of issues.

As the pricing became more aggressive in 1975 so did the issue of levels of oil production. The period 1975–6 saw widespread discussion in the trade press of a division at the highest policy-making levels over what level of output should be maintained. This coincided with the launching of the Second Five-Year Plan and the emergence of discussion as to whether the Saudi social, cultural and political structure could stand the implied pressure. During 1975–8 production was used to maintain a balance in the world energy equation. Saudi Arabia allowed its production to act as the world's stock reserve, with the level of output being adjusted so as to offset the worst of the market fluctuations. Since 1978, more has been said about availability than about prices. In February 1980, for example, Shaikh Yamani indicated that production would be cut unless Saudi Arabia began to receive technology in return for oil.[48] Certainly the Saudi government is continually drawing attention to the country's production of 1 million barrels a day above the 8.5 million conservation limit as a means of securing Western support for Saudi objectives.

Conclusion

The main question to be asked is how far the use of the policy options open to Saudi Arabia has been successful in securing the stated policy objectives? The answer faces one immediate problem. The government of Saudi Arabia favours the channel of secret 'diplomacy' when it comes to the wielding of the policy options. This, of course, is far from unusual but it does mean that it is almost impossible to know how far the policy options have actually been used. An increase in price, for example, is a visible example of a policy option being used, but this is only the tip of the action. Whether the Saudis used the magnitude and timing of the price increases as a bargaining counter, or whether because of some *quid pro quo* the price rise was below that originally intended or even above the original intention, would still have to be established.

In terms of achieving objectives, it is possible to draw some tentative conclusions. Up to 1978 the situation internationally was relatively stable after the 'crisis' of late 1973 and early 1974. Similarly the more domestic objectives of stability and economic diversification also appeared to be achieved, at least on the surface, although it remains to be seen whether or not the economic diversification is real rather than illusory. In the same period, Saudi Arabia's voice certainly grew internationally. As the seeming OPEC 'moderate', Saudi approval was courted on a grand scale by the industrial West; this can be seen, for example, by the country's growing role in the International Monetary Fund.

After 1978, with the lowering of Iranian production, the situation changed somewhat with respect of the objective of stability, since although Saudi Arabia could offset the loss of Iranian output, this left her with no reserve stock with which to manipulate prices. Others, therefore, could push the price higher.[49] Saudi Arabia's international standing, however, remained as crucial as ever by virtue of the high level of crude production.

Overall the policy has been relatively successful. This is in part, however, because the objectives were concerned with maintenance of the *status quo*. Since the major constraints on the use of the policy tools are well known by others, a more radical set of policy objectives, which would have required a more aggressive use of the policy tools, would have been impractical. Saudi Arabia, if she is to survive, must tread a narrowly defined path. Major deviation must mean falling off that path, or more accurately, being pushed off it.

Notes

1. British Petroleum Review of the World Oil Industry (1978).
2. Ibid. and Aramco Reviews (1978).
3. From a study by Dr Odeh Aburdene, *Middle East Economic Survey*, vol. XXIII, no. 28.
4. Much of the recent literature has emphasised this key role of Saudi Arabia both in the present context and the future. See, for example, Ragaei and Dorothea El Mallakh, 'New Policy Imperatives for Energy Producers', *Proceedings*

of the Sixth International Conference of the International Research Center for Energy and Economic Development (ICEED, Boulder, 1980); General Accounting Office (USA), 'Critical Factors Affecting Saudi Arabia's Oil Decisions', *Report to the Congress of the United States* (Washington, May 1978); and C. F. Doran, *Myth, Oil and Politics* (The Free Press, Glencoe, Miami, 1977).

5. It is not clear whether in fact the system being described was in operation at this point. It seems probable that it was not. Quite possibly the banding was introduced subsequently, so that Shaikh Yamani had specific terms of reference.

6. A. Sampson, *The Seven Sisters* (Hodder and Stoughton, London, 1975), ch. 12.

7. For a discussion of differential pricing in the pre-1973−4 situation, see M. A. Adelman, *The World Oil Market* (Johns Hopkins University Press, Washington, 1972), and S. M. Ghanem, *The Pricing of Libyan Crude Oil* (Adams Publishing House, New York, 1975). For the more recent period see J. E. Hartshorn, *Objectives of the Petroleum Exporting Countries* (Middle East Economic Survey and Energy Economics Research Ltd, London, 1979); H. S. Houthakker, *The World Price of Oil* (American Enterprise Institute for Public Policy Research, Washington, 1976).

8. For recent changes in this contract system see F. R. Parra, 'New-style Crude Sales Contracts in OPEC countries', *Middle East Economic Survey*, vol. XXIV, no. 2.

9. This approach has had limited exposure in the literature. M. Adelman covers some aspects in his work, for example, M. Adelman, 'The World Oil Cartel, Scarcity, Economics and Politics', *Quarterly Review of Economics and Business*, vol. 16, no. 2 (Summer 1976); and 'The Clumsy Cartel', *The Energy Journal*, no. 1 (January 1980). For the key differences between the author's approach and that of M. Adelman, see P. Stevens, 'The Interaction between Oil Policy and Industrial Policy in Saudi Arabia' forthcoming as part of the *Proceeds of the First International Area Conference on Saudi Arabia* (ICEED, University of Colorado). Finally, for attempts to examine the approach in the context of optimisation models, see S. Hammoudeh, 'The Future Oil Price Behaviour of OPEC and Saudi Arabia', *Energy Economics*, no. 4 (October 1979).

10. See, for example, US Department of Energy, 'The Iranian Petroleum Supply Disruption', Analysis Report DOE/EIA−0184/13 (July 1979).

11. For example see the interview by Shaikh Yamani in *Al-Sharq Al Awsat* (29 May 1980).

12. See, for example, O. Aburdene, *Middle East Economic Survey*, vol. XXIII, no. 28; and F. Al Chalabi and A. Al Janabi, 'Optimum Production and Pricing Policies', *Journal of Energy and Development*, vol. IV, no. 2 (Spring 1979).

13. For further details see General Accounting Office (USA), 'Critical Factors Affecting Saudi Arabia's Oil Decisions'; and A. H. Taher, 'The Role of State Petroleum Enterprises in Developing Countries: The Case of Saudi Arabia' in United Nations Centre for Natural Resources, Energy and Transport, *State Petroleum Enterprise in Developing Countries* (Pergamon Press, London, 1980).

14. Not to be confused with the Higher Petroleum Council. Also the title perhaps makes it sound more formalised than it actually is.

15. 'Petromin' in the series of OPEC publications on National Oil Companies (February 1980).

16. Ibid.

17. *Saudi Arabia Newsletter*, no. 15 (January 1980).

18. *Middle East Economic Survey*, vol. XV, no. 23.

19. For a detailed discussion of the technical factors see General Accounting Office (USA), 'Critical Factors Affecting Saudi Arabia's Oil Decisions', ch. 3.

20. *Saudi Arabia Newsletter*, no. 23 (May 1980).

21. *An-Nahar Arab Report and Memo* (30 April 1979).

22. Interview in *Al Siyasah* (16 April 1977).

23. *Middle East Economic Survey*, vol. XXI, no. 20.

24. For details see *Middle East Economic Survey*, vol. XIX, no. 31, and vol. XX, no. 34.

25. For a discussion on some of the possible interactions see J. Roeber, 'The Rotterdam Oil Market', *Petroleum Economist* (April 1979).

26. *Middle East Economic Survey*, vol. XXIII, no. 16.

27. *Saudi Arabia Newsletter*, no. 12 (November/December 1979).

28. Ibid., no. 10 (October/November 1979).

29. *Middle East Economic Survey*, vol. XX, no. 27.

30. For a discussion of the impact of revenues on development, see D. G. Edens, *Oil and Development in the Middle East* (Praeger, New York, 1979).

31. *Saudi Arabia Newsletter*, no. 12 (November/December 1979).

32. Ibid., no. 10 (October/November 1979).

33. Ibid., no. 17 (February 1980).

34. *The International Currency Review*, vol. 9, no. 2.

35. For details see P. J. Stevens, *Joint Ventures in Middle East Oil, 1957– 1975* (Middle East Economic Survey and Energy Economics Ltd, London, 1979).

36. See Edens, *Oil and Development*; J. A. Hanson, 'The Leading Sector Development Strategy and the Importance of Institutional Reform: A Reinterpretation', *Journal of Economic Studies*, vol. XXI, no. 2 (May 1976).

37. See L. Turner and J. Bedore, *Middle East Industrialization* (RIIA, Saxon House, London, 1979).

38. In the early 1970s a productive capacity of 20 million barrels a day was discussed.

39. *Arab Report and Record* (April 1973).

40. Ibid. (July 1973).

41. The direct foothold in Aramco, with control of 25 per cent of the equity, may also have played a part in generating confidence to use oil.

42. *Middle East Economic Survey*, vol. XVII, no. 30.

43. Ibid., vol. XVIII, no. 27.

44. Ibid., vol. XXIII, no. 33.

45. *The Washington Post* (30 September 1974).

46. *Arab Report and Record* (September 1974).

47. *Middle East Economic Survey*, vol. XVIII, no. 13.

48. *Saudi Arabia Newsletter*, no. 18 (February/March 1980).

49. The others were both producers who wished to take advantage of the apparent shortage and consumers who reacted to the general uncertainty created by Iran.

13 THE SAUDI ARABIAN PETROCHEMICAL INDUSTRY: ITS RATIONALE AND EFFECTIVENESS

H. G. Hambleton

Background

The kingdom of Saudi Arabia has become important by virtue of its great oil exports and the wealth these exports have generated. It has by far the largest reserves of crude oil in the world and natural gas is also abundant. Yet these resources are finite — the output of oil will probably start to decline towards the middle of the next century.[1] While the country can at present meet its needs through the export of crude oil and natural gas, therefore, a long-term development strategy in this sphere rests on creating a petrochemical industry based on the natural gas (which is now largely flared) and the oil resources. Some portion of the resources would need to be set aside for this purpose in the long term.

Figure 13.1: Natural Gas Utilisation

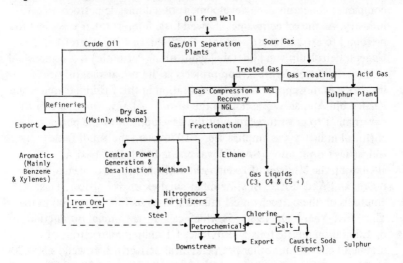

Source: Saudi Basic Industries Corporation.

235

Table 13.1: Proved Oil and Gas Reserves and Production in the Arab
Gulf States

Country	Proved reserves Oil (1,000 bbl)	Gas (10⁹ ft³)	Oil production in 1980 (1,000 b/d)
Gulf Cooperation Council			
Saudi Arabia	167,460,000	116,000	9,900
Kuwait	64,900,000	30,800	1,382
UAE			
Abu Dhabi	29,000,000	20,000	1,350
Dubai	1,400,000	775	349
Sharjah	10,000	—	10
Qatar	3,585,000	60,000	472
Oman	2,340,000	2,500	280
Bahrain	225,000	9,000	49
Neutral Zone	6,060,000	4,800	540
Iraq	30,000,000	27,000	2,638
Total	304,980,000	270,875	16,970
World	648,500,000	2,600,000	59,700

Note: The reserves are those proved using current technology and prices.
Source: *Oil and Gas Journal* (29 December 1980), p. 78; ibid (9 March 1981),
p. 44; *Ministry of Petroleum and Minerals* (15 March 1981).

A petrochemical industry is an old dream in Saudi Arabia. In 1960
the Saudi government was already negotiating with foreign oil
companies concerning the development of a domestic petrochemical
industry. As the oil companies showed little interest other ways had to
be found to attract investment into this field. In 1962, therefore, the
General Petroleum and Mineral Organization (Petromin) was established
to undertake such hydrocarbon projects as did not attract private
investors. State support for industrialisation in this field increased when
Khaled bin Abd al-Aziz ascended the throne in 1975. The desire of the
government to press forward with the development of the petrochemical industry was emphasised in 1976 when the Saudi Basic
Industries Corporation (SABIC) was created with Dr Ghazi A.
al-Gosaibi, the Minister of Industry and Electricity, as chairman of the
board, and Abd al-Aziz A. al-Zamil as chief executive officer. This
emphasis on the petrochemical industry finds its full expression in the
Third Five-Year Plan (1980—5) which calls for an annual production
of 1.5 million metric tons of ethylene, 1.1 million metric tons of
methanol and various other petrochemical derivatives, as well as 500,000
metric tons of urea fertiliser. SABIC has been allocated $7.7 billion
under the Plan for the construction of the petrochemical complexes

and other ventures. The projects, however, are unlikely to come to full fruition until the latter half of this decade.

This desire to move downstream first received concrete expression when it was decided to establish a plant to produce ammonia—urea. The Governor of Petromin, Dr Abd al-Hadi Taher, gained the interest of the Occidental Petroleum Corporation in this venture, and Occidental Petroleum agreed to manage the project. In 1965 the Saudi Arabian Fertilizer Company (SAFCO) was launched. Initially the plant was plagued by technical difficulties, management problems and the falling world price of urea — it did not go onstream until 1970 and then only 24,437 metric tons of urea were produced, less than one-tenth of capacity. The difficulties encountered were extensive despite governmental assistance given to the company: the natural gas feed-stock, the water and the electricity were provided at heavily subsidised prices and the government purchased the output for use in its overseas aid programme. In 1976 SAFCO took over the management from Occidental Petroleum and at the time of writing about half the employees of SAFCO are Saudis, the remainder being composed of nationals of a dozen other countries. In 1979 output reached 298,850 tons of urea, very close to full capacity at 300,000 tons, and this level has been maintained in 1980. The urea is marketed largely in India, Egypt, Bangladesh and Iran, with appreciable amounts going to some twenty other countries. Net profits jumped from SR 37.1 million in 1978 to SR 100.5 million in 1979. Originally 51 per cent of the equity was contributed by Petromin and 49 per cent by the Public Investment Fund (PIF), but in accordance with government policy the PIF equity has now been made available to the general public. The shares are greatly in demand. Today SAFCO proudly advertises itself as 'Saudi Arabia's first petrochemical company, producers and marketers of urea fertilizer and urea since 1970'. Prospects look good.[2]

SAFCO was the first step towards a petrochemical industry. The further development of the petrochemical industry required a more extensive infrastructure and for this purpose the growth poles of Jubail and Yanbu were created. This article will examine the nature of the projects undertaken in Jubail and Yanbu and seek to draw out some of the domestic and international dimensions of the pattern of development adopted.

Growth Poles: Jubail and Yanbu

Al-Jubail, located on the Arabian Gulf half-way between Kuwait and Qatar, has through the centuries been a small port, serving as a centre for fishing and oyster catching, and a point from which travellers crossing Saudi Arabia could initiate and terminate their journeys. The village of al-Jubail had some 5,000 inhabitants in the early 1970s. Petromin saw Jubail as a possible growth pole for petrochemical and other industries because of the proximity of the Berri crude oil and gas field and the deep-water channel, some nine kilometres out, which made it suitable for international shipping. In 1973 therefore, the Bechtel Corporation was called in to draw up a master plan for Jubail, defining the infrastructure requirements, locating industries within the site and setting forth land use and community plans, conceptual designs of components and environmental control measures. The final plan, proposing a prodigious development for the sleepy village, was presented to the King and the Crown Prince in 1975. Crown Prince Fahd threw the full weight of his authority behind the Bechtel Corporation plan. He established the Royal Commission for Jubail and Yanbu (1975), becoming its first chairman, and in June 1976 a management contract was signed with Bechtel covering a twenty-year period. The subsidiary of Bechtel, the Arabian Bechtel Company Limited, was given the responsibility for mapping out the infrastructure of the industrial complex and the city, supervising the granting of contracts after evaluating bids, and actually constructing parts of the complex. The Royal Commission, however, retained responsibility for policy.[3]

Jubail's industrial harbour will eventually be one of the largest in the world, capable of handling 26 million tons of liquid products, mainly hydrocarbons. Roads and pipelines for chemicals will connect the loading platforms to the end of the main causeway, leading on to the petrochemical plants. Further to the south there will be a commercial harbour and a small fishing harbour. Some ten thousand blue and white housing units are now being neatly set out with roads and street lights. Workers are arriving in increasing numbers; by the mid-1980s there could be some 30,000 to 45,000. By the year 2000 this 'industrial city' should have 300,000 inhabitants and boast petrochemical complexes, oil refineries, a steel mill and over a dozen other industries as well as a port area and an airport. The total investment could well reach $40 billion.[4]

Yanbu Al-Bahr, located on the Red Sea some 190 miles north of

Jeddah, has until recently consisted of picturesque old houses with mud walls and wood screens, a few streets with shaded shops, some administrative buildings and the port which had long been a point of landing for pilgrims travelling to or from Medina and on to Mecca. The total population was between 10,000 and 15,000. The nearby town of Yanbu al-Nakhl was similar but smaller. Now the new 'industrial city' of Yanbu is rising some fifteen miles south-east of Yanbu al-Bahr. Under the direction of Dr Yousef Ibrahim al-Suliman al-Turki, the director of the Yanbu branch of the Royal Commission for Jubail and Yanbu, storage tanks now dot this formerly bleak expanse of sand, the natural gas liquifaction (NGL) facility is being prepared for the gas which will arrive by pipeline from the Eastern Province in 1981, and a pier has been built. Saudi Arabian Parsons Limited is acting as project manager for the Royal Commission. Under the eight-year initial development programme the port will be divided into nine areas, one being specifically designed for petrochemicals. Thus by 1988 this port should have the capacity to handle 500,000 tons of petrochemicals a year. By the year 2010 the number of inhabitants could reach 150,000.[5]

If the industrial city of Jubail will be the centre of the petrochemical industry, Yanbu will not be far behind. We will now examine the measures which are being taken to ensure that the petrochemical industry in the two cities will be supplied with the necessary inputs — feedstock, fuel, water, electricity and manpower — and that the capital costs of construction can be met.

Feedstock and Fuel

The industrialisation programme calls for large quantities of gas as fuel and feedstock. This has led to Petromin's gigantic gas gathering, treatment and transmission project — the world's largest engineering undertaking, which will cost some $15 billion. Some explanation of the processes whereby gas is gathered and separated is necessary so as to appreciate the scale of the project. The crude oil from the fields first goes through gas/oil separation plants, which separate the crude oil from the sour gas. Sour gas is normally made up of the following gases: methane 48.1 per cent mol.; ethane 18.6 per cent; propane 11.7 per cent; carbon dioxide 11.1 per cent; butane 4.6 per cent; hydrogen sulphide 2.7 per cent; and nitrogen 0.3 per cent. The gas is treated to remove the sulphur and thereafter the methane, ethane, propane and other gases are separated and recovered. By the early 1980s some 3 billion standard cubic feet a day of gas will be processed to provide gas for industry, power generation and water desalination. The ethane will largely be used as a feedstock and fuel for petrochemical complexes in Jubail and Yanbu. The propane, butane and natural gasoline will be exported.[6]

The gas made available to the emerging Saudi petrochemical industry will be furnished at a small fraction of the world price. Thus ethane, the basic feedstock for the petrochemical industry, will apparently be provided at about SR 1.67 ($0.56) per thousand cubic feet. Abd al-Aziz A. al-Zamil, the chief executive officer of SABIC, observed to the writer: 'no doubt about it, the gas we have will be much cheaper than anywhere else, and that is the whole principle behind our industrialisation. We are using a resource that we have.'

Water and Electricity

Water availability is a major constraint in the industrialisation of the kingdom, since there are no rivers or lakes and little rainfall. The pools of ground water, which underlie parts of the country, are diminishing and are largely non-renewable. The long-term availability of water, therefore, depends upon schemes to desalinate water. The world's largest desalination project is now being implemented in Jubail. After two stages of this project are completed in 1983 the system will be able to produce 235 million gallons of desalinated water a day. Steps to provide Yanbu with fresh water are also progressing. A new desalination plant in the vicinity was opened in December 1980, producing 25 million gallons of drinking water a day. The water reaches Yanbu through a 50 kilometre pipeline while another pipeline goes to Medina. Additional capacity is expected to come onstream in 1981.[7]

The price of fresh water was fixed by the Council of Ministers in 1980 at SR 0.25 ($0.07) per cubic metre. Yet the overall real cost of desalinated water, including the cost of constructing desalination plants, depreciation of machinery, and operation and maintenance, is probably at least SR 7.5 ($2.26) per cubic metre − some thirty times greater.[8] In order to supplement the fresh water secured from the desalination of ground water and sea water, the possibility is being actively considered of using the oil tankers, which at present carry ballast on their journeys to Saudi ports, to bring fresh water. The cost of this water would apparently be considerably below that of desalinated water.[9]

Electricity supply is also expanding. The Consolidated Electric Company which dominates production in the Eastern Province, will expand its load to over 6,000 megawatts by 1983. Electricity is

provided to the public at SR 0.07 (about $0.025) per kilowatt-hour
and to enterprises located in an 'industrial city' at SR 0.05 (about
$0.015). Here again, the real cost of electricity is very considerably
above this charge. In the supply of both water and electricity, therefore,
an important subsidy is provided to industrial firms.

Manpower

By the middle of this decade over 5,000 engineers, technicians and
workers will be needed for the emerging Saudi Arabian petrochemical
industry. Saudis should be available for these positions as they graduate
in increasing numbers from educational institutions in the kingdom and
abroad. The Ministry of Higher Education expected some 3,000 Saudis
to graduate from domestic and foreign universities in 1980. Many of
these graduates entered the hydrocarbon sector, since they must serve
the state for the same period as their education was financed and Saudi
manpower has a special predilection for the hydrocarbon industry. The
government has made arrangements for Saudis to receive special
training in the petrochemical and other industries, qualifying them for
positions with considerable responsibility. Nevertheless, experienced
managers, engineers and other professionals will remain very scarce in
the kingdom. This could place a serious constraint on the development
of the petrochemical industry — a constraint which can only be
overcome through the employment of expatriate labour. The problem
with extensive reliance on the latter is that the cost of specialised
expatriates is high. The median salary for scientists and engineers in
the United States is about $30,000 a year, while the same US
professionals in Saudi Arabia cost about $60,000 a year. It is the policy
of the government under the Third Five-Year Economic Development
Plan (1980—5) to freeze imported labour at the late-1979 level, but
there is some doubt as to how fully this can be implemented.[10]

Capital

Though capital is readily available at concessionary terms for sound
industrial ventures in Saudi Arabia, the actual capital cost of projects
tends to be high. In Western Europe a 500,000 ton per year ethylene
cracker, together with the units to make derivatives, cost about $2.6
billion in 1979. In the Middle East this same complex would cost about
$4 billion, some 50 per cent more. (For a breakdown of the costs
involved see Table 13.2.) The practice now being followed by
Mitsubishi Heavy Industries of shipping the petrochemical units in
modular form may well somewhat reduce the difference in the cost of
materials.[11]

Table 13.2: Comparison of Costs Involved in the Production of an Ethylene Cracker Complex in Western Europe and the Middle East

	(Millions of dollars)	
	Europe	Middle East
Materials	1,500	2,000
Labour	900	1,500—1,900
Other	200	300
Total	2,600	4,000

Source: Author's statistics.

In 1979 the Shell International Chemical Company undertook a comparative study of the construction of a chemical plant in Europe and in the Gulf. This showed that the location alone would make capital costs 35 per cent higher in the Gulf, while if the need for additional infrastructure was taken into consideration then the costs would be 67 per cent higher. Although there can be little doubt that Saudi Arabia can pay the inflated sums required for petrochemical plant in the Middle East, the costs of construction inevitably affect the economic viability of the projects; however, the higher capital costs would be more than offset by lower production costs. Thus methanol could be produced in the kingdom at about one-third the US cost.

International Dimension: Taiwan and Korea

Any evaluation of the prospects of the petrochemical industry in Saudi Arabia must inevitably consider the wider international context: the extent to which the necessary technology can be supplied by foreign companies, and the markets which may be available for the petrochemicals produced. In view of the growing economic importance of Asia — with Japan having surged ahead to join the ranks of the leading industrial nations of the world some twenty years ago, and Taiwan and South Korea now seeking to follow — it seems appropriate to consider first the role which Asian countries can play in the development of Saudi Arabia's petrochemical industry. Lacking natural resources, Japan, Taiwan and South Korea have had cause to pursue outward-looking policies and, despite being net importers of oil and gas, they are themselves now developing an appreciable petrochemical capacity. They are capable of playing a key role in Saudi Arabia's petrochemical development: Japan, the most industrially advanced, can provide technology and markets; Taiwan and Korea can provide technicians and markets. SABIC has already arranged three joint-venture agreements with Asiatic corporations, one of which is Taiwanese and two of which are Japanese. The products agreed are shown in Table 13.3.[12]

Table 13.3: Joint-Venture Agreements in the Petrochemical Industry between SABIC and Three Asiatic Corporations

	Metric tons per year		
Product	SABIC Taiwan fertiliser	SABIC/ SPDC	SABIC Mitsubishi gas
Low-density polyethylene	—	130,000	—
Ethylene glycol	—	330,000	—
Methanol	—	—	600,000
Urea	500,000	—	—

Source: Figures provided by the Saudi Basic Industries Corporation (SABIC).

Taiwan (Republic of China)

Formal ties with the Republic of China date back to 1940, when a Consulate was established in Jeddah. Sixteen years later this Consulate was raised to an Embassy. It was, however, only after the visit of King Faisal to Taiwan in 1971 that real co-operation developed in the economic, political and cultural fields. This co-operation was institutionalised with the creation of the Sino-Saudi Permanent Committee on Economic and Technical Cooperation. It is not without reason that Taiwan now sees Saudi Arabia as its main ally in the Middle East.[13]

The economic structure of Taiwan is such that the relationship with Saudi Arabia could involve a mutual economic dependence. Taiwan has virtually no oil and very little coal. Some 80 per cent of energy products are imported, including about 120 million barrels of oil a year. The most important source of this oil is Saudi Arabia, followed by Kuwait and Indonesia. In 1979 Saudi Arabia exported to Taiwan crude and refined oil products to a value of $2.44 billion and in 1980 the value of these exports is expected to reach $5.5 billion. This dependence on oil can be expected to increase. Under the new Ten-Year Oil Import Plan, Taiwan expects oil imports to grow at an annual average rate of 5.3 per cent. Imports of liquified natural gas (LNG) from Saudi Arabia are also likely to develop.[14]

In the 1960s and 1970s Taiwan imported growing quantities of semi-processed petrochemical products for use in its rapidly expanding synthetic textile manufacturing and plastics industries. A considerable number of plants were established to make nylon and other products from the imported petrochemicals. During this period also the Taiwan Fertilizer Company Limited, employing a labour force of 4,600, was created with state backing. At present this firm has four fertiliser plants which are expected to produce 90,000 metric tons of fertiliser in 1980. The firm is planning to produce melamine, argon and liquid ammonia within the next few years. It is predicted that Taiwan will soon move further upstream, producing polymers and other petrochemicals.

Despite Taiwan's own petrochemical production, then, there could still be a place for Saudi petrochemicals. In 1982, for example, Taiwan is expected to need 701,000 tons of ethylene and domestic production only to reach 618,000 tons, leaving a shortfall of 83,000 tons. Taiwan is also expected to be in the market for urea and some other petrochemicals. The expertise of Taiwan in market penetration could be a valuable asset to Saudi Arabia: Saudi petrochemicals can be used to manufacture synthetic textiles, plastics and other products which can be marketed not only in Asia but also world-wide. It is indicative that synthetic textiles made in Taiwan are already entering Fujian and other provinces of mainland China passing via Hong Kong.

The nature of Taiwanese—Saudi Arabian co-operation in the field of petrochemicals has found concrete expression in an agreement signed on 4 December 1979, between SABIC and the Taiwan Fertilizer Company Limited to establish the Al-Jubail Fertilizer Company, located in Jubail. This joint venture would use methane to produce 1,000 metric tons of ammonia per day, which will be converted to 1,600 metric tons of urea.[15] While Taiwan has highly skilled engineers, technicians and labour, it must rely on US, European and Japanese technology in petrochemicals. The Al-Jubail Fertilizer Company therefore makes use of the Pullman Kellogg and Stamicarbon BV processes, while the construction management services are the responsibility of Bakhsh-Pullman Kellogg Saudi Arabia Limited, located in Al-Khobar. Design and engineering is partly carried out in the Houston offices of Pullman Kellogg. The actual construction on the site in Jubail started in June 1980 and the plant is now expected to go onstream in early 1983. The total investment is estimated at $357 million. SABIC and the Taiwan Fertilizer Company will each subscribe 50 per cent of the shares of the Al-Jubail Fertilizer Company, putting up $100 million at the present time. The balance is being loaned by the Public Investment Fund.[16]

Some 60 per cent of the output of the Al-Jubail Fertilizer Company will be marketed by the Taiwan Fertilizer Company in Taiwan and other places in the Far East. The other 40 per cent will be marketed jointly by the Taiwan Fertilizer Company and SABIC elsewhere. No serious difficulty should be experienced in marketing the ammonia/ urea. Ammonia, being a source of nitrogen fertiliser, is closely linked to agricultural production. Since the world population is expected to double over the next thirty-five years, the output of fertiliser will have to triple just to maintain the subsistence level. The projected global demand for ammonia/urea in 1990 is about 80 million additional tons, such that to meet the increased demand a new plant, with a capacity of 1,000 tons of ammonia per day, would have to go onstream every month. It is possible, however, that in certain regions, such as South-West Asia, a glut may appear. The US Department of Agriculture predicts a urea surplus of 1,250,000 tons in this region by 1985.[17]

Republic of Korea

Prospects for developing economic relations between Saudi Arabia and the Republic of Korea are good, based on mutual economic dependence. The hard work and discipline of Koreans have secured numerous contracts for Korean companies in the kingdom – in 1980 close to 100,000 Koreans were working there. Three-quarters of Korea's energy requirements are in the form of oil and this must all be imported; much of the oil comes from Saudi Arabia. In 1980 the value of Saudi oil exports to Korea reached $3 billion, and it is probable that Saudi liquified natural gas will also soon be exported to Korea.

The Republic of Korea currently has a number of petrochemical plants producing a variety of products which are used downstream. An expansion of this sector is planned, such that by 1986 the output of petrochemicals would reach 1.5 million tons, thereby allowing Korea to meet 83 per cent of domestic requirements. The existing domestic production of petrochemicals is supplemented by imports of organic chemicals, plastic materials, synthetic yarns and fabrics. These petro-chemicals, domestic and imported, are used to manufacture synthetic textiles and fabrics, clothing, garments and footwear. A highly efficient organisation places these products on the domestic market (comprising some 38 million Koreans), and on markets in the United States, Japan, Hong Kong, West Germany, the United Kingdom and other countries – including Saudi Arabia. The garment division of Samsung, one of the most important conglomerates, has recently been involved in the shipment of $100 million worth of uniforms to Saudi Arabia.

Government plans call for a further expansion of the textile and apparel industry to make Korea the most important exporter of textiles in the world by 1986, with $10 billion in exports and one-tenth of the world-market share.[18]

To complement Korea's own petrochemical production the Korean government is now anxious to promote joint ventures in Saudi Arabia in the petrochemical field. The intention would be to use the bulk commodities produced as an input for Korea's downstream industry — transforming them into high value-added products. Current proposals include a joint venture with SABIC to produce 175,000 tons per year of ethylene; a plant to produce 500,000 tons per year of urea; and a joint venture with Petromin for a refinery on the Red Sea coast. In May 1980, when the then President of Korea Choi Kyo-hah visited Saudi Arabia, there was discussion of other possible projects in petrochemicals and fertilisers. Such prospects, however, are for the long term. Neither the ethylene plant nor the urea plant have at present a high priority within SABIC.

While Korea may not be able to offer suitable technology for a petrochemical industry, it can, however, offer highly efficient manpower and eventually an outlet for Saudi commodity petrochemicals. The giant Korean textile industry, with its world-wide exports, could make substantial use of Saudi petrochemical derivatives. Saudi ethylene glycol could be made into polyester fibre and film as well as polyethylene terephthalate resins.

International Dimension: Japan

Economic relations between Saudi Arabia and Japan have developed rapidly since 1973. In August of that year a Japan—Saudi Arabia co-operation organisation was set up under private auspices. A few months later the more all-embracing Japan Cooperation Centre for the Middle East was established with government support. In December 1973, the Japanese International Trade and Industry Minister visited the kingdom. These steps led to the signing in 1975 of a Japan—Saudi Arabia economic and technological agreement, laying down a framework for increased co-operation between the two countries and in the following year joint committee offices were established in al-Riyadh.[19]

Saudi Arabia and Japan have much to gain from a close association. The nature of the mutual benefit has been outlined by the vice-chairman of the Mitsubishi Corporation, Keizaturo Yamada: 'In Saudi Arabia they are interested in securing technology and complete turnkey projects in exchange for their oil exports.'[20] Japan can provide technology for the petrochemical industry that is almost on a par with the best in the United States and Europe. If Japan is not the innovator of a process, as is frequently the case, the technology can often be secured through licensing or other arrangements. Japanese engineering firms, moreover, have a great deal of experience with overseas projects, and the Japanese offer competitive pricing, fast and guaranteed deliveries, back-up services, engineering assistance, onshore warehousing and high-quality design and workmanship. The attraction of Japanese products is evidenced by the Datsuns, Toyotas and Hondas which fill the roads of the kingdom and the Japanese electronic implements which fill the homes. Japan has now become Saudi Arabia's second trading partner, after the United States. The strengthening link is reflected in the number of Japanese in the kingdom: in October 1976 there were 750, but by October 1979 the number had grown to 3,500.[21]

Japan is also becoming an important outlet for investments by Saudi Arabia and other OPEC countries. Large commercial banking institutions and investment firms in Britain and Switzerland are moving petrodollars to Japan and West Germany. It is estimated that by the end of 1980 the OPEC countries will have placed some $25 billion in Japanese blue-chip bonds, convertible debentures, high-technology stocks and top-ranking industrial shares with favourable long-term outlooks. It has been reported that the Saudi Arabian Monetary Authority has agreed to purchase $150–215 million a month worth of Japanese government bonds over an unspecified period. These so-called 'Ohira' bonds would be held on account for SAMA by the Bank of Japan. Indeed, some 15 per cent of Saudi investments abroad are now going to Japan.

The nature of the economic relationship emerging between Japan and Saudi Arabia is most crucially apparent in the interactions between Japan's need for oil, the export market which Saudi Arabia constitutes for Japan's *sogo shosha* (general trading companies), and the role which the latter can play both in constructing projects crucial to Saudi Arabia and in marketing the products of the Saudi petrochemical industry in Asia and other regions. Japan needs to import virtually all of its oil;[22] about 34 per cent of the oil imports come from Saudi Arabia. Some of the implications of this dependence on Arab oil became painfully evident in the aftermath of the 1973 Middle East War when oil supplies to Japan were cut off for three weeks. The yen plunged on foreign exchange markets, stocks collapsed, people began to stockpile and prices rose. The value of Japan's imports of oil stood at $35 billion in 1979 and are estimated to have reached $59 billion in 1980. The Japanese have been quick to recognise the full extent of their dependence on oil. The president of Mitsui and Company has put this succinctly:

> The situation has now completely changed. The single most important fact is this. The Middle East is now important to Japan not only as a supplier of oil; since the oil crisis it has also become one of the most important markets for Japanese manufacturers. Our exports to that area are second only to our exports to the United States, but we're obliged to continue to depend on its oil.

This dependence can be expected to persist. Thus in 1990 Japan will probably be importing some 8 million barrels of oil per day. Ethylene and derivatives are also expected to be in strong demand before the middle of the 1980s, forcing Japan to import.[23] As a counterpart to the increasing dependence on oil the *sogo shosha* are becoming steadily more active in developing links with Saudi Arabia. These giant business conglomerates, without counterpart abroad, owe their strength to close business connections. They are active in marketing, distribution, financing and organising large-scale plant construction. They can marshal the industrial and technical might of Japan behind mega-projects.

The Mitsubishi Relationship

Relations in the petrochemical field between Saudi Arabia and Japan stretch back over many years. In the late 1960s a number of possible joint ventures were under discussion. In February 1969 a Japanese delegation visited the kingdom and submitted several proposals for such ventures with Petromin. This was followed in 1970 by visits to Tokyo by Ahmed Zaki Yamani, the Saudi Minister of Oil and Mineral Wealth, and Abd al-Hadi Taher, the Governor of Petromin, who held talks with Japanese industrialists concerning joint ventures in oils and petrochemicals. A close relationship developed between Petromin and the largest of the *sogo shosha* — Mitsubishi. The Mitsubishi Corporation maintains 140 offices in Japan and 120 abroad, which are staffed by 19,000 employees. Sales in the 1979—80 financial year reached $54.1 billion. The Corporation has 48 subsidiaries and 233 affiliates. If the whole Mitsubishi group's turnover is compared with that of other leading corporations, Mitsubishi is seen to have nearly twice the turnover of Exxon.[24] Mitsubishi has played a key role in Japanese–Saudi relations. Following Taher's visit to Japan, it was agreed that Mitsubishi should construct a refinery in al-Riyadh and increase the capacity of the one in Jeddah. While Petromin was to pay for these plants, Mitsubishi agreed to buy oil equal in value to the cost of the refineries.

After 1973 relations between Saudi Arabia and Japan were greatly strengthened. The Japanese government, through the Overseas Economic Cooperation Fund (OECF), began to throw its support behind closer relations with Saudi Arabia, working in conjunction with Mitsubishi. Mitsubishi soon realised that a chemical company's success in the 1980s would depend almost entirely on whether it had a solid link with a major feedstock supplier. It was necessary to assure long-term stable supplies of crude oil and products such as methanol, ethylene and ammonia. This has led Mitsubishi and various other Japanese firms to look with increasing favour on joint ventures with Saudi organisations in the kingdom. Shoichi Nakase, spokesman of the Mitsubishi Corporation, has asserted:

> We . . . have gained the confidence of the Middle East governments that we are not merely moving to take the money and run. We have shown them that we are really multi-faced business organisations that can put in as much, if not more, than we take out.[25]

Saudi Arabia, through SABIC, and Mitsubishi thus have strong mutual interests in strengthening co-operation in the development of the petrochemical industry in Saudi Arabia.

SABIC/Mitsubishi Gas Complex

It is not surprising, therefore, that a consortium of Japanese companies, headed by the Mitsubishi Gas Chemicals Company, supported by the OECF, decided with SABIC to establish a complex in Jubail, using natural gas as a feedstock to produce chemical grade methanol. The final agreement with SABIC to build the Saudi Arabian Methanol Company (SAMCO) was signed in April 1980. This was to be the first venture by Japanese firms in methanol production outside Japan. The Saudi Arabian Methanol Company is now leasing a 500,000 square metre tract of land in Jubail from the Royal Commission for Jubail and Yanbu. This land was obtained under the national industry protection and encouragement laws. The site will be provided with electricity, water, sewage and communications; sea water will be used for cooling.

The methanol complex is to be on a relatively modest scale, with a capacity of 600,000 tons of methanol a year. Production will be based on the Mitsubishi Gas Chemical Low Pressure Process. The basic engineering is to be done by the Mitsubishi Gas Chemicals Company and the actual construction by Mitsubishi Heavy Industries Limited. A rather unusual aspect of the engineering is that the modular system will be used. Mitsubishi Heavy Industries will make about 100 modules in Japan, ranging from 30 to 1,200 tons, and these will be sent by sea to Jubail, where they will be assembled.[26] In order to effectively implement construction work, Mitsubishi Heavy Industries Limited and Mitsubishi Corporation have established a joint venture with the Olayan Saudi Holding Company (OSHCO). The new company, Mitsubishi Olayan Machinery Industries Saudi Arabia, is capitalised at SR 4 million, with the two Mitsubishi companies each owning 25 per cent and OSHCO the balance. Mitsubishi will thus be able to draw on the collaboration of Suliman S. Olayan, one of the shrewdest and most able entrepreneurs in Saudi Arabia.[27]

The capital investment in the plant is expected to be some $300 million. The Public Investment Fund is to put up 60 per cent of this amount and 10 per cent will come from the commercial banks. The remaining 30 per cent is to be shared by SABIC and the consortium consisting of the Mitsubishi Gas and Chemical Company Inc., Sumitomo Chemicals, Mitsui-Toatsu Chemicals, the Kyowa Gas Chemical Industry and C. Itoh. The Overseas Economic Cooperation Fund of Japan has insured SAMCO against possible financial loss. SAMCO is scheduled to go onstream in 1983. Being a relatively modest undertaking it will require only about 180 employees, including the guards and the general manager.

The Japanese consortium will be responsible for marketing 80 per cent of the methanol — some 480,000 tons a year. Of this amount 300,000 tons will be placed on the Japanese market itself, being used to manufacture formalin for urea resin. While Japan has a considerable domestic production of methanol it should have little difficulty in absorbing the Saudi methanol. Indeed, a study by Chem Systems suggests a shortfall of 1.17 million tons of methanol in Japan by 1990 (see Table 13.4). The other 180,000 tons of methanol would be marketed by the Japanese in the other countries of the Far East. The balance of 120,000 tons would be placed on the world market by SABIC. Given the cheap feedstock and the favourable markets, it would be surprising if SAMCO does not prove to be a profitable venture.[28]

Table 13.4: World Methanol Supply/Demand in 1990

Region	Supply[a]	Demand[a]
United States	5,340	8,070
Eastern Europe	5,620	5,000
Western Europe	4,025	5,960
Japan	950	2,120
Other countries in Asia	1,130	1,087
Africa—Middle East	2,575	100
Australia—New Zealand	360	125
Canada	1,500	312
Latin America	1,641	578
Total	23,141	23,352

Note: a. Supply and Demand columns are measured in thousands of metric tons/year.
Source: Celanese Corporation, from Chem Systems Incorporated data.

SABIC/SPDC Complex

By far the most important joint Saudi—Japanese venture is a large petrochemical complex to be located in Jubail. Using ethane as a feedstock, this complex will, according to tentative agreements, have an annual capacity of 130,000 tons of low-density polyethylene and 330,000 tons of ethylene glycol and 80,000 tons of high-density polyethylene. Considerable capital will be required. Funding will be by SABIC and by a consortium of 54 Japanese firms, formed in 1979, grouped in the Saudi Petrochemical Development Corporation (SPDC). The consortium is led by the Mitsubishi Corporation and 14 other Mitsubishi companies as well as 13 oil companies, 9 power companies, 11 petrochemical companies, 4 banks and 2 gas companies. The Japanese corporate commitment is 7.5 per cent of the capital investment. Another 7.5 per cent will come from the OECF, which classifies the complex as 'national'. In fact, Tazio Wanatabe of the Japanese Foreign Ministry has observed that 'this is the biggest economic co-operation agreement between Japan and Saudi Arabia, and the [Japanese] government feels the realisation of this project is vitally important'.

A pre-feasibility study of the petrochemical complex was made several years ago. The results were rather pessimistic, indicating that the complex would not break even before a decade. Yet, as the price of feedstock continued to rise and as oil entitlements grew in importance, some of the basic assumptions had to be revised. In April 1980 Mitsubishi agreed with SABIC that a new feasibility study had to be made. Chiyoda Chemical Engineering and Construction Company is currently assisting with this study, with the $10 million cost being divided equally between SABIC and SPDC. The Mitsubishi Corporation is now giving top priority to the petrochemical complex project.[29] From planning to plant operation a number of years can elapse; the project is targeted to go onstream in 1984 or 1985 at the latest.[30] Among the aspects of the overall agreement to which the Japanese consortium will be giving closest attention is the oil entitlements. The entitlements to be accorded to SPDC are currently under consideration by the Supreme Petroleum Council. The managing director of SABIC has indicated that these entitlements depend on such factors as:

(a) the equity contributed by the partner;
(b) the commitment of the partner to the project;
(c) the contribution to marketing the product;
(d) the technology transferred.

When SPDC does go onstream, the Japanese consortium will undoubtedly be interested in marketing the output in Japan and other Asian countries. In fact Yosiharo Hongo, the general manager of business development for the chemical department of Mitsubishi, asserted early in 1980 that Japan will be obliged to import ethylene and derivatives from the United States, Canada and Singapore until SPDC comes onstream.[31]

Japanese Accommodation for Saudi Petrochemicals

Faced with rising energy and feedstock costs, as well as the prospect of growing competition from Saudi and other producers of basic and intermediate petrochemicals, Japanese authorities and entrepreneurs are facing the challenge by placing less emphasis on the domestic output of this type of petrochemical product. Thus the Mitsubishi Corporation estimates that a number of smaller ethylene plants will close and the output of ethylene in Japan will ease off between 1980 and 1985 (see Table 13.5). Indeed, already in 1980 the output of ethylene and derivatives fell sharply and the Nippon Petrochemical Company Limited has had to close its plant.

Japan, therefore, is willing to suffer losses in its own petrochemical industry in order to assure the success of its joint ventures with the kingdom. The Minister of International Trade and Industry, Masumi Esaki, declared in July 1979 that 'it is worthwhile going ahead, even if the result is that two or three petrochemical plants in Japan go

Table 13.5: Estimated Pattern of Output of Ethylene in Japan between 1980 and 1985

	Number of plants		Capacity (tons/years)	
Plant size (tons/year)	1980	1985	1980	1985
<100,000	8	4	597,000	300,000
100,000 <200,000	8	6	972,000	778,000
200,000 <300,000	3	3	625,000	625,000
>300,000	11	11	3,575,000	3,575,000
Total	30	24	5,769,000	5,278,000

Source: Author's statistics.

bankrupt'. A number of highly competent and forward-looking industrialists are playing a key role in the shift of emphasis in the Japanese petrochemical industry. One of these is Takeshi Hijkata, the president of both the Association of Petrochemical Industries and of the Sumitomo Chemical Company Limited. He has observed that:

1. Increases in the price of oil, together with the development of petrochemical industries in developing countries, make the capacity expansion of basic and general purpose products such as polyethylene and methanol, less economically justifiable in Japan.
2. We should, therefore, actively cooperate with oil-producing countries by participating in their petrochemical projects for such basic products.
3. At the same time, we should orient our research and development efforts to high value-added speciality products that require more sophisticated technology.

My intention is not to advocate a departure from primary petrochemical products towards engineering plastics or a competition with oil-producing countries. Instead, I wanted to stress the need for international division of labor based on the spirit of mutual collaboration. In this way, I believe, we all can prosper in this age of interdependence.[32]

This move towards concentrating on products with a greater value-added content is now underway. The Honshu Chemical Industry Company Limited and the Mitsui Petrochemical Industries Limited are launching a joint venture, based on the use of phenol, aniline and cresol, which will make products with a greater added value. Teijin Limited is to expand its output of engineering plastics by some 20 per cent a year.[33]

International Context: the United States

The large American oil, chemical, engineering and construction corporations can provide the 'know-how' and the latest technology for a Saudi petrochemical industry. The corporations can also open world markets for Saudi petrochemicals. Process plant projects have grown to an enormous size in the last decade, requiring a billion dollars or more in capital investment and using many millions of engineering and construction man-hours. This is especially true for Saudi Arabia where, in addition to the large process facilities, there is need for a substantial infrastructure, such as permanent housing, port development, roads, support services, etc. To bring petrochemical complexes onstream demands highly specialised skill, perfect co-ordination and faultless timing. To sell the final product requires a highly experienced and extensive marketing system.[34]

The technological leadership of the US in the petrochemical and indeed in the whole chemical field is paramount. This lead is particularly evident in process innovation. The latest ammonia plants designed by Pullman-Kellogg reduce energy consumption by a third. Union Carbide's new Unipol process for low-density polyethylene gives not only a significant saving in energy use and capital cost but also increases safety and reduces the space needed for plant. The United States also leads the world in the latest process of computer-control technology.[35] Corporations which have proprietary rights to technology are not normally prepared to sell their technology. Under certain conditions, however, they may be prepared to license it to other firms with which they have a close working relationship. As the executive vice-president of Dow Chemicals, Robert W. Lundeen, states:

> as far as outward licencing, our posture has not changed. We are not going to licence anyone unless we have a substantial element of management participation in the enterprise that is going to use the technology, so we can see that the shareholders get the maximum benefit out of the licencing of their property.[36]

However, just as Saudi Arabia stands in need of United States technology, so does the United States stand in need of Saudi oil and (possibly) oil derivatives. Saudi Arabia has moved to the first place as supplier of foreign oil to the United States. In 1979 some 1.4 million barrels a day of oil were shipped to the US and natural gas liquids are starting to move to the same market. The value of these exports, which reached $4.9 billion in 1979, are expected to have totalled $6 billion in 1980. The dependence on Saudi oil can be expected to continue. Though US demand for oil may decline somewhat between 1980 and 1990, American imports of oil are expected by the Exxon Company to rise from 8.1 million barrels per day in 1980 to 9.3 million barrels per day in 1990.[37] At the same time US imports of liquified natural gas are expected to increase significantly, reaching 1.2 trillion cubic feet in 1990.

Apart from crude oil and natural gas liquids, SABIC also expects to find a market in the United States for its petrochemicals. In the United States, Europe, Japan and an increasing number of other countries, there has been a revolution in materials. Polyester clothing and polypropylene furniture, plastic automobile parts, plastic milk bottles and toys, synthetic carpets — a virtually endless list of petrochemical-based replacements for natural materials has been produced. In the 1960s and 1970s the production of the petrochemical industry grew at about triple the rate of the Gross National Product in the developed world until it has become a $150 billion industry world-wide. However, the future is expected to see somewhat slower growth rates — in the 1980s and 1990s about 1.5 to 1.8 times the rate of GNP increase.[38] In the United States demand for petrochemicals is expected to grow at an annual average rate of 4 per cent in the 1980s.[39]

Plastics, one of the principal products of the petrochemical industry, illustrates this growth. In the United States production in 1940 stood at 114,000 tons, rising in 1978 to 19 million tons. The Organization for Economic Cooperation and Development estimates that US plastic production will be between 22 and 26 million tons in 1990. World-wide ethylene capacity, which stood at 43.2 million tons in June 1979, reached 46.3 million tons in June 1980 — a 7.3 per cent increase. Much of this increase took place in the United States. While the demand for ethylene can be expected to continue to expand, the four world-scale plants which are scheduled to come onstream should satisfy requirements until 1985. After 1986 the demand for ethylene in the United States could well begin to exceed capacity, as a recent study by the marketing research firm De Witt and Company of Houston shows (see Figure 13.2).[40]

With unsettled conditions prevailing in the Middle East and other parts of the world, the major US oil and chemical corporations are

Figure 13.2: US Ethylene Capacity v. Demand

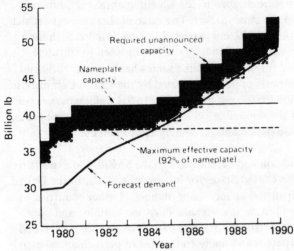

Source: Author's statistics.

looking for assured supplies at competitive prices. Thus the feedstock manager of Essochem Europe declares: 'To be a factor in this business, you must have access to adequate supplies of feedstock at competitive prices. If not, you are out of the business.'[41] Even where an investment in a joint venture by a foreign corporation in Saudi Arabia does not have an acceptable rate of return, therefore, the broader picture also has to be taken into consideration. If the rate of return on a specific venture is low, it can be compensated by supplies of oil or other hydrocarbons at an attractive price or simply by an assured source of supply. The strategy of oil entitlements as an incentive to invest was clearly underlined by Shaikh Ahmed Zaki Yamani in February 1980 when he stated that in future Saudi Arabia will only grant oil contracts to customers willing to help build up industry in Saudi Arabia.[42] Well might former United States Senator William Fulbright assert that 'Saudi Arabia is the most important country in the world to the United States'.

The 'Six Sisters'

Saudi Arabia has long had close working relationships with some of the major world oil corporations — especially those based in the United States. Standard Oil Company of California first secured a concession in Saudi Arabia in 1933. This concession was assigned to the Arabian

American Oil Company (Aramco) in 1944. In order to secure additional investment capital and marketing outlets, Aramco brought in Texaco, Exxon and Mobil as partners. While Petromin has now virtually taken over Aramco, relatively secure supplies and favourable prices – the so-called 'Saudi advantage' – continue for the moment to be accorded to these majors.

Shortly after the establishment of SABIC in 1976 Dr al-Gosaibi approached some of the leading oil and chemical corporations to interest them in establishing joint-venture petrochemical complexes. Since the kingdom was particularly deficient in management and marketing expertise, not to speak of markets, it was essential to draw on the experience of major corporations. These corporations had great misgivings. Doubts existed concerning the adequacy of the rate of return, as to whether satisfactory markets could be found for the petrochemical products, and as to whether or not the political risk in the Gulf area did not preclude any important financial commitment. Evantually six major American corporations did show serious interest – the Mobil Oil Corporation, the Shell Oil Company, the Exxon Corporation, the Dow Chemical Company, the Celanese Corporation and the Texas Eastern Corporation. At the present time it has been tentatively agreed with the six US corporations to produce certain petrochemicals (see Table 13.6).[43]

The American corporations which will participate in joint ventures with SABIC plan to contract much of the work in engineering, procurement and construction. This will largely be done by the Badger Company Incorporated, the C. F. Braun Company, the Dravo Corporation and Pullman Incorporated, with its different divisions such as the Pullman-Kellogg division, Bechtel and the Fluor Corporation. These are firms with great experience in the petrochemical field. Thus Badger, based in Cambridge, Massachusetts, has a staff of some 3,000 and has 23 offices in the United States and other countries, including the Arabian Badger Company in al-Khobar.

SABIC/Mobil Complex. Mobil is a very powerful partner. The Mobil Oil Corporation, with its 75,000 employees and annual sales of over $30 billion, is one of the largest corporations in the world. From their offices in New York they control subsidiaries in the United States and in many other countries in the world. In November 1980 Suliman S. Olayan was elected to the Board – the first time that a Saudi national has been named as a director of an oil corporation with interests in the kingdom.

Table 13.6: Petrochemicals Which Six US Corporations Have Tentatively Agreed to Produce with SABIC

Petrochemicals	SABIC/ Mobil	SABIC/ Shell	SABIC/ Exxon	SABIC/ Dow	SABIC/ Celanese– Texas
Ethylene	450,000	656,000	–	500,000	–
Low-density polyethylene	200,000	–	260,000	80,000	–
High-density polyethylene	91,000	–	–	70,000	–
Ethylene glycol	220,000	–	–	–	–
Ethylene dichloride	–	454,000	–	–	–
Caustic soda	–	377,000	–	–	–
Styrene	–	295,000	–	–	–
Ethanol	–	281,000	–	–	–
Methanol	–	–	–	–	660,000

Source: Author's statistics.

As far back as 1946 Mobil came to the kingdom to produce and distribute oil under the aegis of Aramco. In 1974 it began to examine with Saudi authorities the possibility of establishing a petrochemical industry in the kingdom. In August 1976 an interim agreement was signed between Mobil and SABIC envisaging a feasibility study for a petrochemical complex, an economic assessment of the project and negotiations for the establishment of a joint-venture company. Since those days some $31 million has been spent on different studies related to the proposed complex. In April 1980 the final agreement was concluded between Mobil (Mobil Saudi Arabia and Mobil Yanbu Petrochemicals Company) and SABIC. The Yanbu Petrochemicals Company (YANPET) was duly established on 26 September 1980, covering a concessionary period of thirty years. This, Dr al-Gosaibi observed, was 'a major landmark in our industrial development history'.

Basic to the Mobil/SABIC petrochemicals complex is the gas-gathering and transporting network. The natural gas liquids pipeline, linking Shedgum in the Eastern Province with Yanbu, some 625 miles west, should start carrying 270,000 barrels per day of natural gas liquids in December 1981. The fractionation plant in Yanbu will separate the liquids into ethane, butane, isopentane, propane and natural gasoline. This ethane will then be sold to YANPET for feedstock and fuel at a special subsidised price, probably about one-fifth of the world market price. YANPET will use the ethane to produce annually 450,000 tons of ethylene. Licensing arrangements have already been completed and in November 1980 SABIC signed a contract with

Bechtel Limited covering the engineering and supervision of construction. The ethylene will be used in turn to make 200,000 tons of low-density polyethylene and 90,000 tons of high-density polyethylene. In addition 220,000 tons of ethylene glycol will be produced.

The capital of YANPET is placed at $672 million, with the Mobil Yanbu Petrochemicals Company and SABIC each holding half of the equity. Each party only has to provide 15 per cent of its share of the equity in cash. The balance can be borrowed from the Public Investment Fund of Saudi Arabia at a very advantageous rate of interest and the rest from private banks. Saudi Arabia is also making available, as an added inducement to invest, an oil entitlement.

This venture shows every sign of being viable. A Shell study comparing the production costs of ethylene glycol and low-density polyethylene in the Gulf and in Europe determined that if ethane was priced at about 35 cents per million BTU in the Gulf and naphtha at about $250 per ton in Europe and due consideration was given to the cost of fuel, other manufacturing, capital, freight and duty, then these two petrochemicals had a considerably lower production cost in the Gulf.[44] YANPET is expected to come onstream in 1985. About 1,200 people will be needed to staff the complex. Initially about 40 per cent of the employees will be Saudis and 60 per cent expatriates. By 1990 it is hoped that these percentages will be reversed. It is to be feared, however, that there could well be a dearth of administrative personnel with real executive talent.

YANPET will market its products in Europe, along the eastern seaboard of the United States, in the Arab world, in Africa and in Saudi Arabia itself. Three-quarters of the sales will be handled by Mobil. When the plant is at full capacity this will mean that Mobil will increase its petrochemical production by one-third. Mobil is now taking steps to expand its marketing distribution so that when the project comes onstream all the production can be handled.[45]

SABIC/Shell Complex. The Shell Oil Company, with some 11,000 employees and sales of $14 billion in 1979, is 69 per cent owned by the Royal Dutch–Shell Group and this forms part of one of the largest industrial groups world-wide. The company, which is based in Houston, has been negotiating with SABIC to build a giant petrochemical complex in Jubail, to be known as the Saudi Petrochemical Company. An interim agreement between SABIC and Pecten Arabian Limited, a subsidiary of the Shell Oil Company, was reached in 1976. It was, however, not until 28 September 1980, that a formal agreement was

signed. Using ethane and methane the Saudi Petrochemical Company
now intends to produce 656,000 tons of ethylene per annum. Based on
this ethylene a slate of derivatives will be produced, comprising
295,000 tons of styrene, 454,000 tons of ethylene dichloride, 281,000
tons of crude industrial ethanol and 377,000 tons of caustic soda, as
well as ethyl benzene and chlorine as intermediary products.

The Fluor Corporation, one of the largest engineering and construction companies in the United States for the petroleum, petrochemical
and power industries, was selected in 1976 as the managing constructor.
They are now proceeding with the engineering, procurement and
construction. At the same time Fluor Technical Services, a subsidiary
of the Fluor Corporation, is handling engineering for the off sites and
auxiliaries. In order to work more effectively in the kingdom, Fluor
Mideast Limited has joined with Ibrahim Al-Juffali & Brothers to
establish Petrochemical Engineering Ltd in al-Khobar. Of the SR 4
million equity, 70 per cent will be held by Fluor and the balance by the
Al-Juffali brothers.

The capital cost of this complex has been set at $3.3 billion. It is
hoped that the cost of the ethane cracker, estimated at $900 million,
could be shared with the SABIC/Exxon venture in return for part of
the ethylene. SABIC and Pecten are each to invest $400 million in the
complex. The major part of the balance will be funded by the Public
Investment Fund, which is prepared to make available 60 per cent of
the total cost of the complex on terms which allow a period of grace of
five years and set the rate of interest at between 3 and 6 per cent.
Commercial banks are also being brought into the financing.[46] The
joint venture will pave the way for Shell to receive the special 'incentive'
oil entitlement. Liftings could start in 1981 and the entitlement is
expected to increase by increments of 20 per cent a year over the period
of construction of the Saudi Petrochemical Company. While the
Supreme Petroleum Council has yet to arrive at a final decision on the
level of the oil entitlement, this will largely depend, as the President of
Shell has indicated, 'on the amount of capital invested and technology
transfer'. And, he might have added, on the degree to which Saudi
manpower is used in the Saudi Petrochemical Company and on the
success of the efforts to market the products. The political stance of
Shell concerning Arab issues could even be taken into consideration.

It is now hoped that the return on equity of the Shell/SABIC
complex could be some 15 to 20 per cent a year. This is inevitably
highly speculative. While it is true that interest charges and the cost of
feedstock and even energy will undoubtedly be particularly low, at the

same time much depends on the volume and value of the sales by the Saudi Petrochemical Company – always particularly difficult to forecast. The petrochemicals produced by the complex will be divided 50 : 50 by SABIC and Shell. Initially Shell will market not only its own share but also that of SABIC, and for this it will receive a marketing fee. The slate of products which the Saudi Petrochemical Company intends to place on the market should find a ready outlet. There is, for example, likely to be an increasing demand for ethanol, which is being used more and more in a 10 per cent blend with gasoline to make the automotive fuel gasohol.

Eventually SABIC will market directly its share of the petro-chemicals both in Saudi Arabia and abroad. The growing downstream activity in the kingdom should assure a growing outlet. Even before this complex has come onstream, SABIC is considering an eventual expansion in the slate of products produced by the Saudi Petrochemical Company. The possibility of producing polystyrene and polyvinyl chloride is being considered. Here, however, SABIC might seek another partner.

SABIC/Exxon Complex. The Exxon Corporation is by far the largest American industrial corporation, with 127,000 employees and sales of $79.1 billion in 1979. Formerly Standard Oil of New Jersey, Exxon first came to Saudi Arabia in 1946 as a partner in Aramco. The kingdom soon became a major source of oil for Exxon and the corporation benefited greatly from the sale of this oil. In the 1970s SABIC raised the possibility of a joint venture to produce low-density polyethylene. After an interim agreement signed in March 1977 a number of feasibility studies were undertaken. SABIC, the Exxon Corporation and the Exxon Chemical Company finally concluded an agreement in April 1980 to proceed with the low-density polyethylene complex.

The SABIC/Exxon complex, to be known as Al-Jubail Petrochemical Company, will use ethylene as a feedstock, with the ethylene coming from a cracker shared with the Saudi Pecten Petrochemical Company. Some 260,000 tons of low-density polyethylene will be produced a year. The engineering will be done by the Fluor Corporation. The cost of this project has been put as $1,100 million, the equity being shared equally. Exxon will, as an additional incentive, probably receive a commitment from Saudi Arabia to provide 500 barrels a day of crude oil for each million dollars invested in the Saudex venture. The total personnel of this plant should be about 350. When the plant starts up between one-third and one-half of the personnel is expected to be

Saudi, the balance being expatriates. A number of Saudis are now with Exxon in the United States for training; their number will gradually increase. The plans for the plant have now been approved and it is scheduled to go into operation in 1984.

Some nine-tenths of the 260,000 tons per annum of low-density polyethylene produced will be marketed by Exxon. Abd al-Aziz al-Zamil has underlined that, while the transfer of technology and management expertise is important, what is critical is 'undertaking the responsibility for marketing the products'. Exxon too sees the most important part of the agreement as that which relates to feeding the plants' product into Exxon's marketing network. Production, then, will be channelled into world markets, presumably including Europe. Thus Essochem Europe will undoubtedly be called upon to place at least some of the low-density polyethylene in Europe. SABIC, which is establishing a marketing department, will initially market the remaining one-tenth of production in Saudi Arabia and abroad. The proportion marketed by SABIC will gradually increase as the years pass. While the exports of low-density polyethylene will undoubtedly face some competition abroad, there can be little doubt that the marketing will be successful. It is not anticipated that these sales will create any glut on world markets.[47] Saudex is expected to give preference to Saudi shipping when exporting.

SABIC/Dow Complex. The Dow Chemical Company, with 53,000 employees and sales of $9.3 billion in 1979, is a giant in the American chemical industry, manufacturing industrial inorganic and organic chemicals, plastics, pharmaceutical preparations and a variety of other products. Though Dow Chemical is a relative newcomer to Saudi Arabia, the company is now showing great interest in developing relations with the kingdom. After an interim agreement signed in February 1977, a number of economic and financial studies were carried out. A major feasibility study was completed in January 1980.

The basic feedstock to be used in the proposed SABIC/Dow complex would be ethane. Using the Dow Chemical processes this complex would produce 500,000 tons of ethylene, 80,000 tons of low-density polyethylene, 300,000 tons of ethylene glycol and 70,000 tons of high-density polyethylene per annum. Dow Chemical would also do the engineering. The plant should be virtually identical to one recently completed in Canada, and the cost is estimated at $1,300 million. Negotiations are still in progress. It is reported that the venture will be approved by Dow Chemical in the near future. It is hoped that this complex would go onstream at least by 1986.[48] It has been reported that the Saudi Arabia Monetary Agency has made a loan to Dow Chemical.

SABIC/Celanese–Texas Eastern Complex. The Celanese Corporation, with 33,000 employees and sales of $3.1 billion in 1979, is one of the leading American manufacturers of fibres, chemicals, plastics and polymer specialities. The corporation is now joining up with the Texas Eastern Corporation, which engages in the production and distribution of petroleum products, to launch a joint venture with SABIC to produce methanol in Jubail. On 24 February 1978, Texas Eastern Arabian, a subsidiary of Texas Eastern Corporation, agreed with SABIC to make a detailed feasibility study; start preliminary engineering design; and negotiate agreements for a joint-venture company. Considerable progress has been made since that time. It has been decided to establish a world-scale complex – one that would use the local methane to produce 660,000 tons of methanol a year. The engineering would be done by C. F. Braun and Company.[49] The cost of the plant is now estimated at $350 million, which may be compared with the $215 million which Celanese is to spend for a similar plant in Canada with a capacity of 235 million gallons of methanol a year. Celanese expects to hold 25 per cent of the equity in the Jubail complex, with SABIC as a partner. The plant is now expected to go onstream in late 1984.

This venture would seem to have particularly good prospects. Methanol is becoming a key product for Celanese. Total demand in the US is expected by Celanese to triple over the next decade. As the price of oil rises, methanol should become increasingly important as a fuel. It can be readily adapted for use in cars, power stations and blast furnaces, and has the further advantage of being more readily transported than natural gas. Methanol may also eventually be used as an edible protein. Just for use as a fuel, being blended with gasoline or alcohol, the US demand could well increase a hundredfold over the next ten years, from 23 million gallons in 1980 to 2,300 million gallons in 1990. While US domestic capacity will probably triple during this period, imports could move as shown in Table 13.7.[50] The 230 million gallons produced by the plant in Saudi Arabia could, therefore, be absorbed in the United States. There is, moreover, also the West European market, where demand will considerably exceed supply (see Table 13.4).

The prospects of Saudi Arabia finding markets for its methanol (and other petrochemicals) is complicated by the possibility that the

Table 13.7: Estimate of US Imports of Methanol between 1980 and 1990

Year	US imports of methanol (million gallons)
1980	33
1982	132
1985	241
1987	622
1990	690

Source: Author's statistics.

United States and European countries may impose stringent quotas and import duties. Opposition to the import of methanol can be expected from those European and American producers which do not have interests in the kingdom. It is symptomatic that the European Chemical Federation, the European Council of Chemical Manufacturers' Associations, and the associations in individual countries (such as Britain's Chemical Industries Association) are pressuring the European Economic Community to modify the 1981 proposals under the Generalized Scheme of Preferences (GSP). Under these proposals eleven chemical products would be protected by quotas or ceilings, while all other chemicals would not be subject to import duties for GSP beneficiaries. The associations are now asking the European Economic Community to add eleven more commodities to the 'protected' list, including ethylene glycol and low-density polyethylene.[51] Yet, given the very considerable leverage that the kingdom can exert on oil-importing countries, it is doubtful if European or especially American authorities would be prepared to completely exclude Saudi petrochemicals from their domestic markets.[52]

The Saudi Polymer Processing Industry

It is an integral and vital part of the Saudi industrialisation policy to move from the production of crude oil and gas to the manufacture of polymers and then, further downstream, to the processing of these polymers. As Dr al-Gosaibi states, 'we are not ready to stay forever mere producers of raw materials, witnessing these materials leave our shores, to come back to us at higher prices'.[53] The further one moves from the original feedstock to the final consumer — that is moving downstream — the more value is added. Thus the principal thermo-plastics, such as high- and low-density polyethylene, polyvinyl chloride, polypropylene and polystyrene, have a value between two and five times that of the feedstock; the price of thermoplastics is now in the region of $1,000 a ton.

Strong support is given by Saudi authorities to private enterpreneurs who are prepared to establish enterprises — provided they qualify under the Protection and Encouragement of National Industries Statute. Various incentives are offered. Exemption is accorded on customs duties for imported machinery and equipment, spare parts, raw or semi-processed materials, and packing materials; there are protective tariffs or quotas on competing imports; there is long-term leasing of industrial sites — called 'industrial cities' — at a nominal rent; there is preferential treatment for locally manufactured goods in government procurement; there is assistance in the identification of viable projects through market research and feasibility studies; and, above all, there is the assistance provided by the Saudi Industrial Development Fund (SIDF), which grants interest-free medium- and long-term loans to industrial firms. While Islamic conceptions require the interest-free nature of SIDF loans, a 2 per cent 'administrative fee' is charged. The SIDF can finance up to 50 per cent of the capital requirements of a project, or, in the case of a joint venture, of the Saudi equity. Virtually all lending has been for amounts of over SR 2 million ($600,000). The only problem has been in the time taken before a commitment can be secured — up to one year.

A considerable number of entrepreneurs have been taking advantage of the generous incentives. Over the period between 1974 and 1979 the SIDF has committed itself to a total disbursement of SR 669 million ($200.7 million) in the chemical, domestic gas, rubber and plastics sectors. Some four-fifths of this total has already been disbursed. The growth of the downstream activity in Saudi Arabia is again reflected in the imports of raw materials for these sectors — artificial resins, plastic materials, cellulose esters, rubber and synthetic rubber — which increased from a value of SR 114 million in 1972 to SR 1,496 million in 1978. In real terms this represented a tripling of imports. By 1979 there were some 80 plastics, chemical and allied products plants in the kingdom. These are mostly relatively modest undertakings, using a few thousand tons of raw materials a year, with an equity of somewhat over a million dollars and employing a few dozen employees. Many of the employees are expatriates, frequently Jordanians, Syrians and other Arab nationals. The enterprises tend to be concentrated in the larger cities and towns such as al-Riyadh, Jeddah, Mecca, Medina and Damman. The newer firms normally take advantage of the industrial parks established on the outskirts of these centres.

One of the leading producers of plastics in al-Riyadh is the Saudi Plastic Products Company (SAPPCO), established almost a decade ago to manufacture plastic pipes and fittings. The British firm Chemidus was brought in to provide the technology and part of the equity. Since then the output and the profitability of SAPPCO has grown steadily. Today there are eleven extruders and two moulding machines, 350 workers and 50 office staff are employed, and 22,000 tons of PVC are used annually. In order to enter into the field of polyurethane insulation panelboard — which is particularly suitable for roofing insulation on institutional, commercial, industrial and even private residences — SAPPCO has linked up with Texaco Saudi Investment Incorporated, a wholly owned subsidiary of Texaco Incorporated, to set up the firm SAPPCO–Texaco Insulation Products (SAPTEX). The new undertaking is to be likewise located in al-Riyadh. As the managing director of SAPPCO asserts, 'this partnership will provide Saudi Arabia with manufacturing technology for products which previously have been available only through imports'. For Texaco, on the other hand, the venture is viewed purely as a profitable undertaking, since some 40 per cent of the raw materials going into polyurethane is accounted for by benzene which is readily available in Saudi Arabia. When the plant goes into production towards the end of 1981 it will have a capacity of 100 million square feet of polyurethane insulation panelboard. The cost of the enterprise is estimated at $30 million; 60 per cent of the equity will be held by SAPPCO and the other 40 per cent by Texaco Saudi Investments Incorporated. While SAPTEX is now only interested in the domestic market, exports could eventually be very significant. World demand for polyurethane in 1980, estimated at 6.7 billion pounds, is expected to grow at 7 per cent annually, bringing demand to 9.4 billion pounds in 1985 and to 13.1 billion pounds in 1990.[54]

Another of the larger enterprises is Modern Industries Companies, established in Dammam in 1980 to manufacture and sell detergents. The capital is $10.8 million, half of the equity being subscribed by the Swiss firm Detergent Products and the other half by the Saudis.[55] More typical of the downstream enterprises is Babtain Polyurethane, which was established in Dammam and went onstream in 1980, making polyurethane furniture. The capital of $1.3 million is subscribed by the Josef Egli Company of Switzerland, which provides the technology, and by members of the Saud Al-Babtain family.[56]

A very considerable potential exists for the Saudi polymer processing industry to expand current output and even to introduce new products. Foreign markets will, however, have to be developed in order to assure adequate profit margins. Typical of the possibilities is the potential for synthetic rubber production in the kingdom. In 1978 55,000 tons of rubber was imported from Japan and other countries. According to a study by the Australian firm W. D. Scott & Company, Saudi demand for rubber is expected to reach 90,000 tons by 1983; 93 per cent of the demand will consist of that for tyres and tubes. Little wonder that a joint-venture tyre plant is now being considered. Thus, in not so many years, 'Made in Saudi Arabia' will without doubt be seen on products in many parts of the world.

Joint Efforts by the Arab Gulf States

An evaluation of the Saudi petrochemical industry must inevitably involve some consideration of the regional context — as the kingdom is attempting to co-ordinate its plans (and carry out some joint projects) with neighbouring Gulf states, and as the production of petrochemicals in other Gulf states inevitably affects the balance of supply and demand for petrochemicals on the world market.

Despite the political divisions of the peninsula, a free flow of manpower, capital and goods among the constituent states has been maintained over the years. Iraq, as a brother Gulf and Arab state, is now also being drawn into this framework of close economic co-operation and contact. It has been a corner-stone of Saudi policy to encourage co-operation. Thus in 1973 and 1974 the foreign ministers of the Gulf states discussed the means to enhance political and economic economic co-operation. The drawing up of a single economic plan for the area was even envisaged. Later, in 1976, the ministers of industry of Saudi Arabia, Kuwait, Bahrain, Qatar, the United Arab Emirates, Oman and Iraq gathered in Doha, Qatar, and called for greater industrial co-ordination and co-operation. The possibility of joint ventures was proposed.

One of the practical results of these meetings was the creation of the Gulf Organization for Industrial Consulting (GOIC) in 1977. The GOIC was given responsibility for collecting and publishing documentation dealing with industrial development policies and projects; examining possible joint projects; proposing measures to co-ordinate projects; co-ordinating and promoting technical and economic co-operation between companies and corporations; providing technical assistance in the preparation and evaluation of projects; and preparing data and studies related to industry. Dr Ali al-Khalaf was appointed Secretary General of the GOIC and a staff of some 70 employees was established in Doha. Over the years since then the secretariat has carried out a number of studies dealing with the petrochemical and other industries. In some cases consulting firms have been called in to assist. Thus Chem Systems International Limited undertook a study for the GOIC entitled 'Petrochemical Marketing Strategies'. The findings of this study, dealing with the demand for petrochemical products in different regions of the world and with the surplus or deficit of these products, are summarised in Tables 13.8 and 13.9.

A seminar dealing with the marketing of Gulf petrochemicals was held in Doha under the auspices of the GOIC in May 1979. Using the marketing study as a basis for discussions, the seminar concluded that, due to the availability of raw materials in the Gulf, the states of the area will have a great and increasing advantage relative to the production costs, especially for synthesis gas-based derivatives such as ammonia, urea and methanol. The possibility of a common pipeline for ethylene in the region was considered. An aggressive marketing strategy was suggested, to be implemented in consultation with such other major producers as Algeria and Libya.

When the planning ministers met in May 1980 they once again pressed for greater co-operation and co-ordination and suggested joint marketing of specific products. This time, however, some practical measures followed the discussions. First, Saudi Arabia shelved plans for an aluminium smelter in Jubail so as not to be in competition with others in the Gulf. Second, Saudi Arabia's SABIC, Kuwait's Petrochemical Industries Company (PIC) and Bahrain's Bahrain National Oil Company decided to launch a joint petrochemical venture in Bahrain, to be known as the Gulf Petrochemical Industries Company (GPIC). This project stems from the recommendation of the GOIC that it is advantageous to produce synthesis gas based on derivatives (ammonia, urea and methanol) in the Arab Gulf states. The GPIC, therefore, plans to produce 1,000 tons a day of methanol and 1,000 tons of ammonia. The contract for the licence and basic engineering has already been awarded to Uhde of West Germany. While the ammonia process will be designed by Uhde, the methanol process will be installed under sub-licence from the UK's Imperial Chemical Industries. The complex, which is expected to go onstream in 1984, is to be built over a 600,000 square metre area reclaimed from the sea at Sitra. Total investment is

Table 13.8: Demand for Petrochemical Products Forecast for 1987

Product	Western Europe	North America	Japan	Middle East and Africa	Asia	Latin America
Ethylene and derivatives						
Ethylene	15,700	20,030	6,225	2,452	2,230	2,890
Low-density polyethylene	4,865	5,780	1,515	1,154	1,121	1,320
High-density polyethylene	2,240	3,470	710	595	596	430
Vinyl chloride	6,165	4,595	1,880	970	1,285	1,090
Polyvinyl chloride	5,300	4,270	1,550	1,194	1,332	1,130
Monethylene glycol	1,045	2,535	600	261	473	372
Synthesis gas derivatives						
Ammonia	15,220	19,410	2,680	6,460	10,070	4,150
Urea	2,975	5,610	580	1,490	8,840	1,650
Methanol	4,860	5,670	1,510	135	657	462
Aromatics and derivatives						
Benzene	6,240	8,625	2,675	557	782	1,495
Othoxylene	1,035	700	285	56	144	250
Paraxylene	1,030	2,475	885	155	420	420
Dimethyl teraphthalic/teraphthalic acid	1,310	4,010	960	392	1,270	810
Styrene	3,695	4,865	1,600	255	431	860
Polysterene	2,260	3,030	905	190	490	540

Note: Products are all measured in thousands of metric tons.

Source: Gulf Organization for Industrial Consulting, *Petrochemical Marketing Strategies for the Arab Gulf States in the 1980s* (Doha, Qatar, 1979), pp. 43, 53, 62, 69, 70, 80, 87, 95, 101, 108, 113, 117, 118, 127, 128.

Table 13.9: Surplus or Deficit of Petrochemical Products Forecast for 1987

Product	Western Europe	North America	Japan	Middle East and Africa	Asia	Latin America
Ethylene and derivatives						
Ethylene	+1,190	+1,045	0	+ 823	− 220	+1,694
Low-density polyethylene	+ 535	− 10	−100	+ 64	− 366	+ 225
High-density polyethylene	+ 495	+ 195	− 25	− 307	− 219	+ 63
Vinyl chloride	+ 115	+ 345	− 90	− 305	− 320	+ 142
Polyvinyl chloride	+ 520	+ 85	− 20	− 197	− 171	− 53
Monethylene glycol	+ 220	+ 385	0	+ 194	− 128	+ 58
Synthesis gas derivatives						
Ammonia	+ 250	−2,210	+ 30	+1,345	+1,660	+ 540
Urea	+ 605	−1,670	+320	+1,925	− 210	+ 225
Methanol	−1,355	− 840	−250	+2,985	+ 197	+ 760
Aromatics and derivatives						
Benzene	+ 905	− 195	0	+ 53	− 2	− 74
Othoxylene	+ 30	+ 75	0	+ 96	− 11	+ 2
Paraxylene	+ 90	+ 555	−150	− 25	+ 6	+ 169
Dimethyl teraphthalic/teraphthalic acid	+ 395	+ 45	+105	− 209	− 610	+ 19
Styrene	− 285	+ 235	− 40	+ 440	− 190	− 11
Polysterene	+ 450	+ 150	− 10	− 8	− 78	− 15

Note: Products are all measured in thousands of metric tons.

Source: Gulf Organization for Industrial Consulting, *Petrochemical Marketing Strategies for the Arab Gulf States in the 1980s* (Doha, Qatar, 1979), pp. 45, 54, 63, 71, 73, 82, 89, 96, 102, 110, 114, 120, 122, 129, 131.

estimated at $400 million, to be shared equally between the three parties. The products would be marketed in the United States, Western Europe, Japan and other Asian countries, Africa and the Arabian Peninsula itself. In the view of Dr al-Gosaibi, the venture is

> a turning point in the history of economic integration in the Gulf. We have moved up from dreams to realities. The fact that we are sharing in the creation of this petrochemical project indicates a certain intellectual maturity and a conviction that we should not be wasting our resources in duplication when we can set up successful industries capable of competing with others.[57]

Concern at the possibility of duplication among the Arab Gulf states in the petrochemical field emerges from the pattern of petrochemical development currently underway in the different states. Iraq, Kuwait and Qatar all have relatively important petrochemical projects. In Iraq the Basrah Petrochemical Complex No. 1, built for the Ministry of Industry and Minerals of Iraq by C. E. Lummus and Thyssen Rheinstahl Tecknik, was to have gone onstream in 1980. After the severe damage inflicted during the Gulf War construction has now come to a standstill. The complex was to have had an annual capacity of 130,000 tons per year of ethylene, 60,000 tons of polyvinyl chloride, 66,000 tons of vinyl chloride, 70,000 tons of low-density polyethylene, 30,000 tons of high-density polyethylene, 43,200 tons of caustic chlorine and 42,000 tons of flake caustic soda.[58] Iraq is already the largest producer of urea fertiliser in the Gulf.

In Kuwait the Petrochemical Industries Company is planning to establish a plant in Shuaiba to produce 1,000 metric tons per day of ammonia, 280,000 tons per year of benzene, 350,000 tons of ethylene, 135,000 tons of ethylene glycol, 340,000 tons of styrene, 60,000 tons of orthoxylene, 86,000 tons of paraxylene and 130,000 tons of low-density polyethylene. This complex is expected to go onstream in 1983 and 1984.[59]

Qatar, that flat desert peninsula with its great humidity and stupefying heat, probably has one of the largest gas fields in the world – the North West Dome field with possibly 100 billion cubic feet. This gas may form the basis of a substantial petrochemical industry. The Qatar Fertilizer Company (QAFCO) will soon, with expansions, be producing 1,800 tons a day of ammonia and 2,000 tons a day of urea. The ammonia and urea will be going largely to Asia – India, Pakistan and China – as well as to the United States and Latin America. Spurred on by the relative success of QAFCO, the partly state-owned Qatar Petrochemical Company (QAPCO) has been launched. Using associated gas, QAPCO will produce 280,000 tons per year of ethylene. This will allow 140,000 tons of low-density polyethylene to be produced annually, as well as 200 tons per day of sulphur. Technip of France, Coppee-Rust of Belgium, Turbotecnica of Italy and Japan Gasoline are all participating in this project. The cost of the venture is estimated at $641 million. The state will own 84 per cent of QAPCO, and the remaining 16 per cent will be owned by CdF Chimie of France. A marketing agreement has been signed with CdF Chimie, such that the latter company will export the products – largely to the Middle East and the Indian Ocean area. An entry to the European market might also be gained through a petrochemical company in Dunkirk, Copenor, established by the Qatar General Petroleum Corporation and CdF Chimie. The plant should go onstream in 1981. QAPCO has now decided to expand its activity by erecting a plant to produce 70,000 tons per year of high-density polyethylene. The cost of this plant is estimated at $48–58 million. The process to be used and the engineering work are now being negotiated.[60]

In the United Arab Emirates the great industrial growth pole of Ruwais is gradually taking shape under the agis of the Abu Dhabi National Oil Company (ADNOC). Already plans for an Abu Dhabi Fertilizer Company are being implemented. This enterprise would have a capacity of 1,000 tons per day of ammonia and 1,500 tons per day of urea. It is being undertaken as a joint venture by ADNOC and the Compagnie Française des Pétroles, with much of the construction being done by Chiyoda Chemical Engineering in association with Mitsubishi. In the distant horizon the possibility remains of a petrochemical complex.[61] No production of petrochemicals is at present envisaged in Oman. There is, however, some downstream activity. The Aniantit Oman firm, affiliated with the Swiss Eternit Group, produces PVC and polyethylene pipes;[62] it is located in Rusail.

Resolute and forceful measures are needed to rationalise the production and marketing of petrochemicals of the Arab Gulf states. The main potential markets for these petrochemicals – the Far East, Western Europe and the United States – all have appreciable domestic production or have alternative sources of supply. Saudi Arabia, Kuwait and Iraq do enjoy a considerable negotiating power, since they can link crude oil sales with the distribution of petrochemical products, but Qatar and some of the other Arab Gulf states have only limited crude oil to offer as an incentive. A Gulf common market, therefore, may prove attractive to the less favoured producers. The formation of such a common market is high on the agenda for the new Gulf Coordination Council.

Conclusion

As the different petrochemical complexes come onstream, Saudi Arabia will have gradually increasing amounts of petrochemicals and urea to place on world markets. By 1985 the kingdom should be producing about one million tons of methanol, representing some 8 per cent of world production. Given the cost advantage of producing methanol with cheap feedstock, the sharp increase that can be expected in demand, and the fact that much of the marketing of the Saudi methanol will be handled by two particularly well-entrenched corporations – Mitsubishi and Celanese – this product will almost certainly find adequate sales outlets. Much the same can be said for ethylene glycol and ethanol. A somewhat greater marketing effort may be required for both high- and low-density polyethylene and for some of the other products. Resistance to the entry of Saudi petrochemicals could well develop in Western Europe and even in the United States. Several measures may be taken to reduce the likelihood of the European countries or the United States taking protective measures. First, trade pacts may be in order – calling for duty-free entry of petrochemicals in exchange for assured supplies of oil. Second, the Gulf states should continue to co-ordinate the production and marketing of petrochemicals with other Arab Gulf states. This co-ordination could in due course be extended to include all the Arab states and, eventually, the other Islamic states. Third, Saudi Arabia might be well advised, for the present, to continue to concentrate on the production and marketing of large-volume commodity petrochemicals, leaving the more industrially advanced countries to specialise in higher technology and added-value products. This would allow changes in the distribution of world petrochemical production in favour of the Gulf region to take place within a framework of stability, and therefore forestall the development of protectionist sentiment.

It is important for the Western world to place the emerging Saudi petrochemical industry in proper perspective. The production of the major petrochemicals in the non-communist world is 86 million tons per year, while Saudi production will only amount to a few million tons – a relatively insignificant proportion of the total. Even in Saudi

Arabia itself the output of petrochemicals will only play a minor role over the next decade. The total value of the petrochemicals produced by the middle of the 1980s will not exceed $3 billion a year. This may be compared with a Gross National Product of some $160 billion and foreign exchange earnings of over $100 billion in 1980.

In retrospect one cannot but be struck by how a seemingly impossible dream of the 1960s is now taking a concrete form. King Khaled, Crown Prince Fahd and a small but dynamic group of technocrats of the Saudi administration, as well as executives from Mitsubishi, Mobil, Shell, Exxon, Dow, Celanese, Texas Eastern and other corporations, are creating a giant new industry on the desert sands of the kingdom. Their efforts are backed by those of a host of engineers and other professionals in Saudi Arabia, the United States, Japan and other countries. A firm foundation for the emerging petrochemical industry is being laid which will, in turn, form the basis for further industrialisation.

Notes

1. There may well be some 530,000 million barrels of oil under the ground in the kingdom, but only about half of this, that is 248,100 million barrels is recoverable. There are, nevertheless, varying estimates of oil and gas reserves. Gas reserves should, in any event, be able to last for another 40 years at the present rate of extraction. Cf. E. O'Sullivan, 'Gas', *Middle East Economic Digest – Saudi Arabia* (July 1980), p. 19; Sheikh Ahmed Zaki Yamani, 'The Politics of Oil', *Saudi Business and Arab Economic Report* (9 May 1980), p. 39.

2. 'Urea production up', *Arab News* (29 October 1980), p. 2; 'SAFCO production increases', *Arab News* (20–21 November 1980), p. 2.

3. *Today's Bechtel*, vol. 7, no. 5 (January 1980).

4. Saudi officials and the local press estimate the cost of the infrastructure and basic industrial facilities at between $20 and $30 billion. However American businessmen tend to put the cost higher – as much as $45 billion. Cf. James Buchan, 'Jubail progress report', *Saudi Business and Arab Economic Report* (22 February 1980), pp. 31–4; Royal Commission for Jubail and Yanbu, *Annual Report* (al-Riyadh, 1980).

5. E. O'Sullivan, 'Yanbu industrial port: contract awards start', *Middle East Economic Digest* (29 August 1980), pp. 3–4.

6. K. Stock, M. A. Arahams and A. R. Rhoe, 'More petrochemicals from crude', *Hydrocarbon Processing* (November 1974), p. 158.

7. E. O'Sullivan, 'Gas', pp. 3–4; 'King to open water plant', *Arab News* (9 November 1980), p. 1.

8. The Saline Water Conversion Corporation estimates the cost of fresh water at $1.70 to $2.00 per cubic metre. On the other hand, Mohammad ibn Brahim Al Karim, the director of water for the Riyadh Sewage and Water Department, places the real cost of fresh water at between $2.38 and $2.98. Cf. *Saudi Business and Arab Economic Report* (9 May 1980), pp. 3, 23.

9. Hokaji Mino, 'Return-trip tankers could solve Mideast water problem', *Business Japan* (September 1980), pp. 64–5; R. Bailey, 'Japan's waterfalls –

ready to supply Gulf needs', *Middle East Economic Digest* (3 October 1980), p. 15.

10. US Corporations are paying up to four times more for Americans in Saudi Arabia as for Americans in the US. Thus the Bechtel Corporation offers an engineer a base salary of $30,000 to which is added 72 per cent in various bonuses, such as an allowance for hardship, overtime for a longer working week, a completion bonus, and to this is added a cost-of-living allowance. Cf. E. Larson, 'Saudi rigors toughen task of recruiters', *The Wall Street Journal* (15 October 1980), pp. 31, 39; J. Whelan, 'Manpower Training', *Middle East Economic Digest – Saudi Arabia* (July 1980), pp. 13–14.

11. P. Sterbenz, 'Who's building in HPI', *Hydrocarbon Processing* (June 1980), p. 36–C.

12. These figures indicate nameplate capacity. A plant operating at full capacity would not be able to operate at more than 90 per cent of this capacity. Also see J. Rossant, 'Downstream in Arabia', *Saudi Business and Arab Economic Report* (2 May 1980), p. 25.

13. *Middle East Economic Digest* (7 December 1979), p. 53; *Free China Weekly* (9 December 1979), p. 1; ibid. (20 January 1980), p. 4; *Saudi Business and Arab Economic Report* (28 March 1980), p. 13.

14. Oil reserves in Taiwan are only 10 million barrels of oil and 650×10^9 cubic feet of gas. Oil production in 1979 was 5,000 barrels a day.

15. Ammonia plants using the latest technology require some 30,000 cubic feet of natural gas for each ton of ammonia. In the US gas accounts for about 70 per cent of the production cost. Cf. A. S. Brown, 'Is the ammonia cycle obsolete?', *Chemical Marketing Reporter* (17 November 1980), p. 9.

16. *Middle East Economic Digest* (7 December 1979), p. 53; *Free China Weekly* (9 December 1979), p. 1; ibid. (20 January 1980).

17. 'Malasia plumbs depths for petrochemicals', *Chemical Week* (5 December 1979), p. 52.

18. Metro Consulting Group, *South Korea. Business Opportunities in the 1980s* (Metro Consulting Group, London, 1980); US Department of Commerce, *Marketing in Korea* (US Department of Washington, DC, 1980).

19. Hokaji Mino, 'Country by country countdown on Japan's Mideast relations', *Business Japan* (August 1980), pp. 45, 47.

20. 'Japan and the Middle East', *Middle East Economic Digest* (November 1979), p. 26.

21. Japanese innovative technology is expanding rapidly in the chemical industry. Nevertheless, Japan imports about three times as much technology from the United States as it exports. Much the same is true for Europe.

22. Japanese oil reserves as of 1 January 1980 were 55 million barrels and gas reserves were 600×10^9 cubic feet. Oil production was only 10,000 barrels a day.

23. *Middle East Economic Digest* (16 November 1979), p. 25; Economic Models Limited, London.

24. Dodwell Marketing Consultants, *Industrial Groupings in Japan 1980/81* (Tokyo, July 1980).

25. J. Lewis, 'Japan's tilt to the Middle East', *Far Eastern Economic Review* (28 December 1979), p. 36.

26. P. Sterbenz, 'Who's building in HPI', p. 36–C.

27. 'Company Briefs', *Journal of Commerce* (14 October 1980), p. 3; W. G. Shepherd, 'Suliman S. Alayan – A Saudi's stake in US banking', *New York Times* (19 October 1980), p. 8F.

28. *Middle East Economic Digest* (16 November 1979), p. 40; 'Tighter belts fatten Japanese CPI's profits', *Chemical Week* (26 September 1979), p. 62; *Saudi Business and Arab Economic Report* (22 February 1980), p. 34.

29. 'Japanese trading company plays leading international role', *Business Japan* (August 1980), pp. 30–1.

30. Hokaji Mino, 'Return-trip tankers could solve Mideast water problem', p. 47.

31. *World Methanol 1979; Chemical Week* (26 September 1979); *Saudi Business and Arab Economic Report* (15 February 1980), p. 29.

32. Takeshi Hijikata, 'Management of my company in the 1980s – its problems and perspectives', *Sekiyu Kagaku Shimbun* (1 January 1980). Also letter to author dated 14 May 1980. The same view is expressed by Akira Tsukamato of Mitsubishi Chemical Industries. See 'Outlook for Japan's chemical industry', *Hydrocarbon Processing* (August 1980), pp. 52 F–N.

33. E. V. Anderson, 'Petrochemicals in Japan face troubled future', *Chemical and Engineering News* (15 September 1980), p. 24.

34. Pullman-Kellogg, *Engineers of Energy* (no publishing details available), p. 8.

35. C. A. Gerstacker, however, warns that 'perhaps the most serious problem that faces the US chemical industry in the eighties is the threat of losing its technological leadership in the world. If we use our resources foolishly, that is a very real possibility. In fact, US domination of the world chemical technology,is already a thing of the past in many areas', *Chemical and Engineering News* (26 November 1979), p. 49; D. A. Lee, 'Curbing the appetites of energy-intensive chemicals', *Chemical Marketing Reporter* (25 August 1980), pp. 46, 51.

36. *Chemical and Engineering News* (10 March 1980), p. 23.

37. *USA's Energy Outlook 1980–2000* (Exxon Publications, Houston, December 1979), pp. 14–17.

38. OECD, *The Petrochemical Industry* (OECD, Paris, 1979), p. iii; 'US petrochem feed role eyed for LPG imports', *Oil and Gas Journal* (10 December 1979), p. 36.

39. See G. W. Weismantel, 'Feedstock vs. gasoline: What will happen next?' *Chemical Engineering* (25 August 1980), p. 37.

40. Ibid., p. 39; T. Wett, 'US leads ethylene capacity gain', *Oil and Gas Journal* (1 September 1980), pp. 59–64.

41. D. A. O'Sullivan, 'Essochem Europe strengthen plastics position', *Chemical and Engineering News* (21 April 1980), p. 16.

42. *Saudi Business and Arab Economic Report* (22 February 1980), p. 6.

43. See note 13.

44. See E. O'Sullivan, 'Heavy Industry', *Middle East Economic Digest – Saudi Arabia* (July 1980), pp. 22, 25.

45. 'SABIC accord signed', *Arab News* (10 November 1980), p. 3.

46. S. Cameron, 'Shell in $3 billion Saudi Arabia deal', *Financial Times* (9 July 1980); J. Rossant, 'SABIC, Shell sign $3 billion complex accord', *Arab News* (29 September 1980), p. 1; J. Rossant, 'SABIC, Shell sign petrochemical pact', *Saudi Business and Arab Economic Report* (10 October 1980), pp. 14, 16.

47. J. Rossant, 'Downstream in Arabia', *Saudi Business and Arab Economic Report* (2 May 1980), p. 23; D. A. O'Sullivan, 'Essochem Europe strengthen plastics position', p. 14.

48. *Hydrocarbon Processing – Construction Boxscore* (June 1980), p. 47.

49. 'Global methanol market to double in the 1980s', *Chemical and Engineering News* (7 April 1980), p. 16.

50. Ibid., p. 16.

51. 'UK chemical men fear EEC rules for Third World', *Chemical Marketing Reporter* (10 November 1980), pp. 5, 34.

52. Ibid.

53. *Saudi Business and Arab Economic Report* (7 March 1980), p. 32; ibid. (31 March 1980), p. 31.

54. *Journal of Commerce* (15 July 1980), p. 5; *Arab News* (19 July 1980), p. 2; *Journal of Commerce* (27 August 1980), p. 5 and (12 September 1980), p. 3.

55. 'New Companies', *Saudi Business and Arab Economic Report* (12 September 1980), p. 42.

56. 'New Companies', ibid. (29 August 1980), p. 42.

57. 'Three states establish SR 630 million Gulf plant', *Arab News* (31 May 1980), p. 1.

58. E. A. Kelly, 'Iraq's newest industrial complex', *Hydrocarbon Processing* (June 1980), pp. 36–0–36–I.

59. *Hydrocarbon Processing – Construction Boxscore* (June 1980), pp. 46–7.

60. 'Industry – going ahead fast', *Middle East Economic Digest – Qatar* (November 1979), pp. 6–7; 'European help for plant to help grow plants . . .', *Achievement* (June 1979), pp. 8–11.

61. See J. Whelan, 'Ruwais sets the pace for Abu Dhabi', *Middle East Economic Digest – United Arab Emirates* (December 1979), pp. 25–6; 'Oil is the key as industry struggles against the odds' and 'Gas finds exploited', *Financial Times* (23 June 1980); JAW, 'Ruwais central to Abu Dhabi's plans', *Middle East Economic Digest – United Arab Emirates* (October 1980), p. 30.

62. *Middle East Economic Digest – Oman* (November 1980), p. 21.

14 THE EVOLUTION OF THE SAUDI BANKING SYSTEM AND ITS RELATIONSHIP WITH BAHRAIN

Rodney Wilson

Introduction

With banking, as with any other service activity, a country's need for facilities will clearly depend to a large extent on its economic structure. In Saudi Arabia even a cursory glance at the economic structure would suggest that the need for banking facilities is likely to be greater than that of countries at a similar level of development, especially given the openness of its economy to trade and financial flows. The almost total dependence on imports, for virtually all local consumption requirements and domestic investment projects, naturally implies a high level of demand for trade finance. Moreover, as much of the kingdom's workforce is made up of expatriate labour, the banking system has to cope with enormous volumes of remittances destined not only for neighbouring Arab states such as the Yemens, Jordan and Egypt, but also further afield in South Asia, the Far East, Europe and North America. In addition, the scale of local multiplier effects generated by domestic government expenditure puts substantial potentially investible funds into the hands of individual Saudi citizens, funds which the commercial banking system could effectively channel into projects at home or in overseas markets.

Against this background, the capacity of the Saudi banking system appears hopelessly inadequate, indicating a severe imbalance in demand and supply. The inadequacy of the present system manifests itself primarily in terms of the limited spread of branch banking, but also, although admittedly to a lesser extent, in terms of the range of services which the domestic banks provide, and in the efficiency with which the services are conducted. One objective of this paper is to explain how the present situation has arisen, by examining the recent history of the banking system. Another objective is to explore the implications of the present demand and supply imbalance for the ability of the central monetary authorities to effectively control the system, and to outline its consequences for the Saudi economy generally. A third objective is to consider the extent to which the development of Bahrain as an

278

offshore banking centre merely results from domestic banking deficiencies within Saudi Arabia, or whether the island has a real comparative advantage in the banking field. It is hoped that this examination of the Saudi banking system will provide some insight into the overall functioning of the Saudi economy.

Emergence of Modern Banking

The development of banking in Saudi Arabia parallels the recent economic history of the kingdom, as might be expected. Prior to the exploitation of oil, much of the Saudi Arabian economy was of a subsistence nature based on agriculture, and the only region of the country to be extensively monetarised was the Hijaz, where the annual influx of pilgrims led to some demand for money-changing services. Jeddah, as the nearest convenient port for Mecca, was the centre of much of the commercial activity associated with this pilgrimage traffic, and it was there that money-changers such as the Mahfouz and the Musa Kaki families carried out many of these services, as well as other lesser known families such as the al-Subeaeis, the Qawis and the Bamaodahs. The latter three families are still represented in the Jeddah *suq* today.[1] Elsewhere in the country there was little money-changing activity, although the al-Rajhi family had a small establishment in al-Riyadh as early as the 1920s and in Medina and Taif some of the gold and silver merchants had diversified their businesses to include money-changing.

In relation to the needs of the country before the advent of oil revenue, the money-changers satisfied most financial needs concerned with external trade and many bazaar merchants were prepared to grant credit to established customers, which constituted the main domestic financial demand. It is notable that at the end of the last century and in the early years of this century, when much of Arabia was under Ottoman rule and the Ottoman Bank (unlike the Empire) was in its most vigorous expansionary phase, no branch was established within what later constituted Saudi Arabia. There would have been little difficulty in establishing such a branch, as the bank already had branches elsewhere in the Arab world, including Egypt, Palestine, Syria and Iraq. The main factor inhibiting the Ottoman Bank must have been lack of potential business, rather than any qualms about operating in Islam's holiest place, as the Ottoman authorities would undoubtedly have encouraged rather than discouraged the bank's presence.[2]

Saudi Arabia's laws are, of course, based on the *shari'a*, and there were no banking statutes during the first three decades of the new kingdom's history. With no provision for banking institutions, most financial business for Jeddah's small European community was carried out by the trading firm of Gellatly Hankey, which was quite active in the 1920s. The Dutch Bank, which was to be the forerunner of Algemene Bank Nederland, had a seasonal office for pilgrims from Dutch Indonesia, and the Banque de l'Indochine et de Suez performed a similar function for those visiting Mecca from the French colonies, but neither of these institutions could officially serve the local market. The attitude of the authorities to banking was made apparent in 1936 when the Egyptian Bank Misr made a bid to enter the kingdom, but was turned down.

Nevertheless, the meagre role played by foreign banking institutions was one of the factors which prompted two of the country's leading money-changing families, the Mahfouz and the Musa Kaki families, to petition the King to let them establish a bank. Thus the National Commercial Bank was established in 1938, with the Mahfouz family owning a majority shareholding (51.5 per cent) and two branches of the Musa Kaki family, and their relatives the Abdel-Aziz Kaki family the remainder. The families believed that the establishment of the new institution would serve to increase their share of potential financial business at the expense of the existing money-changers. It would also result in them being well placed to act as bankers for the kingdom's rulers, for no central monetary authority existed until 1952 when the Saudi Arabian Monetary Agency (henceforth referred to as SAMA) was founded. To a large extent these two enterprising Jeddah families succeeded in these objectives, and have been rewarded handsomely for having had the foresight to establish a modern, Western-style financial institution at such an early date. It is worth remembering that the National Commercial Bank was only the third wholly indigenous bank to be established in the entire Arab world; the forerunners were the originally Jerusalem-based Arab Bank of Abd al-Hameed Shoman, an essentially Palestinian institution, and Bank Misr of Egypt, which was designed for a much more specialised function.[3]

Although during the 1938–50 period the National Commercial Bank was the sole local commercial bank operating in the kingdom, its expansion was fairly modest. It was not until the late 1940s that branches were opened outside the Hijaz, in al-Riyadh and al-Khobar. To some extent this rather slow start may have been due to the advent of the Second World War and its disruptive effect on commerce, but of at least equal significance was the continuing competition from the traditional money-changing establishments. This meant that the bank was far from being in a monopolistic position as far as the provision of financial services was concerned. Indeed, as commercial activity in Eastern Province started to expand as a consequence of the new oil wealth, it was largely the al-Rajhi family's money-changing establishments that captured most of the business rather than the Hijaz-orientated National Commercial Bank. Given the wealth of the large land-owning al-Rajhi family, moreover, it is debatable which institution was more soundly based, even if as a legally-constituted financial institution the National Commercial Bank published details of its paid-up capital and assets — which the al-Rajhi establishments did not.

Perhaps surprisingly, it was only in the post-war period that the British-owned Bank of Iran and the Middle East became involved in Saudi Arabia. This institution was later renamed the British Bank of the Middle East when its Iranian operations were suspended in 1952 during the Mossadeq period.[4] Its offices in Jeddah and al-Khobar started business in 1950, initially mainly to serve the needs not only of the British community but also of those Americans and Europeans whose financial institutions were unrepresented. As was the case with its operations elsewhere in the Arab world, the British Bank of the Middle East concentrated on trade finance, and soon its customers included both suppliers from the industrialised countries and the Saudi merchants who handled these supplies. The latter were encouraged to open accounts. It is possible, however, that the new Saudi customers were not engaging in banking for the first time but, rather, were using the British Bank of the Middle East's services to complement the facilities they already had with the National Commercial Bank and their local money-changing establishment. In Saudi Arabia, then as now, account-holders with foreign affiliated banks often kept a separate account with a national bank.

With the expansion of Saudi economic activity resulting from the increase of oil production in the 1950s, and with imports booming as government expenditure trickled down into private hands, it became clear that the kingdom was underbanked, and that there was scope for new financial institutions to enter the market. SAMA was mainly concerned with managing the note issue in its early years, but in so far as it served as a banker's bank it found itself only dealing with one local and three foreign institutions, the latter providing only limited banking services. In response to the obvious gaps in the financial system, a group of *shaikhs* from the Central and Eastern Provinces, principally from the al-Suwailem, Abu Dawoud and Binzagr families, decided to found a new bank, the Riyadh Bank, which would seek to challenge the hegemony of the National Commercial Bank. Despite its name, and in recognition of the position of Jeddah as the kingdom's commercial centre, the new bank's headquarters were established in Jeddah in 1957. A rapid series of branch openings followed over the next five years.

The expansion in business by the Riyadh Bank, viewed in retrospect, appears to have been too rapid in this early period, given the financial and human resources at the new institution's disposal. In its over-ambitious effort to win new customers and enhance its position *vis-à-vis* the National Commercial Bank, it accumulated a significant amount of bad debt by the early 1960s. In 1964, as rumours started to spread in the small and closely interwoven financial community of Jeddah, there was a loss of confidence in the bank, and a spate of withdrawals of deposits. The bank was forced to turn to SAMA for help, but the young agency had difficulty in dealing with the crisis due to its own inexperience. Despite the kingdom's wealth,[5] SAMA encountered considerable problems in raising the necessary resources for the rescue, but eventually succeeded in doing so. In return for its assistance, SAMA demanded a say in the running of the Riyadh Bank, and since that time, when it took a 38 per cent equity stake in the bank's capital, it has nominated one of its staff to sit on the bank's board of directors, usually the manager of its investment department. To some extent these events reinforced the existing conservatism of SAMA and resulted in it having a rather cautious attitude towards new banks planning to enter the kingdom's financial market. If the agency was to be forced into playing the role of lender of the last resort, then it wanted to be sure who it was supporting.

SAMA only permitted foreign banks to establish themselves within the kingdom if the countries from which they originated had significant numbers of nationals employed in the Saudi workforce, or if there was a considerable volume of bilateral trade. The mere fact of a bank handling a large amount of Saudi investment funds in overseas markets was not a sufficient criterion for the Monetary Authority to grant permission for it to operate domestically. In addition, as a general rule, only one commercial bank was permitted from each country; a rule that was adhered to with only two exceptions. The first was Lebanon, as both the Banque du Liban et d'Outre-Mer and the Lebanese Arab Bank were allowed to open offices in Jeddah, and in the case of the latter, offices in Damman and al-Riyadh as well. One explanation for this exception may be that large numbers of Palestinians with Lebanese passports used these banks, and in the Saudi Arabian workforce there were large numbers of Palestinians as well as Lebanese, so in a sense the banks represented two nations rather than a single state. Another, perhaps more significant, factor may be that there was a minority Saudi ownership stake in both institutions, which in the case of the Lebanese Arab Bank was quite substantial. The second country from which two banks were permitted to operate was Pakistan, but in this case each bank was limited to one office: the National Bank of Pakistan was confined to an office in Jeddah, while the United Bank was confined to one in Dammam.

A financial institution which also served the Palestinian community in Saudi Arabia was the Amman-based Arab Bank, a wholly Palestinian-owned and run institution, as already indicated, but the sole representative in the kingdom of Jordan's financial institutions. Other countries with expatriate groups in Saudi Arabia, and therefore with banks to handle remittances and provide ancillary services, included Iran (Bank Melli), Korea (Korea Exchange Bank),[6] Egypt (Banque du Caire), the United States (Citibank) and the Netherlands (Algemene Bank Nederland). Interestingly there were no Japanese or German banks in Saudi Arabia, despite the significance of their trade with the kingdom as the second and third largest import suppliers respectively.

Current Banking Structure

As a consequence of the restrictive attitude of SAMA regarding the entry of foreign banks, by 1976 (prior to Saudi-isation) there were only 14 such banks maintaining offices within the kingdom, compared to over 40 in Abu Dhabi and almost 50 in Dubai, where the market for financial services was much smaller than that of Saudi Arabia, and where the future potential was extremely limited. The major reason for the restrictive attitude of SAMA to foreign banks was of course political, to some extent reflecting the nationalistic spirit within the country. A second factor was the view that it would be unseemly for the country in which Islam's holiest places were sited to aspire to becoming a major international financial centre, with all that that implied concerning interest-rate policy and financial wheeling and dealing generally. A third factor may have been the conservatism of SAMA itself, which was reinforced by the problems of the mid-1960s referred to above. There was certainly no desire to attract fringe financial undertakings of dubious standing into the kingdom. Finally, there may have been some worry on the part of SAMA, especially prior to the 1974 expansion of its own reserve base, that even if it was successful in attracting major Western banks into the kingdom, the sheer economic power of the latter would have made them difficult to control, especially if their world-wide assets were many times greater than those of SAMA itself. The latter is a recurrent theme in the literature analysing the relations between multinational companies and developing countries generally.

Although only 14 foreign-owned banks had been licensed to operate in Saudi Arabia by the mid-1970s, such a number would have been more than sufficient to dominate the domestic financial scene had it not been for the attitude of SAMA as the regulatory authority, on the one hand, and of local clients, on the other. SAMA in most cases confined the activities of the foreign banks to Jeddah and al-Riyadh; most banks were only granted permission to open one branch, although the British Bank of the Middle East and the Banque de l'Indochine et de Suez both ran two branches in the oil-rich Eastern Province, largely to serve the expatriate communities resident there. The latter institutions, as the first in the field, had a clear advantage over the later arrivals, and it appears that SAMA's attitude towards the expansion of foreign banking in the kingdom hardened as time passed. Citibank, in particular, felt frustrated by what it saw as a rather inflexible attitude on the part of SAMA regarding its activities. As the sole United States bank within the kingdom it naturally wished to expand its operations in the Eastern Province, where the majority of the American expatriates resided — including most of the highly paid Aramco technical experts. It was only permitted to operate from one branch in al-Riyadh, however, and was prevented even from opening an office in Jeddah where most of the other foreign banks competed.

The extent to which foreign banks would have been able to penetrate the Saudi market in the absence of SAMA's restrictions must be a matter of conjecture, as certainly Saudi citizens would have had some degree of loyalty to locally-based institutions.[7] Even in the United Arab Emirates, where there is less sense of national identity, and where the monetary authorities were willing to license virtually all potential foreign entrants until the late 1970s, locally-based institutions still maintained an overall majority of the market share (in terms of the total value of deposits and the number of accounts from local citizens, although not of expatriate accounts). The data on market shares published by the central monetary authorities in the Gulf and Saudi Arabia, moreover, refers only to licensed banks and not to money-changing institutions. The inclusion of the latter establishments is likely to raise appreciably the share of locally-based institutions in the domestic market.

Simply by comparing the published accounts of the National Commercial and Riyadh Banks with the consolidated figures published by SAMA for all the banks operating in Saudi Arabia, it is possible to ascertain the dominance of the two indigenously-based institutions in the local banking system. On the basis of deposit data for 1979, it appears that the National Commercial Bank alone accounted for over 60 per cent of the Saudi total, and the Riyadh Bank for over 20 per cent, such that the other fourteen foreign-affiliated banks together accounted for less than 20 per cent of the total. These proportions appear to have remained broadly constant over the 1970s, illustrating the significance of the local 'duopoly' throughout the period. It should again be stressed that the data only refer to enumerated deposits with commercial banks, and that in Saudi Arabia money-changing establishments are of even greater significance than they are in the smaller Gulf states. Thus the Saudi market in financial services may be much more competitive than the basic data suggest.

There is little doubt that the money-changers are a powerful force in Saudi Arabia. Their role in absolute — and perhaps even relative — terms has expanded enormously in recent years, although their precise significance is difficult to gauge in the absence of reliable or comprehensive data. The functions they fulfil are certainly much wider than the money-exchanging operations which they seem to dominate. As deposit-taking institutions they are probably of only limited importance, but despite their lack of substantial deposits they seem to be prominent in credit provision, providing advances for industry, agriculture, commerce, building materials, timbers, etc.[8] They play a major role in assisting neighbouring traders in the *suq*, with whom they have much informal as well as formal contact, and in recent years the financial support they have given to the local construction businesses has grown enormously with the building boom of the latter half of the 1970s. Much of this funding is financed by the money-changers' own reserves, or funds generated within the family businesses, rather than from deposit-taking.

It is often difficult to distinguish the banking roles of money-changing establishments clearly from their other activities. The al-Rajhis, for example, have their own building-supplies company, and much of the credit they advance is in kind rather than in cash. Even where money-changing establishments have not diversified into other activities, such tying of loans is not uncommon and borrowers are often expected to purchase supplies from other clients of the money-changers. Ordinary commercial banks, of course, seldom put such constraints on borrowers, being more concerned that borrowers purchase supplies from the optimum source from the point of view of their business's profitability – as this determines the client's capacity to repay. Nevertheless, in a banking and business community as small as that of Saudi Arabia, bankers may well suggest the names of potential suppliers, whom they know personally, in the course of discussions with borrowers.

Inevitably it is as foreign exchange dealers that the money-changers are most well known, especially to the expatriate community within Saudi Arabia. As exchange dealers they offer more competitive rates than the commercial banks, often provide a speedier service, and have the advantage from the client's point of view of being open longer hours. In addition, the larger establishments, particularly the al-Rajhi group, offer just as extensive a range of correspondents abroad as the commercial banks, and can handle remittances with ease and efficiency.[9] In fact, not being a registered bank has advantages, as money-changers have no reserve requirement obligations and hence do not have funds unprofitably tied up with SAMA. In addition, operating expenses are generally lower; money-changers pay their employees below bank rates and maintain less prestigious establishments for the most part.

Recent Banking Developments

Despite the competitive vigour of the money-changing establishments in the market for banking services, SAMA has become increasingly worried over the last decade about the state of the market and the dominance of the National Commercial Bank and Riyadh Bank duopoly. One way of increasing competition would, of course, have been to permit the existing foreign banks to expand their operations, and to encourage newcomers, but nationalistic factors militated against such a policy. The decision was therefore taken in 1977 to Saudi-ise the foreign banks already operating in the kingdom, and then permit them to expand their activities. Saudi-isation is not to be confused with nationalisation, which the Saudi authorities, favouring free enterprise, oppose on ideological grounds. Rather than the state or SAMA taking a share in the ownership, the 60 per cent majority stake was to be held by private Saudi citizens.

The procedure for the foreign bank take-over was that one-third of the shares to be Saudi-ised should be offered to so-called 'founder members'. These were defined as important Saudi clients of the particular bank, the selection being left to the banks themselves. Any left out could appeal to SAMA. All shares were offered at their current value, which represented particularly favourable terms for the purchaser as current value took no account either of a bank's goodwill (which was worth a considerable amount) or of the extent to which value would be enhanced once restraint was taken off new branch openings.[10] The remaining two-thirds of the Saudi-ised shares were to be offered to the general public, with each bidder receiving shares in relation to the size of the offer he or she made, rather than on a first come, first served basis. This was designed to ensure as diverse a degree of private owner-ship as possible and to avoid ownership being concentrated, as was the case with the National Commercial and Riyadh Banks.

The first bank to be Saudi-ised, the National Bank of Pakistan, attracted little public interest, perhaps because the public were unaware of what a good purchase the shares were. As a result the founder members were given further share options, and their holding in the reconstituted institution, the Bank Al-Jazira, now amounts to 35 per cent, while the National Bank of Pakistan retained 35 per cent, and the wider Saudi public 30 per cent.[11] By the time the local Dutch and French banks came to be Saudi-ised in 1977, however, over one year after the formation of Bank Al-Jazira, Saudi investors had had a chance to observe the rapid appreciation of the value of Al-Jazira shares. As a consequence the 40 per cent public issue of shareholdings in the newly constituted Al-Bank Al-Saudi Al-Hollandi was more than eleven times oversubscribed, and the shares in Al-Bank Al-Saudi Al-Fransi were oversubscribed tenfold. A similar situation arose with the British Bank of the Middle East, which had its branches Saudi-ised in 1978, the negotiations taking longer because of the bank's more extensive involvement in the kingdom.

The final and most reluctant bank to be Saudi-ised was the United States institution, Citibank, which feared that any take-over of its Saudi assets might set a precedent for other countries to follow. At first when Citibank learnt of the government's intentions it threatened to withdraw altogether. Later, on re-consideration of the potential of the local market and the extensive opportunities once the restrictions on opening new branches were lifted, the decision was taken to stay and comply with government policy. Citibank did, nevertheless, succeed in making the take-over negotiations last as long as possible. It was only in 1980 that the new Saudi American Bank was constituted. These delaying tactics owed much to the efforts of Adnan Khashoggi, one of Citibank's most important customers and a founder member of the Saudi American Bank, as well as owner of the prestigious building in al-Riyadh in which the new bank's headquarters was located.

From the bank's point of view these delaying tactics had several merits, not least the advantage of retaining the Citibank name within the kingdom for as long as possible.[12] A further advantage was that it gave the bank's staff time to prepare for the launch of the new institution, both through staff training and through research into local banking needs. The latter research enabled the new bank to identify key groups to which advertising and credit marketing could be directed. In addition, services geared to perceived domestic market preferences could be organised, including the establishment of separate banking facilities run by women for women. The introduction of separate banking facilities for women is now well advanced in Saudi Arabia, with the National Commercial Bank, the Saudi Cairo Bank and Bank Al-Jazira already operating women's branches. This service saves Saudi women the embarrassment of dealing with male bankers, and ensures privacy in financial transactions regarding any wealth they have inherited by right under Islamic law. Details of the current numbers of domestic branches operated by Saudi commercial banks may be found in Table 14.1.

A Profile of Banking Activity

The data presented in Table 14.2 illustrate the consolidated position of Saudi Arabia's commercial banks; the activities of the money-changing establishments are excluded, as the latter produce no published accounts. The picture of the growth of banking activity is therefore only partial – in some developing countries the growing assets of the commercial banks, for which enumerated data are available, merely reflect a switch from the traditional money-changing sector and not a rise in banking activity as such. The sheer scale of the expansion in enumerated activity in Saudi Arabia, however, indicates that such switching effects are likely to be minor. Private sector loans and investments have increased almost twentyfold in money terms over the 1965–79 period, as the table shows. Despite the virtual quadrupling of retail prices during the period under discussion,[13] even in real terms the rise has been remarkable.

Table 14.1: Number of Domestic Branches of Saudi Arabian Commercial Banks[a]

Bank	No. of domestic branches
National Commercial Bank	70
Riyadh Bank	50
Saudi British Bank	10
Bank Al-Jazira	8
Al-Bank Al-Saudi Al-Fransi	7
Al-Bank Al-Saudi Al-Hollandi	6
Arab National Bank	5
Saudi Cairo Bank	5
Saudi American Bank	3
Lebanese Bank	3
Bank Melli Iran	1
Korea Exchange Bank	1
United Bank (Pakistan) Limited	1
Banque du Liban et d'Outre-Mer	1

Note: a. Includes seasonal branches for pilgrims.
Source: Authors' statistics.

Table 14.2: Growth of Commercial Banking Activity in Saudi Arabia

	1965	1970	1975	1979
Assets				
Claims on private sector (loans and investments)	1,014	1,667	6,722	19,739
Foreign assets	193	535	3,617	12,962
Liquid assets (cash and deposits with SAMA)	253	321	4,845	17,298
Unclassified assets	73	406	528	2,561
Liabilities				
Current account deposits	570	868	7,427	29,476
Time and savings deposits	116	561	1,610	4,165
Letters of credit	97	113	815	2,836
Guarantees	78	107	984	2,155
Foreign liabilities	185	181	1,786	5,699
Capital and reserves	143	178	679	1,990
Unspecified liabilities	271	833	1,945	4,502
Foreign currency	73	88	466	1,737
Total liabilities = total assets	1,533	2,929	15,712	52,560

Note: All numbers are in million riyals.
Source: Saudi Arabian Monetary Agency, *Annual Report 1399* (SAMA, 1979), Table 6a, pp. 124—7.

On the asset side of the balance sheet, domestic loans and investments accounted for over 40 per cent of the total in 1979, a
proportion which fluctuated around 5 per cent of that amount
throughout the 1970s. Most of this is made up of loans, for despite the
Islamic preference for direct equity investment, Saudi commercial
banks, like their Western counterparts, strongly favour revolving credits
rather than longer-term commitments.[14] In some respects this is
fortunate; given the monopolistic structure of the banking system, too
much equity involvement by the National Commercial Bank and the
Riyadh Bank in particular would have had serious implications for
competition in Saudi business generally. From the bank's point of view,
in any case, the reluctance to become involved in the boards of local
companies stems partly from their shortage of experienced and
competent staff. It is difficult enough for them to find staff to run
their own operations, let alone anyone else's.

Total foreign assets of the Saudi commercial banks amounted to
almost 13 billion riyals in 1979, as shown in Table 14.2. Most of these
assets are in the form of deposits with other banks in the principal
world financial centres, particularly London. Saudi Arabia's two
indigenous banks have only recently extended their operations outside
the country, and their external operations are largely confined to the
wholesale inter-bank market rather than retail banking. The foreign
assets are largely in the form of liquid placements, mostly withdrawable
on demand. They are deposited with a few major Western-owned banks
and with consortium banks under mixed Arab and Western holding,
such as the Union de Banques Arabes et Françaises (UBAF).[15] Despite
the liquidity of these foreign assets, it is only domestic assets which
SAMA permits to be counted as liquid assets, in line with normal
central banking convention. As the table indicates, the domestic liquid
assets were almost as great as loans outstanding in 1975 and 1979. This
reflects the commercial banks' large cash holdings and deposits with
SAMA, in excess of the 15 per cent reserve requirement.

On the liabilities side of the balance sheet, Table 14.2 highlights the
overwhelming importance of current-account deposits, on which no
interest is payable. The sheer magnitude of these deposits, and their
growth over the last decade, indicates that they are well in excess of
what depositors require for transactions or even precautionary purposes.
Clearly many customers are using current accounts for savings
accumulation, ignoring the opportunity costs involved – a situation
which benefits the bank rather than the depositor. The value of time
and savings deposits, on which a fixed commission is paid in lieu of

interest to the depositor in accordance with Saudi law, remains relatively modest. There seems little desire to change the relative balance of current and savings accounts on the part of customers, however, and the banks for their part seem reluctant to promote savings schemes.

This reluctance to encourage savings schemes is understandable, given the greater profitability of current-account deposits *vis-à-vis* savings deposits from the bank's point of view. A growth in savings deposits, however, may not necessarily be at the expense of current accounts, as Saudi funds might be attracted which would otherwise have been deployed abroad. A further factor explaining the lack of savings promotion may be concern about antagonising the more conservative sections of the community. Vigorous promotion by offering high premiums for savings could be viewed as an indirect form of interest incentive. Nevertheless, there is no reason why religious principles should be undermined, so long as the higher charges are not passed on to borrowers. Muslim concern is with any hardships that might be inflicted on the latter, rather than with the potential gains that might be made by depositors.[16]

Commercial banks in Saudi Arabia charge comparatively low lending rates. The rates charged by the National Commercial and Riyadh Banks, for example, gravitated between 8 and 10 per cent during 1979–80, which could scarcely be considered usury. Nevertheless, the relatively high differential between these lending rates and virtually zero deposit rates is perhaps surprising, given the sensitivity over interest-rate questions. To call the lending rates service charges is mere semantics. The high differential reflects in part the lack of competition within the Saudi banking system. It is not clear, however, that the recent structural changes in the banking system will drive lending rates down, for the newly Saudi-ised institutions charge even higher rates — often over 15 per cent. SAMA seems to tolerate such rates largely because it sees the need for prices to play some part in credit allocation. By keeping up lending charges, moreover, the agency hopes that borrowers will not merely seek credit in Saudi Arabia which they can redeploy for speculative purposes in international financial centres, as even with rates at existing levels there is already considerable evidence of such practices.

A breakdown of the lending by the commercial banks in Saudi Arabia is presented in Table 14.3. From this it is evident that trade credit takes the highest proportion of lending, accounting for over one-third of the total in 1978. Much of this is to finance local

Table 14.3: Saudi Arabian Commercial Bank Credit by Economic
Group (1978)

	Amount (million riyals)	Share (percentage)
Agriculture and fishing	93	0.7
Manufacturing and processing	1,433	10.7
Mining and quarrying	117	0.9
Electricity, water and other utilities	469	3.5
Building and construction	2,930	21.9
Commerce	4,520	33.9
Transport and communications	316	2.4
Finance	225	1.7
Services	426	3.2
Miscellaneous	2,821	21.1
Total	13,350	100

Source: Saudi Arabian Monetary Agency, *Annual Report 1399* (1979), Table
19, p. 36.

merchants' stocks of imported goods, as they often have to meet the
payment to the foreign supplier before the goods are actually sold.
Banks can, of course, provide letters of credit and guarantees, but these
are usually for short periods only, and it may take a considerable time
for a Saudi importer to offload his stocks. Although Saudi traders may
be more likely than traders elsewhere to self-finance their own stock-
holdings, and although they can also raise funds from the traditional
money-lenders, it is evident that the commercial banks are now playing
a growing role in this area. Between 1977 and 1978 alone the value of
trade credit increased by over one-third, and even if a substantial
allowance is made for inflation, the real increase must have been
considerable.

The second most important use made of bank lending is for construction finance, accounting for over one-fifth of the total in 1978. At first
sight the extent of commercial bank lending for construction is
surprising as the state-run Real Estate Development Fund provides
interest-free loans to private home buyers and the Credit Fund for
Contractors gives highly subsidised short- and medium-term loans to
Saudi building firms. Housing and other facilities for immigrant workers
are not covered by these funds, however, and the mid-1970s boom in
the construction of apartment buildings (for the rent of apartments to
immigrant workers) was therefore financed by the commercial banks.
The ending of this boom in 1978, in response to the stabilisation and in

some cases the decline in rents, was reflected in a fall in commercial bank credit to the residential construction sector. Bank lending for the construction of commercial premises and other urban non-residential development, nevertheless, has continued to soar, as governmental bodies do not cover financial needs in this field.

Despite the generous financial provision made for manufacturing ventures through the Saudi Industrial Development Fund, commercial bank lending to industry is increasing rapidly in both absolute and relative terms. The State Industrial Development Fund contributes no more than 50 per cent of the finance available for the ventures it backs, and its finance primarily covers medium- and longer-term fixed capital formation.[17] As a result borrowers have to turn to the commercial banks for assistance with the finance of working capital, a situation that suits the banks well, given their usual preference for shorter-term lending. From the borrower's point of view, dealing with the commercial banks has its advantages in any case, even if the cost of borrowing from this source is well in excess of the 2 per cent service charge levied by the Saudi Industrial Development Fund. The banks provide a relatively speedier service, have easier application procedures, and do not normally delve as deeply into the accounts of the borrower's business. The latter is particularly important in a country where a high value is placed on privacy, even with respect to non-personal finances.[18]

Bahrain Banks and Saudi Finance

There seems little doubt that to some extent the rise of Bahrain as a financial centre is a result of the deficiencies in the Saudi banking system. The dominance of the local banking system by the National Commercial Bank and Riyadh Bank duopoly has resulted in a competitive gap, which the Bahrain-based institutions have sought to fill. This has been facilitated by the absence of any exchange controls, which means that Bahrain can be used both as a deposit base and as a source for borrowing. Bankers in Bahrain can extend credit to clients in Saudi Arabia secure in the knowledge that there are no government controls that can be used as an excuse for failure to make repayments on loans. In addition the *laissez-faire* attitude of the Bahrain Monetary Authority, in contrast to SAMA, has resulted in banks based on the island being able to offer more attractive rewards to depositors. Interest rates offered in Bahrain respond to world market forces and the authorities impose no constraints, unlike in Saudi Arabia, where no interest is officially allowed and the commissions given are usually well below the rewards available in Bahrain. In Saudi Arabia the dilemma for the banks is that they have to comply with the spirit as well as the letter of Islamic law, and if commissions were changed too often, or raised too far, then their role as a proxy for interest would be evident for all to see.

The attractiveness of Bahrain to Saudi depositors is obviously greatest when international interest rates are high, as they were from mid-1979 through to the end of 1980. In February 1980 depositors holding dollar accounts in Bahrain were able to earn up to 17 per cent there, and the resultant exodus of funds from Saudi Arabia caused liquidity strains. Paradoxically the world's leading oil exporter and holder of official reserves actually found itself short of funds for private lending, especially as the relatively low rates in the kingdom encouraged borrowing. Some individuals may have taken advantage of the differentials, by borrowing funds within Saudi Arabia cheaply — and then re-depositing them in Bahrain or other centres for higher returns. As Saudi-based banks, respecting their clients' privacy, seldom question their more important customers too thoroughly about the purposes for which funds are being borrowed, it was difficult to prevent such export of funds.

It seems, however, that the shortage of funds for lending affected the newly Saudi-ised institutions more than the National Commercial and Riyadh Banks. Three possible reasons can be suggested for this. First, depositors with the foreign-affiliated banks are more likely to be the sort of clients who are aware of opportunities outside the kingdom. Second, the newly Saudi-ised institutions in their drive to attract new customers were unwilling to turn away any potential borrowers with reasonable security to offer, and they probably over-extended themselves. Finally, the National Commercial Bank, which had deposited some of its surplus funds with the foreign-affiliated banks within Saudi Arabia in the past, substantially reduced these deposits in 1979 and generally cut back on inter-bank lending.[19] This made more funds available for its own private borrowers, but squeezed the Saudi-ised institutions.

SAMA found difficulty in responding to the liquidity shortage, as it could not raise domestic interest rates (or their equivalents) in line with those of Bahrain. Its initial reaction was to hint that the Saudi riyal might be revalued, which would result in exchange losses for those holding deposits of foreign currencies in Bahrain and elsewhere. As there was actually a minor depreciation of the riyal against the dollar in 1979,[20] those exporting capital did not see this as a significant threat. Saudi exchange-rate policy, in any case, is constrained by the fact that oil prices are denominated in dollars, and the kingdom's official reserve holdings, valued at almost 65 billion riyals this year, are mostly held in dollars. Any appreciation therefore reduces the riyal value of both the kingdom's oil revenues and its overseas asset holdings. Besides, many of the Saudi deposits in Bahrain were denominated either in riyals or in regional currencies such as the Bahrain dinar, the Kuwait dinar, or the United Arab Emirates dirham. As the various Gulf monetary authorities keep their currencies in line with the riyal, there is therefore no risk of exchange loss.

Table 14.4 gives a breakdown of the assets and liabilities of the Bahrain offshore banking units. More than 60 per cent of the $16 billion in deposits which were recorded by the Bahrain Monetary Agency as coming from other Arab countries in 1979 originated in Saudi Arabia. Funds from Kuwait, the Emirates and Qatar accounted for most of the remainder. Although most Saudi funds are placed in dollar accounts, in recent years there has been an increasing tendency to leave the funds in accounts denominated in riyals. These offshore riyal (or Euro-riyal) deposits constitute the major portion of the regional currency deposits recorded in Table 14.4 under the currency classification of section (B). Bahrain overseas banking units attract not only the deposits of private individuals but also a significant portion of the overseas deposits made by Saudi banks.

There is little doubt that the existence of such a large volume of offshore riyal deposits causes SAMA some anxiety, especially as most are lent back into Saudi Arabia directly or are taken up by foreign companies carrying out extensive business with Saudi Arabia. Even the Saudi banks, including the foreign-affiliated institutions, are concerned about the extent of the Bahrain market. The Saudi American Bank, for instance, was annoyed to discover that Citibank of Bahrain had been seeking borrowers within Saudi Arabia to find an outlet for its riyal deposits, without informing its al-Riyadh-based affiliate. For SAMA the main concern is not that the existence of the Bahrain market creates unwanted competition – such pressures are viewed as healthy – but that it reduces SAMA's ability to control the domestic money supply, and hence ultimately internal inflation.[21]

In order to curb the growth of the offshore riyal market, it was decided in autumn 1979 to stop denominating major Saudi Arabian government contracts in riyals, and instead to fix dollar prices.[22] This, it was hoped, would reduce pressure on the riyal; foreign contractors

Table 14.4: Bahrain Offshore Banking Units: Assets and Liabilities

(A) Geographical Classification

	Arab countries	North America	Western Europe	Offshore centres	Other
Assets					
1976	2,487	13	1,129	1,241	1,344
1977	7,065	468	3,904	1,888	2,376
1978	11,688	277	5,301	2,971	3,204
1979	14,739	477	6,917	2,243	3,388
Liabilities					
1976	2,578	414	2,277	923	222
1977	8,255	419	4,995	1,539	493
1978	11,666	1,891	7,018	1,850	1,016
1979	16,143	828	7,873	1,936	984

(B) Currency Classification

	US $	Regional currencies	Deutsche Mark	Swiss Franc	Other
Assets					
1976	4,387	1,196	183	318	130
1977	11,594	3,242	319	389	157
1978	16,031	6,075	501	389	445
1979	18,216	7,440	524	637	947
Liabilities					
1976	4,471	1,168	175	258	142
1977	11,269	3,567	252	330	283
1978	15,459	6,720	383	295	584
1979	17,538	8,113	609	546	958

(C) Maturity Classification

	Up to 7 days	8 days to 3 months	3 months to 1 year	Over 1 year
Assets				
1976	1,059	2,426	1,609	1,120
1977	2,259	7,718	3,676	2,048
1978	2,793	12,444	5,382	2,822
1979	3,953	14,005	5,829	3,977
Liabilities				
1976	1,714	3,618	830	52
1977	3,344	9,730	2,477	150
1978	5,078	13,503	4,471	371
1979	6,212	15,485	5,444	623

Note: All numbers refer to US $ million.

Source: Bahrain Monetary Agency, *Quarterly Statistical Bulletin*, vol. 5, no. 4 (December 1979), Tables 14–16, pp. 16–18.

would no longer need to take forward cover in riyals against exchange risks. It was expected that through these means the size of the Bahrain offshore market in riyals would be reduced, and Saudi Arabia's internal liquidity problems would thereby be eased. The rise in interest-rate differentials between Bahrain and Saudi Arabia on riyals, however, minimised any possible effect of SAMA's actions. In 1980 there was both a continuing rise in the value of offshore riyal deposits in Bahrain, and an increase in dollar and other currency deposits.

The only other action that SAMA has been able to take towards solving the fund-shortage problem in the kingdom has been to reduce the reserve requirements of the commercial banks. These were reduced in May 1979 from 15 per cent on all deposit liabilities to 12 per cent on demand deposits and 2 per cent on time and savings deposits.[23] In 1980 a further reduction on demand deposits was agreed, and the ratio of liquid assets was reduced to a mere 7 per cent. It was hoped that this action would reduce the competitive position of the Bahrain banks *vis-à-vis* those of Saudi Arabia, as of course one of the main attractions of operating from an offshore banking centre is the absence of any reserve requirements, and the lack of other interference by the monetary authorities. So far, however, these measures appear to have had little effect on the comparative strength of the Bahrain market. The conclusion must be that the island's competitiveness *vis-à-vis* Jeddah and al-Riyadh reflects inefficiencies in the provision of services within the kingdom, and not merely differences in regulatory regulations.

It is important to bear in mind that the attitude of Saudi Arabia towards Bahrain is basically protective. This must explain the tolerance shown towards the island's development as an offshore financial centre in the first place, as well as the subsequent reluctance to take actions that might seriously damage Bahrain's position, in spite of the internal problems caused in Saudi Arabia itself. There is a realisation that Bahrain needs to diversify its economy if it is to prosper, given its limited oil resources, and any discontent on Saudi Arabia's borders would be far from welcome. Although only 119 Bahrain citizens are directly employed in the offshore banking units,[24] there is little doubt that local spending by the high-earning resident and visiting expatriate bankers brings substantial benefits to the island's service-based economy, even if non-property owners have some misgivings about the rising real-estate prices and rentals. The Saudis also realise that if Bahrain did not act as an offshore banking centre, then most of the funds currently held there would, in the absence of exchange controls, migrate elsewhere. SAMA can at least exercise some influence with the

Bahrain Monetary Authority, whereas further afield outside the Gulf its control over events is likely to be much less.

There does, nevertheless, remain some concern in Saudi Arabia about the long-term stability of Bahrain as a financial centre, despite the fact that the island is now well established in its new role. This concern is partly with overall socio-political factors beyond the scope of this paper, such as the Shi'a–Sunni religious divide in the Bahrain community and the radicalism which has arisen, perhaps inevitably, amongst some elements in what is the oldest urban society in the Gulf. Of more immediate concern is the stability of the offshore banking market itself; the maturity structure of the market is monitored closely not only by the Bahrain Monetary Agency but also by SAMA. As section (C) of Table 14.4 shows, there is no justification for alarm at present, but there has been some tendency for the banks to lend for longer periods than those for which their deposits are placed. If this tendency became more marked, and the still thin Bahrain market showed signs of being volatile, a threat could arise not only to the Bahrain banking sector, but also to the stability of the riyal and the Saudi financial system generally.

In spite of these nagging doubts, several factors would appear to favour Bahrain's future as a regional, and even an international, financial centre. First, there is the range and geographical spread of the 70 banks already represented there – including some of the most respected international financial institutions.[25] Second, communications are excellent, both in terms of telecommunications and air-travel facilities; a new causeway will soon link the island physically with the oil-rich Eastern Province of the Saudi mainland. Third, Bahrain (unlike the United Arab Emirates) is in the same time zone as Saudi Arabia, which is convenient for the financial communities in both centres. Moreover, Bahrain's time zone enables it to function as an international currency market after Singapore closes and before London opens, although admittedly dealings tend to become brisker later in the morning when the European exchanges open and currency trends become more obvious. Finally, historical factors should not be ignored; Bahrain was always important as a trading centre in the Gulf and to some extent its establishment as a major financial centre can best be viewed as an extension of that role into the modern world.

Conclusion

The analysis of the Saudi Arabian banking system given above provides some insight into the broader problems facing the development of the Saudi Arabian economy. Although banking is the area of economic activity where Islamic principle is most likely to affect economic policy, there is little evidence that the nature or operation of banking in the kingdom has been substantially affected by this. Concern with respecting Islamic principle, rather, has emphasised some of the more fundamental structural problems in the banking system — especially those following from the domination of the sector by a very small number of institutions, whose ownership is narrowly based. The overall effect has been to render the sector uncompetitive in international terms, even within the Gulf area itself. The superior facilities offered by the Bahraini banking sector, the absence of exchange restrictions between the two states, and the consequent ability of Bahrain-based financial institutions to attract very substantial funds from Saudi Arabia, raises an important question: whether, in the long term, the forms of economic unity currently in force among Gulf states — involving the free movement of trade and capital — can continue to exist without a more unified overall economic policy.

Notes

1. Where they continue to trade in close proximity to each other.
2. A detailed account of Ottoman Bank activities in this early period is given by A. Du Velay, *Essai sur l' Histoire Financier de la Turquie* (A. Rousseau, Paris, 1902), especially pp. 189 f.
3. A profile of the Arab Bank was presented in the *Financial Times* on 18 June 1976 by Robert Graham. For an account of the role of Bank Misr see Marcus Deeb, 'Bank Misr and the Emergence of the Local Bourgeoisie in Egypt' in Elie Kedourie (ed.), *The Middle Eastern Economy: Studies in Economics and Economic History* (Frank Cass, London, 1976).
4. The British Bank of the Middle East, *A Brief History of the British Bank of the Middle East* (Aurora Press, London, 1974), p. 2.
5. And in view of the fact that the kingdom's financial affairs were far from being healthy at the time, with government expenditure exceeding oil revenues.
6. The Korean Central Bank also maintains representation in Saudi Arabia, but only to represent South Korean state interests *vis-à-vis* Korean companies involved in the kingdom. It carries out no commercial banking functions and its presence merely reflects the particularly close links between government and industry in Korea.
7. This would not, however, have precluded clients from maitaining two accounts, which, as already indicated, was the case with the British Bank of the Middle East in its early years.
8. The al-Rajhi group openly advertise these services.

9. Including remittances by South Asian, Far Eastern and European expatriates, and not only those being sent to other Arab countries.

10. Share prices have already doubled for some of the newly Saudi-ised institutions.

11. This was the only bank not be Saudi-ised on a 60–40 per cent basis.

12. The new headquarters bears the Citibank name, even though it was only occupied after the Saudi-isation was agreed.

13. As indicated by the Ministry of Finance and National Economy cost of living index. See SAMA, *Annual Report* for 1979, Table 26(a), p. 161.

14. Interestingly there is no Islamic Bank in Saudi Arabia providing domestic finance like those in Bahrain and Dubai. The Islamic Development Bank, an inter-governmental institution, provides external assistance only.

15. The Riyadh Bank has a small equity stake in this French-based institution (1.81 per cent), and the National Commercial Bank has a similar stake in the Luxemburg holding company that owns one of its main rivals, the European Arab Bank.

16. For a wider discussion of these issues see Rodney Wilson, 'The Economic Consequences of the Islamic Revival', *Contemporary Review*, vol. 236, no. 1372 (May 1980), pp. 240–5.

17. The author carried out interviews at the Fund. A useful account of its activities is given by Nigel Harvey, 'SIDF's First Five Years', *Saudi Business*, vol. 3, no. 49 (7 March 1980), pp. 31–5.

18. It is far from easy to distinguish personal from business borrowing in Saudi Arabia.

19. The 1979 accounts show deposits with other banks declining from 309 million riyals to 77 million riyals, and loans to other banks falling from 511 million riyals to 150 million riyals.

20. From 4.27 riyals to the dollar in January to 4.43 riyals to the dollar by December, a depreciation of around 3.7 per cent.

21. A point emphasised by most observers, including Peter Field of *Euromoney* writing in the 1979 *Middle East Annual Review*, p. 137.

22. A brief discussion of the implications of this decision was given by Nigel Dudley of *Middle East Economic Digest* writing in *The Times* 'Special Report on Arab Banking' (11 March 1980), p. 6.

23. SAMA, *Annual Report* (1979), p. 35.

24. Information supplied by Bahrain Monetary Authority.

25. Including Saudi Arabia's National Commercial Bank and the Gulf Riyadh Bank, a joint venture 60 per cent owned by the Riyadh Bank and 40 per cent owned by Credit Lyonnais.

APPENDIX: OPENING REMARKS OF ABDULLAH AL
SAUD (DEPUTY SECRETARY-GENERAL, ROYAL
COMMISSION FOR JUBAIL AND YANBU) TO THE
SYMPOSIUM ON STATE, ECONOMY AND POWER IN
SAUDI ARABIA, CENTRE FOR ARAB GULF STUDIES,
UNIVERSITY OF EXETER, 4–7 JULY 1980

I wish to express my appreciation to the Centre for Arab Gulf Studies
of the University of Exeter for this opportunity to address such a
representative gathering on the opening day of the symposium on
Saudi Arabia. It is a pleasure to be here and to have an opportunity to
participate in a discussion that promises to be exceptionally wide-
ranging and informative.

It is important that all aspects of Saudi Arabian society be examined
and understood at home and abroad. For although we are not unaware
of our problems and our mistakes we can profit from the knowledge
of others. But Western countries should have a realistic grasp of the
kingdom's unfolding history and not be influenced by ill-intentioned
misinformation or journalistic sensationalism whose true objective is
not understanding but notoriety and commercial profit. That is the
reason why this symposium can play such a useful role in providing
insights into the complex process of socio-economic development and
the effects on the kingdom's traditional society. I hope that I can
contribute to achieving this. The range of topics to be discussed at this
symposium is very wide indeed. I shall briefly comment on certain
aspects of Saudi Arabian history and society that are especially
important, in my view, to an understanding of contemporary state and
society in Saudi Arabia.

Modern Saudi Arabia can not be understood without the required
historical perspective. For it was over two centuries ago, in the
eighteenth century, that the Saudi political system was first established.
It was based on an alliance of the religious scholar, Muhammad Abd
al-Wahhab, who preached the return to a purified Islam, and Muhammad
ibn Saud, the Amir of Dar'iya near al-Riyadh.

This Saudi-Wahhabi alliance led to the successful conquest of
al-Riyadh, all of the Najd and al-Hasa and finally the Hijaz with its
holy places, as well as parts of Iraq, Yemen, Asir and Oman. It was only
the intervention of the Ottoman Turks that curbed the power of the

301

alliance in the early nineteenth century. Thus, from the very beginning, the legitimacy of Saudi rule was clearly established. It can be argued, in fact, that the roots of Saudi political legitimacy are deeper than are the roots of legitimacy in many European states, whose present political systems emerged in the late eighteenth century (France), the nineteenth century (Italy) or after the Second World War (Germany).

What we are witnessing in the twentieth century is the third revival of Saudi power and the emergence of Saudi Arabia as a modern state which began in 1902 with the capture of al-Riyadh by Abd al-Aziz ibn Saud in an attack launched from exile. By 1926, Abd al-Aziz had taken the Hijaz. In 1927, he was declared King of the Hijaz and Najd, and in 1932 the new state was renamed the Kingdom of Saudi Arabia.

Throughout this period Abd al-Aziz ibn Saud faced the problem of forging a unified, orderly, stable society out of the chronically warring, independent tribes of the Arabian peninsula. He was aware that his authority was based on his personal charisma, the long-standing prestige of the Al Saud, the historical association with Wahhabism, and the tribal alliances he had so skilfully established. Abd al-Aziz knew that most of the Saudi kingdoms established before his had failed to outlive their founders, and that tribalism could not serve as the basis for a stable political order.

There can be no authentic understanding of modern Saudi Arabia without a profound study of the life, character and politics of King Abd al-Aziz for he was not only the driving force of the new Saudi state but he left the stamp of his personality, his pragmatism, caution and flexibility on the monarchy as well as his interest in economic development and the maintenance of Islamic values which has been continued by his successors. His conquest of much of the Arabian peninsula during a quarter of a century of struggle is an epic story, but his greatest feat was to forge a unified, secure state under his rule which ensured modern development under stable conditions.

However, now as in Abd al-Aziz's day, the aspect of Saudi society which deserves special attention is the part that Islam plays as a shaper and motivator of state and society. It is particularly difficult for non-Muslims to understand Islam's pervasive role throughout the Middle East, and the special place it has in the life of Saudi Arabia. For the devout Muslim, the *shari'a* is the only legally accepted code. Islam dictates the political, social, legal and cultural system. Saudi Arabia's historical legacy and cultural heritage is closely identified with Islamic civilisation. In part this Islamic religious awareness stems from the presence of the two holy cities of Islam, Mecca and Medina, within the kingdom's borders.

But the central importance of Islam in the daily life of the kingdom, is reinforced by the strict discipline whose principles were embodied in the Saudi political and social system by King Abd al-Aziz ibn Saud. Islam not only pervades social customs but it also motivates government policies. This is especially difficult to grasp by the secularised Western intellectual trying to understand contemporary Saudi Arabia. Islamic countries not only understand this but they expect Saudi Arabia to uphold the practices and defend the principles of Islam.

The highest principle guiding the government's development policy is the preservation of the religious and moral values of the Saudi Arabian people. The kingdom's policies — whether towards education, industrialisation, telecommunications or social services — are all shaped by that guiding rule. We believe that it is possible to maintain our traditional Islamic values while creating a modern industrial society with high levels of material welfare available to all citizens. The interaction between traditionalism and modernisation — between the ideals of Islamic society and the imperatives of material progress — undoubtedly creates social and spiritual tensions. But we believe they are manageable with intelligent and sensitive direction on the part of the responsible authorities.

We, in Saudi Arabia, are very much aware of the challenge that rapid socio-economic change brings in its wake. The development of a modern infrastructure and industry, the creation of new institutions, the expansion of the state bureaucracy solves old problems but creates new ones. It places strains on traditional values and institutions. The kingdom's heavy investment in education, raising the level of professional and administrative skills, and expanding the supply of trained national labour is creating a new professional technocratic—bureaucratic middle class settled in the urban centres of the country. The rapid growth of the manufacturing industry, and the installation of heavy hydrocarbon-based industries, is spawning an urban industrial labour force whose problems and aspirations require attention by the authorities.

Western journalists and scholars often raise questions about whether the kingdom's unprecedented economic development is not eroding traditional institutions, such as the direct links between the leadership and the people. It is sometimes alleged that, as the kingdom becomes more bureaucratised, the tradition of the *majlis* — which ensures the population direct access to the leadership, including the king, for the redress of grievances, the resolution of disputes, and all kinds of assistance — is being weakened. There is an element of truth in these arguments, but the leaders of the kingdom are aware of the need for maintaining channels of communication with the people at all levels. An effort is being made at different levels to identify the problems of the people, to ensure they have continued access to governmental leaders, and to devise new ways of meeting the people's needs. Let me assure you that the *majlis* still plays a most important role in our life.

I would like to end these brief comments on domestic and international policy with a few words about the importance of a better, more accurate understanding of Saudi Arabia. The kingdom is a complex, and in many ways unique, society. The political system has deep roots in the history of the Arabian peninsula, and in Islam. The role of Islam in the political, social and legal structure is all-pervasive and fundamental. It is a society undergoing rapid economic development while trying to preserve its religious and moral values. It has emerged as a major financial power since the mid-1970s, and is more deeply involved in regional, inter-Arab, Islamic and international affairs than ever before. It is dedicated to improving the material welfare productivity of the people of Saudi Arabia. And it is taking steps to meet the challenge of the next century when the oil resources are exhausted and the prosperity of the kingdom will depend entirely upon the education, skills and talents of the Saudi Arabian people.

Yet as I survey the vast and growing literature on Saudi Arabia – particularly recent journal and newspaper articles on the kingdom – I am rather more dismayed than enlightened. Where, I ask myself, did these journalists and so-called experts on the kingdom obtain their information? How do they know what views and attitudes pervade such diverse social groups as the new middle class, the government bureaucrats, the technocrats, the bedouin in remote areas, the armed forces, and the royal family? They talk confidently about the most sensitive and difficult matters. But have these foreign observers had a long and intimate association with a cross-section of the groups concerned? Have they lived amongst us for many years and gained entrée to the social groups about which they write? Have they designed any analytical framework which does justice to the complexity of Saudi Arabian reality? Or have they simply applied inappropriate Western or class analytical concepts to a unique Islamic society, thereby doing violence to reality?

These 'instant experts' depend upon a narrow, unrepresentative segment of Saudi society – businessmen, public officials, members of the royal family – or foreigners living within the kingdom for their information about what is happening. It is not surprising that much of what they publish is based on the flimsiest evidence. All too often the results are highly speculative, inaccurate and sometimes nonsensical. For all these reasons I very much look forward, as I am sure all of you do, to the deliberations that will follow over the next few days.

GLOSSARY OF ARABIC TERMS USED IN THE TEXT

'abaya: cloak.

amir: strictly speaking, commander. In Saudi Arabia, however, the term is more often used to mean prince.

'aqida: belief, faith or creed.

beiah: a popular oath of allegiance.

bersim: alfalfa.

bid'a: innovation (implying, in the religious context, heresy).

da'wa: literally, call. The term is used, in a religious context, to signify the message put across by a religious teacher or reformer.

dira: grazing territory associated with or controlled by a specific nomadic tribe.

fakhd: section of a tribe.

fatwa: an authoritative statement by religious leaders, which can form the basis of court decision or government action.

ghazi: warrior, member of a tribal raiding party.

hadith: tradition based on the Prophet Mohamad's words and deeds, serving as one of the sources of Islamic law.

hajj: pilgrimage.

hijra (plural *hujar*): literally, migration. Used in this text for the agricultural settlements to which the *ikhwan* migrated.

'ibada: the canonical rites through which the relationship of the worshipper to God is expressed.

ikhwan: literally, brothers. Used in this text for the brotherhood of ex-bedouin settled in the *hujar* and playing a military role in the expansion of the Saudi state.

imam: a leader determined to revive the observance of religion.

jahiliya: state of ignorance. To orthodox Islam this refers to the period prior to the Prophet Muhammad.

jihad: the struggle to establish the law of God on earth, often interpreted to mean holy war.

madhab: school of Sunni religious law.

mahdi: literally, a guided one; in common use, the expected deliverer of Muslims from oppression and guide to the way of pure faith. (The Islamic justification for this belief is found in a *hadith* of the Prophet, not in the Koran.)

majlis: council. In this text it generally refers to the audience of the king or shaikh, open to citizens or tribespeople for adjudication.

mufti: religious jurist, interpreter of Muslim law.

mujaddid: renewer of the faith; a preacher determined to revive a
failing observance of religion.

mulhaq: postscript.

mutawa' (plural *mutawa'in*): literally, volunteer. The term is used for
the religious teachers who spread Wahhabism among the bedouin,
and latterly for the so-called religious police authorised to assure
obedience with Wahhabi teachings.

muwahhidun: literally, those who proclaim the unity of God; here,
followers of the *al-tawhid* teachings of Muhammad Abd al-Wahhab.

qadi: judge in *shari'a* law courts.

shari'a: Islamic law.

shirk: polytheism – the association of any one or any thing with God.

subhanahu: glory be to (God).

sufi: a Muslim mystic. The term was first applied to Muslim ascetics
who clothed themselves in coarse garments of wool (*suf*), and is now
broadly used for those who seek a direct experience of God.

sunna: custom, tradition of a custom of the Prophet.

suq: market.

tariqa: literally, path or way. Used in the religious context to refer to a
sufi order.

tawhid: literally, unification. Refers in this text to Muhammad Abd
al-Wahhab's teaching on the oneness or unity of God.

'ulama (singular *'alim*): religious scholars/leaders.

zakat: taxation based on Islamic precepts.

CONTRIBUTORS

Abdullah Al Saud is Deputy Secretary-General of the Royal Commission for Jubail and Yanbu.

John Duke Anthony is Associate Professor at Johns Hopkins University, Washington.

J. S. Birks, formerly Research Fellow at the Department of Economics, University of Durham, is currently working for the International Bank of Reconstruction and Development.

James Buchan is a journalist working for the *Financial Times*. He was formerly the paper's correspondent in Saudi Arabia.

Ugo Fabietti is a social anthropologist from Milan. He was employed recently on a research project in Saudi Arabia organised by the Societé d'Études pour le Développement Économique et Social (Paris).

Fred Halliday is Associate Director of the Transnational Institute (Amsterdam and Washington).

H. G. Hambleton is Professor of Economics at the Université Laval, Quebec.

Derek Hopwood is Middle East Bibliographer, University of Oxford and St Antony's College, Oxford.

Shirley Kay is the author of two recent books on Saudi Arabia: *The Bedouin*, and *Saudi Arabia Past and Present* (co-authored with Malin Basil).

Tim Niblock is Deputy Director of the Centre for Arab Gulf Studies, University of Exeter.

Clive Sinclair is Research Fellow at the Department of Economics, University of Durham.

Peter Sluglett is Lecturer in Middle Eastern History at the University of Durham. Marion Farouk-Sluglett, his wife, has worked on the modern Middle East.

Paul Stevens is Lecturer in Economics at the University of Surrey.

Rodney Wilson is Lecturer in Economics at the University of Durham.

Rosemarie Said Zahlan is author of *The Origins of the United Arab Emirates* and *The Creation of Qatar.*

INDEX